PHILOSOPHY OF THE SHORT TERM

Also Available from Bloomsbury

Simultaneity and Delay, Jay Lampert
Deleuze and Guattari's Philosophy of History, Jay Lampert
The Many Futures of a Decision, Jay Lampert

PHILOSOPHY OF THE SHORT TERM

Jay Lampert

BLOOMSBURY ACADEMIC
LONDON • NEW YORK • OXFORD • NEW DELHI • SYDNEY

BLOOMSBURY ACADEMIC
Bloomsbury Publishing Plc, 50 Bedford Square, London, WC1B 3DP, UK
Bloomsbury Publishing Inc, 1385 Broadway, New York, NY 10018, USA
Bloomsbury Publishing Ireland, 29 Earlsfort Terrace, Dublin 2, D02 AY28, Ireland

BLOOMSBURY, BLOOMSBURY ACADEMIC and the Diana logo
are trademarks of Bloomsbury Publishing Plc

First published in Great Britain 2024
This paperback edition published 2025

Copyright © Jay Lampert, 2024

Jay Lampert has asserted his right under the Copyright, Designs and
Patents Act,1988, to be identified as Author of this work.

For legal purposes the Acknowledgments on p. viii constitute
an extension of this copyright page.

Series design by Charlotte Daniels
Cover image: Art inspired by Architecture study and a figure.
(© Penta Springs Limited / Alamy Stock Photo)

All rights reserved. No part of this publication may be: i) reproduced or
transmitted in any form, electronic or mechanical, including photocopying,
recording or by means of any information storage or retrieval system without
prior permission in writing from the publishers; or ii) used or reproduced in
any way for the training, development or operation of artificial intelligence (AI)
technologies, including generative AI technologies. The rights holders expressly
reserve this publication from the text and data mining exception as per
Article 4(3) of the Digital Single Market Directive (EU) 2019/790.

Bloomsbury Publishing Inc does not have any control over, or responsibility for,
any third-party websites referred to or in this book. All internet addresses given
in this book were correct at the time of going to press. The author and publisher
regret any inconvenience caused if addresses have changed or sites have
ceased to exist, but can accept no responsibility for any such changes.

A catalogue record for this book is available from the British Library.

A catalog record for this book is available from the Library of Congress

ISBN: HB: 978-1-3503-4796-0
PB: 978-1-3503-4800-4
ePDF: 978-1-3503-4797-7
eBook: 978-1-3503-4798-4

Typeset by Newgen KnowledgeWorks Pvt. Ltd., Chennai, India

For product safety related questions contact productsafety@bloomsbury.com.

To find out more about our authors and books visit www.bloomsbury.com
and sign up for our newsletters.

Jennifer Bates and Hector Lampert-Bates

CONTENTS

Acknowledgments	viii
INTRODUCTION TO CONCEPTS OF THE SHORT TERM	1
Chapter 1 PHENOMENOLOGICAL SHORT TERM (KANT, HEGEL, HUSSERL)	25
Chapter 2 THE SHORT TIME REMAINING UNTIL DEATH (DE BEAUVOIR, SCHOPENHAUER)	39
Chapter 3 SHORT TERM HISTORY (RICOEUR, BRAUDEL, HEGEL)	59
Chapter 4 SHORT TERM MEMORY (COGNITIVE PSYCHOLOGY)	87
Chapter 5 SHORT TERM MEASURED BY QUANTITY (TIME ATOMS, HEGEL)	101
Chapter 6 SHORT TERM ETHICS (SOCRATES, CYRENAICS, UTILITARIANISM)	121
Chapter 7 SHORT TERM IN PRACTICE (PSYCHOTHERAPY, INVESTMENT, POLITICS, MISSIONS, AND ROMANCE)	143
Chapter 8 SHORT TERM AESTHETICS (EPHEMERAL ART AND THE FREE USE OF TEMPORAL CONSTRAINTS)	167
Chapter 9 "HAVE SHORT IDEAS" (DELEUZE AND GUATTARI): A GENERAL THEORY OF TEMPORAL SEGMENTATION	189
Notes	211
References	227
Index	241

ACKNOWLEDGMENTS

I would like to thank Dan Selcer, chair of the Philosophy Department at Duquesne University, for his generous, friendly, and intelligent support over the years.

A much different version of Chapter 10 appeared in Spanish as "*Ideas de corto plazo y segmentación temporal*" (translated by Juan Rocchi and Iván Paz) in *Las Potencias del Continuo: Deleuze: Ontología Práctica*, Volume 3 (edited by Sebastián Amarilla, Giorgina Bertazzo, and Gonzalo Santaya), Buenos Aires: RAGIF Ediciones, 2022: 201–24. I would like to thank Julián Ferreyra and all the organizers of this project for many Deleuze discussions and for their hospitality.

INTRODUCTION TO CONCEPTS OF THE SHORT TERM

Life is short, and every part of it is shorter than that, including the parts that are too long for what they are. Time is continuous and, to put it mildly, long, but all our experiences of time are in short term segments. How do we segment time, and why do we do it?

What does it mean for the nature of time if some of it can be short? What does the idea of the short term[1] mean? What makes a temporal term short? What makes a time segment terminate? Is the short term a quantitative idea, or qualitative, or functional? When are events short term? When are short term decisions good?

My previous book (*The Many Futures of a Decision*) argued that open-ended decisions presuppose a future with many possible continuations, overlapping virtual branches that diverge and converge. I argued that we live out many decisional futures over the same period of time. We might think of that as an ultra-long term future, doubly long in the sense that it is dense with concurrent time lines. In this book, I argue for irreducible functions of the short term. How can the short be good if the long was good?

Of course, I am not primarily talking about what is good, but about how time is structured. Understanding time—the time it takes for events to start and finish; the lived time of memory, perception, and expectation; the social use of time in historiography and politics—requires analyzing both short and long time segments, both the segmentability and the indivisibility of time. There is no tension between saying that multi-layered long term futures exist, and saying that short term processes are cut out of the time continuum. In fact, the book I wrote before the current book and *The Many Futures of a Decision* argued that simultaneity and delay—events that happen at the same time and events staggered across time—are part of the same temporal dialectic. I argued that events over time are both contracted into virtual co-existence and also distributed across temporal locations. To the extent that delay spreads out into the long term and simultaneity describes the relative temporal proximity of events and their consequences, the immanent relation between simultaneity and delay leads directly to correlated studies of short and long terms. I am not advocating that we should always value the short term and never sacrifice the short term for the long. It would be a waste of temporal resources to always value one temporal structure over another. Instead, my idea is that every temporal structure gives us additional temporal resources for acting however we choose. In Husserlian terms, we could call this eidetic variation for time concepts; the poet Vladimir Mayakovsky calls it "laying in rhythmic supplies."[2]

As in the last two books in this series, I explore a subcategory of time by weaving together a variety of philosophical approaches and interdisciplinary connections. Three methodologies are employed: (1) I gather and analyze diverse phenomena of the short term. I draw short term phenomena from such diverse fields as film editing and tense logic, history and physics, literary narrative and climate change activism, religious teaching and financial instruments, mathematics and romance and ritual, and poetry and technology. (2) I explore discussions of the short term in the history of philosophy, from Plato and Aristippus to Hegel, Bentham, Husserl, Ricoeur, and Deleuze. The methodologies I use most often are Husserlian eidetic variation, Hegelian dialectic, and Deleuzian micro-political multiplicity. Husserl, Hegel, and Deleuze may not have appreciated each other as much as I appreciate them all, but I have argued elsewhere[3] that their triple forced encounter gives rise to powerful conceptual forces. (3) I aim to systematize these results into a general theory of temporal segmentation in order to schematize an overall philosophy of the short term, and to draw implications from short term temporal segments for a general philosophy of time.

In this introduction, I lay out distinctions, disambiguations, and variations that go into the analysis of the short term. Each small subtopic in a book like this (every book is like this) could spin off. The book is a short version of a longer term possibility.

Argument

The concept of the short term is not a single measure of temporal quantity, but a set of interactions between temporal quantities, qualities, and functions and covers a wide range of structural variations.

Temporal Segmentation

The category of the short term draws a line between one segment of time and the next, isolating the period between the beginning of the segment and its end. Of course, time as a whole does not end when that time segment does. Indeed, the very idea of the short term presupposes that time goes on past the end of the term. But even the relative division of time is problematic. How can time be segmented?

I use the term "temporal segmentarity" in order to repurpose Deleuze and Guattari's theory of segmentarity in micropolitics (Chapter 9). Segmentation might sound like it presupposes linear accumulation of temporal parts, but as we will see, the cuts, thresholds, and leakages across the cutting points between temporal segments escape the whole-part dichotomy of temporal modeling.

What Does "Short" in "Short Term" Mean?

Shortness is not the same as short term. There are processes that are typically long term but that only last a short amount of time (a long sea voyage that ends abruptly during a storm on its second day)—that is, short long term processes. There are, conversely, long short term processes. For example, a long period during which nothing happens is not something we would normally call a long term event: it is long but not long term. Neither is long term the same as the whole of time, and short does not mean the same as part. There can be short wholes, and a part of a whole can be long.

In some cases, short and long terms are defined simply by temporal quantity. A short term romance lasts one night, whereas a long term one lasts decades. But in other cases, short and long term are not defined quantitatively but by qualities and functions. For example, short term memory is often understood as working memory, and long term memory as storage memory (Chapter 4). Some working memory may last a longer quantity of time than some storage memory; some qualitatively short term memory lasts a quantitatively greater amount of time than some qualitatively long term memory.

In still other cases, short and long term are defined neither quantitatively nor qualitatively, but rather in terms of the interventions that cause them to be long or short. For example, some jobs last into the long term by default, because there is no time limit imposed in advance, whereas temp work is short term by definition because the contract explicitly from the start cuts off the employment at an agreed date; what defines such a job as short term is that there is a targeted intervention that causes it to be short, whereas long term processes do not require an intervening cause to make them so. In other cases, a process may naturally run out of steam and hence be short term by default (as an electric car uses up its battery charge), so that it takes a targeted intervention to re-charge and extend that process for another term. One of my most general theses is that the difference between long and short term is not just a difference between amounts of measured time but between different principles for measuring time. The concept of the short term thus implies the co-existence of interacting temporal sequences and interruptions, which we might call a dialectical conception of time.

One paradigm that shows that quantity is not always the determining factor in whether a time segment is short or long term involves the time remaining before a person dies (Chapter 2). If a person is told they will live for only thirty more minutes, the time remaining is surely a short term period. If a person is told they will live for only another 1,000 years, the time remaining, if you ask me, is also a short term period. The remainder of life is short no matter what its quantity is. Sartre, writing of some of his fictional characters who are not at all old, ascribes to them an attitude that De Beauvoir's *Coming of Age* attributes to those who are: "They pass their time ruminating on their youth; they only conceive short term projects, as if they only had five or six years ahead of them."[4]

Narrative

How much do interpretations of short and long term depend on narrative? To know that something is a short term instance of its kind, like a short term romance or a short term loan, we need to know how such events are normally initiated and redeemed, and what progressions and vicissitudes they undergo. A theatrical run is judged short relative to expectations, receipts, reviews, and business models and will be re-evaluated if there are revivals at a later date.

This becomes complicated when two or more national or personal narratives pertain to the same events over the same period of time. A six-year war is relatively long in a single person's life, but relatively short, though important, in the life of the nation. We might wonder whether the whole idea of the short term is dependent on whose story we are telling, what our values are, and how the narrative is organized. Does narrative dependence undermine the ontology of the short term?

Relative versus Definitive Short Terms

Skeptics might argue that as long as the universe continues to exist, short term refers only to the succession of one part of a process by another, not to the definitive end of a process. No doubt, living beings come to an end, qualities are dialed down to zero, actions are interrupted, and vectors diverge. But the skeptic might say that in the final analysis, every process is part of a long term. Distinguishing short term processes would be a way of thinking that only works in the short term.

Still, the distinction between relative and definitive short terms is not entirely correlated with the distinction between subjective and objective short terms. There are cases where shortness is objectively relative, as a 100-minute movie is short relative to a 120-minute movie and long relative to a 70-minute movie. There are relative length periodicities, like solar year-long cycles relative to lunar month-short cycles. (A year of twelve lunar cycles is eleven days (one "epact") shorter than one solar cycle.) These objectively relative length cycles may in turn be expressed in different narrative forms: myths and fables respectively.[5]

There are other cases where shortness is subjectively relative, as a 100-minute movie can feel short or long depending on how much one is enjoying it, in contrast to how much one looks forward to what will happen afterward (though the connection between enjoyment and shortness is not obvious). Experiences of whales, oaks, and Ents are slow changing, relative to ours, whereas fruit fly experiences are fast and short. Furthermore, subjectively, the longer the whole, the more its parts qualify as short term: in a two-hour event (writing an exam), the first hour is a good chunk of time, but in a fifty-hour event (driving cross-country), the first hour is a drop in the bucket.

There are short term phenomena that seem less directly dependent on narrative, subjective, relative description, as for example the brain's limited capacity for short term memory, or events that last a few zeptoseconds, or the fact that unrecorded performances are lost to the future. Of course, I am telling of these phenomena too in narrative sentences, but it is not the narrative form that makes them end after a short term, it is the temporal fact. So while some events can be called short only under a certain narrative, others are short because the events themselves terminate.

Subjective or Objective Time

There is a vast objective science of time measurement. "Minimalization problems" in physics measure the shortest time in which an event can occur.[6] Fermat's "Principle of Least Time" says that light goes through space from point to point in least time—that is, in a "geodesic" (the shortest path between two points in a Riemannian manifold). A "brachistochrone" (Greek for "shortest time") is a curve that maps movement from point to point in the shortest time.

Indeed, the fact that there are different forms of time measurement (McLuhan distinguishes societies that measure time by seasons, by clocks, and by electronics[7]) blurs the distinction between subjective and objective definitions of the short term, since each society has its own rules for the objective measure of short and long events, from meals to deals.

On the one hand, one might think that objective time passes without division and that it is only in subjective representation that we attend to one period of time separately from the rest. On the other hand, one might think that the measurement of time is based precisely on objective metrics (from the earth's rotation to atomic clocks), so that it is rather subjective time that is an unbroken stream, and only objective time divides into short term segments. In brief, one might think either that continuity is objective and segmentation subjective or that continuity is subjective and segmentation objective.

The linguist Émile Benveniste takes the former view, but in a complicated way[8]: "The physical time of the world is a continuum that is uniform, infinite, linear, and segmentable at will (*segmentable à volonté*)" (Benveniste 1974: 70). In contrast to physical time, the "interior duration" of psychic time is divided up by subjective interests and interpretations. We might read this as meaning that physical time is indivisible and psychic time is divisible. But we may also read it as meaning that physical time can be segmented in ways that subjects are free to choose. Both objective time and subjective time do continue through time and both can be segmented for various purposes. My own view is that the relation between continuity and segmentation is a problem for every kind of time: both socio-phenomenological time and objective-physical time.

Short Events versus Short Descriptions of Events

There are short experiences, and short descriptions, of long term processes and long experiences, and long descriptions, of short term processes.

Short Term as Defined by the End, the Middle, and the Beginning

A short term segment is defined, first of all, by its termination, its end. In some cases, an event is known in advance to be short term (like a short term contract). In others, the fact that an event is short term comes as a surprise at the end (like a short-lived dynasty). But even when the end of a term is known from the beginning, it is still the end that defines it as short.

The middles of events are generally not relevant to whether the events are short or long. While tempting, it is misleading to associate short term attitudes with being in the middle of things. It is true that being in the middle of things stands for a criticism of teleology, and this does resonate with the short term. But what defines a short term is not its middle as such, but the amount of middle between beginning and end. This means, in turn, that its beginning is as crucial to the short term as its end, though it is only at its end that its beginning counts as one end of a short term status.

To be short, an event is normally cut at both ends. There might be an exception at the cosmological scale: suppose the cosmos goes infinitely far back in time, but will come to a finite end. Is that a short term universe? In a sense, yes, since it ends and could have been longer; in a sense, no, since how can something already infinitely long be short term? In any case, with this possible exception, short term events have beginnings, middles, and ends, but are defined by the end.

Measured from the Beginning of the Event to the End versus Measured from Now (the Time of Measurement) to the End

Sometimes, the short term is measured not by the entire length of a process from beginning to end but from the moment a stopwatch is set until its end. For example, a person who has been teaching for thirty years and plans to retire in one more year will be teaching for the short term relative to now, whereas a person who has been teaching for one year and plans to teach for thirty more will be teaching for the long term, even though both teaching careers have the same length.

Short Term as a Relation to the Present versus Short Term as a Relation to the Future

Some processes are experienced to be, or predicted to be (rightly or wrongly), short term before they start. Others are judged short term while in progress. Still others are only judged short term after they end. It might appear as though the idea of the short term is focused on the present, whereas the long term is focused on the future. But the end that defines whether the process is short or long term is in both cases the afterward.

The fact that current time segments are measured only by the future when they will end is one of the reasons that Bergson objects to the whole idea of temporal segmentation (Chapter 1), on the grounds that it ignores time while it is being experienced. But a phenomenologist should not reject the idea of measuring the short term just because it requires positing an end that will take place afterward; rather, the very oddity of measurement delay highlights the problem of short term ontology.

Last Moments before the Cut: Last Chance, Too Late

The idea of cutting a temporal segment off at a certain point entails that there are a few final moments before the cut: these are the last things you see, and the last chances you get, before things move on. We do not need to think of this as the epsilon in calculus, the interval smaller than any interval before the cutoff—it can be longer than that, as long as it is the last bit of time inside the time segment before it ends. In fact, the termination of a temporal segment is defined both by the last part of time inside the segment before it ends and by the fact that the segment is cut right after that last part of time. (In the same way, in defining the set of numbers from 1 to 10, we need to say both that its final member is 10 and that it ends before it includes 11.) There may be a regress in defining the "last" bit of time in a segment, since that depends on defining the second last, and so on, but regressions are unavoidable in part–whole analyses of time and space.

Instances include "the last thing you see" (before you fall asleep or before you are murdered), "the last thing you do" (before you get married), and "the last chance you get" (with the net empty). After the cut, "it is already too late." There is sometimes a feeling that it was already too late almost before it started, as in Mandelstam's poem *The Age* (1923), which Badiou quotes in *The Century*[9]: turn-of-the-twentieth-century innovations in science, politics, art, and love, despite being brilliant humanist inventions, made a new kind of war possible, thanks to which the century's hopes already ended, too soon, by 1918.

Short Term as Discontinuity

Short versus long term is not the same as discrete event versus process. When processes linger, they seem opposed to the short term spirit. Yet one can linger just for a moment, which shows that even leisurely processes can be short term even though they are open-ended, as long as they are not open-ended for too long.

Sometimes, short term events are unimportant, as when the main event gets interrupted by a short pause for a commercial break or a power nap: time out, give me a minute, just a sec, take a breather, *pause café*. In positive terms, it is a fragment; in terms of what it puts on hold, it is a gap. In fact, a gap may be filled with great stuff, like "gap years" and sabbaticals. Alternatively, a gap may be a quiet but significant moment, as in the Japanese concept of "Ma," a "twinkle of time," when the emptiness of the void leads to Enlightenment.[10] The case of sudden Enlightenment (assuming it really happens) suggests that a very short term event can be a glimpse of, or entry into, eternity (assuming there is such a time). Psychedelic experiences may be interpreted in a similar way,[11] as might Marion's saturated phenomena. The point is that whereas a simple short event is short in temporal quantity, a doubly short event is both short and also discontinuous with its context, and a triply short event is one that is short, and also discontinuous with its context, and also empty of events, though possibly still significant.

Short versus Fast

As long as the beginning and end positions of a spatial movement are invariant, moving fast across the space will take a shorter amount of time than moving slowly. In that obvious sense, short is correlated with fast and long with slow, as in phrases like "in the blink of an eye" or "two shakes of a lamb's tail." (Based on the lamb's tail idiom, nuclear physicists define a "shake" as 10^{-8} seconds—the time it takes for each neutron in a chain reaction to cause a fission event.) A blink of an eye episode may be over before one even notices it had begun. A person acts in the blink of an eye when they intercede in a fast movement with a fast and short move of their own, like catching the snitch. In Paul Morand's novel, *The Man in a Hurry*, being "pressed for time" means "shortening the distances that separated you from the moment at which you could drink."[12]

But the correlation of short and fast is not universal. Some short events are slow, like a turtle chewing, and some long events are fast, like interstellar travel will be. In some cases, both fast and slow are on the side of the short against the long, as evidenced by the fact that both very slow talkers and very fast talkers share the inability to finish sentences.[13]

In social applications, relations between fast and short, and long and slow, are complicated. Sometimes, if a technology is added slowly to a society, its effects are delayed over the long term, whereas if it is added quickly, its effects come sooner. But sometimes, portions of slow-moving events have immediate but short-lived effects, whereas a fast event that occurs at a distance does not have its effects until a long time has passed (and these effects may in turn linger for a long time).

Filmmakers know that if they want to highlight a few seconds out of a film's duration, they can do so equally well by running a scene in fast motion or in slow motion. In the great Kitchen scene in Bryan Singer's *X-Men: Days of Future Past* (2014), we see Quicksilver (the fast mutant) running fast to save his colleagues by diverting a hail of bullets one by one. Quicksilver is moving superfast, but since the audience cannot see that fast, it has to be shown to us in slow motion. So from the viewer's standpoint, Quicksilver is moving at normal human speed around the kitchen, while the shooters are shown moving in slow motion. We see a relation between two rates of speed (humans slow, Quicksilver normal), and infer a different relation (humans normal, Quicksilver fast), on screen at the same time. The result is a scene that is famous on its own, a stand-alone 2:28-minute clip on YouTube. The slow, crosshatched into the fast is the source of the cutdown from full-length movie to autonomous short clip.

Slowing down can add or intensify content (the "slow cooking" movement enhances both flavor and taste) or, alternatively, can reduce content to a minimum, and thereby shorten by slowness. In Krasznahorkai's novel *Baron Wenckheim's Homecoming*,[14] a character conceives the need to remove false presuppositions from his thinking. So as not to miss the tiniest error, he slows down his thinking in order to examine every little piece of every thought:

> Questions should be *deaccelerated* to the greatest possible degree of which the thinking mind is capable, indeed, to put the brakes on these questions to such an extent that the best thing for us is to not even budge an inch, and in this way we won't make the mistake of missing a step, or of failing, in the meantime, to take notice of something; the proper method of liquidating thought is, therefore, the standing position.

The "standing position" is not motionless—in fact, it does "budge an inch"—but it is so slow that it evaluates each sub-thought in a process of its own. If a process is slow enough, it isolates each sub-event into a time segment that comes to a full conclusion before the next is allowed to begin. The slow, in this way, can be a source of the short term.

Short Events with Long Effects

Marketing generates lasting brand impact out of short commercial advertisements, as with product placement at a child's birthday party (the quintessential one-off, short term event).

Short by Success versus Short by Failure

Some short term phenomena are inherently short, like blinking. Others are usually but not necessarily short, like orgasm. Others are contingently short or not short, like dieting.

Some short term events are successful: they reach their end after a short time. But other attempts at keeping an event short fail, and the event gets long.

Short Termism, or the Value of the Short Term

The short term is sometimes taken to imply low value, as in "small time actors" in vaudeville. Alternatively, though, "short term" can be a value-positive temporal designator for minoritarian politics. We might call societies attuned to short interventions micropolitan.

Human rights should always be established in the short term. It should never have taken so long to end colonization, slavery, and patriarchy. The sorry arguments of times past, and sadly sometimes present, to the effect that people are not ready for freedom, or not ready for others to have freedom, that moral policies need to wait until more stable times, that fairness takes time, that humanity is a long term project, and that patience is a virtue all violate the human right to the short term. I argued elsewhere that there is a time for the politics of delay.[15] But it is difficult to deny Fanon's argument that colonizers rely on delay as their primary means of maintaining power over the long term and that that very withholding of the short term justifies the use of violence. Justice comes on the scene when the question "When do we start?" is answered: "Without delay."[16]

Still, the designation "short termism" is most commonly used in political discourse by its critics, who almost without fail call it "myopic." To be sure, it is wise to be critical of short term thinking in arenas like freshwater management, genetic modification of crops, incarceration, rent control, peace treaties, and filibusters. But while it is important to seek benefits in the long term, it is equally important to receive benefits in the short term. Both short and long term values are essential to any activity, so we need to know how both function.

The problem of the short term pertains both to the content of decisions and to the status of decision-makers. It is sometimes held that people who participate in a society only for the short term do not feel responsible for making good decisions for it. Universities, for example, give this excuse for limiting the participation of students in decision-making (short term defined by how long into the future students will remain registered), and nations give the same excuse for discriminating against recent immigrants (short term defined as how long ago in the past they arrived). Almost every immigrant group has been described by some bigot or other as lending their primary loyalty to the nation they came from, as if no matter how long they live in their adopted country, they are inherently in passage short term. Yet nations do not generally prohibit old people from voting merely on the grounds that they will not be around long enough to experience the effects of their votes. In fact, many short term participants are highly motivated: tourists on a sailboat in a storm, for example. Indeed, the YOLO perspective (You Only Live Once) suggests that short term thinking can be the most value-intensive. In the final analysis, short term thinking is neither less nor more conducive to reasonable values than long term thinking.

The flip side of temporal value is the weaponization of both short and long term. Short term employment can be an instrument of employers' long term gain. Conversely, Kafkaesque delays disenfranchise people in legal and civil systems, relegating them to the long term where nothing happens. On the one hand, "When do we want it? Now." On the other hand, "Don't Steal My Future" (anti-Brexit slogan).

It is natural to want it both ways, as expressed in book titles found on Amazon.com (I leave out the specific topics, preserving just the time-related subtitles): *How to Think Long-Term in a Short-Term World*, by Roman Krznaric (The Experiment, 2020); *Long-Term Thinking for a Short-Sighted World*, by Jim Brumm (Muse Harbor, 2012); and *A Context-Sensitive, Short-Term Retentionist, Long-Term Revisionist Approach*, by Jeremy Pierce (Lexington Books, 2004).

Short Term in Best Practice Epistemology

Steven Pinker complains that people overthink the daily bad news they see in the media and underestimate long term progress.[17] Over-valuing the short term can certainly prevent us from seeing long term trends. On the other hand, under-valuing punctual events in the short term present can prevent us from noticing something new. That is, under-valuing the short term might make us think that the future will resemble the past, and thereby prevent us from seeing the long term in the making. Under-valuing the short term might thus prevent us from seeing the true relation between the short term and the long.

Variations

Virtually every phrase with the word "short" in it contains an interesting aspect of the short term: short stop, short straw, short fuse, short division, short list, short order, short supply, caught short, fall short, run short, come up short, short acting, short-sighted, short notice, short wave, short turn, play a short game, a few slices short of a loaf ... No time to deal with them all.

My premise is that temporal concepts, like all concepts, are defined not by isolating a single trait as the common denominator across phenomena but by eidetic variation. Husserl's method of eidetic variation covers a wide range of cognition. Everyday experience figures out pragmatically what to call a tree and what to call a bush; theorists experiment with criteria for defining terms of art; phenomenologists describe relations between perceptions of fact and abstract conceptualizations. In some cases, variation is a procedure that consciousness uses in order to formulate precise concepts; in others, concepts themselves are names for varied phenomena; in others still, a thought is precisely a procedure for producing, varying, and loosely organizing an open-ended stream of contents. Deleuze appeals to Husserl's term "vague essences"[18] as an instance of conceptual assemblage, and while Deleuze probably exaggerates its role, Husserl does advocate vague essences when describing fields where intuition is involved, presumably including temporal intuition.[19] This is close to the use I make of eidetic variation. My method is to assemble a concept in this sense: imagining related patterns, to see where a range of phenomena comes to a limit, where it begins to exclude or conflict with phenomena that have ostensibly similar patterns, and conversely, where it overlaps with, becomes indiscernible from, or transforms into, phenomena that would not at first have seemed similar. Variations on the essence of chair should, in this way, come into a fuzzy zone in relation to bench, hillock, and toilet. The concept is itself this process of assembling, destabilizing, experimenting with, varying, and allowing the circulation of elements within, a zone of connected, shifting, converging, and diverging, definientia. So also for the essence of short term. The method of variation is both analytical and genetic, dialectical and diagrammatic. The crucial thing is that variation is not merely a means for producing invariant essences; in some cases, open-ended variation in the circumscription of a field of activity is the concept itself.

Some Phenomena

The following is an open-ended list of twenty-five eidetic variations on the short term.

(1) Contractions:

Short terms are often generated by short cuts,[20] cutting corners, abbreviation, condensation, compactification, synopsis, abridgment, or miniaturization. These terms are short because they have been shortened, for example, by shorthand or short-spoken speech (an effect of aphasia). Some events are called short just because they are shorter than others of the same type: Thomas De Quincey refers to "what are called the 'short terms'" at Oxford, relative to those of other colleges.[21]

Abridgment is an art of shortening: Orson Welles's *Mercury Theater of the Air* radio play (1946) of *Moby Dick* runs about thirty minutes. This is hardly comparable to the time it takes to read the novel, but who could resist the comparison? Occasionally, a long film based on a novel, like Fassbinder's sixteen-hour *Berlin Alexanderplatz* (1980), can make the original novel seem short by comparison, even though reading Alfred Döblin's novel (1929) takes far longer. Early twentieth-century magazines ran abridged versions of popular novels, so their readers could pretend to be well-read. (Stephen Leacock wrote humorous parodies of these in a book appropriately called *Short Circuits* (1929).) Humor, radio, and film have this in common: creativity under the constraint of the short term.

(2) Deadlines:

Mortality, term limits, and prison terms are limited by deadline, as are some research projects and vacation rentals. There are dated deadlines ("due on the twenty-first"), action deadlines (De Quincey had seventy seconds to stop the out-of-control mail coach before sudden death—"Between eternity and life, by human calculation, there was but a minute and a half"[22]), anniversary deadlines ("twenty-one days till Christmas"), and finality deadlines ("be prepared when Jesus calls" counts, but "when Hell freezes over" does not). These are not condensations of longer processes but naturally or reasonably cut off by a temporal boundary. Exceptionally, one may be granted an extension on a deadline, and the end of a tied game may be prolonged by sudden death overtime. But such extensions to the short term are typically short. Sometimes all there is, is the last minute, the nick of time.

(3) Modularities:

Some events are short term in the sense that they are separable modules of a segmented process, like one-step-at-a-time sequences, hinged actions, and serial desires.

(4) Acceptability thresholds and shelf life:

Many qualities are desirable within a certain time limit, beyond which the quality still exists, but without value. Childhood is fine for children, but ought not to drag on indefinitely. (Why not? One might well ask.) Testing a hypothesis can go on forever, but there is a threshold beyond which evidence provides diminishing returns. Knowing when to fold 'em is a phase of the art of the deal that not every wheeler-dealer is good at. Beta versions of new technologies are released to the public only for the short term, until a better version is ready, like Google Cardboard's 2014 stand-alone VR goggles. The thing has value until further notice. Administering shelf life can take a great deal of decision-making in advance, for example, in order to harvest, assign, and convey organs after the death of a donor.[23]

Soon:

"Soon" is the temporal equivalent of the spatial "just over the horizon."

(5) Repetition and recursion:

In every kind of repetition, from counting integers, to manufacturing widgets on an assembly line, to dreaming a recurrent fantasy, each episode is a short microcosm. Some repetitions start a new instance of the type (buying a new car to replace the old heap), but others extend the life of the same instance for more time (renewing a lease). Sometimes it is prudent to opt for a series of short renewable time-periods rather than commit to one long time period, like buying parking tags hourly instead of annually.

(6) Singularity:

An event that happens only once is not the same as an event that ends soon after it starts. Nevertheless, its presence is short in the sense that we will never see it again. Our capacity to see it is time sensitive. Some events are quasi-singular, like once-in-a-lifetime business opportunities, or (once-in-a-)hundred-year floods. A once-in-a-hundred-years event could be interpreted as a singularity, or it could be interpreted as an event that repeats one year out of every hundred, that is, 1 percent of the total time. Nowadays, a hundred-year storm happens every other year.

(7) Shortest intervals:

I do not normally count temporal instants (if there were such a thing) as short term, since they endure for no term at all. But it is difficult to say whether time-periods characterized as the shortest possible, like infinitesimals, vanishing points, or "time atoms" (Chapter 5), are too small to count as short term. The point is that any time segment is an interval between two time posts, after x and before y, like the period when Alcibiades starts to grow a beard: after he had none and before he has one.

(8) Meanwhile:

Often, we designate a single process as short term: we go on a diet until we reach an ideal weight, then stop. But in other cases, doing something in the short term means doing it precisely "while" something else is happening: we ride a bike to work while the car is in the shop. We engage with a given process just until some other process ends. The short term project is a temporary side project, which will be outdated and obsolete when the other process ends. The shortness of that process is grounded in the timetable of some other process.

The structuralist Gérard Genette distinguishes temporal segments that end for a while to be picked up later, that is, which end due to a "pause" or "ellipsis" ("some years passed, after which …"), from segments that end definitively due to "diachronic limits" ("between the end of June and the end of September in the year 1890").[24] We might call the latter a short term in-itself and the former a short term for-another.

(9) Temporariness:

The attitude that the temporary is less real than the permanent is, for good reasons, outdated. Temp work, one-night stands, short prison sentences, and short term loans are very real. Finance is filled with temporary realities: "Short-term paper" consists of "financial instruments that mature in less than nine months." "Commercial paper" is "an unsecured form of promissory note … typically issued by large banks or corporations to cover short-term receivables and meet short-term financial obligations, such as funding for a new project."[25] Or to cite an example from a different field, we can set the "history" cache on our web browsers to keep track of the websites we visited over the last hour, or the last week, after which they no longer appear on our drop-down list. For cybersecurity, you should limit data to a short life span on your computer. When the digital information age was young, we had the cultural idea that it offered the advantage of extending the life span of information. But we have learned that some information about ourselves is best erased after a time.

(10) Manageability:

Take it five minutes at a time. Put one foot after another. Work only on tractable problems. Play the short game (baseball, golf).

(11) Fleeting and ephemeral (*ephemeros*: "for a day"):

Some people, if they discovered that the world will end, or that they will die, tomorrow, would find it pointless to do anything today. The vanishing present seems to them to be both illusory and valueless because it dissolves into flux. Yet the journal *ephemera: Theory and Politics in Organization* studies such important topics as pandemics, repairs, comics, secrets, branding, authenticity (it is a nice point to call authenticity ephemeral), failed universities, sandcastles, and consumption. Bonnie Lambourn, a middle school teacher, designed a curriculum for teaching teens to build and compare ephemera like sand mandalas and time capsules.[26]

(12) Provisionality:

Being hired for a probationary period means being tested to see if one is good enough for the present, with the expectation of later improvement. Short term provisionality is valued for future capacity.

(13) Keeping up:

Keep up with the newest news, techniques, styles, and memes, before an even newer thing comes along. Fads express the perpetual process of catching up and getting (and staying) ahead.

(14) Early:
Getting something early (like the vaccine) often means getting to use it for a longer time. If time to arrival is short, time to expiry is long. Sooner thus implies later. Poet-historian Charles Olson: "Know the new facts early."

(15) Holding Out/Lasting For:
People can hold their breath longer if they know they only need to hold out for ninety seconds than if there is no end in sight—likewise for wearing masks, if we know the vaccine is coming by Spring. Empowerment generally lasts for a short term and dissipates if the term is either too long or indeterminate.

(16) Nothing more/nothing left:
The French expression *tout court* ("all short") means "without qualification," "without anything further." The short term is the one with the fewest extensions and appendices.

(17) The mood most conducive to the short term:
For people who prefer to keep their human interactions short, novelist Enrique Vila-Matas recommends insolence.[27] To lengthen relationships, try guilt.

(18) Planned obsolescence:
Designed to break; hence, to be replaced before it breaks. Useful things are designed for a determinate purpose and, therefore, have a determinate term value. Whereas useful things are gotten rid of when they cease to be useful, there is no reason to get rid of useless things, so they stay on the shelf indefinitely. Useless things, like the Odradek according to Kafka,[28] are for this reason a source of anxiety; only useful, therefore short term, items provide comfort.

(19) Fizzling out:
Many things decay or undergo density loss without help from anything else, the way soft drinks lose their bubbles. At the end of the day, a person gets tired.

(20) Decay by prolongation:
We tend to think of the short term as a process that could have gone on longer but gets cut short. But the other mechanism of the short term arises by lengthening rather than by shortening. Short term memory decay works like this: we perceive a certain event; the longer we continue to perceive new events, the less we remember that earlier event. This prolongation of perceptual tasking is the measure, and even the definition, of short term memory storage. The short term can thus be the result of extending an event until it decays, as much as it can be the result of cutting it back.

(21) Absorption:
Short term events often transform, as a larva becomes a butterfly or a vibrating bridge collapses. This is not decay but the conversion of energy from one process to another.

(22) Abandonment:
   An author may, for no apparent reason, stop working on a book.
(23) Relay:
   Many multistep processes include serial episodes, as when a triathlete performs three qualitatively different short term actions in a row, or when four members of a relay team perform four qualitatively similar short term actions in a row, or when a series of producers try to get a failing movie project back on track.
(24) Quick:
   Speed dialing, instant cereal, fifty-meter races, "Be right there." Not all fast things last only for a short time, as we have said, but these do. A few processes may even be short just because they are fast, on the condition that there is no way to do them more slowly, and that there is no way to do the fast thing for a longer time, as in a chemical explosion. In modern English, "quick" suggests that a process will soon be finished, as in "quick-change artist." In Old English, "*cwik*" meant "lively," without the implication of soon being finished.[29]

   In some cases, high velocity combines with small spaces to make small amounts of time. When novelist Robert Walser suffered from writer's block, he found that if he gave himself only a small piece of paper to write on, he could fill it with "microscript" before he even noticed he was blocked.[30]
(25) Getting it over with:
   Websites offer philosophy in five-minute segments.

I present these twenty-five variations to indicate a range of parameters, operations, and formal patterns. Some short term phenomena end by themselves, others are made to end; some are fast and complex, others are slow and simple, still others are fast and simple; some are better short, others would have been better long; some have no long term implications, others have crucial implications for human history. If we mix and match parameters, we might analyze a phenomenon that is short, fast, dangerous, autonomous, and condensed; or another that is short, slow, funny, interactive, and layered. In my general view, time is an ontological framework that does not have a single form but is a network of variations across interactive parameters. This is what I mean by eidetic variation. The short term is a network of operations, and it functions alongside other temporal categories that are likewise networks of variable parameters.

Short Term Depends on Something After It

Some short term phenomena are single events, but in the bigger picture, the end of one event is defined by the beginning of the next. As we will see in Hegel (Chapter 1), a temporal limit, like any limit, both excludes the time outside it and is also shaped by the contours of the time outside it. A time segment, like a spatial area, lifted out of a whole, has exactly the shape and size of the hole left in the whole around it. In addition, most short term processes contain at least one element that is long term, that spills over the limit of the short term (psychotherapy ends, but insights continue). The topology of the segment includes the long term around it. This raises the most general problematic of the short term. How is it ever possible, reasonable, or advisable to stop short?

The whole point of the short term is that it ends when it could have continued. It does not come to finality, but ends short. Paradoxically, precisely by ending, the short term ends in the middle, albeit a middle that does not continue. To that end, I have not focused on the entropic phenomena of winding down, that is, never completely finishing a project but spending less and less time on it. I have not focused on giving in. As a Toronto graffiti artist put it in the 1970s, "Don't give in, give up."

But a cut-off is also a switch, the overflow of some part of a process across the threshold from one time segment to the next. It is easy to say that from the perspective of what comes after, what looked like a previous cutoff was in fact a switch. But my method is not to use the long term to describe what happens at the end of the short term. I want to use the short term as the perspective to describe what happens at its own termination point, to describe when and how some continuing process leaks out of its end point to enter into a new segment that, from that short term standpoint, is still to come.

Short Term and Tense (Logic and Fantasy)

One way to define the cutoff between one temporal segment and the next is under the formula "until X." The tense logic interpretation of "until" focuses on the finite scope of time during which a proposition is true. The "Until" operator, pUq, could be read as: "p is true until the time at which q is true."[31] Inserting operators like "until" into tense logic recognizes that temporal categories like past and future, and the distribution of properties of objects over time, do not simply locate events and predicates in time but distribute time-sensitive truth values "just until," "as long as," or "during the interim" by attributing truth to a proposition only from $t1$ until $t2$. It should also be possible to distribute truth values across variable time segments in the form (Ex)pUx ("There exists some time up until which p is true") without designating what that time is. Or to say it differently, "p is true in the short term."

John Mbiti[32] argues that many African languages (like Swahili and Gikuyu) do not have a verb tense to refer to the distant future, that their future tenses refer only to a near future, a short term future defined by the continuation of a process or cycle already begun. The near future tense can be used to talk about a baby that will be born to a woman already pregnant, but not to the Final Judgment, or to a far-off future envisaged by science fiction. It is not that those languages cannot speak of a long term future at all, but they need extra locutions to do so.[33]

This makes us wonder whether it might be possible to invent additional verb tenses, which do not yet exist in any natural language. Macedonio Fernandez, in *The Museum of Eterna's Novel (The First Good Novel)*,[34] proposes a "minimal tense," which sounds like a specifically short term verb tense. One of his examples describes the condensed short term: "Five minutes of film, in which the entire case of Hollywood has to run, falling over themselves in order to convert all of the disgraces in two hours of film—marriage, kissing, the unmasking of false virtue—into happiness" (Fernandez [1967] 2010: 43). His other example is more puzzling: "measuring this [minimal] tense by another standard, the tense of rescuing a black hat that had been forgotten on the black seat of a chair, during the forthcoming visit of a recently arrived guest" (Fernandez [1967] 2010: 43). The confusions of past, present, and future in this sentence may even be essential to short time segments, since in a very short term event, the present makes the future so proximate to the past that we might almost say they coexist. I am not sure how to put this "verb tense" into a sentence, but it does seem to be an alternative to "until." Perhaps the short term could be expressed in a "future already" tense, or an "already not yet" tense, or a "distant hereafter now" tense. In any case, there are tense resources for analyzing the short term in surrealism and fantasy fiction.

Short Term Does Not Simply Continue After the End of It

The hard question is not how a process can continue past its time limit but how it can stay within its limits. What is there on this short side of the infinite? How can a thing's expansion, dissolution, absorption, *Aufhebung* be delayed? In topology, places have a periphery; in biology, organisms have skin. But temporally, how does a bounded period have integrity?

In Hegelian terms, this is like asking how each stage in the dialectic maintains a sphere where it works, given that every stage ends by being transformed into all the others? After all, the point of the dialectic is to exhibit the scope of, but then sublate, everything. Yet each category is supposed to do actual work and give life (good or bad) to the system, for a time, despite the fact that it is destined to be repealed and replaced in the long run. In a system of the outer limit, the trick is to preserve in some way the inner limit.

The solution will be that a given time segment is both its own whole and a part of another whole. There must be two co-existing time measures operating simultaneously in order for the concept of the short term to work.

A short term segment depends on a plurality of co-existing staggered temporal segmentations. Sometimes, one process is cut short because of another process on a different time scale. Many scientific analyses involve interactive measures, where different aspects of a situation change at different rates of speed. "Short run causality measures" predict what happens on one time scale based on what happens in another. "The Granger causality test is a statistical hypothesis test for determining whether one time series is useful in forecasting another."[35]

For example, Rachel Carson shows that human technology changes too quickly for some species in the environment to adapt to.[36] "Phylogenetic trees" graph such interactions: a species gets too good at hunting its prey, which makes the prey species go extinct, which in turn makes the hunter species go extinct. One series is short term because other short and long term series squeeze them out of their niche.

We tend to think of cutting something short on the model of snipping a piece of yarn off the spool and leaving the rest, or on the model of excerpting a passage of music for performance and leaving the rest on the page. But a "cut" in the game of Go is different: a line of black stones may be loosely connected on a diagonal, and a line of white stones may cut across the line of black stones at that diagonal. White's cutting stone cuts one segment of black's line off from the other segment. The cut is mutual, since white's line is also cut by the same diagonal made by black's stones. If either side can capture one of the other's groups of cutting stones, its line will be restored, but if not, then black and white have to operate with two lines each. A cut, on this model, is not simply the shortening of a line, but a cross-cut between two lines, a prolongation of each line on the other side of the cutting point.

Furthermore, most segments can be cut again into smaller segments. It is not only that a longer time segment can be cut into fractions but also that the same time span can be cut into many overlapping segment schemes, like overlapping time signatures and polyrhythms in the same musical composition. Temporal segmentation is rarely just one pair of cuts at the start and end of a segment but most often an overlapping set of potential cuts and even multiple criteria of segmentation.

Zizek is thinking of interpretation rather than temporality when he talks about short circuits,[37] but this passage is applicable to cross-cut temporal circuits:

> A short circuit occurs when there is a faulty connection in the network—faulty, of course, from the standpoint of the network's smooth functioning. Is not the shock of short-circuiting, therefore, one of the best metaphors for a critical reading? Is not one of the most effective critical procedures to cross wires that do not usually touch: to take a major classic (text, author, notion), and read it in a short-circuiting way, through the lens of a "minor" author, text, or conceptual apparatus?

In electrical short circuits, the path of electrons is shortened, and the result is a failure to reach a goal, which shorts out the process by stopping it too early. In Zizek's description, the short circuit cuts one thing short only to switch the circuit to another. It makes a plurality of circuits overlap, and where one circuit cuts across another, the elements are forced into a shorter circuit.

Because the very idea of the short term implies a plurality of staggered segments, some longer and some shorter, along the same temporal continuity, it is not always obvious whether a given process is short or long term. We tend to assume, for example, that people concerned about climate change are concerned with the long term, whereas people who are concerned about the economic cost of preventing climate change are concerned with the short term. Certainly, there is some truth to this. After all, climate change deniers claim not to believe in long term predictions. But it is also possible to think of the two positions with reverse temporal associations. Climate change is already having its effects, so people who want to deal with it without delay can be said to be those most concerned with the short term. Conversely, people who affect not to be concerned with climate change hope that something will somehow happen to save the day at some unknown future time—that science will solve it or that large-scale planetary cycles will someday swing back to normal. In this picture, it is deniers who posit a long view unrelated to the local events of our time and climate activists who take the short term view that current causal sequences need to be engaged as soon as possible.

It is sometimes also difficult to distinguish a complex short term desire from a simple long term desire. For example, when an animal desires only to eat, does it have a series of short term desires to eat or does it have one long term desire to eat? Some people have a short-lived desire to perform a long term action. Yet there are some clear cases. The desire to write an encyclopedia from scratch just cannot be a short term goal; the desire to draw one more breath simply cannot be a long term goal.

Applications of the Concept of Short Term

Just as it is not always clear whether a thought is short or long term, so it is not always clear whether short term thinking has better effects, both short and long term, than long term thinking.

The most common practical topics that come up in a *Google* search for "short term" are (1) short term psychotherapy, (2) short term investment, (3) short term religious and medical missions, (4) short term politics, and (5) short term relationships. It may seem dubious whether psychological problems can be cured, economies develop, faith grow, and romance bloom in a few days. Yet some human activities can probably be carried out more quickly than they usually are. I do not generalize either by praising all short term practices for their efficiency or by condemning them all for selfishness. The important thing is that practitioners of the short term conceptualize, operationalize, and evaluate detailed procedures, and the theory of the short term can gain all sorts of concepts by investigating their practices (Chapter 7).

Are Events in the Modern World Getting Shorter?

It is tempting to think that the world today is undergoing accelerating technological developments that humans lack the time to understand and assimilate. But it is also true that many basic technologies have stalled. As Marshall McLuhan complained in the early 1960s, transportation still relies on the wheel.[38] Getting on a passenger airline feels like re-entering the 1930s. It is true that smart devices are new, but the devices that are getting smart are telephones and refrigerators, which are not very new. The most discouraging fact ever about the human spirit is that humans traveled to the moon in 1969, leaving the surface of the rock to explore the cosmos, and within a few years lost interest. The newest of all possible things was at our fingertips, and we lost interest in two shakes of a lamb's tail. Can we trust SpaceX to persevere for X amount of time?

Corollary to the generalization that our age only looks ahead to short term futures is the generalization that our age only has a short term future or, in the extreme version, that our age has no future. Mathias Nilges's challenge to the allegedly futureless present age begins with a story about temporal resistance: in 1996, the "Long Now Foundation" began building a huge clock in a mountain in Texas designed to click for ten thousand years. The project is to counter "our moment of history aimed at the short term."[39]

Of course, we should acknowledge the things that are new—AI medical diagnosis, Zoom dinner parties, hacked elections—and those still to come—cloning, efficient solar energy. But innovative periods of human history, when the new is short-lived, can themselves be short-lived. The truism that the world moves fast these days may be outdated.

Similarly, it is tempting to think that the Metaverse presents us with more and more short term episodes, Instagrams, and Snapchats. Yet digital media also allow us once again to watch movies without the commercial interruptions of old TV, to binge full seasons rather than twenty-two-minute segments interrupted by a week of other things, to collect footnotes online one after the other, rather than in short flurries of archival work separated by slowly flipping through cards in catalogues. Again, this is not to understate those phenomena of screentime that are short and fragmented but to suggest that the medium itself is capable both of more short term events and also of more long term continua. It depends on who, what, and why: Twitter users think micro-thoughts, whereas the software developers who made Twitter had to think in ultra-long chains, since a single error in its 1.21 million lines of code could crash the system. Phenomena like Twitter increase the gap between humans who work in short term pieces and those who work in long term chains. I would have said that those who make Twitter wield more power than those who use it, but the world's most famous tweet rager made us wonder.

Coronavirus Diary (Discontinued)

In April 2020, I conceived the idea of keeping a coronavirus diary as a concrete example of evolving short term phenomena. It seemed obvious to make use of the planet-wide short term phenomenon at everyone's fingertips. But a few months later, it came to seem too obvious. Billions of people have been keeping the same diary. So I will cut way down on my notes and retain just three entries.

April–May 2020: We do not know how long the lockdown is going to last: two weeks (until the curve is flat), six months (until the vaccine), two years (until after the second or third wave), forever (as climate change leads to more virus mutations). We do not know whether to stockpile toilet paper, to become (or beg the acquaintance of) survivalists, or just reschedule a few things and keep our self-respect by wearing pants every day. The fact that Americans cannot trust their president to convey the truth that experts have told him, and the fact that some governors are opening up faster than the task force advises, means that we are in a term that frequently shifts from short to long and back again.

There are a lot of time-to-effect measurements that everyone now knows: it takes particulates twelve seconds to travel six feet, after which they cease to be airborne; an "R nought" infection rate over 1.1 defines "outbreak"; it takes two weeks for a delivery date to open up at Whole Foods; ten days on a ventilator is the kiss of death for patients over eighty; every day at noon, New York Governor Cuomo refutes the claims Trump made at 6:00 p.m. the day before; you get a lot of reading done in the afternoon, but if you get bored and eat dinner early, the evening stretches on endlessly.

Why should it take so long to make a vaccine? Why is the government not ramping up testing, given that that is the only way to open the economy safely? Why are they trying to open stores in too short a time, and yet not testing in a short enough time? Why does the short term not instigate a plan for getting things done, but weigh down as a question we cannot get a good faith answer to? If only there were a short term in sight.

December 11, 2020. The vaccine was approved by the FDA yesterday. How long before I get it? How long I have already lived, and have left to live, determines how long my wait for the vaccine will be. Am I old enough to get the vaccine early? I think I am going to miss, by a couple of years, the cut-off point at which the time I would have had to wait for the vaccine would have been short. If Trump had purchased the amount of vaccine that Pfizer offered, my wait would have been shorter. A person I have no respect for has made my waiting term less short.

Anti-vaxxers will not line up for the vaccine, which is good for me, as it shortens my wait. But their choice will delay, maybe forever, the point where the virus stops circulating through the population. Happily, as I understand it, I will be safe without them being safe. My short term wait will come to a definitive end independent of whether their continued risk is short or long.

March 18, 2021. I just received the first dose of the Moderna vaccine. I feel immortal. I am scheduled for the second dose on April 19, which should fully protect me by May 3. Then if the Canadian border finally re-opens, I can visit my mother, and if France can get itself together in time, vacation this summer in Marseille, which my family had planned for last summer. The End. Or is it?

[January 2022. Not the end.]

The Last of the Thought

Contrary to the ancient Egyptian saying that "Death made their names forgotten, but books made them remembered!,"[40] most writers know that finishing a book is the end of it, that any readership it might be lucky enough to find (a few reviewers, a few friends, a few dissertation candidates) will likely last a very short time. The thoughts that went into the book persisted for the time it took to write it, which seemed very long. But now that the book is in print, their short tenure on this earth is probably just about up.

Method

A general theory of the short term has a lot of moving parts. It covers ontology and epistemology. The psychology of short term memory is already a complex paradigm. There are urgent ethical/political/social issues that put us face-to-face with the short term. Mathematics and physical sciences measure short term phenomena. The arts (music, cinema, performance art, even painting) formalize strategies of short term constraints. Life is full of short term practice.

As with the previous two books in this series (*Simultaneity and Delay* and *The Many Futures of a Decision*), my methodology is to use a wide variety of theoretical and practical sources in order to study structures and operative functions of the short term. I draw equally from Husserl-influenced phenomenology, Hegel-influenced dialectic, and Deleuze-influenced multiplicities. Classical phenomenology turns out not to say much about the short term (though what it says is interesting), so I spend more time on Ricoeur's phenomenological hermeneutics. Hegel, seen stereotypically as the philosopher of the whole, would not seem to be too interested in the short term. But seen more correctly as the philosopher of interactive sub-systems, Hegel is all about what happens as the limit of one process emits the threshold of the next. Deleuze and Guattari's theory of micro-segmentation, alongside their theory of flows and interruptions, can be repurposed as a theory of temporal segmentation.

In addition to these philosophical mainstays, I extract resources for a theory of the short term from De Beauvoir's phenomenology of aging (the experience that there is not much time left); from ancient and modern utilitarians; medieval time atomists; short speech rhetoricians; old controversies over the philosophical interpretation of calculus; film editing; and many other regions and folds. I schematize short term patterns theorized by various conceptual systems and practiced in various concrete activities and disciplines. I do not think that there is a single definition of the short term (any more than there is a single definition of simultaneity, or delay, or the future). There are many ways to construe the quantities, qualities, and functions that define a term as short in various contexts. The more we investigate temporal concepts like the short term, connecting features that work together and distinguishing those that do not, the better equipped we are for analyzing and using onto-temporal structures.

Because this project is built out of short pieces, it was difficult to be sure where to put each one. We might even define the difference between short term segments and sub-portions of long term events by noting that short parts of long wholes have fixed positions in the whole, whereas short wholes can function out of order. Nevertheless, the reader might find that Chapters 1–3 approach the short term using phenomenological, existential, hermeneutical, and dialectical frameworks; Chapters 3 and 4 focus on the short term in history and memory;

Chapters 4 and 5 deal with the relation between quantity and function in the short term; Chapters 6–8 cover ethical, practical, and aesthetic short term phenomena; Chapter 9, Part 1 uses Deleuze to add further solutions to unfinished topics in previous chapters, particularly ontological and historical–political problems; and Chapter 9, Part 2 produces a general schematic for short term temporal segmentation that can be back-propagated through the book as a whole.

Chapter 1

PHENOMENOLOGICAL SHORT TERM (KANT, HEGEL, HUSSERL)

Argument: The consciousness of a short term phenomenon is constituted by cutting a limited time segment out of the temporal continuum, which in turn implies overlapping temporal measures.

What does it mean to cognize a determinate time-magnitude, to take a limited amount of time as an intentional object, to experience a finite time period marked by a beginning and end? Though we do it all the time, it is not obvious how time lends itself for us to do that to it.

Normally, I would start every topic with the phenomenology of Husserl. But on the short term, we find only a few relevant passages. For example, in Husserl's sixth Logical Investigation, we find the general idea that the fulfillment of any meaning takes place in steps and gradations. To understand the meaning of 50, we break it down and consider 5 and 10, then break those meanings down into 1 + 1 + 1 + 1 + 1, and so on. To see a cup, we move around it one side at a time, synthesizing perspectives in order until we get back to where we started and have a view of the whole. We could take these examples as models for interpreting the short term micro-processes that ground the synthesis of all meaning intention and meaning fulfillment. But while this has all sorts of implications, there is not much direct discussion of the short term in Husserl's work.

A passage from the "Temporality" chapter of Merleau-Ponty's *Phenomenology of Perception* is representative of the way that phenomenology introduces, but then tends not to focus on, short and long term temporal segments:

> [Bergson] was right to stick to the continuity of time as an essential phenomenon ... Instant C and instant D, however near they are together, are not indistinguishable, for if they were there would be no time; what happens is that they run into each other and C becomes D because C has never been anything but the anticipation of D as present, and of its own lapse into the past ... What there is, is not a present, then another present which takes its place in being ...: there is one single time ... which establishes itself at a stroke. [The presence of time ...] is equally this day, this year, or my whole life.[1]

Given that Merleau-Ponty posits time intervals, with distinct beginning and end points, qualified with the length-relative clause "however near," we might expect the particular lengths of intervals to be essential to time and times. But Merleau-Ponty's emphasis on continuity, the unbroken density of time across that interval, and the subjective whole that combines past, present, and future treats temporal intervals more as sliding transitions than as measured segments. Of course, a day is not a year, but phenomenologists often regard time more as continuous elision than as interrupted segmentation. Yet the latter is clearly also part of our experience of time, and just as good a topic for phenomenology.

As we will see in Chapter 3, Heidegger resists the very idea of measuring time. He does advocate that philosophy should only take small steps on a long path, but that is less a preference for the short term over the long term, than a preference of the ontological over the ontic. Husserl too recommends that philosophers aim just for a few small steps to begin with, but Husserl at least wants to get a few concrete results under his belt, whereas Heidegger is ready to stay at the beginning for a long, long time. Husserl in this sense will be somewhat more useful for a theory of the short term than Heidegger.

So what does it mean to pin down a limited amount of time as an intentional object in the midst of a wider temporal horizon?

Generating Determinate Time-Magnitudes: Kant

The goal of Kant's Transcendental Aesthetic in the *Critique of Pure Reason*[2] is to show that the "axioms of time" are not empirical but a priori (Kant [1781] 1929: A31B47). Kant's analysis of time focuses on succession. Although time as a whole is continuous, there are distinct parts of time "one after the other" (Kant [1781] 1929: A32B49). Kant does not zero in on the fact that some series of successive time-parts are shorter than others. Nevertheless, our analysis of the structure of the short term is an attempt to explicate one of Kant's axioms of time.

When Kant schematizes the twelve categories of the understanding according to their time-functions, time-length just barely comes up in passing. Of the four temporal schemata—quantitative time-series, qualitative time-fullness, causal time-order, and modal time scope—only the first, the "Axioms of Intuition," even indirectly considers the difference between longer and shorter time segments. Kant here describes how we construct an extensive magnitude in space over time, which at the same time describes how we construct an extensive magnitude of time.

> I cannot represent to myself a line, however small, without drawing it in thought, that is, generating from a point (*Punkte*) all its parts (*Teile*) one after another. Only in this way can the intuition be obtained. Similarly with all times, however small. In these I think to myself only that successive advance (*sukzessiven Fortgang*) from one moment (*Augenblick*) to another, whereby through the parts of time (*Zeitteile*) and their addition a determinate time-magnitude (*bestimmte Zeitgrösse*) is generated. (Kant [1781] 1929/Kant [1781] 1990: A162–3B203)

Let us focus on drawing a time line. In Kant's description, every length of time, "however small" (and presumably also, however large), moves away from a point at its start and is measured by the distance it extends from that point. The shortest duration is still a duration longer than a point. To generate time, and to understand it, thus first means generating a short duration. As I read it (though I am not sure about this), the parts of time that are added together are not points; only the launch is point-like, whereas the subsequent parts added together to make a longish extended duration are all shortish extended durations. There are a number of tricky questions of interpretation. Is a "moment" (*Augenblick*) in time exactly analogous to a "point" (*Punkt*) in space, or might a "moment" take up a positive extension of duration whereas a "point" has no extension in space? Is the end of a temporal duration as point-like as its beginning (since Kant uses the phrase "from one moment to another"), even though Kant does not say anything analogous for spatial lines, which begin at a point but are not said to end at a point? I am not sure how to solve these technical problems in Kant's interpretation, and for my part, I would rather not commit to "points" one way or another. But we do not have to solve these questions here. What is important for us in the passage, though it is not emphasized by Kant, is that constructing a small time-magnitude requires not only adding parts together one after the other but also cutting off that generation of parts at a certain limit, so that a "determinate time-magnitude" results. If we just keep adding parts without stopping, there will be no magnitudes at all, no way to measure time, no meaning to the question "how long?," just ongoing increase: continuous quantity, perhaps, but not discrete quanta. It is possible that Kant believes there may be such a thing as continuous infinite magnitude without discrete quanta (though Kant's antinomies are skeptical about that). But what Kant is interested in here is "determinate magnitude," and this is by definition at least one cut shorter than forever. The whole point of schematism is to temporalize the categories of the understanding, and the categories at stake here are Unit (launch point—sometimes this is translated as Unity, but as I understand it, that is not the right idea here), Plurality (successive advance), and Totality (determinate time-magnitude). Cutting off the production of points so that they count together as a determinate length is the schematic generation, the temporal operationalization, and the transcendental functionality, of the category of Totality. (Totality is the category of a finite determinate whole, which is completely different from the so-called idea of infinity.) In other words, the act of cutting the time-length is just as crucial to the synthesis of time-magnitude as the selection of a launch point and the serial generation and accumulation of multiple parts one after the other. But if we then ask Kant how it is that perception, or imagination, or thought cuts off the serial production of temporal parts, even provisionally, there is no description. Maybe it is too obvious to require explanation; maybe it is a given (a fact of consciousness, as Kant's immediate successors would say). Maybe the fact that imagining borders around segments of space and time is a necessary condition for the appearance of objects means that it needs no further operational analysis. It is possible, I think, that cutting into time is in this way a primitive, fundamental, universal, and necessary a priori capacity of consciousness, and hence a transcendental property of all phenomenal reality. Still, this is the step that I am interested in questioning further. How is the cutoff limit accomplished? How does the termination of an extension in space, and especially in time, which divides time into segments, "however small," actually work?

Sooner or Later (Not): Hegel

Hegel's theory of time in *The Philosophy of Nature*[3] shares with Kant's the fact that he mentions, but minimizes the role of, the length of time segments. We might briefly construe Hegel's difficult argument that time is the negation of space (Hegel [1830] 2004: 34) as follows: space is differentiated into places, therefore it must be possible for spatially located things to move through space, and therefore, there must be time in order for one thing occupying space not to be where another space is. Toward the end of his seven pages on time, Hegel challenges the idea that arithmetic, with its abstract categories of equal and unequal, and its numerical intervals, is a proper science for measuring time (Hegel [1830] 2004: 38). Mathematics, the "theory of magnitude," should emerge from the dialectic of reality and (contrary to what Kant thinks) not be prior to it. In other words, time does have magnitudes, but the principles for measuring time should emerge from relations among actual movements in space and time.

Yet while arithmetic is not suitable for describing continuous movement through space over time, there should be some way of quantifying the finite periods during which things rest in a place before moving on. Hegel writes in a *Zusatz*: "All finite things are temporal, because sooner or later [*kurz oder lang*, which we might translate as 'in the short term or in the long term'] they are subject to change; their duration is thus only relative" (Hegel [1830] 2004: 36/ [1830] 1970: 50).

Hegel inserts the "short or long" clause almost as an aside, but it is important that even things that for a long while appear to be unchanging will eventually change. Indeed, short term things seem to be the most normal kind of things, since they change. There appear to be exceptions, since other things seem not to change, but in fact, all things have the property of passing away that short term things have the most. Even long things are like short things. This looks like Hegel privileges those short term things that change without much resistance over short term things that resist change for a relatively long term, and hence that Hegel privileges short amounts of time over long amounts. But this preference for the short term does not last. Ultimately, Hegel's point is that change happens to everything, sooner or later.

Even though "sooner or later" looks like a throwaway phrase inside a discussion of change and finitude, it is effectively a definition of temporality. Time segments may be measured by discrete quanta when we are looking at isolated events, but when we look at the variable magnitude of time as a whole, we ground events in the shifting sands of the "sooner or later."

Nevertheless, there is a reason why the topic of the short term is hard to make visible in the history of the philosophy of time. Philosophers of time spend great effort on the question of whether time is measurable, and therefore divisible. But they do not speculate much on whether, among all the time segments of variable length, some lengths are privileged. That is, philosophers have not traditionally speculated on whether time naturally falls into short, or long, terms. Indeed, that would be an odd controversy to pick a side on. I am not trying to argue that short term time segments are more time-like than long term segments. But I am interested in whether and how the possibility of segmenting time in short spans has implications for the nature of time. I am interested in how the "sooner or later," short and long, may be crucial for understanding how time works. I am interested in variable time-length as a functional property of time passage. And I am especially interested in the way that every time segment, short or long, requires a cut in the temporal continuum, which, in a limited sense, does privilege the shortening function over the lengthening function after all.

Time Cut: Husserl

It is interesting to contrast the phenomenological picture of a short amount of time with research in cognitive science that defines the subjective present as a "three-second window"—not a vanishing instant, and not an elastic context-dependent synthesis of relevance, but a specific amount of time.[4] The typical experiment behind this definition of the present involves finding the ideal experiential duration of an event that people will be able to reproduce correctly at a later time. A person is given a task to perform that takes a certain amount of time, then later is asked to let the same amount of time go by. It turns out that three seconds is the optimal quantity of time that subjects accurately reproduce for the same amount of time at a later time. People asked to reproduce experiences shorter than three seconds spend more than three seconds reproducing it later on, whereas people asked to reproduce experiences longer than three seconds spend too little time doing so. The temporal zone of the living present is thus defined by the length of time that a person can re-live as another present later without a difference.

In fact, it is rather odd that cognitive science would define the feeling of presence by the optimal experiential length that can accurately be reproduced at some later time. After all, there are obviously experiences that last shorter than three seconds, and it is not obvious why those are not typical present experiences. For that matter, phenomenology generally has a very different account of the relation between present time and the way the present is retained afterward. In phenomenology, the present is retained in memory in later time, but that does not mean it is reproduced as another present in later time. Still, even if we are skeptical about the cognitive science thesis that the "present" lasts for a typical quantity of time (whether three seconds or some other amount), we can nevertheless make phenomenological use of one aspect of that thesis, namely that the present is a "window" and not a point. We might think of the phenomenology of time as an analysis of the frame of the window of the present.

Husserl's *Lectures on Internal Time-Consciousness* centers on the running present window and the temporal continuity produced by constantly re-generating retentions of the past and protentions of the future. Time is both continuity and segmentation: "Modes of running-off of an immanent temporal Object have a beginning, that is to say, a source-point" (*Querschnitt*, which could also be translated as "cross-section").[5] Starting and stopping points—engaging and terminating the inner stopwatch of consciousness, even though consciousness always runs past these terminations—constitute the ever-returning periodization of temporal segments. This is the key point in the phenomenology of temporal window-opening. Time passes by temporal markers. We could always refer to a fixed time, of no matter what length, as a temporal identity, but the point of the identity is that points along the way are skipped over in the process that eventually ends at a marked point.

Nicolas de Warren[6] points to the early psychologist William Stern as a source for Husserl's account of the cuts at the beginning and end of time segments. James Dodd[7] points to Dedekind cuts as another source. If a present Now is by definition a cross-section (*Querschnitt*), then a segment of the past is a length-section (*Längsschnitt*). Since the present is not an isolated unit but a portion of a duration, and a duration is not openly continuous but is measured at its ends by relatively sharp limits, the effect of defining both the present and the past as cuts in duration is to reduce the difference between the two most basic forms of time, namely the simultaneity of a moment and the succession of a duration (de Warren 2009: 93). A moment is nothing but the launch point or the landing-point of a duration, and a duration is nothing but the interval between cuts. Continuous time is defined by the limits that make it short term, and discrete time is defined by the extensions that continue past its borders.

As important as his *Lectures on Time-Consciousness* are, the core of Husserlian phenomenology (in my view) is intentional objects, introduced in his first and sixth *Logical Investigations*.[8] In a nutshell, whenever we perceive, or think about, an object, our understanding of it, its meaning, is built on the way we synthesize experiences we may have had of it and with experiences we expect we might have of it in the future under various conditions and from various perspectives. If we go on to achieve some of the perceptual intuitions that we anticipate, we confirm our prior understanding of that object; when we are frustrated in our attempt to achieve those intuitions, we change our minds about what the object was. These "graded syntheses of epistemic fulfilment" over time are the heart of intentionality. As we synthesize more perceptions with each other, we come to know objects more fully. Husserl devotes thousands of pages to clarifying the many elements in this description. The only point I want to draw here is the central importance of what we could call the "next" perception. If I am climbing stairs to the top of the Eiffel Tower, I expect my next perception of the Seine below to take up just a bit less of my visual field than it did in the perception before it. If I am experiencing the climb upward and yet see the Seine take up more of my visual field, something will be very wrong with my understanding of the objects in the world around me. And if the river on the ground got *too* much smaller with just one upward step, then once again, it is perceptual blooey. This is the nature of perspective, and perspective is the zero point of orientation of all finite experiencing subjects like ourselves. The centrality of perspective is not just that we perceive things from a spatial point of view but also that we perceive spatial things in temporal order, with some (albeit imperfect) degree of continuity. When I turn a coffee cup around from left to right in my hand, then unless something has gone wrong (which of course it might), I see the cup's "next" profile along that pathway; when I hear a melody or a rhythm, I hear the next tone, or the next beat, next;[9] when I climb the steps, I see, in the next moment in time, the next thing in space. The entire phenomenological apparatus of subjectivity and objectivity, space and time, and, if we draw out all the consequences, intersubjectivity and lifeworld, not to mention anxiety toward death, hangs on the concept of the "next" experience. The next, the supplement (*Ergänzung*), and the psychic demand for supplementation (*Ergänzungsbedürftigkeit*) ground the transcendental procedure that turns empiricist sense data into phenomenological intentionality. To move from having a particular sense impression in our subjective visual fields, to experiencing a real object in the three-dimensional world, we anticipate what the object will look like next, and next after that, from a plurality of changing points of view. Ideally, we might like to anticipate what an object would look like if it were fully present, if we were to somehow accomplish a perception of it from all possible points of view at once. But of course, that is not possible. We cannot see an object from all points of view at once; there is not even such a thing as what an object would look like from all points of view at once. The object has no such look. All we can do is to anticipate what it will look like exactly next. And this is all we need. As long as we can synthesize different perceptions in order, remember the sides of the cup that we have seen so far, confirm with each new perception over time that it appears more or less to be the one we expected next, and eventually find after an appropriate amount of time that we are looking at the same side again that we saw at the beginning, so that we will by then have seen the whole cup in the round over time, then we can judge, with all the perceptual reason available to any perceiver, that the object, based on the evidence so far, is what we thought it was. It all hangs on the "next." And the next, to finally state the moral of the story, is the perception we will get after an interval of the shortest term possible. It would not be enough for perception if we experienced each new perception some time after the previous one—the next one has to be right after the last, as soon as it can be after the last as perception is over. Phenomenology certainly also relies on long term memory. But procedurally, transcendentally, and *wissenchaftlich*, the role of the next perception commits phenomenology to the shortest of terms.

In Husserl's *Crisis*,[10] a more particular present is at stake: the "modern" one. The problem with the modern, Husserl says, the reason it is in crisis, is that this present we are currently living through is failing in its retention–protention practices. Husserl may or may not be right to think his own present times were worse in this respect than all the others. It was certainly extremely bad (ours is no great shakes either), and perhaps as a transcendental philosopher, Husserl is allowing that every age is in crisis in its own way. In any case, the point is that it is not trivial that the present in a social world, a modernity, is the cutting edge in any historical duration. As a cutting point, the modern has a long history, but defines recency. The modern is a termination point for the time being, it culminates a long term and defines a short term. And of course, it is critical in part because there may be something we can do about it—a socio-temporal "I can"—and what we might be able to do about it might be doable in a short enough term that we could save the modern from itself, to make the modern less isolated from the past and at the same time less stuck in it, so that the future will be free to use temporality in full retention–protection mode. The modern presents a problem we need to deal with in the short term, using evidence from the recent term, to free the next period of socio-historical time.

Husserl is interested in the way all people make use of the past, but since he is concerned with the philosophical worldview that modernity is mired in, he is especially interested in the way philosophers draw from the past. And he contrasts the way philosophers draw from the distant past with the way they draw from the recent present:

> The situation is complicated. *Every philosopher "takes something from the history"* of past philosophers, from the past philosophical writings—just as he has at his disposal, from the present philosophical environment, the works that have most recently been added and put in circulation, takes up those that have just appeared, and, what is possible only in the case [of the present], makes more or less use of the possibility of entering into a personal exchange of ideas with still living fellow philosophers. (Husserl [1936] 1970 *Beilage* XXVIII: 392)

It may seem that there is no structural difference, only a quantitatively relative difference, between retrieving something from long term retention and retrieving something from short term retention. But once the crisis of modernity is at stake, it may make all the difference whether something recent, or only something uncontaminated by the recent, or only something even more recent than the recent past will be of assistance.

Husserl's *The Origin of Geometry* pursues the puzzling implication of the fact that we have the writings of distant past authors in our libraries today, but if we read their ideas in today's context, they appear merely as *"ready-made* concepts" (Husserl [1936] 1970: 366). Reading the past in the present way means that paradoxically, old texts appear as if their original meaning-creation were irrelevant, as if they appeared out of nowhere as assertions; the old ideas appear as if they were inventions of the present, without context or motivation, without experiential intentionality; the old ideas appear in the present without anything in the present to give them meaning other than the dictionary meanings we would find if we looked up the words on *Google*. To restore their meaning, they would have to appear again as *made* (signed by a thinking subject) but *not ready*-made, or to put the same point in the opposite way, to appear as *ready* (for use) but *not ready-made*.

The main issue in the reconnection of the present and the past is thus not just the amount of time elapsed but how the two moments of subjectivity, past and present, along with the interval between them, are co-present. Sense-making is a process of "historical backward reference" (Husserl [1936] 1970: 370). Subjectively, it is a process of "co-consciousness constructed through human activity" (Husserl [1936] 1970: 370). Structurally, co-consciousness with the authors of the past, to be sure, shares something with co-consciousness with contemporary authors. In both cases, a philosopher reads works that have been put into circulation and enters into a personal exchange of ideas with fellow philosophers. The difference involves the "recency" of the other's contribution. Of course, communication with a philosopher who is still alive, whose recency is ongoing, may be more lively. But the similarity between engaging with long-dead, recently dead, and still-living philosophers whose works have been recently published is that in all cases, there are relations between me-now and the having-been of the works of others, and between me-here and the lived-ideas of the others. In all cases, the way that the ready-made becomes lived, that is, becomes unready-unmade, is by means of pairing: pairing one subject with another-subject, and pairing now with not-now. Reading and understanding are in this way not acts of solo consciousness but of co-consciousness. Even if both writer and reader coexist in the present, there is still a division within the present, between the current present subject and the "recently added" other; and the two have to have been put into simultaneous circulation together. Even if a writer wrote a book a long time ago but the reader is just seeing it now, there still has to be a juxtaposed contemporaneity, so that the long term gap in existence functions effectively as an encounter with something one has just come across recently. In the final analysis, the co-consciousness between writer and reader does not make the length of time between them irrelevant, rather it constructs their dialogue out of the dialectic of long and short term.

This is the deep phenomenology of historical term-making. A long period of history appears synthetically as history only when the long term circulates in the short term of the present reader; and a reader only thinks in the lived present when the short term divides into a distanced temporality that keeps the given, and the interpretation of it, from collapsing.

It is not that there is no phenomenological difference between the short term and the long term other than by degrees that are not very important. It is that the lived present, the synthesis of currency and distance, is a synthesis, in the short term, of the long term and the short term. Still, for there to be a synthesis of short and long term, we need a way to characterize the limit of the short term and a way to characterize the limit of a segment of time even when time surpasses that limit in joint contemporaneity.

Time Limit: Hegel

The problem of limit is the guiding thread of Hegel's *Science of Logic*.[11] Schematically, the problem of limit works like this: coming-into-being and passing-out-of-being splits the process of becoming into two directions; each implies the movement of the other, so the inner constitution of each is located inside the constitution of the other outside of it.

This model of the interactive limit at the border of a thing and its counterpart can be applied to just about everything, from geometrical figures up to cosmopolitan onto-sociology. It provides the logic of Husserl's idea of the alter ego as the alien consciousness present yet inaccessible within our own consciousness; of Lacan's idea that the unconscious is the desire of the other; and of the Ubuntu proverb that "I am because we are."[12]

Short term temporal segments are simpler than intersubjective polemics, so I will start with a straightforward picture of limit and draw out a few of Hegel's theorems applicable to a theory of the short term.

Any finite something is what it is because it shapes itself (spatially, qualitatively, and functionally) against and alongside something else. Its determination is constituted at its border with the other, and the shape of each is immanently shifted as the shape of the other at its border shifts. This is easiest to see when a shape is cut out of a spatial field: the border of the shape, which defines its interior area, is exactly the same border as the one that defines the area on its outside. Time and space do not always have the same structures, but in this they do: whatever amount of time is taken out of a twenty-four-hour day for sleeping, the part of the time left over to be awake is exactly the remainder left behind in the twenty-four-hour whole. Hegel is not only, and not even primarily, concerned here with quantitative divisions. His discussion of limit is deliberately positioned under the category of Quality, to be used in examples like the limit of redness between green and violet, or the limit of law between criminality and despotism. The type of limit present in short temporal segments would for Hegel be only a subordinate case. Nevertheless, the things Hegel says about limit in general are indispensable for our account of the short term.

Because each thing is affected by changes in the determinations of the other outside it, each thing is constituted by, and at, its "unstable surface" (Hegel [1812] 1989: 124). Some philosophers might prefer to say that things change only accidentally at their surfaces and not in their nature. But since Hegel defines the being of each thing in terms of its changing borders, the alter-ability of each thing via changes in the other is inherent in its own self. A thing is always-already the incorporation of the thing that is its other. As Hegel puts it, "determinate being has *passed over* into otherness, something into other, and something is just as much an other as the other itself is" (Hegel [1812] 1989: 125). This is Hegel's definition of limit: "something has its determinate being *outside* of its limit" (Hegel [1812] 1989: 127). To put this back into the vocabulary of Kant's Axioms of Intuition, in the generation of a temporal duration, it is the instability of the point, its lack of autonomy relative to the parts around it, that has already shot it into its next part. We do not need to ask what motivates a subject looking at a point to draw a line from it; each point is already where it is because of where the next point is sitting beside it, so each point is already becoming a line (Hegel [1812] 1989: 128).

The "already," either in the explicitly temporal sense of pre-existence or in the transcendental/ontological sense of "always-already," suggests another way to think of the ultra-short term. For Hegel, the logic of conceptual transition is that a new conceptual development has already taken place within the conceptual system that led up to it, before it was explicitly "posited" as such. This, after all, is the nature of "pre-supposition," namely that something is posited-as-pre, posited to-be-in-advance-of-itself, constituted after the fact *as* having been there earlier. Historiography operates this way: we study history not just to find out what has been shaping us but to let ourselves have become shaped by it all along. Following a similar line of thought, Husserl[13] interprets the "prior" in "a priori" transcendental givenness in this way: I observe an object, and in thinking backward to what makes up that experience, I constitute, by my enquiry, the a priori givenness of presentation that I will have been experiencing all along.

The point of the always-already event is that when a change happens, something new arises, in such a way that it has already happened. In the vocabulary of the short term, the virtual end of the process arises a priori along with its beginning. Normally, of course, a time period's end must come after its beginning. Even an always-already event, like the learning process whereby a society realizes/decides that it is/will-have-been subject to the heritage of something that happened in the past, starts the process before ending it—obviously. But as a transcendental a priori made real in the course of self-reflection, it is a process so short that its accomplishment will have been in the past just as soon as a subject is conscious of it in the present. It sounds paradoxical, but that is the nature of any always-already: it takes place in an event that is so short term that its time span is effectively shorter than zero. In all other cases, time spans, short or long, are greater than zero; an event which occurred in no time at all (I do not think such a thing is possible) would take place instantaneously and would not count as a time span at all; but in the unique case of an event of transcendental conditioning, whose end will already have been accomplished before the process that constitutes it in backward synthesis has begun, the accomplishment occurs in a time span of less time than zero. The same might be said about backward causality—but few people seriously believe in that.

This possibility of short terms that occupy less than no time is interesting. However, this moves into topics of transcendental conditioning and away from temporality as such, so I am going to leave it behind here and return to the simpler problem of how a time line is drawn from end to end.

If Hegel can explain better than Kant how line-generation begins (since the first point will already have moved beyond its limit), he creates an even more difficult problem of how line-generation ends (since the supposed end point should already be expanding beyond its limit). Does every line go on forever? Everyone knows Hegel's discussion of the bad infinite: if the being of one thing is found in the next being over, and the being of that thing is in turn in the next being over beside that one, then progress is an endless regress. It does not help to posit some overall total being outside all the finite particulars defined by their others, since the so-called total being would itself again be shaped by what it is on the other side of, so the problem of generating endless other sides is just repeated. And it is not enough to concede that there just are an infinite number of other-defined beings, even though strictly speaking that is accurate. We need in addition to describe the positive character of the infinite system. We need to describe the "good infinite" in contrast with the bad one. The solution, for Hegel, is that the "good" finite–infinite relation has the form of "being-for-self" (Hegel [1812] 1989: 157). Each limited something is not just shaped by something external to it; rather, by being shaped by something outside it, that outside becomes something *for* it. The good infinite is the "for" structure of the series of others. The "for" structure turns the bad infinite good. While we keep expanding and moving through the time line, we also keep affirming its continuity with each new movement. Each now, though it is the not-now (or the for-another) of its antecedent and of its successor, is the yes-now for the time being (the for-itself). Admittedly, this does not explain a lot about temporal segmentation. But it does say something. The productive affirmation of the Now does not end a temporal period, it does not cut it out, it just distinguishes the continuation of time at one moment from the continuation of time at another moment. But this is precisely all we wanted it to do. We do not really want a theory of temporal segments to tell us that time segments are separate pieces of time—that would be a terrible theory, counterintuitive, contradicting the most basic evidence that time undergoes succession. The small amount of segmentability in Hegel's idea that each passing-over is "for" itself is just enough and not too much.

From the idea that in drawing out time we mark each non-autonomous advance as an interval for itself, we can unveil the next Hegelian topic, namely quantification: the quantification of lines, series, and durations.

Hegel's argument is that since there is actual otherness, real exteriority in the for-other relation, it follows that being-for-self is operationalized in the field of many ones (Hegel [1812] 1989: 159). This point is common sense. The finite–other relation, namely the structure by which one thing leaves off and the next begins, introduces the question of quantity.

Hegel's analysis of quantity in his *Science of Logic*, starting with continuous and discrete magnitudes and ending with ratios, proportions, and multiple measuring criteria, is hundreds of pages long. We cannot go through the whole analysis here, obviously, though every page of it is interesting for the problem of the short term. In Chapter 5, I will say a few things about Hegel's understanding of the limit in calculus, but for now, I will just pick out five particular theses.

First, temporal segments and temporal continua are mutually dependent. We might have thought that discrete magnitudes would be described by particular quanta, whereas continuous magnitudes go off vaguely in all directions. But in fact, continuous magnitudes also start and finish at particular points, so they too are measured by determinate quanta (Hegel [1812] 1989: 201). Both discrete and continuous magnitudes are segmented. Or to put it in reverse, a discrete quantum is a quantity that has started somewhere, then becomes continuous up to another point; conversely, a continuum is undivided up to a certain point and is then "broken off" at that point (Hegel [1812] 1989: 203), so that the end point is a discrete quantum. Every quantity is both cut at a short term and continuous up to that termination, beyond which a different quantity continues its vector. For example, the cardinal number 100 is just where the 100th ordinal number breaks off the count. Indeed, much of Hegel's dialectic of quantity hangs on the idea of "breaking off the count" (Hegel [1812] 1989: 206).

Second, the functions of equal and unequal break a complex number into elements, which are in turn broken up into other elements, and so on indefinitely (Hegel [1812] 1989: 210). Quantities, in other words, are made up of other quantities, either by multiplying a number by itself (squares and powers); or by breaking it up into fractions, ratios, and inverse ratios; or by functioning in differential equations (Hegel [1812] 1989: 253). Each extension can always be broken into shorter extensions and the shorter multiplied into longer. Irrational numbers exemplify this process in its extremity.

Third, it follows that every number is made up of other numbers. There is no such thing as a stand-alone number. Numbers, and other quantitatively measured segments, including short terms in time, are degrees in a scale, that is, intensive magnitudes (Hegel [1812] 1989: 218). Determinate quantum "consists in undergoing increase or decrease" (Hegel [1812] 1989: 225). This is ultimately why mathematics is more concerned with relations between variables than with constants (Hegel [1812] 1989: 246–7).

Fourth, as long as we only look at quantities as degrees on a single scale of measure, it might seem that limits, which describe the size of an interval, are calculated in single numbers. But once we look at quantities that involve two or more scales of measurement at once, the whole issue of the short and the long gets complicated by nodal lines (Hegel [1812] 1989: 366–7). Typical cases include the way that a liquid, measured by temperature, may increase gradually, and at a certain point of that temperature increase, the same liquid, under the measure of density, changes suddenly into gas; or in Marx's example, discontented workers, measured by number of people, increase gradually, and at a certain point on that increasing scale, the same people, under the measure of social power, change suddenly into a revolutionary army. Hegel says that the classical thesis that "nature takes no leaps" may be true for continua on a single scale but is not true for continua measured on more than one scale at a time (Hegel [1812] 1989: 369). And almost all real-world phenomena, both in nature and in culture, are of the latter type.

Hegel offers an interesting example from music. A piece of music is not just a number of tones in succession; it is also a harmony measured simultaneously. The way Hegel puts it is that "while successive notes seem to be at an ever-increasing distance from the keynote, or numbers in succeeding each other arithmetically seem only to become other numbers, the fact is that there suddenly emerges a return" (Hegel [1812] 1989: 369). In the course of a note-by-note melody, notes return to the tonic at the octave, and dissonances are resolved in major chords. Judged on the measure of individual tones, the melody just goes on and on; judged simultaneously under the two different measures (melody and harmony), there are points that end a phrase, restart, and return. The crucial thing for us about the Hegelian dialectic of quantity is that defining segments in music, and in anything else, depends on the interaction of multiple measures. The short term is not measured by one number but by a combination of numbers.

Hegel says provocatively that the return to the octave during a melody is a case of "*actio in distans*," action at a distance (Hegel [1812] 1989: 369). This is something like Raymond Bellour's definition of segments in film (Chapter 8), where a character laughing early in a film falls into a segment pair when the character laughs again later in the film; it is also much like the way that a memory is not a single experiential phenomenon but a coordinate pair of phenomena, namely one original perceptual experience and one subsequent retrieval experience (Chapter 4). Our conclusion is that many short term segments can only be spotted when we measure phenomena on two measuring scales at once. To put it provocatively, a short term temporal segment can be composed of a bit of time here plus a bit of time there. Or even more radically, a short term temporal segment can be cut off by a continuing succession of tones crossing a continuous succession of intervals, in such a way that the discontinued segment is cut by the cross-point of the two continuities. Music is thus a paradigm for the way short segments overlap in a staggered way and reconnect at a distance. Interference patterns across multiple measures are essential to the structure of time.

This has been the moral of a number of our stories: the logic of segments is generally operationalized not in simple cuts but in cross-cuts, temporal cuts across multiple measures of time-content.

Finally, fifth, since numbers are not settled without ongoing comparison with other numbers, quantities are more like "problems" to be solved than they are like facts (Hegel [1812] 1989: 227). We can consider the whole field of quantity as the problem of how the short term is possible and how the short term is a limit that makes other terms possible.

We have been analyzing the determinate temporal limit using a broadly dialectical transcendental phenomenology. But phenomenology often yields its most powerful structures in the context of more concrete experiences. We now turn to de Beauvoir's concrete phenomenological analysis of the experience of having only a short amount of time left to live.

Chapter 2

THE SHORT TIME REMAINING UNTIL DEATH
(DE BEAUVOIR, SCHOPENHAUER)

Argument: The short term is experienced dreadfully (or is it?) as the short amount of time remaining in one's life. The short term remnant of life in turn impacts other temporal forms of consciousness, including the sense of past, present, and future; the sense of memory and projects; and the sense of genealogy and legacy.

A person gets to the age when they realize that they have only a relatively short amount of time left to live. Of course, people from a young age may feel that life is short, but the question is whether and how the feeling that life has become shorter than it used to be has an effect on time-consciousness in general, and on the short term in particular. This chapter focuses on aging as a mode of noticing the short term, but phenomenology of the biological clock for fertility or the phenomenology of death row would have made equally good chapters.

Existentialist discussions of the short term often concern whether the recognition of finitude gives rise to a greater, or lesser, sense of urgency or enthusiasm around projects for the future. Schopenhauer, as always, draws the pessimist conclusion; Seneca (Chapter 6) and Kierkegaard offer qualified optimism; De Beauvoir chooses, as is her wont, ambiguity. I do not have any wisdom to offer about what a person ought to feel about it. My goal is primarily to schematize the vicissitudes of the consciousness of the short term remainder, to clarify the temporal resources available to us.

It seems natural for the consciousness of a short future to interact with consciousness of the past, that is, for anticipation to interact with retention. But there is no single pattern in which this happens. There is an obvious way that productive memory opens possibilities for the productive future. And conversely, the twin but opposed age-related phenomena of memory loss and dwelling on the past lead in different ways to an under-developed future. But important as the relation between memory and futural projection is, there is a point where the topic of the short future is separate from the topic of memory. After all, everyone of a certain age is going to feel that future time is short, no matter whether they are generating too much, too little, or just the right amount of memory.

To examine what is involved in the short term remaining, phenomenology needs to bracket stereotypes of what old people feel. For example, the famous list of the seven stages everyone supposedly goes through when they are told their death is immanent (denial ... anger ... acceptance) is simplistic, reductionist, and objectionable, both to those who will not go gently and to those who were accepting from the beginning. As with every topic in phenomenology, the experience of the short term of life remaining should be described in terms of its possible variations, not as an invariant structure.

Aspects of shortened life-remainder that I will not talk about at length are afterlife, suicide, hospice, and doomsday.

I am not going to discuss belief in an afterlife, except to note that some studies purport to show that aging people with religious backgrounds on average feel more optimistic and have a greater sense of "well-being" than aging people without.[1] Yet other studies purport to show the exact opposite.[2] Some surveys claim that religious people cope with impending death by contemplating the meaning of life and society, whereas atheists cope by means of humor and pharmaceuticals. But these findings have limited relevance to our topic, since hope, fear, and indifference are not the same as the sense of time and may or may not affect an aging person's sense of the short term.

The temporal sense in contemplating suicide is another topic I mention only to leave it out. Roman Jakobson (controversially) categorizes suicide within a wide range of phenomena where death limits futural time-consciousness (summarizing themes in Majakovsky's poetry): "child-murder and suicide are closely linked: these are simply two different ways of depriving the present of its immediate succession."[3]

Though the act of suicide itself cuts a person's time short without further ado, there is commonly a short term gap between the moment of contemplating suicide and the moment of committing it. According to a study in 2001, the time between the moment when people seriously contemplate suicide and the time they attempt to carry it out is quite short (shorter than I thought).

> A Houston study interviewed 153 survivors of nearly-lethal suicide attempts, ages 13–34 ... They were asked: "How much time passed between the time you decided to complete suicide and when you actually attempted suicide?" One in four deliberated for less than 5 minutes!
> Duration of Suicidal Deliberation:
> 24% said less than 5 minutes
> 24% said 5–19 minutes
> 23% said 20 minutes to 1 hour
> 16% said 2–8 hours
> 13% said 1 or more days[4]

We might define suicide as the choice to make the time before death more short term than it would otherwise be. Some advocates of "physician-assisted suicide" prefer to call it "physician-hastened death."[5] This not only removes the moral stigma, it also emphasizes that the question is not whether a person will die, but how short a term is desirable.

There is a natural concern that after a person decides upon physician-hastened death and the physician then takes steps, the person might change their mind "at the last minute," when it is too late to reverse the course. The idea of "the last minute," which pertains to all sorts of situations, from backing out of a wedding to ducking a punch, refers to the heel end of the short term, to the last moment of what was already a short term. Ethically, of course, we need to allow for last-minute changes of heart, but we cannot block every choice merely on the grounds that one might undergo a last-minute reversal. The short term reverse decision is a real phenomenon, and yet not every decision is reversed. This is another way of saying that the short term is a special kind of temporal region for authentic decision-making.

Yet another subtopic I will not treat involves hospice care for those whose very short time to death can no longer be temporarily lengthened. It would sound in poor taste to put end-of-life care into the category of short term therapy, but forthrightness after all is the point of hospice care. Caregivers for a given patient accept that they will soon go on to care for other patients. The point of hospice care is that its short term character does not diminish the importance of each individual under their care.

Again, my goal is not to give edifying advice for what people ought to do with their remaining days when they are given a life sentence (by disease, penalty, age, or The World Coming to an End), though it is a good topic for novels and movies, from Akira Kurosawa's sublime *Ikiru* (1952) to the ridiculous Rowan Atkinson vehicle, *Dead on Time* (1983).[6]

Short Life Counted as Long: Kierkegaard

Before discussing the effect that impending death has on aging peoples' diminishing measure of the future term of life, we need to consider the thesis that impending death gives Dasein a sense of urgency for the time remaining. Rather than discussing Heidegger's well-known account, I look at Kierkegaard's 1845 discourse, "At a Graveside."[7]

Death cuts into what was otherwise a duration, with the decisive moment at which "Now all is over" (Kierkegaard [1845] 1993: 79). "Death does not dabble with the decision as if there were still a little left over … the word is: Up to here, not one step further" (Kierkegaard [1845] 1993: 78). All other short term events in life precisely do leave "a little left over," namely the term that follows the end of that temporal segment. Death, in contrast, leaves no leftovers. The End. Anyone who imagines they can "postpone" death is a hypocrite (Kierkegaard [1845] 1993: 79). "Death produces the scarcity of time" (Kierkegaard [1845] 1993: 84).

But even short amounts of lifetime deserve to be filled by some valuable activity. All time during life, long or short, is time, and the person who decides to live in time "rejects no time as too short." Life as a whole is too short not to make full use of its shortest parts. The marketing world knows this: "Life's too short for sensitive teeth" (Sensodyne toothpaste ad).[8] It is as if time has us under surveillance: "Only thinking of the short term, time was looking back at me" (Cosmo Sheldrake lyric).[9]

In short, all lifetime is short, but no time is too short to do something in and with. The shortest time is time enough for living in. In this sense, what the recognition of death assigns highest value to is precisely the short amount of time. Just as the scarcity of a commodity makes it expensive, so also, "Who has not heard how one day, sometimes one hour, was jacked up in price when the dying one bargained with death!" (Kierkegaard [1845] 1993: 84). Expressed as a bargain for extra time, this sounds like the already dismissed "hypocritical" hope of postponing death. But adding an extra hour after the presumed end is not really what is at stake; what is at stake is that "the earnestness of death has helped to make a final hour infinitely meaningful" (Kierkegaard [1845] 1993: 84). I do not know about "infinitely," but it is interesting to measure the value of life by the last hour before the end, the way that any temporal segment is defined by its final sub-segment.

Hence the paradox of the long and short term through the effect of value on quantity: "To make a long life as meaningful as in a time of scarcity" (Kierkegaard [1845] 1993: 84). One way of formulating this is to say that all life spans, whether quantitatively long or short, are qualitatively extended, due to the value of the short: "Earnestness becomes the living of each day as if it was the last and also the first in a long life, and the choosing of work that does not depend on whether one is granted a lifetime to complete it well or only a brief time to have begun it well" (Kierkegaard [1845] 1993: 96). Since the baseline is that even a long life is life under temporal scarcity, the "choice of work" makes a long life valuable just by means of its shortness or, alternatively, makes a quantitatively short life qualitatively long because it is valuable.

One might reduce Kierkegaard, or Heidegger, to the slogan that we should treat every hour as our last (or as the first). But the short term is not just a generalization about the value of every hour; it is a specification of the singular hour that draws to the end. The point is that the short term of some years of life is operationally short in quantity and existentially big on meaning, all because of the hour at its end. Of course, the last hour of life is not really better or more important than all the other hours. But it is the last hour that makes life short, and that is what makes all those other hours valuable in themselves. And while this is not Kierkegaard's concern here, the effect of the last hour for the other hours should have a particular meaning for those aging people who can start to see the last hour coming. The problem, according to De Beauvoir, is that awareness that one is arriving at one's last hours generates a diminishing sense of temporality in general. Let us evaluate this hypothesis.

The Sense of Having a Short Amount of Time Remaining in Life: De Beauvoir

The methodology of Simone De Beauvoir's book *Coming of Age*[10] (*La vieillesse*, which might be translated as *Old Age*, or *Aging*) includes both reflective sociology and what I would call researched phenomenology. Her ethico-sociological aim is to show that old people are treated badly in many world cultures and that there are alternatives. Her existential–temporological aim is to uncover structures similar to what Kierkegaard called temporal scarcity.

De Beauvoir's topic is aging, not death. "Old age is life's parody, whereas death transforms life into a destiny" (De Beauvoir [1970] 1996: 539). Death is an end to temporal concerns, in a way that old age is not at all. De Beauvoir barely mentions the anxiety some people have about actually being dead, no longer existing, the possible impossible, nothingness. And she barely mentions fear of an afterlife, monsters of the underworld, hell, forlornness forever, infinite pain, or, conversely, infinite bliss. Rather, she is focused on the topic I am interested in, the experience of having only a short amount of time remaining.

I focus on the phenomenological experience of the short time remaining, rather than on society's ethical responsibility toward the elderly, which is hard to argue against (though it is also hard to argue with the Russian futurian, aka formalist, Velimir Khlebnikov, when he demands in 1913[11] that old thinkers get out of the way of the young. "All who are closer to death than to birth must surrender! They must bite the dust when we attack like wild men in this time-war").

Defining the Old

De Beauvoir discusses at length dozens of authors (philosophers, novelists, politicians) who have described old age, some autobiographically and some in general. A typical example is her citation of the sixty-two-year-old Jonathan Swift's thesis that he no longer has as much future as he used to (De Beauvoir [1970] 1996: 369). There are quite a few generalizations in *La vieillesse*. The book develops subtleties, variations, and exceptions too, but it has a tendency to generalize about the sense of time among people for whom time is objectively running short on account of age. De Beauvoir does not determine a single age that counts as old, which is good, since as she acknowledges, even taking into account cultural and historical differences, some very old people have the same attitudes about time as some young people. There are many parameters onto which one might pin old age. One might say that "old age" names people who are old enough to retire (which depends also on class); or people who begin to experience physical ailments involving eyesight and hearing, arthritis, muscle loss, sexual dysfunction, organ failure, and wrinkles; or people with grandchildren; or people whom others treat *as* old; or people who do not keep up with progress. A given person may fall under some of these headings and not others.

The most important definition of old age for De Beauvoir is based on the phenomenology of self-attribution. In this mode, a person is old exactly when they think they are old, namely when they think to themselves that they have only a relatively short time remaining to live. Then, considering just those experiential subjects, we can ask what that implies for the other aspects of their sense of time. Do people who feel they do not have much time left to live thereby lose interest in conceiving and contributing to long term projects? Do such people dwell more on the past than on the present or future? Do they focus on the distant past or the recent past? Or do they lose their sense of past too and drift along in the present? Or do they instead dwell on their legacy in the long term future?

It is difficult to feel comfortable with any generalization about the effect of having a short future on other aspects of the sense of time. I, for my part, know that I have a limited time remaining. When I hear generalizations that at my age, I should be losing interest in finishing my book, or in writing another, or in traveling the world, or making new friends, I want to object. Not that I have any more access to my attitudes than the next guy, and in twenty more years (a big If) I may say something different, and for that matter, perhaps my knee-jerk tendency to object to generalizations is a professional deformation of philosophers, but whenever I hear a generalization about people in a certain category, I am inclined to think of a counterexample, and the counterexample is me. As insightful as De Beauvoir often is, we should take her generalizations, which are after all meant to be flexible, even more flexibly, less as structures than as variabilities.

Recognizing One's Age and Preparing for the Short Future

De Beauvoir spends a seventy-page early chapter on "The Discovery and Assumption of Old Age," the "surprise" that most people feel when they first realize they are old. In itself, this self-recognition is a very short experience, which reveals to a person that from then on, for as long a term as they still live, their status has changed to old. For as long as the time left is, it is henceforth short. It is a short term experience that recognizes a long term status that will come to an end, probably within a shorter period of time than the amount of life they have lived so far.

Some people who see the future shortening against their will take an interest in taking control of that fact, imposing their ego over that lack of control. Some people attempt to take control over the death that is out of control by cognitively intending death as an even more immanent event than it actually is (De Beauvoir [1970] 1996: 371), obsessing over their last will and testament, for example (De Beauvoir [1970] 1996: 379). Just as vertigo makes a person want to throw themselves over a bridge rather than submit to the contingency of an accidental fall, an aging person figures: if it is going to be short, I will make it shorter. Short begets shorter.

All the more normal, then, when old age diminishes a person's projects for the future. The old often do have ambition for honor, reliability, an impressive estate, legacy, and posthumous imitators (De Beauvoir [1970] 1996: 454, 466), but that is not the same as having goals to work toward. Alternatively, an aging person might choose a different form of project reduction, by undertaking a large number of pseudo-projects, dilettante-style, each of which lasts only a brief time without being synthesized into an authentic project.

One might try to be optimistic by arguing that old age itself is a project. But let us not fool ourselves. "Undergoing age is not an activity" (De Beauvoir [1970] 1996: 540). True, a person can "prepare" for old age (saving money, reserving a retirement home, training for a hobby, stocking up their home entertainment center), but the way to preserve a life of projects is to commit to those projects for their own sake, not to do so for the sake of one's age. It may sound odd to hear an existentialist say of a stage of life that "it is far better not to think about it too much" (De Beauvoir [1970] 1996: 541), but it is right to point out that committing oneself authentically to a project is not the same as thinking about what an authentic old person looks like, then imitating that ideal. If an old person thinks a lot about how being old is itself a project, it is for that very reason not a project.

At any rate, if authentic old age is possible, one's projects should still be intense. And in an authentically humanist society, ageist discrimination against older peoples' projects "would be virtually non-existent" (De Beauvoir [1970] 1996: 543). De Beauvoir's aim is not simply for there to be better old age policy regarding pensions, health insurance, and housing but for "the whole system [of intersubjective age-consciousness] … to change life itself" (De Beauvoir [1970] 1996: 543). Sadly, there are all sorts of ways for both individuals and societies to go wrong.

De Beauvoir cites dozens of human interest stories culled from newspapers. In 1968, a sixty-five-year-old farmer killed his son for having modernized the family farm, then killed himself and the rest of his family (De Beauvoir [1970] 1996: 383). De Beauvoir describes this under the heading of old people not being able to keep up with progress (she counts herself in that category), "falling behind" the times (De Beauvoir [1970] 1996: 382), and therefore feeling like "a dead man under suspended sentence" (De Beauvoir [1970] 1996: 385). This brief story contains many themes. A person with few years left is enthusiastic about extending himself after death (admittedly, in a dubious way) through his children's lives. But when he realizes that his children will carry on in their own manner (almost every child modernizes the family farm without their parents' consent, after all), even this secondary way of converting his short term remainder into something longer term is undermined. So he takes the relatively short remainder of his own life and ends it right away, after ending the long remainder of his son's. The short term was not going to get long in the way he wanted, so he made it even shorter. Trade-offs of long for short, and short for long, need not be zero sum, but they are always paired in temporal negotiation in which no temporal choice comes free of charge.

Does Long Memory Imply Short Future?

The most important chapter of *La vieillesse* is Chapter 6: "Time, activity, history" (De Beauvoir [1970] 1996: 361–447). It begins with a Sartrian premise (with citations to *Being and Nothingness*):

> For human reality, existing means existing in time: in the present we look towards the future by means of plans that go beyond our past, in which our activities fall lifeless, frozen and loaded with passive demands. Of course, young people too experience obstacles to their projects; typically, the adult world delays their admission to the community of action. But the temporality of delay that the young face is very different from the temporality of retirement and relaxation

that the old face. Age changes our relationship with time: as the years go by, our future shortens, while our past grows heavier. (De Beauvoir [1970] 1996: 361)

What does it mean for the past to shorten the future? De Beauvoir's descriptions are most interesting and useful as eidetic variations in the fourfold interplay between short and long pasts and short and long futures.

Different ways in which people have lived their lives, and have constructed their pasts, result in different schemata for the future. People can construct their past as a possession, which they can freely at their leisure "inspect from every side." Alternatively, they can construct a past that they are possessed by, which binds them in the future. The past can be by degrees either more limiting or more a resource. Of course, we never literally retrieve past events by means of memory: memory at most entertains, then may or may not guide future action. In fact, a past event never just meant one thing, or just had one possible continuation in the first place; it had its own ambiguities of meaning and so is an ambiguous, and ineffective, guide. But even that ambiguity, for better or worse, can be marshaled for the future too.

There is a lot to say about the image of the past: as a montage of re-imagined representations; as a kind of dream for psychoanalysis to interpret; or as a narrative to tell ourselves and ask others to fill in the gaps (De Beauvoir [1970] 1996: 362). Memory has a wide range of alternately passive and dynamic forms.

De Beauvoir's thesis is that independent of whether memory is rigid or gap-filled, the finitude of life span entails that a long amount of past is correlated with a short amount of future remaining. The long past has this reducing effect on the future no matter what our psychological state, our moral attitude, or our balance of memory and forgetting. Indeed, if memory declines altogether, by disease or stroke, it will have the same effect of emptying future projects as excessive memory has. Both over- and under-determined memory can equally undermine the future projects that a normal amount of memory normally underwrites. For that matter, memory and forgetting are rarely all-or-nothing, and normality can be simulated with variations. For example, when aging people lose their recent memory, they sometimes "invent an immediate antecedent" to fill the gap. Not recalling what they had been doing that morning, they will lie to themselves: "I've just seen my son" (De Beauvoir [1970] 1996: 501). For hope-oriented subjects, if there were no past, they would have to invent it.

Variations can be structurally complicated. At the same time as forgetting the past can impoverish future planning (too little knowledge of what one has constructed can lead one to lose the use of memory's construction materials), too much recollection of the past can also impoverish the futural attitude (too much construction can lead to the sense that the construction of one's life is already complete and nothing remains to be done). Too deep pasts and too shallow pasts can thus have the same effect on the future. This means that deep futures and deep pasts do not always have the same reciprocal effects. A deep future does not always make the past shallow; deep future can instead make the past full (full of potential). But a deep past (long in facticity) can also make the future shallow (short on potential).

The paradox is that an over-determined past in one sense makes me too much myself to have a free future; but in another sense, an over-determined past gives me too little to do with it. From both directions, I end up feeling that "'my history is not me'" (De Beauvoir [1970] 1996: 365). This is another Sartrian point. No person is her past self to herself. My authentically free self is being in the form of non-being, with negation built into its positivity; so if the past is over-determined and my history has the form of being, without non-being built in, then the past presents itself as non-being in the form of being: some other past self, who used to be me, bossing me around.

The paradox of a person shaped by projects that had been lived at a time that is no longer is that while events in the past were originally lived "toward the future," their futures have already been lived through. That is why we cannot make a "pilgrimage" to the past. We can recollect the facticity of the past, but we cannot recreate that aspect of the past that, at the time, projected toward an unknown and unaccomplished future. That futural direction was essential to the past experience, but that essence of the past is not what we re-experience when we re-experience the past in memory. What we hoped for in the past has by now already come about (or not), so the past's future is no longer future. Indeed, since so many events lead to disappointment, most attempts to live in the past are doomed to disappointment too (De Beauvoir [1970] 1996: 366). But even when the past's future goal was achieved as desired without disappointing, it no longer presents as the future. So as a project, it disappoints anyway (De Beauvoir [1970] 1996: 368). The conclusion is that a lively memory for the past may have looked like a resource for future projects, but it is a dubious ally—even more so when we take intersubjective phenomenology into account.

One salient case of interpersonal temporal dissolution occurs if an aging person's children die before they do, in which case their own hopes for the future can seem pointless (De Beauvoir [1970] 1996: 366). A more common case is when the aging person's contemporaries, with whom the aging person faced events in the past and worked through their common future, die off one by one, expressed in a spate of funerals, infrequent at first, then sadly more frequent, then more sadly, infrequent again, and the aging person loses the interactivity of intersubjective futures. To be proactive in the face of this, aging people may cut off communication with others, falling into deafness, bad temper, and detachment (De Beauvoir [1970] 1996: 471, 475). In some cases, peer die-off can even feel like revenge. That frenemy of your youth, whom you wished would just die soon, will, now that you are old and will die soon, also die soon.

To add yet further parameters, there are also interactions, though not invariant correlations, not only between the density of memory for the past and the fullness of future projects but also between these and the speed of change in events, as well as the sameness and difference across those events, as well as the fullness and emptiness of temporal segments. Having a long future (as the young do) means that there will likely be many quickly occurring changes of self to come. For the aging, time means a less changeable self (De Beauvoir [1970] 1996: 375). Having fewer short term changes to look forward to means that the future is one long sameness. In other words, the long (full) future intensifies short futures; the poverty of short futures intensifies the long (empty) future. More long means more short; less short means more long.

In cases where a person experiences, in the present, a future possibility, but only because the idea to do so arose in the past, it is as though their past has a future but they themselves do not. Consequently, the abstract future of the past turns the future into a kind of timeless imagination. It is as if "time no longer has a hold" on them (De Beauvoir [1970] 1996: 376). The same youthful future has been made to last a long time, it is true, but it is a long time that is timeless—not eternal, but indifferent to the time one is actually living in. In this picture, the future is time's hold, and time holds with the urgency of short term concerns of the present. The downside for young people having a living future is that actions are pressing, so they are "ruled" by time, since there is "not enough" time. The less time there is to squeeze one's urgent actions into, the more one is governed by time. Less time is more powerful time. But the upside of having a youthful future, made stressful by the present, is that being ruled by time is being in time, having the right to make a promise and a project in time, hence ruling over time. Being ruled by time thus allows us to rule time. Without a youthful project, a person is not ruled by time, so they do not rule over time.

In sum, the young have a lot of time but do not feel like it is enough, because they have so much to do; the aging do not have enough time but feel like it drags on because they have so little to do. From the perspective of the aging, not only do their own futures seem short, the futures of the young seem pointless, hence short, as well. If some aging people dote on their grandchildren more than their children (De Beauvoir [1970] 1996: 475), it is partly because their grandchildren have projects so unrecognizable to them that the grandparents are not as embarrassed at having so little to contribute to them. And this in turn means that the grandparent's projects are obsolete. "Tomorrow [time] will destroy what was built yesterday. The trees the old man has planted will be cut down ... Small firms are either taken over by monopolies or they fail. The son will not re-live his father's life, and the father knows it" (De Beauvoir [1970] 1996: 380).

De Beauvoir cites Hegel's thesis that only when the past is transformed by the present is the future determinate and immanent (whether the future succeeds in its particular goals or not). The problem is that aging people are not able to use this ontology in their working lives any more. For the old, life is no longer a summa but a break, a hardening, a rotting away (De Beauvoir [1970] 1996: 380).

We said that when a person either remembers few events from the past or anticipates few events in the future, it constitutes the "poverty" of time (De Beauvoir [1970] 1996: 375). But there are at least partial ways to compensate for this. Nostalgia might empty out their future, but they may still take pleasure imagining childhood, the time of their most "boundless future" (De Beauvoir [1970] 1996: 376). And for those (few?) old people who do retain their spirit of novelty and enthusiasm for new projects (De Beauvoir names Rousseau, Disraeli, Grandma Moses, and, no surprise, Sartre, sixty-five at the time), their capacity for creativity is tied to the fact that their "childhood is there, still fully alive in the person it formed" (De Beauvoir [1970] 1996: 402). People get an added advantage if they had an idea in their youth that was so strong that it remained fresh their whole lives long. Composers and painters have a better chance at this than scientists, because art develops fresh ideas out of old, whereas old science just becomes outdated (De Beauvoir [1970] 1996: 405–6).

The issues we have been considering concern the interaction between having a short term future and some exaggeration of the past (either in the direction of dwelling too much on the past or in the direction of remembering too little of the past). Given the phenomenological corollary between memory and anticipation, it is natural to think that it is precisely the over-determination of the past that creates the sense of having only a short future, or conversely, that it is precisely the sense of having only a short future that distorts our sense of the past. One might wonder, though, whether the issue of the short term future has been hijacked by the issue of memory. Might it be better to disentangle the short term future from the over- or under-determined past?

Schematizing the Dialectic of the Long and the Short

Leaving aside the issue of long or short memory, let us analyze long and short futures as such. In this subsection, admittedly, I am schematizing more than De Beauvoir does. The primary structural point is that the old person's future is "doubly finished" (De Beauvoir [1970] 1996: 373): it is (a) short and (b) closed. In general, the more closed, the more short.

To analyze this, we need to use the distinction between relatively full and relatively empty time segments, whether the time segments are short or long. We might think of short and long futures as a dichotomy, that either a person experiences a long future or they experience a short future. But it captures more of the reality of experience if we think of short and long futures dialectically, in that the more short term futures one experiences, the more that will extend into the experience of long term futures, and vice versa. The premise behind this dialectical way of thinking about the long–short pairing in connection with the full–empty pairing is that short and long futures are not just quantitatively different, they are also qualitatively different. The very idea of a short future is of a future filled by some important change. If there were no change, then either no experiential time would pass at all, hence there would be no intentional future of any length, or else a stable condition would last past the end of that short period and continue into a longer period, in which case there would be no point in talking of a short but only of a long term future. In sum, short term futures are inherently filled with significant change. The idea of a long term future, in contrast, could be meant either as a long future with nothing much happening or else as a long future made up of many events, possibly many short term events, but at least made up of events that generate significant changes over that long length of time.

This is the non-symmetrical conclusion: A long future can enhance short futures, but lacking short futures need not diminish a long future. Lacking short futures diminishes only the filled long future but does not diminish the empty long future. Long futures may be filled or empty. Short futures, by contrast, have only one type: all short term futures are filled. But the only long term futures that short term futures are compatible with are filled long futures; the only long term futures that the absence of short futures is compatible with are empty long futures.

We might schematize this set of relations: (a) less long term leads to (i) more, or (ii) less short term; (b) less short term leads to (i) more, or (ii) less long term. The (a(i)) case refers to the intensified importance of short term events. The (a(ii)) case refers to pointlessness. The (b(i)) case refers to the long view. The (b(ii)) case refers to there being no way to get there. To spell it out: Having a shorter time to live can make some people feel like (a(i)): time is running out fast; but it can make other people feel like (a(ii)): they face a long slow drift into boredom and decline. The former can make them feel like they have to quickly complete their legacy; the latter can make them feel like nothing is worth doing. Conversely, the feeling that there is plenty of time left can make some people feel like (b(i)): there is room for complex development; but it can make others feel like (b(ii)): the world is too big for them to work with. The former can make them feel like they can take their time, making a bit of progress each day toward a big project; the latter can make them feel like even modest projects will not be completed for ages and ages.

I put the schematism in these ways in order to indicate that there is no one form of short and long term projection; there are all sorts of combinations and variants. There are long projects with many short stages, projects with a small number of long stages, short stages with subroutines that carry over into successive stages, and so on. In my view, every element of a theory of time should be expressed in this way: as eidetic variations rather than as an invariant pattern.

De Beauvoir imagines an old person imagining they did have a longer future: "If I were given health and another hundred years to live, I should be able to launch into fresh undertakings" (De Beauvoir [1970] 1996: 377). (It is surely possible, if not in the best of faith, to imagine magically getting a new multiyear lease on life.) The more years a person imagines they have left, the more they are inclined to launch new projects, and soon. The imaginary long term future provokes a projected short term future. There are twists and variants here too. Aging people without a long future will have no short futures. But if they are able to establish short futures, they may thereby project toward a filled long future in spite of not having enough years to make it in. They may generate a long future ex temporal nihilo, out of the pure act. The long future cannot create a short future out of nothing, but the short can make the long out of a short amount of time. The short is in this way the cause of the long. For the aging, that is. The young do not need this device; their long future is given naturally, so they can make short futures or not, as they will. The aging have only the one way of making the long, namely with the short.

This only works existentially. Psychologically, if a person only has a short time left, they cannot plan for the future, and so they have no long future. Existentially, though, following Kierkegaard, they can make the long out of the short. Of course, they cannot really make themselves live longer (probably, at least not that much longer); they cannot by will make their future quantitatively longer. But they can make their short term be the short that if only they could live longer, would have been long, and that is something.

Unfortunately, when all is said and done, too many older people tend to fritter away their time, De Beauvoir says. Their long hours go by quickly without being marked by much of anything. "The paradox is that this hellish speed does not always protect the old person from boredom: far from it" (De Beauvoir [1970] 1996: 376). And again, this is doubly paradoxical. The time of the aging is endless, in that there are few aims to accomplish in the urgent future, but by the same token, their time is bounded by an impending finish, "asphyxiated" by the diminishing air of the future (De Beauvoir [1970] 1996: 379). To put it simply, either there is nothing more to do or there is no time to do it in. Both are short in fact, and the feeling of shortness exaggerates both the quantity and the quality of shortness: the first is a short term that feels extra long, the second a short term that feels extra short.

To sum up, "the older one grows, the faster time runs" (De Beauvoir [1970] 1996: 373). And the shorter the remaining time gets, the faster it gets still shorter. For a child, an hour seems long; for the old, short.

Temporal Scarcity, Acceleration, and Variability

But this is the sort of generalization I am skeptical about. De Beauvoir herself has described aging people for whom time stretches out too slowly. In reality, the problem with losing future projectability is not that it has one single temporal consequence, but that time segments get out of step with the usual measure of time, and so it is natural, and dialectical, that it feels both too long and too short. A future that is too short to get to a goal will be too long as a waiting period to nowhere. Yet even with this more flexible interpretation, De Beauvoir's generalization still sounds too general. Why is it not possible for people, like me, to come right up to the end of their time and still measure time in the same way they always did? Why must it be the case that if the future remainder of life measures short, every other measure of time duration is distorted? I can see that it seems natural to think that a life with little time left may affect a person's whole attitude toward time. But if durational relations are structured by patterns of variation, as I have been suggesting, rather than by fixed implications, then all possibilities should equally be part of the same theory of the phenomenological measure of temporal durations.

To make the temporal description more complex, since the phenomenology of temporal duration is not limited to quantity, or even to quantity plus quality, we could analyze the short time remaining in terms of the four Kantian temporal schemata: quantitative (extensive) time-series, qualitative (intensive) time-fullness, inter-causal time-relations, and modal time-potentials. Each of these time measures may vary independently of the others in different experiences. A smaller extensive magnitude in the time-series may not always mean less intensive magnitude in time-fullness, or fewer causal effects in time-order, or less potential in the time scope. It may often happen that a quantitatively short time means less temporal quality, order, and scope, but there are obvious cases where short events are all the more intense, or where short events cause long effects, or where short events leave latent possibilities for later. It is not just that the aging do not have enough future in general but that they do not experience the most elastic balance between the four categories of short term future.

There is no doubt some experiential basis for De Beauvoir's generalized conclusion that aging people do not have enough "tomorrow" (De Beauvoir [1970] 1996: 380), or at least that their tomorrows do not have tomorrows, or at least that they do not feel those tomorrows as their own. After all, the fact that as individuals each with our own personal experience of time passage, we will die, and soon, is not in dispute. "Old people, even if they do believe in the future, the long-term future, do not reckon on being present when the change is brought about" (De Beauvoir [1970] 1996: 413). They are dead "under suspended sentence" (De Beauvoir [1970] 1996: 385). To mix metaphors, the aging are like actors who cannot get roles, and if they do get roles, cannot remember their lines (De Beauvoir [1970] 1996: 386).

To generalize even more, De Beauvoir argues that the loss of the short term future is not only a problem for the aging but a general problem for modernity. (Modernity makes us all old.) Modernity's "acceleration of history" (De Beauvoir [1970] 1996: 380) means that everyone feels like their projects will come to either fruition or destruction without them, before they have had a chance to carry out any deliberate action. It is as if time reaches the long term future without passing through the short term, thereby taking time out of our hands. De Beauvoir's occasional Heideggerian miso-modernism is questionable. But there is no question that new technology challenges people who lived most of their lives with old technology. Aging people, she says, feel new worldviews rushing past them. They think of themselves as "outdated ... while they are still living" (De Beauvoir [1970] 1996: 380). Even if they had the energy to learn a new science, they would have to go back to learn the new "language" for it first, and that is just too much (De Beauvoir [1970] 1996: 390). Only the young have the energy to move forward from the "practico-inert" temporal resistance of their own minds (De Beauvoir [1970] 1996: 390). She appeals to Bachelard,[12] arguing that old age is an "epistemological obstacle" to scientific development (De Beauvoir [1970] 1996: 391). Indeed, the very fact that aging scientists have extensive knowledge prevents them from following the future of their own field (De Beauvoir [1970] 1996: 393). They may be interested in new technology, but like that farmer are unable or afraid to retool.

De Beauvoir leaves little to look forward to. That is the point of aging, after all, to look forward less. The stereotypical advantages of old age—serenity, liberation from desire, contemplation, and wisdom—are bogus. The aging do not really possess the wisdom of experience, or truths about the human condition, or the grand synthesis. They are not statesmen who "foresee the present" with the breadth of the past, they cannot learn from the past to make good judgments about the future, they do not even remember most of what they read during their lives (De Beauvoir [1970] 1996: 381). They typically descend into anger, jealousy, resentment, and melancholia (De Beauvoir [1970] 1996: 494–5). Still, there are a few compensations. Occasionally, they overcome the two opposite tendencies of misguided youth: self-aggrandizement and subservience. Aging peoples' anger can on rare occasions present as a peculiar form of dignity, and their lack of shame can under special circumstances lead to useful political boldness. Some aging women become free to ignore taboos against drinking red wine and staying up late (De Beauvoir [1970] 1996: 485–9).

Where Am I on the Time Line Now?

De Beauvoir sometimes suggests that old age starts around sixty-five. At the time I am (now) taking notes on De Beauvoir's text, I am sixty-two (the same age, coincidentally, as De Beauvoir when writing her book); at the time I am (now) revising those notes in chapter form, I am sixty-four. I turn sixty-five in three weeks. (Now, final revisions: sixty-five.) So it is not yet quite me she is talking about. But I am feeling it. I do not feel most of what she says old people feel, my interests are still lively, and I am still picking up new interests at a rate faster than I can carry them out. But I take her point that old people get surprised when they feel old, and I am starting to expect to be surprised. In under four years (from now)? Next year/last year (from now)? No, there is plenty of time; maybe I will never feel that. Maybe I count among the few biographies she cites of many-year-old people who never get phenomenologically old. There should be a named category for the near-old (everyone is relatively "near" to old age, of course, including children who shiver at the thought of ever being as old as grandma, and even God (De Beauvoir cites Goethe for the speculation that God may tire of the world in His old age), as well as anyone who realizes that the long future one still has does not have that much longer to go). People of my age are certainly conscious of Alzheimer's. I might have dementia already without realizing it, as De Beauvoir hints in an attempt to frighten her reader. Fear of early symptoms looks like responsiveness to possible futures, but it can also lead to the opposite: over-reaction and paranoia, which are after all typical of aging. Every slip of the tongue "foretells disaster" (De Beauvoir [1970] 1996: 479). For the aging, she says, good health itself is an "insulting mockery" (De Beauvoir [1970] 1996: 477), a concession soon to be withdrawn.

It is difficult to draw a solid conclusion from de Beauvoir's observations, analyses, and generalizations. An aging person's recognition that they have only a short term remaining in life is clearly a real subjective phenomenon, based on objective fact. And short term futures clearly do generate, and interact with, long term futures, long term pasts, short term pasts, and forgotten pasts. It is just that the many varied phenomena that de Beauvoir cites in her long book, and the many more that each of her readers can add from experience, as well as the combinatory that can be generated structurally when we diagram interactions between short and long, past and future, filled and empty, fast and slow, changing and unchanging, personal and intersubjective, psychological and technological, and other distinctions pertaining to temporal phenomena, lead us to a more variation-based phenomenology of the short term future than de Beauvoir's narrative sometimes suggests. Yet it is precisely Beauvoirian investigation that leads to eidetic variations on the experience of the short time remaining in life of the sort I have experimented with.

On the Vanity of Existence: Schopenhauer

De Beauvoir is not always a pessimist, but when she is, Schopenhauer is her pre-interpreter, and now that we have started down this path, we should see it to the end. When an older person, feeling that their time remaining is short, also feels that the time remaining is not worth making projects in, and so feels that quantitatively short time is qualitatively empty, they are not just judging the time-length of the rest of their life, they are assigning a value to the very idea of the short term. The assumption made both by some aging people and by some phenomenologists of all ages is that short times are worth less. They assume that as a result of age constraints, all is vanity. Schopenhauer's "Additional Remarks on the Doctrine of the Vanity of Existence" begins:[13]

> This vanity finds its expression in the whole form of existence; in the infinite nature of time and space as opposed to the finite nature of the individual in both; in the transitory and passing present moment as reality's sole mode of existence; in the dependence and relativity of all things; in constant becoming without being; in constant desire without satisfaction; in the constant interruption of efforts and aspirations which constitutes the course of life until such obstruction is overcome ... Time is that by virtue of whereof at every moment all things in our hands come to naught and thereby lose all value. (Schopenhauer [1851] 1974: 283)

This litany of valuelessness contains a number of distinct theses: (1) life is short relative to infinite time; (2) the present passes; (3) becoming never arrives at being; (4) even if a project lasts for a short but appreciable amount of time, it gets constantly interrupted during the time it lasts. Some of Schopenhauer's other complaints have less to do with time as such. For example, he laments that our desires cannot be satisfied and that achievements have value only relative to other better goals that we have not achieved. But his key points concern the shortness of time, particularly the shortness of our time relative to infinite time, the infinite time we wish we could survive through as individuals, and the infinite time it would take us to achieve our desires.

The second and third points above occupy the second paragraph of the text: "What has *been* no longer *is*; it as little exists as that which has *never* been" (Schopenhauer [1851] 1974: 283). The past is so much gone that it is as if it never took place, and since everything good and pleasurable is immediately experienced, time passage is tantamount to nothing ever being good. The present "has the advantage of reality" (Schopenhauer [1851] 1974: 283), but it passes right away and so loses the advantage of reality as soon as it has it. This anti-substantialism, indeed, is the foundation of idealism, the theory that there is no reality but the appearance of reality, and, for Schopenhauer, "this is why Kant is so great" (Schopenhauer [1851] 1974: 283).

But more important than a philosophical theory of temporal transience and the vanishing present and, a fortiori, the vanishing past is the human experience of it. An infinite amount of the past has always-already vanished, and this is a dreadful experience. "To his astonishment, a man all of a sudden exists after countless thousands of years of non-existence and, after a short time, must again pass into a non-existence just as long. The heart says that this can never be right" (Schopenhauer [1851] 1974: 283). The idea that the anxiety of non-existence pertains just as much to the contemplation of the countless time before birth, as it does to the countless time after death, is an idea we associate with Arendt's turn to the philosophy of birth from Heidegger's philosophy of death. Schopenhauer turns De Beauvoir's consideration of the devaluation of life that comes with old age to a devaluation of life that begins with the youngest age. The force of Schopenhauer's thesis that life occupies only a "short time" is that the human heart knows that the short term of life is just not right.

To be sure, we can sometimes get ourselves to believe that enjoying the present is the "greatest *wisdom*." Believing otherwise would "drive us mad." But this so-called wisdom "could just as well be called the greatest *folly*" (Schopenhauer [1851] 1974: 284). Whether we persuade ourselves to like it or not, we are stuck with the temporal fact that "we resemble a man running downhill who would inevitably fall if he tried to stop, and who keeps on his legs only by continuing to run" (Schopenhauer [1851] 1974: 284). It is not just that life is short, but that everything we do runs at full speed toward cutting it short. "Thus, restlessness is the original form of existence" (Schopenhauer [1851] 1974: 284). Psychologically, we experience this in the form of "hunger and the sexual impulse, aided a little perhaps by boredom" (Schopenhauer [1851] 1974: 285). The thrilling unhappiness that Schopenhauer takes from this is the phenomenological recognition of the short term.

There is a paradox. On the one hand, it is difficult to enjoy events while they are in the midst of happening and easier when we see them at a distance: "The scenes of our life are like pictures in rough mosaic which produce no effect if we stand close to them, but which must be viewed at a distance if we are to find them beautiful" (Schopenhauer [1851] 1974: 285). I do not know if this is true, but if it is true, the other hand creates the paradox, since, "When at the end of their lives most men look back, they will find that they have lived throughout *ad interim*" (Schopenhauer [1851] 1974: 285). Put together, these two theses mean that we do not find our lives beautiful until we get to the point where we also find those events to have slipped by "in the interim." Value is visible only afterward when we look back into the interim, yet as a mere interim, it loses its value.

Schopenhauer effectively has two reasons for saying that all is vanity. There is the reason everyone knows, namely that "every satisfaction creates a fresh desire and its craving, eternally, insatiable, goes on forever" (Schopenhauer [1851] 1974: 286). His more original line of reasoning is that satisfactions are so short that they have been ended by the time they become visible. The everyday reason hangs on the long term of unsatisfied desires; Schopenhauer's special reason hangs on the short term of satisfied desires. If some young people already experience the vanity of life, that just means that we all of us humans are old in spirit and short on time.

In sum, what is the point of having done something well, and of having satisfied desires, in the past? By now, whatever was good about it will just be "the shriveled-up mummy of a memory" (Schopenhauer [1851] 1974: 289). We might like to think that memory preserves good things for us, but it does the opposite. If we had a memory "microscope" that could see past events up close, even though they have receded into the past, that would be one thing, but the mental microscope that we humans have does the opposite: it interposes countless events between past and present, so the past event gets smaller and smaller the longer our mental microscope attends to it. And if we add to the tininess of the past event, the "fluctuations" we are going through while we look at it, the shrinking of the past event is further "accelerated." "We then become aware that we have only a quasi-existence" (Schopenhauer [1851] 1974: 289).

Like de Beauvoir and Heidegger, Schopenhauer sees a parallel between the shortness of human life and the short term attitude toward the world that defines modernity: "the present period of intellectual impotence" (Schopenhauer [1851] 1974: 286). Modernism is the attitude that the "Now" is the highest end of history (this is, in my view, the best definition of modernism), but since the current world's mediocrity cannot be denied, the modernist has to keep his standards low. Now is the best, but the best is slim pickings. And after all, our times are not very different from any other times. Nice as our best is whenever we achieve it, its mediocrity is shameful. It is not just that we cannot preserve the good of an event over a long time, it is that we do not really want to preserve it over a long time, since it is not really that good. The short term is bad relative to what we would like to get out of the long term, but at least the short term is better than what we actually get out of the long term.

Worse even than the fact that pleasant events are a burden to maintain is the fact that they get boring, that the drawing out of time itself turns them into events with "no *genuine intrinsic worth*" (Schopenhauer [1851] 1974: 287; emphasis in the original). As nobody but Schopenhauer could think to put it, "Human existence must be a kind of error" (Schopenhauer [1851] 1974: 287). It happened for such a short time, therefore it did not happen at all. The short term is not less time, it is no time at all, the empty form of time, as Kant, Schopenhauer says, said (of course, meaning something else). "Existence in itself would [at least] fill our hearts" (Schopenhauer [1851] 1974: 287). But interimic time implies precisely non-existence. It is not just desire and its satisfaction that is vanity, it is existence as such that is vanity. Pretty things like jewels and finery, lovers and honor are attempts to cover over the lack of existence in the emptiness of time.

This is vintage Schopenhauer. Our "will-to-live" is so devalued by the shortness of the time of achievement and the immanent "necessity of death" that even suicide is pointless (Schopenhauer [1851] 1974: 288). Schopenhauer is not altogether against suicide. He does not think it should be a crime (Schopenhauer [1851] 1974: 306), and he does not think that love of life should count as a virtue in the first place (Schopenhauer [1851] 1974: 307). Suicide is even interesting as a phenomenological "experiment," though it is an awkward experiment, since the experimenter will not see its results (Schopenhauer [1851] 1974: 310). But his main point against suicide is that it does not solve the problem of temporal precariousness that prompts it. Since the problem is that we have already been cut short, how could it help to cut short the future? At any given time, the time for suicide is long past.

In sum, human life "is like a drop of water, seen through a microscope and teeming with *infusoria*, or like an otherwise visible little heap of cheese-mites whose strenuous activity and strife make us laugh. For, as in the narrowest space, so too in the briefest span of time, great and serious activity produces a comic effect" (Schopenhauer [1851] 1974: 290). The short term is not even nothing; it is just funny.

Walter Benjamin goes yet a step beyond Schopenhauer's view that long times might as well be short, with the casual attitude that says, "Who cares how long it takes? Short or long, it makes no difference." Benjamin[14] is thinking about societies where people are bad at making plans to meet at a particular time (like Russia, he generalizes). When they do make a plan, they forget it; when they do remember it, they still miss it; when they miss it, they do not apologize—in such societies, time cannot be said to fall into short or long segments. Benjamin does not especially criticize this lack of a "feeling for the value of time." Indeed, he seems rather pleased with it: "[Russians] fritter everything away. (One is tempted to say that minutes are a cheap liquor of which they can never get enough, that they are tipsy with time)" (Benjamin [1927] 1999: 31). The breakdown in time measure does not simply mean that rendezvous takes an extra-long time to happen. On the contrary, it means that "The real unit of time is the *seichas*. This means 'at once'. You can hear it ten, twenty, thirty times, and wait hours, days, or weeks before the promise is carried out" (Benjamin [1927] 1999: 32). In other words, when the time remaining to the end of a promissory time segment is unspecific, every time segment is precisely short, "at once," and immanent, even in cases where it takes a long time to bring it to a close. To say it less paradoxically: without time measure, short and long are indistinguishable. To say it more paradoxically: if the end of every time segment is delayed by an unknown quantity, then we have to be alert that any given time segment, at any given moment of its progression, might as well, as far as we know, be just about to end shortly—or not.

Speaking of periods of time we do not take seriously, Adorno adds yet another carefree attitude toward short times, namely "free time."[15] Adorno is skeptical about the temporal "oasis" (Adorno [1972] 1991: 189) of free time, or "spare time" (Adorno [1972] 1991: 187), which employees are granted under capitalism: short amounts of after-hours time between work days and short annual vacations. Sadly, because bourgeois education and employment discourage imagination, we know of few ways to use our free time and rely on the light entertainment industry to occupy it for us. Our temporal freedom is short and in truth falls more under the heading of the "miscellaneous" than of freedom. Adorno pairs "free time" with one-off public events, like royal weddings, described in German as *einmalig*: "unique experiences," or "once in a lifetime events" (Adorno [1972] 1991: 196). Both free times left empty, and exceptional times filled with spectacle, reduce authentic time to short and vacuous sub-segments.

As with De Beauvoir's descriptions of the time-consciousness of aging people, I find I do not share very many of Schopenhauer's experiences. But if we take his speculative observations not as theses about transcendental time-consciousness for all organic beings but as structural variations and diverging response mechanisms to temporal patterns, we can draw more useful conclusions about the temporal variability of short term functionality. Old age and the vanity of life are correlated in various possible ways: when the elderly lose their sense that life is valuable, it makes some of them enter a less happy phase of life, but it can make other aging people, at least those with an anarchist personality, happier and freer, knowing that they have no further responsibility to live well.

How Short Is It?

The founder of immunology, Elie Metchnicoff, wrote in 1908[16] that the amazing longevity of Bulgarians is thanks to yogurt. Why are we not all extending our life spans with fermented dairy? Going all in on extended longevity, the idea behind cryogenics is that death itself is a short term problem in human evolution. A person who is ill or injured is to be placed in low temperature stasis to induce anabiosis, suspended animation. When medicine later figures out a cure, they are to be revived. Anabiosis can be called "temporary death" and the cure "healing by death."[17]

With the application of robotics to cryogenics, there is a view that longevity will soon be behind us. Russian "entrepreneur" Dmitry Itskov founded the "2045 Initiative" in 2011, devoted to engineering technology to download a human personality into a "non-biological carrier" (a digital memory disk), then later uploading it to an avatar, hence rendering humans electronically immortal by the year 2045.[18] Itskov's open letter[19] begins, "Fellow Immortalists!" The technical problems are daunting, but happily, all we have to do is invent learning machines that can solve those problems themselves, and that should not be too hard. Many billionaires are invested, but the AIs will also figure out how to make immortality affordable. Disappointingly, not all roboticists think that electronic immortality is either technically or phenomenologically possible, and a few cranky sticklers think there might be ethical issues.[20] It seems we will continue to need phenomenology of short term life for a while still.

Chapter 3

SHORT TERM HISTORY (RICOEUR, BRAUDEL, HEGEL)

Argument: Short term events are dialectically interwoven with long term trends, as controversies in historiography show. The relation between segmented historical periods and the repeatable influences of events at a temporal distance shows how the long term is a functional effect of the segmentable short term.

Ricoeur's three-volume *Time and Narrative*[1] offers extensive resources for our topics, by using narrative to explain the historical synthesis of short episodes into long contexts. Ricoeur values long term historiography, siding with Fernand Braudel against François Simiand. Though I give more value to the short term than Ricoeur does, Hegel's critique of both short and long term history cuts across the dichotomy. In setting up his account of historiographic narrative, Ricoeur passes through Aristotle and Augustine, and Husserl and Heidegger, and all of these together will aid us in analyzing the measurement of long and short temporal segments.

Measurement in Temporal Experience and Poetics

The classical view, according to Ricoeur, is that "measurement is a genuine property of time" (Ricoeur 1985: 3:12). But Augustine raises a paradox (Ricoeur 1985: 3:8).[2] The problem is that we measure time in the present, but the present is neither long nor short; it is constantly passing. If a long time, like a year, were present, then all the times during that year would be simultaneously present, which is absurd. The same holds even if only a short time were present all at once. Therefore, the present cannot be long or short. Only a future or a past segment of time can be short or long. Yet the only part of time that exists is the present. So the only parts of time that can be measured do not exist. How, then, do we measure the length of a past (or future) event?

Augustine's well-known solution appeals to the mind's "distension," which Ricoeur interprets phenomenologically, as the consciousness *of* extended time. Memories exist *in* the present; but those memories tell a story *about* the past. Likewise, expectations *exist in* the present, but *tell of* the future. When the mind measures future time, it is just measuring time as it imagines it. To expect something will happen in the future is to imagine some long or short narrative. The future is not real, but the present is; so, if I can put it this way, one end of the interval between present and past (or future) is real, which makes the measurement of the time between now and the past (or future) a half-real measurement.

On Ricoeur's construal, mental distension is the soul telling itself a narrative about its future and its history. As the present passes, the narrative distance to an expected future becomes shorter, and the narrative distance to a remembered past becomes longer. It might seem as though we are always getting closer to the future, as though the time to the future always gets shorter, and the time from the past always lengthens. However, we can pick different futures and pasts to measure our distance from, so there are both long and short futures as well as long and short pasts, each of which is variable, cumulative, and subtractive.

To analyze time-quantities in narrative more concretely, Ricoeur turns to Aristotle's poetics. Aristotle prescribes that a tragedy should tell a story lasting not much more or less than a day. The reason for constraining its minimal and maximal temporal "magnitude" (Ricoeur 1985: 3:42) is that a tragedy must be "complete" enough to get the character to happiness (or not); and it must be long enough to include the "reversals" that permit catharsis. Without reversals and completion, a play would be merely a series of "episodes" (Ricoeur 1985: 3:41).

The standard narrative of time measure is thus poetic, but time measure itself is defined more technically in Aristotle's *Physics*. Time is measured when a "numerical relation is added" to succession (Ricoeur 1985: 3:16): measurement counts how many times a given moment is succeeded by other moments. Number is what converts the general before–after narration into particular intervals, either discretely short or long, or relatively shorter or longer. And counting in turn requires temporal units. Without a cut, a "now," a dated point, a break between before and after, there would not be separate ones to count up. In fact, as everyone knows, Aristotle regards the infinite number of breaks or divisions in time as potential rather than actual. This weakens the thesis that time is measurable into the more modest claim that time is potentially measurable. But what sort of cognition can actualize the potential for temporal division, counting, and measure? It is fine to say that time is measured by units, but how do we define the unit? Ricoeur thinks that the only way to count temporal units is to pick out and individuate events that change the description of the world, and that this depends on narrative. How certain is it that time measurement requires narrative? Could there be nonnarrative experiences of temporal units?

Aporias of Time Segmentation in Phenomenology: Husserl and Heidegger

Husserl's *Lectures on Internal Time-Consciousness* largely do without narrative. On Husserl's account, we have direct experience of temporal nows, successions and simultaneities, temporal continua and units. Husserl thinks we can direct our attention to temporal experience itself, bracketing the narrative history of objects and their changes. For Ricoeur, Husserl's method of redirecting attention away from narrative temporal content toward nonnarrative temporal form is itself a meta-narrative. This is typical of the aporias that Ricoeur finds in temporal measurement: temporal experience seems to be measured without narrative, but saying so seems to presuppose a meta-narrative about experience.

If time in this way has a double reference, subjective and objective, it is natural that there would be two kinds of memory and two kinds of time measurement. The memory of an internal stream of nonnarrative subjective time-consciousness (as when an idler watches the clouds roll by) will consist of a simple retention of its past. It will be measured simply by the feelings of shorter and longer time passage. The temporal stream will feel longer or shorter even if the experiencing subject is not explicitly calculating how long a segment of time is. In contrast, the narrative experience of empirical objects (as when a teacher paces himself getting through a certain number of points in a lecture) is remembered in explicit recollections, and is thus subject to explicit measurements of temporal distance. Subjective retention measures distance from the past by the number of nows that have drifted into the past since the process started; objective recollection measures distance from the past by a narrative that describes in stages how an earlier event has been accomplished and succeeded. There are thus two different operations that measure short and long. Both operations result in temporal objects of determinate length, some shorter and some longer. But only one of those operations is narrative.

In both cases, appealing to the length of temporal segments suggests "identities of temporal position" and intervals of unambiguous quantity, but we should be careful about these presumptions (Ricoeur 1985: 3:38–9). There may be more than one measure of the length of a given time segment, technically, due to the observer's time-space frame of reference; or semiotically, due to alternative units of measure; or relatively, due to its comparison group; or pragmatically, due to its potentiality to be shortened or lengthened. Ricoeur's view is that ultimately, Husserl is less concerned about univocal temporal lengths and more with the "unity of the flux" of time-consciousness (Ricoeur 1985: 3:41–2). To my mind, though, phenomenology must value both fuzzy continuity and discrete breaks in the time stream. Time-length measured by the subjective feeling of how long we have been experiencing the time stream and time-length measured by the sequence of objective episodes in a story simply produce different measures of time.

Ricoeur considers whether the duality of subjectively intuited time and objectively narrated time might be resolved by Heidegger's existential projection. After all, existential care is both subjective and narrative. When a person "takes the time to" carry out a project, they are measuring both subjective perseverance and objective obstacles at the same time (Ricoeur 1985: 3:62). But if Heidegger's existential projection might have provided a way of measuring time both subjectively and objectively at once, Heidegger himself is generally not interested in "how much time" an event takes up (Ricoeur 1985: 3:75). In contrast, Ricoeur (and I) think that care always has to work within a certain amount of time, so that time measurement should always be on the table for Dasein. Every project requires a "long enough," action-sensitive, time period. Occasionally, too, we have to set aside an amount of time that is "short enough," like if we start making supper too early, and the risotto dries out before the guests arrive. Either way, Dasein meets its finitude in time segments of particular lengths.

Heidegger thus in principle offers a way to think subjective and objective temporal segments and continuities under a single projection. The fact that Heidegger does not pursue this possibility is due to the basic tension in Heidegger's account of existential time. On the one hand, there is a final end to Dasein's temporal period, namely death; on the other hand, being-toward-death is the continuous projection of time (Ricoeur 1985: 3:67). The first is a termination point of all experience whereas the second is the narrative construction of the term. Death is the ultimate term limit, but it is unique, and therefore not a paradigm for any other partial cutoff of life processes. Because death does not strictly exist within time, coming-to-term does not strictly happen during life. One might think that the phenomenology of projected decisions also requires temporal segmentation this side of death, an explanation of how durations get constructed and sized. In short, the Heideggerian conception of temporality and care would seem to require temporal measurement. However, Heidegger shows limited interest in that.

Heidegger generally has contempt for "the extensible character of time that makes us speak of a long time or a short time" (Ricoeur 1985: 3:71). He thinks determinate time segments are ontic and vulgar, "the expression of a leveling off" of concern for authentic projects (Ricoeur 1985: 3:71). Measuring time, he thinks, whether short or long, flees from the existential call of Being. When we look further into Heidegger's own text, we find that Heidegger's lack of interest in temporal measurement leads him to a special disdain for the short term in particular.[3] Most people today, Heidegger complains, are "too short-sighted" (Heidegger [1938] 1999: 31) and exhaust their attention on events that are both short-lived and trivial. The very fact that someone would choose to measure an event to see how long or short it is shows that that person has only a short term attitude toward events and their world-historical inheritance. They only want to know how to gain benefits from events, how to make them last longer, or how to get past them, not how our being speaks through them. The most painful effect of the short term attitude is thus the wreckage it makes of historicity: "History now seems to be taken to be the gloomy chasing after self-devouring events, which can only be fleetingly held by means of the loudest of noises" (Heidegger [1938] 1999: 25).

For Heidegger, temporal measurement as such is to blame. "The frenzy let loose in the domain of machinations and numbers" (Heidegger [1938] 1999: 68) results in "a total lack of questioning" (Heidegger [1938] 1999: 76). It is alright to "calculate" how long a machine will work before it breaks (Heidegger [1938] 1999: 76), but existential events, like self-conversions in thought, which make up authentic historicity, do not have a shelf life. Indeed, the very "struggle for measure" generates mismeasure. It biases historians toward calculations that are either too large or too small, since temporal measure gives them too easy an opportunity either to over-value or under-value their own society's temporal movement. That is, the urge to measure tends either toward imagining that social history is "accelerating" or else toward imagining "the gigantism of the *slowing down* of history" (Heidegger [1938] 1999: 311). Assessments of historical changes either as temporally large or temporally small are both symptoms of the same arrogance in the face of events. Fleeing from social boredom (accelerationism) and gloating about the end of history (decelerationism) result from the same error—too much temporal measure (Heidegger [1938] 1999: 84).

Heidegger's diagnosis of this error (like Bergson's) is that the very idea of "timespan" (*Zeitraum*) wrongly understands time in spatial terms, and therefore, whether in subjective form ("from now to then") or objective form ("a hundred years") is "blind and useless" (Heidegger [1938] 1999: 264) and without "anticipatory resoluteness." He disparages the image of an "interval between a 'since then' and an 'until,'" along with the concepts of "lapse of time" and "temporal extension" (Ricoeur 1985: 3:83). By implication, Heidegger looks down on calendar dating (Ricoeur 1985: 3:82) for being calculative and, worse, public. In short, time can only "shelter" events as long as it is not quantified (Heidegger [1938] 1999: 271).

In sum, Heidegger thinks that the measure of time into short and long segments assumes a false ontology of time, a short-sighted and trivial view of events, a complacent and dogmatic attitude toward history, an arbitrary calendar, a flight from true finitude in death, and an abandonment to public norms. He thus opposes the "ordinary time" of "simple succession" (segmentation and length), and as a result, for all his interest in historicity, Heidegger shows little interest in actual world history (Ricoeur 1985: 3:78). For Ricoeur (and me), Heidegger in this way under-values being-within-time (Ricoeur 1985: 3:72).

Heidegger occasionally seems poised to overcome his blanket criticism of temporal measure and to suggest new authentic uses of short and long term. Resoluteness, after all, means keeping it up. We may not know how long when we set off, but we undertake "perhaps a long sojourn" (Heidegger [1938] 1999: 3). Not definitely a long time, but "perhaps." Not a term but a "sojourn." With the right attitude, perhaps there could have been an existential way to reinterpret the measure of short and long, an existential dialectic of quantity and quality.

But unfortunately, in the short term, which is as far as Heidegger wants to predict, the short and long terms are likely to continue having the trivial sense that they have had for quite a while now. "Today," the enemy of existential time is winning: "those who have nothing more ahead of them and nothing more behind them" (Heidegger [1938] 1999: 66). But perhaps at an earlier time …, and in a time to come … Perhaps with a different sense of the scope of human history, a new short and long term could have been, and could be again. That other thinking, "inceptual thinking, locates its enquiry into the truth of be-ing *very far back* into the first beginning as the origin of philosophy" (Heidegger [1938] 1999: 41). Sadly, that past, the existential moment at which a sudden event could have become a long sojourn, has been forgotten, though it might one day be revived in the form of "futural steadfastness" (Heidegger [1938] 1999: 41). Existential philosophy holds for the longest of terms, but it has only a fragile hold upon it. Its fragility might sound like it finds the authentic long term attitude only in rare short term periods. But Heidegger leaves not even this much room for authentic short term periods.

Indeed, the worst thing about short term attitudes is that they interpret the long term inauthentically. Every kind of short term is destructive of historicity.

To challenge Heidegger on this point, we can begin by considering whether there might be authentic uses of the temporal technologies that Heidegger disparages the most: clocks and calendars (Ricoeur 1985: 3:105–9). For example, the observation that it has been raining for four days can be taken either as an inauthentic expression of data or as an existential expression of mood (Ricoeur 1985: 3:84). Similarly, under an existential interpretation, "'centuries' [might] no longer designate just chronological units, but 'epochs'" (Ricoeur 1985: 3:210) or "horizons of expectation" (Ricoeur 1985: 3:208). Another calendar/existential hybrid is that "the average age for procreation—let us say thirty years" or, more generally, "the notion of a generation" is both statistical fact and a source of heritage (Ricoeur 1985: 3:110). Matthias Fritsch thus describes generations "taking turns with the earth," which relay being-in-the-world in overlapping short terms.[4] Indeed, it is a fundamental fact of being-with-others that some people are old while others are young: "the compensation of rejuvenation and aging takes place in each temporal division of the period defined arithmetically through the average life span" (Ricoeur 1985: 3:112).

But for Heidegger, the ultimate argument against this sort of existential re-interpretation of temporal measure is that death is the ultimate and only paradigm of authentic temporal concern. Death is in each case one's own, and therefore the ground of authenticity. In contrast, the measure of time is not one's own, it is public. Therefore, the measure of time is inauthentic (Ricoeur 1985: 3:87). But Ricoeur offers the reverse twist: we would not be impressed with death, or "speak of the shortness of life, if it were not for the immensity of time" (Ricoeur 1985: 3:93). Anxiety toward death depends on experiencing the mismatch between the short term of Dasein and the long term of public time.

I would go one step further. The paradigm of finitude cannot pertain to the whole of life without also pertaining to its parts. In my view, temporal coming-toward must come toward points that are still in time, not just toward a death that is an impossible experience for time. There must be at least some authentic experiences of coming-toward that come toward an end, reach that end, experience something else after that end, and then, to use Heidegger's terms, hand that end back down to itself. Coming-toward, in all cases where it is not the finality of death that it comes toward, comes toward a relative short term. The conclusion to the synthesis of subjective and objective temporal measurement is thus that the short term needs to be one of the basic structures of existential temporalization.

We now apply these results to short and long term historicity, which Ricoeur discusses in Volume 1 of *Time and Narrative*.

Narrative and History

Historians almost always spend either more or less time narrating events than the events themselves take. Likewise for time position and time-order: narratives can be enunciated during, shortly after, or long after (or sometimes before) events. They can be enunciated in the same order as the events, or in reverse, or shuffled. Some narratives anticipate a future, others do not (Ricoeur 1983: 1:67). Using Kant's contrast between a person drifting on a raft in a river, who can only move downstream, and a person touring the rooms of a house in any order they choose, the writer of history is like the homebuyer. The historian chooses time span, time position, and time-order, without instruction from the events themselves, though she cannot help presenting episodes in some order or other, and cannot prevent general themes from emerging (Ricoeur 1983: 1:66). Different narrative forms balance episodic plurality with running themes in different ways: folktales emphasize episodes without much synthesis, whereas moral tales culminate. Which patterns of synthesis should historical narrative adopt?

The fact that historians can make such choices raises questions about the very idea of describing historical events in narrative form. Does narrative not add more order, totality, and coherence than historical events themselves have? Does narrative storytelling exaggerate sharp beginnings, decisive turning points, and satisfying endings? Does it artificially segment history? These are genuine concerns, but would it not be just as biased to assume that historical events in themselves are temporally unformed? Ricoeur finds these questions unanswerable, since any evidence used to solve them will be circular (Ricoeur 1983: 1:72). For example, citing any given event (e.g., the 1918 Armistice) as the end of a historical period in order to prove that historical processes come to an end begs the question. If we do not assume that wars come to an end, an Armistice will not count as an end, and the narrative will drift along without taking shape. The ultimate question of whether history should be described in narrative leads to an aporia.

But this aporia does not simply mean that we cannot know whether the meaning of historical events is revealed by narrative. It means rather that writing the narrative of historical events interacts with the historical events themselves, so as to confer a kind of unity upon those events precisely by letting human subjects interpret their past, which is only natural. We might think of this as constructive idealism. The narrative is the "(as yet) untold story" (Ricoeur 1983: 1:72), where historical events themselves have the potential to be synthesized into a narrative, but where the narrative needs to be told explicitly in order to connect events. Hermeneutically, "To follow a story is to actualize it by reading it" (Ricoeur 1983: 1:76). The choice of how long a segment of history lasts, and thus how long a historical period one ought to study, depends on how long a story people living at a certain moment in history want to tell to and about themselves and their times. Term length is auto-poietically decided by the ones asking how long a term's length is.

Long and Short Term Historical Narratives (the Braudel Problem)

Though Ricoeur in the end is more sympathetic with long term history, his position is that both short and long term historiography in isolation fail to fulfill the needs of narrative. Ignoring short term episodes conceals the details of history. On the other side, when "positivist" historians collect only short term episodes, they conceal context. Indeed, the positivist attitude to short term events does not really treat them as short term events at all, but only as data points (Ricoeur 1983: 1:96, 1:101). Long term history is narrative history, but fails to narrate in detail; short term history, qua positivism, is not narrative, and therefore leaves both long and short events meaningless.

However, Ricoeur's contrast between narrative long term history and positivist short term history cannot be quite right, since short term history is not necessarily positivist. Ricoeur's premise seems to be that short events are isolated, therefore positivistic statistics can simply collect them, whereas long trends are interactive, and are therefore likely subjects for narrative interpretation. But it is already misleading (though common) to associate long term history with "trends" and short term history with "events." In reality, events can be long, and trends short. Events can be interpreted, and trends treated as data. Ricoeur himself sometimes acknowledges this: "the long time-span is just as much about an event as is the short time-span" (Ricoeur 1983: 1:170). In any case, the problem of the short and long term in history depends on what an "event" is.

Ricoeur begins with a deceptively simple definition: an "event" is "what actually happened" (Ricoeur 1983: 1:96). He acknowledges more complex features of events besides their actuality: their contingency, singularity, human causality, and cultural specificity. But even the more complex definitions do not answer the most important dispute: should events be defined as inherently connected phases of a single phenomenon over a long time, or as discrete phenomena each occupying a limited time, or both?

Ricoeur does not refer to Sartre's *Critique of Dialectical Reason*,[5] but Sartre's paradigm of "totalization without totality" could be helpful here. On Sartre's analysis, each segment of history carries out local, quasi-totalizing activities, without there ever being a completed totality. Long term history can only consist of serial quasi-totalizations, since no matter how long history continues, it can never complete an actual totality. History is the dialectical work societies do to reach a limit, posit the end of a term, and, by doing so, to move on, continuing into the next term.[6] Moving on (*dépassement*) makes each phase short term, but also makes it pass beyond its limit and become long term. Sartrian history does not fall into exclusively short term pieces, but it makes the long term short term-friendly. At times, Ricoeur expresses a similar attitude and seems happy that "the most recent history seems to be seeking a new dialectic of short spans of time and long ones" (Ricoeur 1983: 1:249).

However, some of Ricoeur's comments are less dialectical: for him, the choice of short and long historical focus is ultimately decided by coming down on one side or the other of the question: is history event-centered or trend-centered?

Yet Ricoeur knows that the border between these two sides is porous, and that it is not always obvious when a change is just a fluctuation within a longer trend and when it transitions to a new trend. This vacillation over whether the long term takes priority over the short term, or whether long and short terms overlap, is found over and over in Ricoeur's analysis of historical time and narrative. Sometimes it simply seems like Ricoeur wants it both ways—he wants to side with long term historiography, but he needs to acknowledge all the concrete roles that short term episodes have in history. In the final analysis, I think this vacillation is intentional, since for Ricoeur, the whole point of narrative is that it confronts a plurality of events and tries whenever it can to synthesize them into a historical continuity. An explanation of a historical phenomenon has to explain both short and long parts of it, and so at least to some extent, it "renders irrelevant the distinction between a pointlike event and a long time-span" (Ricoeur 1983: 1:191). For that matter, different historical phenomena incorporate different relations between short and long processes. On the one hand, there are occasions when a relatively quick event in history (e.g., when clocks replaced church bells in Europe) expands into a long-lasting worldview (Ricoeur 1983: 1:109). (The European idea precisely about the measure of time emerged within a short term.) On the other hand, even trends that take a long time change the world and are in that sense "quasi-events" (Ricoeur 1983: 1:109) and so, we might say, quasi-short term. The consequence of these cases is that we should expect that every time a long term trend is being built up, short term provisos will intervene and make the continuity more complicated. This is why Ricoeur is so helpful for developing a working theory that builds into the fabric of time-inevitable resurgences of short term segmentation.

In fact, there are other parameters, besides the frequency and importance of changes, that could also be used to distinguish short term events and long term trends. For example, one could say that events are made by individual agents, and trends by social groups. This would make the short term subjective and the long term objective (or intersubjective). After all, individual lives are short relative to societies (Ricoeur 1983: 1:101). One might conclude that history should not limit itself to short-living individuals, but extend to the life span of civilizations. But even here, a short-lived cause may have long effects, so the fact that human life is brief does not imply either that it is not also long or that the brief is unimportant in history.

Another problem that cuts across short and long term is how to decide whether and when a period of history begins and ends. The beginnings of the French Revolution and of the First World War, for example, are notoriously disputed. Trumpism counts as short term if its beginning was the "Tea Party" of 2009, but long term if its beginning was white supremacy. Dating the "end" of the Trump era will be disputed for quite a while. The short can seem awfully long under the wrong circumstances. The clickbait website *Listverse* names "10 Historical Events That Were Much Shorter Than You Thought," including: "The Aztec Empire Didn't Even Make It to 100" (#9), and "Julius Caesar's Reign Was Shockingly Brief" (#1).[7]

By extension, both short and long term raise the problem of how much earlier than an event's beginning was its first proto-cause, and how much later its epilogue. The problem is not just when the time segment begins and ends, but when the relevant causal series before and after it begins and ends. To take the familiar extreme case, the entirety of human history occupies a short blip of time relative to its prologue in planetary history. Each human is a blip in the blip, and each action a blip in the blip of the blip. This perspective on the ultimate beginning of series makes everything in human history seem short. One might prefer to avoid the "obsession with origins" (Ricoeur 1983: 1:222), but beginnings clearly have relevance to history, short and long. The aporias and conflicting perspectives on what is short and what is long are unavoidable.

Endings likewise make all events short relative to the time afterward. Ricoeur describes a finite human lifetime as "the long time span shortened" (Ricoeur 1983: 1:218). But as with any judgment of relativity, instead of saying that the long looks short in the big picture, we could say in reverse that scanning many short events looks like one long "acceleration ... covering long spans of time" (Ricoeur 1983: 1:219).

A simple solution would be to construe the beginning as the first cause of a series, and an end as the point where that cause runs out of effects. But causal historiography introduces its own problems for defining long and short. First, causal explanations of history rely on time-neutral "covering laws" of the form: "poverty causes rebellion." The problem with such causal laws is that history is full of exceptions (in spite of poverty, there was no rebellion against the beloved queen). Sometimes exceptions can be explained by a secondary law ("nobody rebels against a leader who is beloved"), but it is not obvious whether finer and finer exceptions can always be explained with finer and finer laws. As philosophers from Hume to Hegel point out, the more a law refers to a particular series of empirical facts, the more it is not a general rule at all, but merely a restatement of the facts themselves. If there has to be a different law for every particular event, each particular event becomes the law for itself (Ricoeur 1983: 1:126). Added to this is the problem that causal laws only explain a particular situation if we know all of that situation's relevant pre-existing conditions, which is clearly not feasible in historical knowledge. Causality thus does not by itself solve the problem of beginnings and ends of historical periods, so it does not clearly differentiate short vs long term. If the distinction between short and long term is still possible, causal explanation will need to be supplemented by humanistic, narrative interpretations of the meaning of events.

Does the form of narrative supply laws for measuring the length of historical events?

Narrative Form

Which features of narrative might be able to constitute events as short term? How does narrative extract, or embed, a temporally segmented episode into a longer series of changes over time?

Perhaps the principal advantage of narrative description is that it adds motives to causal explanations. Motives do help to make actions coherent, but they also lead to a new puzzle. Since motives are more individualized than causal laws, and have their impact primarily at the beginning of an event, Ricoeur has to concede that at least sometimes, large-scale historical phenomena are consequences of short individual interventions (Ricoeur 1983: 1:131). The long term narrative description would thus cover the consequences of short term interventions. Whereas long term causal series were supposed to look like smooth continuities, long term motivated series look like extended discontinuities. Of course, the role of motives does not mean that events are exclusively located during the short time when the motive is formulated. Motivations need not imply that there are intentional "gaps" between events, each of which is short. A plurality of agents' motives may also connect events "meaningfully" in a long humanist arc (Ricoeur 1983: 1:131). Still, narrative description does make the motive into a short phase that initiates the beginning of a sequential logic that includes both short and long segments.

The longer Ricoeur spends developing his account of historiography, the more complex its logic becomes, and the more interconnections it reveals between long and short term histories. In addition to allowing both the humanism of short term motives as well as a modest degree of explanatory power for long-ranging causal laws, Ricoeur also has an affinity for branching tense logic,[8] that is, for historical events as "finite state spaces" (Ricoeur 1983: 1:133–4). A state-space is a different kind of short term: "a fragment of the history of the world" (Ricoeur 1983: 1:134). A state-space (or state-time) is an action-node on a branching tree of possibilities. The short motive-event is on the before-side of a divergence point, and the long term is the after-side. Both humanist historiography with unforeseen consequences and state-space logic with branching futures use the contingent future to double the short term event-space into a dense serial short term on a larger scale.[9]

Events are "time-separated" (Ricoeur 1983: 1:145) not only because they happen one after another but also because other events occur in the "intervals" between them, and within each. For Ricoeur, the implication of the fact that there are dense series of events crossing over, and running through, other series is that the description of any one past event is folded into history "as a whole," or "of a piece" (Ricoeur 1983: 1:144). Historical [short] space-states are pieces whose crossovers operate "of a [long] piece." In one sense, the layers of history separate events' temporal locations, but in another sense, they map conducting lines between them. A narrative is thus "followable" (Ricoeur 1983: 1:150), not because the story is fully continuous (since motivated individuals are inevitable exceptions to continuous history) but because the layering of events provides clues for re-constructing connections when the plot has been lost. In my terms (not Ricoeur's), long term history proceeds by filling in short term segments a few at a time. Once the long term is broken up into divergences, intervals, and time-separated layers, then even long term history is constructed via the functioning of layered short term relations.

When we add the what-ifs and as-ifs of history, its unactualized potentialities, we get an even more complicated picture of long and short term categories. The intentionality of motivation is almost always constituted by imagining what "might be better" than what is currently actual (Ricoeur 1983: 1:184). This implies that potential alternate-history follow-throughs expand any given short term actuality into longer term modality, and conversely, that long term possibilities are projected out of short actualities. The ideas of short and long term tend to assume that a time segment has one length and not more. But qua potentiality, each event has several different lengths depending on which of its modalities are taken into account.

The actual/potential distinction pairs with the other two-folds we have been considering that also affect short/long measurement: individual/social, motive/cause, time-separation/branching, and so on. Whichever parameter we choose for measuring time, events are always one level more complicated than that. If we choose to measure time according to social meanings, for example, we find that that produces not just one measurement but many. The same period of world history might be "cut up" into time segments of difference lengths, depending on whether it is cut up into the rise and fall of empires, or into economic ups and downs (Ricoeur 1983: 1:196), and whether the cuts are made by traditionalists, or revolutionaries, or scholarly outsiders. And as we will see in Hegel, if we choose to measure time segments according to the model of the rise and fall of empires (already a subset of the social model of measurement), we will find still more sub-models by which the same period of history is measured in different time segments (so many years per dynasty, so many years per king, so many years per first minister, etc.)

Ricoeur's conclusion from the inevitability of multiple time scales is that, "for me, the event is not necessarily brief and nervous, like some sort of explosion. It is a variable of the plot" (Ricoeur 1983: 1:217). This is Ricoeur's best formulation, in my view. It allows for the possibility of the long term, but without always prioritizing the long over the short. Assuming the usage in which "event" designates short term history, this means that the short term event is not necessarily brief. What makes the short term short is rather that, unlike invariant trends that keep a plot on track, the short term is a variable, a divergence, "a change in fortune" (Ricoeur 1983: 1:224), moving the plot dialogically. "Short term" is the name for any element, brief or lengthy, that pluralizes a dense overlapping field of plot-lines and plot-levels. Variables of temporal length will always arise from modalities and instabilities in the political and economic order. Ricoeur speaks of "relay stations" (Ricoeur 1983: 1:200) across the ontological and hermeneutical levels of history and historiography, not only of plots and characters but also of "quasi-plots" and "quasi-characters" (Ricoeur 1983: 1:200). For the same reason, we should properly speak of "quasi-short terms" and "temporal quasi-segments."

On this model, the length of an event is not a one-term predicate, like "six years," but a coordinate pair like "(1939, 1945)" or "(1914, 1939)." "Any event can be analyzed into sub-events or integrated into a larger-scale event. In this sense, the difference between short term, middle term, and long term is simply the temporal aspect of the relation of part to whole that predominates in historical explanation" (Ricoeur 1983: 1:202). "If the long time span did not lead us back to the [short term] event ..., it would be in danger of severing historical time from the living dialectic of past, present, and future" (Ricoeur 1983: 1:224). Each event thus has at least two lengths, one necessarily shorter and the other necessarily longer, and asking how long an event is involves two or more interdependent problems.

However, for all his success in explicating multiple temporal layers in history, Ricoeur ends his chapter on historical narrative, and thus Volume 1 of *Time and Narrative*, with a general preference for long-duration history. In France, he notes approvingly, writing in 1983 (forty years ago), "long time-span" historiography has won the day against short term evental history (Ricoeur 1983: 1:207). If short term events had won the day, detail would have overrun overview, and the overly pluralist study of history would have lent itself to conspiracy theories (Ricoeur 1983: 1:223). (It is not clear to me why conspiracy theories would result from over-pluralization, rather than from an excess of coherency.) While short term details and discontinuities are also necessarily part of history, in all the ways we have outlined above, the best historiography, Ricoeur judges, synthesizes potentially divisive plurality into "a virtual plot" (Ricoeur 1983: 1:216), and in this final statement, the "plot" is meant to connote the long term.

In sum, for Ricoeur, both long and short terms need to be synthesized, but it is the long term that performs that synthesis: "the long span of time brings about the transition between structure and event" (Ricoeur 1983: 1:208). My view is that the short term is also in its way a synthesis of long and short terms. But the important point, which I share with Ricoeur, is that for both syntheses, the temporal character of a time segment is not just its measure, but its capacity for multi-layering and re-ordering a web of temporal patterns.

It is time to look more closely at the advocates for long term and short term history, Braudel and Simiand respectively, then the synthetic critic of both: Hegel.

Long Term History: Braudel

Ricoeur spends thirty-five pages on whether historians ought to study history in long or short term periods (Ricoeur 1983: 1:96–111, 1:206–25). The best-known advocate for long term history is Fernand Braudel. Braudel's 1960 essay, "History and the Social Sciences: The *Longue Durée*,"[10] focuses on slow-moving and long-acting trends. His premise is that if a socioeconomic situation changes only slowly, then it counts as one long process rather than many short ones. As we said, slow is not the same as long, and fast is not the same as short. There are fast, even accelerating, processes that go on for a long time (like the expansion of the universe), and slow processes that can be distinguished into shorter sub-processes, like stages of the decline of an empire. Braudel's paradigm case is both slow and long: cyclical interactions between mountain dwellers and plain dwellers over a long period of the European Middle Ages. There were of course some short-lived fluctuations within that period, but in Braudel's view, historians should not allow these to obscure long term patterns.

Long term advocates like Braudel often assume that short term advocates, proponents of *histoire événementielle*, are only interested in cause–effect relations between discrete episodes immediately proximate in time. This is why Ricoeur likes Braudel, for preferring narrative over causality. I do not think, however, that cause vs narrative corresponds to short vs long. Causality is equally good for, and bad for, understanding short term history, just as it is both good and bad for long term history. In my view, the short term needs its own definition, independent of other parameters. Furthermore, we will see that Braudel's practice of synthesizing short events into long ends up not being so different from analyzing long events into short.

Braudel thinks that research into long-duration events will, among other benefits, ward off a danger he saw emerging in 1960: overspecialization in the social sciences.[11] At the same time, he also thinks it will be an antidote to a lot of "traditional history," which, as he sees it, is "oriented to brief time spans" (Braudel [1960] 2009: 173). I think most readers today will be surprised to hear "traditional" history defined this way. Many books on the philosophy of history in our own times, for example, have an Index entry for "long term history," while few have entries for "short term history." Perhaps short term history was never as likely to take over the discipline as Braudel feared. In any case, his concern is that short term history rewards fad-driven readers who seek out "short-term dramas" that leave them "breathless" and who lack the stamina for "more rigorous temporalities" (Braudel [1960] 2009: 173, 178). Worse, it glamorizes financial speculators who rise and fall with daily fluctuations (Braudel [1960] 2009: 174), draining society of its vigor.

Braudel acknowledges that historians who focus on "events" might not admit that they are only interested in the short term, since they can stretch the term "event" to cover longer chains. But Braudel thinks this is a bad faith trick. What event-historians really think is that small events constitute the whole of history. He calls that a "clever and dangerous" position and, strangely, attributes it to Sartre (Braudel [1960] 2009: 174).

Braudel begins with an unambiguous but surprising distinction between short- and long-duration history. He does not primarily define short term by its quantitative duration. He instead associates the short term with the quality of newspaper headlines calling out "the trivial happenings of everyday life: a fire, a train accident, the price of wheat, a crime, a theatrical performance, a flood" (Braudel [1960] 2009: 175). Braudel writes as if short means the same as trivial. In fact, it is surprising that he calls floods and prices "trivial," since Braudel's own insightful analyses of ordinary life in Europe (admittedly over the long term) are sensitive to the effects of natural disasters and economic turns. Braudel admits that recent historians of the short term have done the good deed of discovering some overlooked details in history. And of course, he has to acknowledge that "everyone realizes that there exists a short term in every sphere of life" (Braudel [1960] 2009: 175). But he is worried that the data of the short term will get assembled as a "mass of details" rather than "thick reality."

Braudel's argument is that details can be deceptive, in one of two opposite ways: either in making it appear that a temporary fact is defining for a longer phenomenon; or in making it appear that a temporary fact is just one episode out of an unconnected pile of thousands, and so has no role in defining a longer event. In other words, if we start with details, we end up making the details either too important or too unimportant, for the whole. It would be better to start with the whole, then details will be seen in their proper role. The problem with short term analysis, then, is not that there are no short terms in reality within the long term, but that overemphasizing the short term fails to connect it systematically to the long term. The goal is to synthesize short and long terms (as Ricoeur also says), and for "the salvation of our craft" (Braudel [1960] 2009: 176), we have to prioritize the long term.

It gradually turns out that Braudel's division between short and long term is not the clear dichotomy he starts with. He allows that different spheres of life fall into "inter-cycles" of different lengths. In politics, he says, power generally changes hands in a few days, whereas in economics, prices and interest rates take decades to rise or fall (not the most convincing example; Braudel [1960] 2009: 176). The point is that some historical research projects justifiably investigate short cycles while others go long. "History is the sum of all possible histories" (Braudel [1960] 2009: 182). Even so, Braudel advises we not get "bogged down" in varied measurement scales. What is important is that the different "growth rhythms" (Braudel [1960] 2009: 177) be connected, which ultimately returns to the long-duration scale.

I agree with Braudel that the overlay of different time scales means that in one sense, short terms are embedded in a longer term. But I think it also means conversely that the long term is assembled out of overlapping non-synchronous cycles. The fact that Braudel constructs the long term by "going beyond temporal limits" (Braudel [1960] 2009: 177) indicates that the long term happens at the edge-limits of the short term. For Braudel too, this generates a mixed-level model. "The time of today is composed simultaneously of the time of yesterday, of the day before yesterday, and of bygone days" (Braudel [1960] 2009: 182). The same process can rightly be seen as a one-day event, a two-day event, or a multi-day event. Just as a yardstick can measure distances shorter than a yard, we cannot understand the long-distance events that had been leading up to 1960 for hundreds of years, unless we include the short-distance events of 1959 among them.

Still, for Braudel, the "structure" of long duration is not the accumulation of short term events but the "trend" (Braudel [1960] 2009: 178). What makes a trend irreducible is not just quantitatively that it "goes on for a long time," and not just that it "can only slowly erode." The essence of a trend is its ontological substantiality, namely that it "restricts" the flow of historical changes (Braudel [1960] 2009: 178). For example, social organizations devoted to preserving heritage, like religions and monarchies, marginalize dissenting phenomena and prevent them from taking hold. The long term trend is thus not just a quantity of time, it is a force, an "obstacle" to transitory "events," a resistance to change. In contrast, the short term situation is porous; it lets new events into the social series without resistance; it is easygoing, receptive, and weak (though obviously, not every short term situation concedes without a struggle).

Braudel admits that long term trends are not always healthy. (The Medieval period, after all, was not always healthy for the people who lived in it.) The long term may even in some cases be a temporal "prison" (Braudel [1960] 2009: 179). But history tells things as they are, for better or worse, and the truth is that the long term is a force. Of course, even while a trend is in operation, there will be short term crises: "a thousand ruptures and upheavals" (Braudel [1960] 2009: 180). But for Braudel, the very fact that ruptures happen within a recognizable society, and are combated by it, shows that the long term trend is not just a backdrop but a stabilizing force.

The subsection of Braudel's essay whose subtitle sounds the most important (but is more snarky than meaty) is "The Quarrel About the Short-Term" (Braudel [1960] 2009: 183). There are two ways, he says, to under-value the long term: by over-valuing the timeless or by over-valuing the short term. The error of over-valuing timeless patterns is exemplified by structuralism, whether it posits mathematical models, unconscious forces, or language-like systems. Braudel thinks that all of these structuralist models of historical explanation take the appreciation of stability too far. (Ricoeur thinks that Braudel himself already goes too far by effectively positing "cosmic time" (Ricoeur 1983: 1:266); I too think Braudel goes too far, but I do not think Braudel goes that far.) The reason why Braudel thinks timeless models of history are inadequate is that structural models themselves only convince historians for limited time spans. It is not just that no one model fits the entirety of world history (Braudel [1960] 2009: 195) but also that models do not last long enough to keep historians focused on the long term for the long term. In sum, timelessness might appear to be about the ultra-long term, but Braudel calls this "the *too longue durée*" (Braudel [1960] 2009: 197). The structuralist image of "the eternal man" (Braudel [1960] 2009: 196) is not really about the long term, since it is not about any temporal term, short or long. The too-long term (the model) is too abstract and therefore misses the concrete long term (the trend).

The second way, more important to us and more straightforward, that historians have under-valued the long term has been to over-value the short term. The short term attitude toward history, he says, "presentizes" events, "disdains history," and relies on "on-the-spot surveys" (Braudel [1960] 2009: 183, 200). Braudel ridicules the "pretty" diagrams of statistics and throws in digs at *Sciences-Po* (Braudel [1960] 2009: 187).

To me, these are straw man construals of the short term. First, the idea of presentization suggests an exclusive concern with instantaneous states of affairs, and even short term historians do not focus on that. To be sure, there are roles for both synchrony and diachrony in history.[12] But the short term is just as diachronic as the long term, just shorter. Furthermore, short term historians are interested in short events whenever they occur, not just in the present.

Second, Braudel ridicules on-the-spot surveys, as we might today ridicule "Breaking News." It claims to be the newest news, but in practice repeats clichés. To be fair, though, historians who employ surveys need not be naïve about it. They generally combine data collection with pre-survey and post-survey analysis. For that matter, while surveys are obviously not a complete methodology for history, knowing what people think of current events is not uninteresting. And not all surveys need be taken at the very place and time of the event (the "spot"), since a historian can also consult surveys taken in the past. In the big picture, short term historiography uses all same methods as long term historiography: documentation, causal analysis, humanist interpretation, temporal inter-cycles, and so on.

Braudel's main skepticism about surveys is that people who live in the present, who will be the survey subjects, often have distorted views of the past: the opinion of such people "teaches nothing" (Braudel [1960] 2009: 184). Why bother surveying uneducated people today about what happened during the French Revolution? Worse, people in the present often have only a short term interest in the past. They just want to use a historical name (Lincoln or Hitler) to win a rhetorical political battle in the present. Happily, Braudel says, we do not need surveys of people in the present day in order to understand history, since plenty of evidence direct from the past is available: "Is the past really so dead?" (Braudel [1960] 2009: 184). It is true, he says, that there are challenges in "reconstructing" evidence from unfamiliar times, but confronting the unfamiliar is a good thing, both for self-understanding in the present and for understanding what it means to have a history, not to mention for multicultural recognition (Braudel [1960] 2009: 185). In fact, the confrontation between different historical standpoints over the long term is a good hermeneutical foundation for the study of both long and short term historical events.

It seems to me, contrary to Braudel's overview, that prioritizing unfamiliar standpoints (the past read by the present without presentism) emphasizes differences between time-periods even while bridging them, and so emphasizes the relative short term even more than the stable trend. At least, it focuses on turning points where standpoints change (whether it has been a long or short time since the last change), rather than durations (long or short) when they do not. At times, Braudel's view on this problem sounds complex and hermeneutical: "Historians and social scientists can eternally pass the ball back and forth between the dead document and the too living testimony, between the distant past and the too close present" (Braudel [1960] 2009: 186). But immediately, he retracts the long–short dialectic: "I do not think this is the fundamental question" (Braudel [1960] 2009: 186). I think it is.

Braudel ends his essay with a plea for historical context in the social sciences. We might have hoped he would define context as a plurality of time scales. But he ends by criticizing sociology for positing too many time-forms: phenomena fast and slow, cyclical and irregular, regressive and avant-garde, accelerating and anachronistic, explosive and static (Braudel [1960] 2009: 200). This kind of variability seemed allowable in some of the earlier pages of Braudel's essay, and his own historical investigations into the Middle Ages are flexible in just these ways. But Braudel instead asks: "How can this be convincing to a historian? With such a wide range of colors, it becomes impossible to reconstitute unitary white light, which is indispensable to him" (Braudel [1960] 2009: 200; Braudel oddly cites Marx as an ally). The short term is like a chameleon, and also like the Aeolian wind (Braudel [1960] 2009: 200). Historians should be taught (it is hopeless to try to teach this to sociologists, he says) to resist the multiplicity of perspectives and term lengths.

It seems to me that once advocacy for the long term turns into a polemic against variable term lengths, it undermines descriptive historiography altogether, and becomes a reductio ad absurdum against the long term. Dividing lines between long and short term, blips and trends, norms and exceptions, are often, as Ricoeur might say, aporetic. Is a retreat in battle a tactical withdrawal coherent with a long term strategy, or is it a sudden change in the balance of power? Is a monarch subsumed in a dynasty, or is she an individual voice?[13] Is counter-culture part of culture, or a temporary autonomous zone? Even if we do not go to the lengths of Alfred Jarry's pataphysical "universal science of exceptions"[14] (and I am not saying that we should not), or to the lengths of Carl Schmitt's thesis that "sovereign is he who decides on the exception"[15] (and here I am saying that we should not), we do sometimes need to give exceptions a decisive role in history, which means allowing for exceptions to long term history, in the form of fragments[16] and *ars inveniendi*.[17]

Before we follow up on inter-cyclic interventions, let us give equal time to an advocate of short term history.

Short Term History: François Simiand[18]

François Simiand is interested in "*La psychologie sociale des crises et les fluctuations économiques de courte durée*" (1937): short term economic fluctuations. The prompt for this research was that on many occasions during the previous hundred years of European and North American history, culminating in the Great Depression, pronouncements about the good health of the economy were shortly followed by an economic crash. At the particular level, such errors are due to overconfidence in prediction, particularly regarding one's own future. At the general level, the error is due to misunderstanding the nature of the future. Materially, to avoid such errors, one should study economic fluctuations; formally, it requires understanding the short, medium, and long term (Simiand 1937: 7). Yet in spite of the reference to *courte durée* in his title, Simiand is interested less in temporality than in the plurality of economic inputs and outputs. He gets interested in time as a way of sorting out the large number of relevant causes, effects, and statistical formations in economic history. His method of prioritizing the short term is neither positivist nor presentist, and he does not utilize on-the-spot surveys. His aim is to prioritize complexity over rules (pre-systems theory).

The economy is complex in the sense that it includes a plurality of production sources, distribution mechanisms, consumer destinations, inventions, administrative centers, and pricing negotiations. Different industries require different amounts of time to plan, produce, and sell (Simiand 1937: 16). CEOs, entrepreneurs, safety testers, salespeople, consumers, and shareholders negotiate around different time scales even within the same industry (Simiand 1937: 17). Different companies have different corporate cultures around time-management, as do bankers who speculate with other peoples' money. Different nations' economies have different temporal paces, independent of how "evolved" they are (Simiand 1937: 27). An economic system is a web (*tissue*); up to a point, it can be repaired if torn, but after that point, there is no way to know where the threads lead (Simiand 1937: 25). Interactive events produce gaps, delays, and polyrhythms in time (*décalages dans le temps*, Simiand 1937: 25). Markets, without a command center, fluctuate on every parameter and reduce long term explanations to "estimates" at best (Simiand 1937: 9).

One practical effect is that long term credit is high risk, both for lenders and borrowers. Many industries, like farming and shipbuilding, require long gestation time, and since the longer a term is the more volatile the fluctuations there are, the long term is the biggest source of risk (Simiand 1937: 12). But short term opportunities are no better for the risk-averse. Even the most similar simple and short situations are too complex to reliably fall into place the same way every time. Insurance mitigates risk a little, though if it is expensive (like medical malpractice insurance today), it too risks ruin (Simiand 1937: 21). Nassim Nicholas Taleb's "Black Swan" strategy[19] gambles on crisis, but Simiand does not offer any short term strategy to compensate for long term unreliability. His judgment, for example, is that the American imposition of price controls in the 1920s, attempting a quick fix, was not only doomed but was even one of the causes of the Depression (Simiand 1937: 24–5). Hitler and Roosevelt, he says, made the same mistake of thinking they could control the economy, either in the short run or the long (Simiand 1937: 30). For Simiand, the short term does not support any investment or policy strategy; it recognizes the unstrategizable economy. Yet he is not pessimistic, since he associates the short term with "free production and free consumption" (Simiand 1937: 29–30), that is, with societies that are "more lively, more mobile, and more democratic" (Simiand 1937: 26).

Simiand's pluralistic and fluctualist method can be seen in a variety of spin-offs. Recent Italian "Microhistory," for example, studies events that run their course within a single day; it is interested in popular culture, people without power, minorities, and local events; it makes use of anecdotes, not only official documents; it acknowledges lacunae in source materials. His short term micro-focused method is also consistent with Nietzsche's claim in *Human, All Too Human* that it is a virtue that historians can only understand their own times, and that their times are short. "Everything uttered by the philosopher on the subject of man is, in the last resort, nothing more than a piece of testimony concerning man during a very limited period of time."[20]

Comparing Braudel and Simiand suggests nice, but not simple, similarities and differences between long and short term history. Long term history, whether long or short, for Braudel, expresses unitary temporality; short term history, whether long or short, for Simiand, expresses polyrhythmic temporality. Paradoxically, the long is not one length (long) and the short another length (short). The long is unitary length; the short is a plurality of lengths. Braudel occasionally acknowledges the plurality of lengths across historical events, but the last word of his essay separates the long and the short. The last word of Simiand's 1935–6 lecture series promises to reconnect the short term with the long in the next season's lectures.

Speaking of 1936, the reader must have been jolted when I was. When Simiand says (in 1936) that Hitler and Roosevelt shared the same idea about political economics, something has gone wrong with his sense of history. Perhaps the problem is that Simiand posits the short term as the genuine sphere of economic events, but then does not think of the short term as a locus of intentional action, for urgent politics, for ethical decision, or for a philosophy of time. The solution to the presence of short term events cannot simply be to abandon oneself to them. We need to say more about how short term action intervenes in the long.

Aufhebung *of Both Short and Long Duration: Hegel*

One might expect Hegel to side with Braudel's long term over Simiand's short. But Hegel never fits easily into one side of a dichotomy. His philosophy of history[21] offers a dialectical interplay of variable temporal lengths and measures, devaluing both short and long term phenomena in favor of transitions that are more about contact and absorption than completion and succession. Neither long term "duration" nor short term "transience" captures historical reality (Hegel [1830] 1900: 221). Hegel's rejection of both short and long durational lengths allows for some relatively quick, short, qualitative re-shaping of history.

In drawing from Hegel's lectures on the *Philosophy of History*, I exclusively select passages where Hegel writes about short term events. There are not many. I am not interested in the stereotypical generalizations about Hegel's philosophy of history (that it is totalizing, that it posits Prussia as the end of history). When Hegel says the truth is the whole, he certainly did not mean, as critics sometimes assume, that the truth is general; he means that the truth is intricate interactivity (*Wechselwirkung*). It is true that Hegel sometimes metaphorically treats human history as an eternal expression of Genesis and pictures the Christian Church as the "the goal and the starting point of history" (Hegel [1830] 1900: 319). On that picture, every kind of time, both short and long, appears secondary to history's eternal qualities. But I am interested less in macro-Hegelianism than in micro-Hegelianism.

The first relevant passage in Hegel's text rejects the idea of ruptures in history. There is only one kind of gap in history, and it is rare: periods of happiness. "Periods of happiness are blank pages" (Hegel [1830] 1900: 26); no antithesis, therefore no development. There are, no doubt, "contingencies" in world history due to "personal aims" (Hegel [1830] 1900: 29), but these are part of the flow of history, not breaks in it. One might easily take this continuism as a sign that Hegel valorizes long term development. But in Hegel's historiography, development does not take the form of "periods," and this undermines long term segmentation as much as short term. The very idea of a "period" is pre-historical:

> Periods—whether we suppose them to be centuries or millennia—that were passed by nations before history was written among them—and which may have been filled with revolutions, nomadic wanderings, and the strangest mutations—are on that very account destitute of *objective* history, because they present no *subjective* history. (Hegel [1830] 1900: 61)

Only self-conscious societies have history. Hegel is Ricoeur's precursor on this point: without collective and reflective subjectivity, time passes, and mutations occur, but there is no story to tell. Therefore, periods are objectively senseless unless there is a continuously developing society to learn from its past. By definition, duration means the inheritance of a standpoint, and anything that exists only within its own limited period is by definition not the self-education of world history but the self-delusion of a geopolitical empire. "Empires belong to mere space, as it were (as distinguished from time)—unhistorical history" (Hegel [1830] 1900: 105). Therefore, history is made up of qualitative "worlds," not quantitative periods. History is composed of dynamic forces in lifeworld consciousnesses rather than temporal segments. It is true that Hegel organizes early Chinese history by the dates of dynasties (Hegel [1830] 1900: 116–17), but he does so only in order to highlight Chinese historians' own mistake in periodizing themselves numerologically.[22]

This point of Hegel's interpretation, however, is difficult, since Hegel himself occasionally appeals to periods (Hegel [1830] 1900: 306) when talking about divisions. The Roman world, he says, had three periods: state, war, despotism (Hegel [1830] 1900: 281). And the first period is further divided into two stages: monarchy, republic (Hegel [1830] 1900: 296). Then the stage of monarchy subdivides into the reigns of seven kings (Hegel [1830] 1900: 296). Further, each stage within each period undergoes a fluctuating opposition of forces: "the chief point in the first [stage of the first] period" is the back-and-forth struggle between patricians and plebians (Hegel [1830] 1900: 303). Increasingly finer divisions of historical phenomena like these are unavoidable. Even Braudelian historiography that posits long term trends and Hegelian historiography skeptical of both short and long term segmentation still have to describe fine-grained changes over time.

Consequently, Hegel has some use for short term events in history. Nevertheless, at times he resorts to the stereotype of short term events as uninteresting "minute details" (Hegel [1830] 1900: 405): it would be "wearisome" to describe the endless details of old battles between principalities, since "they are in themselves unimportant" (Hegel [1830] 1900: 304). Yet on the same criterion of tediousness, Hegel also dismisses long term trends: "Respecting this first [Germanic] period [of barbarian wanderings], we have on the whole little to say, for it affords us comparatively slight material for reflection" (Hegel [1830] 1900: 347). The point, for Hegel, is that history is the self-reflection of peoples, and reflection does not segment sub-temporal subtopics. Reflection is free to connect events from history across as short or long a time span as it finds revealing.

When Hegel occasionally violates his own principle, and cites world civilizations as if they were defined by finite temporal periods, it leads to his worst work. His notorious view that African cultures belong only to the past (Hegel [1830] 1900: 99) is ignorant and biased. His view that "America is the land of the future" (Hegel [1830] 1900: 86) is outdated. But even the distortions in Hegel's statements about cultures too limited to the past, or too displaced into the future, show that Hegel was right in the first place when he said that societies are not defined by their temporal duration but by how they pick something up and are picked by something up.

Of course, individuals, nation states, and new technologies come and go, and such temporally delimited factors do play important roles in history. But individuals and nations are participants in something that periods do not capture, namely "the life of the ever-present Spirit as a circle of progressive embodiments" (Hegel [1830] 1900: 79). This does not mean that "political revolutions are matters of indifference" (Hegel [1830] 1900: 154). Revolutions are indeed the form and content of history. The point is just that they are not characterized by linear time segments but by circular embodiments.

What Hegel replaces periodized beginnings and endings with are socialized convergences and absorptions. Even in cases where Hegel does put a time limit on a historical event, as when he says that "Persia was the first empire that passed away" (Hegel [1830] 1900: 173), he defines transition not as the threshold between temporal segments but as "contact" across worlds: "the historical transition takes place when the Persian world comes in contact with the Greek" (Hegel [1830] 1900: 221). Stated conversely, the incorporation of the foreign is the condition for Greece (Hegel [1830] 1900: 224). When Hegel uses a phrase like "This is the date of" (Hegel [1830] 1900: 233), his point is more to register the convergence of two histories at a crossing-point than to fix the event on a time line. The important thing is that while Hegel is obviously not an advocate of short term events, he is equally not an advocate of the long term: "We must banish from our minds the prejudice in favor of duration, as if it had any advantage as compared with transience" (Hegel [1830] 1900: 221). Of course, Hegel affirms that freedom develops step by step over the entirety of human history, which is a thesis about the long term. And he freely speaks of civilizations (Chinese, Greek, Germanic), which is long term thinking. But for Hegel, history is the history of freedom, and freedom is not a datum, it is a deed.

When Stefan Skrimshire applies Hegelian historiography to the history of climate change, it is with this problem in mind.[23] On the one hand, the long overview is essential to climate history. But the danger is that the long view might reconcile us with the inevitability of climate disaster, in which case "human agency has been swallowed up in a 'larger temporal narrative'" (Skrimshire 2011: 325). Long term history can lead to disillusionment, the feeling that there is no freedom in history, and then to the escapist desire for lighthearted pleasure in short term consumerism (like "climate change chic" accessories, Skrimshire 2011: 325). For Skrimshire, in order to keep a "long term and potentially never-ending narrative of catastrophe" (Skrimshire 2011: 329) from devolving into apocalyptic despair, "deep time" needs to be something agents can intervene in, and this is where Hegelian freedom in history can be relevant. Free agency in times of crisis is a short time intervention into deep time. Freedom is both the means by which subjectivity overrides temporal segmentation, both long and short, and is, at the same time, the short term intervention into the long term for the sake of the long term.

Just as Hegel converts the vocabulary of long term history into the vocabulary of cultural contact, so he also converts the short term. Rather than saying that Ancient Greek democracy was short-lived, he prefers to say that it only worked in small cities (Hegel [1830] 1900: 255, not enough intercultural contact), and that it allowed corruption (Hegel [1830] 1900: 267, too much contact with bad people). The closest he comes to saying Athens was short-lived is that it was so beautiful it would not be seen a second time (Hegel [1830] 1900: 273). He talks of the "fall" of the Greek world, but the fall-of-Greece has a name: "Roman power" (Hegel [1830] 1900: 277). Of course, Hegel can still use everyday formulas like "no longer" (e.g., Hegel [1830] 1900: 278). But the topoi of world history do not divide into periods; instead, they gain new names.

It is not just that an event is continued elsewhere when it gets a new name, it is that history consists of events repeated, albeit differently, under different names. Hegel's famous thesis is that

> In all periods of the world, a political revolution is sanctioned in men's minds when it repeats itself. Thus, Napoleon was twice defeated, and the Bourbons twice expelled. By repetition, that which appeared at first only a matter of chance and contingency becomes a real and ratified existence. (Hegel [1830] 1900: 313)

This is common sense: a historical event is defined in part by the reactions to it, by the way "it manifests itself in the following period" (Hegel [1830] 1900: 365). It follows that every event is in turn a repetition of another event, and that repetition is not just a twice-told tale but multi-told. Repetition is "a double external relation—backwards to an earlier world-historical people, and forwards to a later one" (Hegel [1830] 1900: 341). The historical event is repeated in another event; when repetition is doubled, the event is tripled. The important implication is that calling an event short term holds only for the short term. Once the event is repeated, that is, once it is later ratified and becomes real in the first place, then its short term status is replaced with its second place status. Repetition does not mean that the event was continuously long term in the meantime; on the contrary, it is the second short term repetition of the first short term event that makes the category of the short term obsolete. The short term is not opposed by the long term, but by the secondary instance of the short term. Hegel is not saying that one short term event is replaced by another short term event, thereby constituting a plural series of short term events—that is what everyone else's short term theory says. Hegel's account is that a single short term event becomes its own replacement, thereby constituting a single short term event that remains short every time it is instantiated, a short term that is distributed in discontinuous pieces across a long amount of time. Periodicity is disproved not by duration but by repetition. In Chapter 9 we will see Deleuze make a similar point.

Hegel thus uses the very shortness of the short term, the fact that it is a limited segment repeated by another limited segment, to sublate the distinction between short and long term. On the usual stereotypes of Hegelianism, Hegel sides with the long term, or at least uses the long term to sublate the distinction between short and long. But on my construal, it is the properties of the short term that Hegel uses to sublate the distinction between short and long.

Toward the end of his text, in approaching modernity, or the "New Time" (*Neue Zeit*, Hegel [1830] 1900: 412), Hegel refers to "recent times" (Hegel [1830]

1900: 353), that is, to the part of history to which we refer back by means of a short term reference (a century or so). Different temporal distances do matter to him, and to his readers in *"our own time"* (by which he means his time, and we mean ours; Hegel [1830] 1900: 442; emphasis in the original). But short or long, historiography is always the pairing of two times (as we saw in Husserl in Chapter 1), extending an interval in distance and then collapsing it in repetition.

We end with the well-worn problem of the end of history. Some people think that Hegel believes that history has no future, but his lectures on history close by expressing interest in upcoming electoral reforms in England: "This problem [of opposition parties] is that with which history is now occupied, and whose solution it has to work out in the future" (Hegel [1830] 1900: 452). Hegel includes this nearby future within the scope of history. It is true that he also cites the commonplace that "in history we have to do with the past" and asserts that the question whether reason will survive "hereafter" "is a question that does not concern us here" (Hegel [1830] 1900: 350). Yet, like his limiting proviso in the *Philosophy of Right* that philosophy only describes what the world is already, not what it might become in the future, Hegel's program for watching what happens to democracy in the near future shows that he does not mean that history, and our concern with it, comes to a dead stop as of this moment. True, our capacity for knowing the nature and narrative of the world is limited to the short term future, but this does not mean that history excludes the future, it just means that the future that history is about is short term.

And this is to articulate again the ongoing results of this chapter. Complex events come and go and come back in inter-cycles, repeating in layered time lines and staggered measures. In one sense, this means that divisions into short and long term periods are too simple to accurately describe historical segmentation. But in another sense, it means that both longer trends and shorter events take effect by a logic of divergence and convergence, in free and reflective interventions, in the sort of temporal periods that we typically call short term.

Short and Long Term in Fictional Narrative

We cannot leave Ricoeur's discussion of long and short term historical narrative without touching on his parallel account of fictional narrative in Volume 2 of *Time and Narrative*. The temporal possibilities of fictional narrative are more "open" than in historical narrative, since the former is not constrained by truth (Ricoeur 1984: 2:3). Nevertheless, Ricoeur's covering premise, for both history and fiction (and hybrids), is that plot synthesizes episodes in time (Ricoeur 1984: 2:8). He allows many variations, including narratives that begin telling the story from the middle (as Homer does), or that proceed non-chronologically, or that do not end with closure. Temporal synthesis can incorporate breaks, delays, and inconclusive hiatuses (Ricoeur 1984: 2:15)[24] as well as wandering streams of consciousness (or subconsciousness) (Ricoeur 1984: 2:9), as long as it includes both episodes and linkages: events and trends, short and long term.

In the last chapter of Volume 2 of *Time and Narrative*, Ricoeur reads "tales about time" (Ricoeur 1984: 2:101), picking out what we might call microfeatures of short and long terms in narrative form. In Virginia Woolf's *Mrs. Dalloway*, Ricoeur is impressed by the rhythmic alternation of "long sequences of silent thoughts" with "brief spurts of action" (Ricoeur 1984: 2:103). Marcel Proust's *Remembrance of Things Past*[25] opens with "*Longtemps*," "for a long time," followed a few lines later by: "but of late …": one long term and one short, already thematizing the loss and re-capture, and re-loss and re-re-capture, of time. In Thomas Mann's *The Magic Mountain*, characters in a tuberculosis sanitorium lose their sense of time. In the end (spoiler alert), the relative timelessness inside the asylum is suddenly broken by the intrusion of war from outside, which Ricoeur describes as the intrusion of "large-scale history" (Ricoeur 1984: 2:128). The miniaturized time inside the asylum lasts a long time for the characters, and takes a long time for the reader to plow through, whereas large-scale history intrudes into the story only for a short amount of fictional time. Short life can make a long story, and large-scale history can make a short chapter. The narrator even speculates on whether some of his sub-stories "seem too long or too short" in the telling (Ricoeur 1984: 2:114).

There are some more extreme possibilities that Ricoeur does not consider, for example, fiction designed so that the reader cannot read to the end. He does consider extensions beyond the usual constraints on plot, but does not press exceptions to the bursting point, as a philosopher should. We might consider Walter Abish's stories,[26] which consist only of word lists in alphabetical order. Or Dadaist writing, or The Four Horsemen's wordless concrete poetry. Since such cases do involve short and long segments, they therefore count as evidence that some properties of the short term are not found in narrative. I am not going to undertake my own analysis of particular fictions, but I might have picked Schwitters and Pindar, Gertrude Stein and Djuna Barnes, Jodorowski and Ponge, bill bissett and the Egyptian Book of Coming Forth By Day, Darius James and Wakaliwood, Tati and Fagunwa, Germaine Dulac, Lee Chang Ho, and the Transcendent Satrap in Charge of the Extraordinary Commission on Clothing of the Collège de Pataphysique, each of which stretches the temporal synthesis of narrative to, or beyond, the breaking point. The question, to return to the beginning of this chapter, is whether there are forms of short and long temporal segments that are not dependent on, and not captured by, narrative.

Ricoeur thinks not; his stand is that nonnarrative is non-art (Ricoeur 1984: 2:22). It is acceptable for art to be fragmented, but only if the reader has some chance of piecing it together. "Frustration cannot be the last word" (Ricoeur 1984: 2:24). Why not? Again: "Rejecting chronology is one thing; the refusal of any substitutable principle of configuration is another" (Ricoeur 1984: 2:24). Again: "Even Joyce …" (Ricoeur 1984: 2:26)—readers can imagine the rest. Ricoeur concedes there is a slight chance that narrative literature may be dying out in the late twentieth century, but not that some other literature can replace it. I find these to be dogmatic prognoses that fail to save the literary phenomena and fail to test whether short and long terms may exist without narrative.

Ricoeur argues that even if one promotes fragmentary novels, on the grounds that fragmentation is true to experience, one still appeals to truth, and therefore to the order of narrative. I do not think that fiction needs to hold true to life experience. And if non-experiential fiction produces new short term patterns, so that readers then experience temporal forms in reading that they would never have experienced in life, all the more interesting.

So how might short and long temporal durations be constructed without narrative?

Ricoeur's sometime target, structuralism, holds that narrative is a secondary effect of taxonomic structures, and may even be generated from axioms. Ricoeur replies that structures may generate the shapes of plot outlines, but not actual stories (Ricoeur 1984: 2:38). Structural variations may generate character types, but do not embed a character in a motivated situation (Ricoeur 1984: 2:43). Structuralism may want to think of itself as diachronic, and may think it can generate free agents and their quests, but their method wrongly assumes that time reduces to logic (Ricoeur 1984: 2:48–50). When structuralism does try to account for the way a character engages their future, as in Greimas's category of "durativity" (Ricoeur 1984: 2:52), it does not really generate time and narrative, but rather surreptitiously presupposes them. A full "adaptation to time" (Ricoeur 1984: 2:52) requires agents deliberating on narrative urgencies.

But to press the question of whether duration in short and long segments can be handled by structure without narrative, let us consider serial music. Schoenberg's aim is to avoid the story-like formula of sonatas, which set out from the tonic of a key, modify keys a bit and vary the melody, and finally travel home to the tonic, consonant and comfortable. To reject the predictable narrative based on the centrality of the tonic, Schoenberg gives all twelve tones on a scale equal value. To make sure no tonal character is privileged, his rule is to write a tone row, or series, using all twelve tones in any order one likes, then to play through all those tones before repeating any. The composition thus has no central tone, no original tone to which it returns. It is permitted to play the tones simultaneously, as chords, or in reverse order, or to invert the intervals between notes upward or downward on the scale, or to orchestrate different tones with different instruments, or in different tempos. Many variations are possible on a single twelve-tone row, and a composition based on a row is still determined by the feelings of the composer. The point is that structurally generated compositions do not have the unity of narrative music, but they have most, if not all, of the same temporal forms. The limited number of structure-governed variations did tend to keep Schoenberg's compositions unusually short, but the conclusion is that structural analysis alone, without recourse to lifeworld narrative, might provide a model of long and short durativity.

A series is twelve notes long, and if each note is played for the same length of time, all twelve-tone rows are equally long. But the twelve notes do not all have to be played for the same length of time. In the generation after Schoenberg, composers of "total serial music," like Stockhausen, had the idea that not only pitch but other parameters, like the length of notes, should also be serialized.[27] Where tonal serialism puts all twelve tones into an ordered series, temporal serialism put all the standard tone lengths (from sixty-fourth notes to double whole notes) into a series, and requires that a composition play through each tone length on that series (it does not matter which pitch, as long as the note has that length) before moving to the note with the next length. Again, the tone-length series can be varied by combinatory rules. This seems like a great idea. But a problem for composition length soon became clear. If a piece of music plays double whole notes as frequently as sixty-fourth notes, it will be a slow piece of music, since the sixty-fourth note passes quickly, and the double whole note takes much more time to pass. Whereas tonal serial music is short, temporal serial music is long. But again, the point is that structure by itself can control longer and shorter lengths of time.[28]

Ricoeur can accommodate some structural time within narrative, in the form of "games with time" (Ricoeur 1984: 2:80). For example, a fictional character's pasts and futures at different distances from the present can be placed on view at the same time. And the reader of a fictional sentence like "Tomorrow was Christmas" (Ricoeur 1984: 2:66) can affix that fictional past of another time line onto their own. Each fictional time interval becomes a "quasi-past" for another time (Ricoeur 1984: 2:64). A narrative's short and long terms can be the narrated character's (or the reader's) long and short terms.[29] Consider a chapter ending with a character about to go on a long voyage to outer space. The reader understands that the next chapter will pick up years later, once the character has arrived. The reader starts reading that next chapter a few seconds after finishing the one before. The fictional character's long term is the reader's short term. Similarly, one fictional character may quickly read in a letter about another fictional character's long travels, which is in turn experienced by a reader who reads half the novel, then is interrupted by long term illness, then picks up the book again where the characters left off.

The deeper the narrative, the more it takes structure to keep track. In some sentences, like "That would come back to haunt her," temporal experience is rendered by grammatical structure: "the conditional is to narrative what the future is to commentary" (Ricoeur 1984: 2:70). Ricoeur can thus give some role to structural temporality. In fact, it is always possible for a writer to choose a temporal structure first, then only secondarily, to find a narrative that fits it. Italo Calvino wrote the nested narratives in his novel *If on a Winter's Tale a Traveler* to fit an algorithm of his own design.[30]

Ricoeur touches on many temporal patterns—condensed time, elongated time, staccato rhythms, iterative events ("every week …"), skipping over dead time—all under the heading "tempo and rhythm" (Ricoeur 1984: 2:79). Even within continuous narrative, there are breaks between chapters, after periods, between subplots, in analepsis (anticipating events) and prolepsis (returning to the backstory). It is common for several times to be telescoped ("Today I can still see …," Ricoeur 1984: 2:83) into anachronies, anisochronies (periodic events with unequal intervals), and omni-temporalities (Ricoeur 1984: 2:84), as well as temporal counterpoint and temporal polyphony (Ricoeur 1984: 2:97).

Surveying the range of possibilities, we can say that short and long term temporal segments overlap without being simplified either into one long term with shorter parts or into many separated short terms strung together. As variations and degrees of exception pile up, I think we have to conclude in a way that forces a proviso into Ricoeur's account of time and narrative: while the interweaving of short and long terms commonly does happen narratively, it sometimes happens structurally.

Historical/Literary Hybrids

Ricoeur's conclusion to *Time and Narrative* is that historical narrative connects objective measurable time with existential time, and fictional narrative "neutralizes" objectivity in free phenomenological time (Ricoeur 1985: 3:127–8). Both the ethics of socio-historical organization and the aesthetics of controlling imagination are mapped by temporal distances along several contemporaneous temporal measures. Diagrammatically, events, containing multiple subjectivities, are shaped by interactive short and long term forces. Insofar as the short term is defined in terms of absorptive and repulsive transitions, we can take the position I attribute to Hegel, namely that quantitative short and long terms are both sublated by the transformational quality of the short. The short term is the temporal segmentation that makes temporal complexity possible.

Chapter 4

SHORT TERM MEMORY (COGNITIVE PSYCHOLOGY)

Argument: Insofar as short term memory means working memory, the same short term memory can keep recurring for a long time. The concept of the short term is thus more functional than quantitative.

Cognitive psychology is not entirely settled on whether there is a genuine distinction between short and long term memory. In this chapter, we focus on the way cognitive psychology deals with memories, namely as the storage of particular former experiences and their explicit recall after a determinate amount of time. These are what Husserl calls secondary memories and Bergson calls recollection images.

A different sort of memory may also exist, which Husserl analyzes as primary retention and Bergson as virtual memory, if it is true that everything that is ever experienced is implicitly retained in consciousness, whether we later become aware of it in a separate recollection-image or not.

In Husserl's *Phenomenology of Internal Time-Consciousness*,[1] "primary retention" is neither short term nor long term, though it does, permanently, retain relative distances between past and present. It marks the amount of time since a past event was experienced, but that mark does not last just for a specific short or long amount of time. Primary retention is the gradual and constant slide of present experiences into experiences marked as past. "In the continuous line of advance, we find something remarkable, namely, that every subsequent phase of running-off is itself a continuity, and one constantly expanding, a continuity of pasts" (Husserl [1928] 1964: 49). Each experience is thereafter experienced as earlier than the present by some degree of temporal distance. The continuity of experience implies also that between any present experience and any given past experience there are other experiences marked as having been in-between the two. Each retained past is always in the process of receding. Some experiences are more distant from the present than others, so one might call them farther back, or longer term memories. But they are not different in principle, either by type or by how long they last as memories, from memories of experiences that happened a shorter time ago. In other words, there are short-distance and long-distance retentions, but not short term and long term retentions. This is the nature of any process that is gradual and continuous: such processes, and their segments, are constantly ongoing without breaks that could divide them into short and long term. Only processes that are inherently different when they are long and when they are short are long or short term in practice.

This idea of permanent memory, independent of questions of recollection, thus bypasses the difference between short and long term memory. I am not going to focus on this sort of memory in this chapter; this chapter is limited to just those cases where we have an experience, then later recall it, after an amount of time that is either short or long.

Concrete memory must obviously include both short and long term memories. There must be short term retentions that make experience feel continuous from one moment to the next, as well as some long term storage of a knowledge base. When we listen to a person talking, for example, we have to retain the beginning of a heard word while we hear the end of it, and we have to know the meaning of the words, which we will have learned a long time ago. This kind of example leads Roman Jakobson to say that, "the role of short- and long-term memory constitutes one of the central problems of both general linguistics and the psychology of language."[2]

The literature in cognitive psychology on short term memory is complicated and disputed. I will draw from two frequently cited survey articles: Nelson Cowan's "What are the differences between long-term, short-term, and working memory?" in *Progress in Brain Research*, 2008;[3] and Bart Aben et al., "About the Distinction between Working Memory and Short-Term Memory" in *Frontiers in Psychology*, 2012.[4] The conceptual speculations below about the meaning of the short term are my own.

Short term memory is memory for a particular experienced image retained (again, in what Husserl calls secondary retention) only for a short amount of time, or to be more operationally precise, memory that can only be recalled a short amount of time later.

One might think that short term memory is memory that simply lasts a shorter amount of time than long term memory. But we will see that most theorists of memory think of "memory" as an equivocal term, naming two different functions (not including "primary retention") that may be performed on an original experience, one of which leads to its short term retention, and one of which leads to its long term retention. Short and long term memory thus tend to be defined primarily by the operations they perform on the original experience, and only secondarily by the length of time the original experience lasts. Theorists disagree on what exactly the operation that counts as short term memory is. But the first point to emphasize is that the short term is not a simple quantitative measure but is constructed out of qualitative micro-functions.

Before laying out the different views on how short term memory works, we should say something about what it means to no longer remember something. The literature takes memory loss, or forgetting, as something of a given, not as an existential condition of being-in-the-world, as Heidegger might say. The experimental literature defines memory loss more narrowly, as an experience that a person was at one point exposed to, but cannot later recall quickly or accurately. Failure of recall means that a person cannot say what they experienced when asked in an open-ended way; failure of recognition means that a person cannot tell whether an image they are shown in the present is the same as one they saw in the past.

In Bergson's view, failure to recall or recognize an image experienced in the past does not entail memory loss as such. In Bergson's view (based on his distinctive ontology of images), no memory is ever lost. Failure of recollection or recall consists only of an incapacity to make use of memories in motor activities, or to convert certain memories into explicit mental or linguistic images. On this understanding, short term memory is more a function of the pragmatics of recollection than of the extent of preservation. All memory on Bergson's account is long term, but retrieval is short term. To put it ontologically: memory is an expression of the past, and the past does not change; retrieval happens in the present, and in the present, everything changes. In a certain sense, of course, time passage happens for a long time, so the short term happens over the long term. But the point is that since the present keeps passing, the long term passing present consists in re-generated, repeated, and individually repeatable short terms. Memory, qua past events, cannot change and cannot be short term; memory, qua current recollections of the past, must change, and can only be short term. In sum, Bergson's more than usually rigorous ontological distinction between retention and retrieval would introduce a lot of problems into the cognitive psychological theory of short term memory. Let us keep this part of the problem simple, though, and just use the vocabulary of experimental cognitive psychology: in the pages below, we will say that a memory is lost if it can no longer be recalled or recollected.

One more note: we talk as though memory preserves previous experiences, but there are also short term memories of experiences that we were never explicitly conscious of in the first place. Cowan's example is that a person might unconsciously start slightly mimicking the Scottish accent of a person she is talking to, reproducing her recent but unnoticed experience of the other's voice. In this case, it is the imitation of the other's voice after they have spoken that makes the listener conscious, for the first time, of that person's accent. The moment of remembering an experience may thus in some cases be the first moment one experiences it at all. The memory act, to this extent, is the primary medium of the prior perception. Retroactive cognition is a fairly common feature of phenomenological description, but it is particularly interesting if short term memory in some cases is not just a secondary image that arises shortly after the original perception, but a kind of experience that is short because of the way it unexpectedly brings a perception to light. It is short not because it ends shortly after it began, but because it cuts itself into the present as a new experience.

But let us go back to asking which operation(s) count as remembering in the short term. Surveying the literature of psychology journals, we find four theories. (1) Temporal decay: where time lapse alone causes a memory to be lost. (2) Attention decay: where as long as the subject attends to something, whether for a short or a long time, it remains in short term memory; once the operation of attention diminishes, the memory is lost. (3) Capacity limit, or "chunk capacity": where short term memory is a storage facility with limited room, like cassette tape answering machines, so that when more new input experiences arrive than the storage capacity can contain, an equivalent quantity of old memories is displaced. (4) Working memory: where experiences currently being used in cognitive processing are placed into a short term memory module; once those experiences are no longer being used, they are removed from the module. Examples of this fourth type take the following form: during the time that a person is reciting a list of words learned a short time earlier, or during the time she is baking a cake she saw her father make a long time earlier, salient memories are placed in an "episodic buffer" where they are subject to "management" by a "central executive" function (Cowan 2008: 3). This quaint administrative metaphor is meant to suggest that the upper-level bureaucrats of the brain facilitate interactions across departments; for example, the face department exchanges information with the name department, so that we can remember a person's name when we see their face. The point is that whereas the first three theories treat memory as a more or less passive mode of preserving experiences (though holding an image steady in attention is not completely inactive), this fourth theory treats memory as active cognitive work.

Short Term Memory as Working Memory

The most common (though not unanimous) of these four views is the fourth, namely that short term memory is the same as working memory. On this theory, it is the working time of the present, rather than the short distance of time from the past, that defines short term memory. Whenever we are working on, putting to use, thinking about, or changing our thinking about something we have experienced in the past, we bring the experience into consciousness for a while. Whenever I visit Montreal, I pull up memories I haven't had since the last time I visited Montreal. As long as we have an experience in consciousness, that is, as long as we are making use of it in current experience, we are activating our short term memory function for it. The long term, by contrast, would be lazy memory. Indeed, the only kind of memories we can use, the only kind we are ever conscious of, are short term memories; long term memories are by definition latent, and we are normally not conscious of them.

Short term memory, then, in the sense of working memory, need not indicate an uninterrupted brief period of time between the moment when something is originally experienced and the time when it has been forgotten. The same short term memory may, and is likely to, arise in bits and pieces over a long period of time, in the way a life-long baker, or a speaker of German as a second language, brings the same memory-region into a short term buffer module each time she needs it. In fact, working memory will be continuously present under high cognitive demands in all medium-long term activities, for example, when we are reading a text for several hours, or playing a long game of Go. Even though working memory is a definition of short term memory, these cases have sometimes equivalently been called "long term working memory."[5] AI research utilizes an analogous procedure: "long short term memory."[6]

The time scope of memories is complicated by the fact that some theorists make a hard distinction between "episodic memories," in which we remember an event that happened to us at a certain time (e.g., the memory of the time we learned the definition of "existentialism"), and "semantic memories," in which we remember the definition of a word (we access our inner thesaurus, and remember the definition of "existentialism" without remembering the time we learned it). Episodic memories are temporally dated; semantic memories are not. Episodic memories are generally remembered in order, and during a time span, roughly similar to the order and span of the original events; semantic memories are remembered in a single moment. Episodic memories are supported by "time cells" in the hippocampus (recently discovered to exist in humans, not just in rodents) that activate segments of the memory in order.[7] However, the distinction between episodic and semantic memories cannot be all that hard,[8] since we obviously use our knowledge of meanings in order to remember episodes. The consequence for us is that all memories, not just some, are tied to the history of our experience, all memories take an amount of time to come into the mind, and so all memories are subject to short and long term measurement.

The important point for us is that memories about how to bake a cake are at work for the time span it takes to bake the cake, after which those memories need no longer be active. These memories (some muscle memories, some conceptual) come back into play for a while, then go back out of play. If short term means precisely the time during which a memory has to be activated in order to accomplish a short term task, then working memory and short term memory are conceptually distinct but closely related. We might say that the potential time scope of short term memory is long term but that its use is short term. It lasts for a lifetime but only denotes short term segments in which it is actualized. The point is that the very concept of the short term requires that there be a flexible relation between time and act. The scale of the short term is neither simply that of decaying memory nor simply that of working memory, but consists of the variability in the relations between them.

Indeed, if we think of working memory as the time between experience and action, we might think of memory as the operation of delayed reaction. Wolfgang Ernst's techno-phenomenological *Chronopoetics*[9] describes memory as the "time channel" of information processing (Ernst 2016: 30–2). Between the time that information is received and the time that it is worked into a result, there is a delay. Qua waiting, delay can be called "processing dead time"; qua work channel, delay can be called memory.

Time Quantity and Its Exceptions

Not everyone agrees with Cowan's assessment that short term memory is activated long term memory. Dennis Morris[10] argues that short term memory performs three functions that cannot be attributed to briefly activated long term memory: (a) Memory for new experiences, that is, for "previously unencountered information," cannot count as activated long term memory; (b) Memory for lists of words or numbers ("storage of multiple items of the same type") is not retained long term; and (c) When in everyday experience, seemingly instantaneously, we attach words to visual experience (the "variable binding problem"), we are creating interpretations on the go, not just restoring connections drawn from long term memory.

Morris also raises the puzzle of what the very idea of "activation" is supposed to mean in the context of memory. For Bergson, this is the central problem of memory: in what sense is anything in the mind non-active? If memories are already active, what could it mean to activate them? For Bergson, memory must be active all the time if it is ever to be active. Of course, that requires additional Bergsonian theses that carry their own difficulties. It requires that all images be actively present in the mind at all times, yet mostly without being consciously recollected or represented. It requires that long term memory be interpreted as still-activated short term memory (rather than short term memory being interpreted as activated long term memory). It requires that memory be understood more as prolonged perception than as storage. And thus, to go full-Bergson, it requires that experiences of the "past" never really pass, or to say it in reverse, that when we remember something, we experience the past live. In terms of phenomenological ontology, I find these claims of Bergson to be surprisingly convincing (see my *Simultaneity and Delay*). But I am not following this approach in the current chapter. Let us instead pursue Morris's position that some short term memories cannot be explained as short-lived working activations of long term memories.

Bart Aben's survey of the same material that Cowan surveys begins with the observation that there is a "remarkable" lack of agreement over whether to identify working memory with short term memory (Aben 2012: 1). As a result, there are all sorts of confusions in experiments when subjects are asked to perform tasks using working memory, which are then interpreted as measurements of short term memory. He proposes the term "holding memory" for memory that is not working at interpreting or applying a knowledge base, but is merely the retention of unintegrated newly gained information. That distinction would validate Morris's view that working memory is not the same as short term memory. However, the distinction between new datum and background schema of operations is not entirely clear, since even the simplest auditory retention requires some sort of "phonological loop," and even the simplest visual retention requires a "visuospatial sketch pad" (Aben 2012: 1). Such loops and slates involve at least some minimal pre-existing capacity for manipulation of information as a mechanism for holding on to it, so there is at least that much working memory going on even in holding memory, and therefore some degree of calculation and decision involved in even the simplest memory record. In addition, since there is a correlation between people who score well on short term memory tests and people who score well on IQ tests, it seems that there is some interaction between the mere attention required for memory and what we call "intelligence" (Aben 2012: 4). As a result, Morris's attempt to separate the merely quantitative shortness of strict short term memory from the functional operation of working memory does not fully succeed.

Still, even to the extent that working memory must be defined operationally, and not just quantitatively, it nevertheless remains the case that quantity—quantity of time lapse, as well as quantity of information—does play an irreducible role in the experimental psychology of memory.

Since Ebbinghaus in the 1880s, it has been typical to experiment on short term memory by experimenting on the way subjects acquire, rehearse, memorize, repeat, and then forget short phrases or number combinations, individual words, or nonsense syllables (Cowan 2008: 1). From a philosopher's point of view, the paradigm of memory of word lists is a poor choice, since it suggests that short term memory is equivalent to memory of unimportant packets of information. It is certainly not a good way to experiment on the short term memories used for baking or for speaking to Germans. Still, memory of word lists does exist, and studying it reveals some interesting features.

The common generalization is that human short term memory for word lists has a time limit (twenty to thirty seconds) as well as a capacity limit (seven, plus or minus two, words). The different theories listed above offer different functional explanations for why there are those limits: it may be because of temporally caused decay, or because of interference in attention, or limits in neuronal capacity, or loss of salience. But even before we get to the explanations, the quantitative phenomena themselves are not so simple. To start with a simple example, subjects reciting items in a word list tend to recall the words in "spurts" of three, so the very idea of counting memories is not obvious. The technique of chunking memories both expands the number of items that can be held in short term memory and extends the amount of time they last. This is a lesson in its own right: time lapse and content assemblage are not independent parameters. The short term is not separate from the short stack.

Furthermore, neither retention nor memory decay is measured in a vacuum. A degree of memory retention or loss will be determined by such factors as the type and number of prior rehearsals, the distinctiveness of the information, and the method of retrieval. To cite a clear case: the length of time a memory for a word list is retained depends on how many times, and for how long a time period, the list had been rehearsed, and, on top of that, on whether the rehearsal time had been interrupted (Cowan 2008: 2). If subjects are given a list of words ("cat adverb gaucho election") and told to rehearse them by saying the word "the" between each word ("cat the adverb the gaucho the election"), then, unsurprisingly, they retain fewer words, and for less time (Cowan 2008: 5). The denser the rehearsals, the thinner the memory, and the quicker the decay. The more you do, the shorter it lasts. There are many similar cases, where inserting an extra process into the memory environment causes a memory to fail more quickly than it would have done otherwise.

Yet this point too needs to be qualified. If a lot happens during a short period of time, subjects tend to remember that period of time (though they may not remember many of the details from that period of time). If little happens during a short period of time, subjects tend not to remember that period of time at all. So dense time is remembered, though not all of its details are, whereas thin time may not make a mark on memory at all. Though yet again, if a period of time is extraordinary for its lack of anything happening, it may be remembered especially for that reason, since an extreme case of nothing feels like something—not for perception, of course, but for memory.

Experimental designs generally either try to force memory into a shorter term by interposing obstacles to retention, or else try to compensate for those obstacles by introducing extra learning techniques to make the short term memory last longer. The question is whether these variations of command and control force nature to tell us what it means for something to exist in the short term, or whether they are the very functions that constitute the short term. The back-and-forth series of qualifications on what will be remembered for how long does not mean that short term memory is random. But it does suggest that short term memory is not defined solely either by the quantity of time passage or by the number of events contained in a period of time but also by the salience of those experiences relative to such criteria as purposiveness, normality, or interestingness. Memory persists in the short term, and decays over time, depending on the different sorts of functionality that the experienced events have over time. Indeed, making memory short term, as a technology of forgetting, is a time-generating act in its own right, not just a fact of time measurement. And this suggests that even when we analyze the quantitative aspects of short term memory, and thereby try to isolate the function of temporal decay, it remains nevertheless that attention span, capacity limits, and the functionalities of working memory are still factors. The point is that both quantitative and qualitative features, and the many variations of each, determine what it means for highly varied types of memory to exist in the short term.

There is another unexpected impact of rehearsal on memory. Normally, rehearsal allows a word list to be retrieved for a longer time than if the list had not been rehearsed. Obviously. However, there are counter-intuitive exceptions. If rehearsal time is too short, for example, if the subjects are told to rehearse the word list but then cut off before they have finished rehearsing, their short term memory for the list will last for even less time than if there had been no time at all to rehearse it (Cowan 2008: 6). A too-short amount of rehearsal time functions as if it were somehow less time than zero.

Rehearsal shows that the operation of short term memories includes actions leading up to the creation of those memories. The short term of memory covers the pre-term of that term. And the amount of time spent preparing to form a short term memory in part determines the amount of time between the forming of the memory and its decay. The point is that the short time limit of memory does not occur instantaneously; it takes a measurable amount of time to build up. It takes a short amount of time in order to make a memory that, subsequent to that, lasts a short amount of time. It takes preparation time to make a short term event possible. Conversely, since the memory is short term in the sense that it will be forgotten, we could also say that it takes a certain amount of time in order to make a memory of such a nature that it can be forgotten. As a character in the Runyonesque movie *St. Benny the Dip* (Edgar Ulmer 1951) asks, "How long does it take for a guy to get amnesia?"

Time Order

As philosophers of time might expect, time-order ultimately outranks time-length in the function of short term memory. For example, everyone knows the Recency Effect: we remember the last items in a word list better than we remember the middle words. At least, this is true in the short term; when asked a long time later, we remember all of the words on the list about equally well (Cowan 2008: 6). This shows the interaction between temporal orderings within the list, and the difference between decay over a short period of time and decay over a long period of time. One might have imagined that an experience is first put into short term memory, then only its best retained parts get transferred to long term memory. But if that were true, long term memory would preserve the Recency Effect present in short term memory. The fact that the Recency Effect diminishes in the long term suggests, oddly, that long term memory is the baseline for direct memory. Short term memory over-concentrates on a small part of the experience, distorting the experience by taking it out of order, as if some of the just-perceived world is almost invisible in the immediate context; but then, after the short term is over, the experience (not all, but more of it) becomes whole again and more likely to be retrieved for a long term.

To take yet another interesting variation: "The availability of short-term memory of an item may allow resources needed for long-term memorization to be shifted to elsewhere in the list" (Cowan 2008: 6). That is, if a subject rehearses one item on a list to preserve it in short term memory, but does not rehearse the other items, it may result in the other items on the list not getting into short term memory at all; yet that very omission from short term memory retention may actually help those other items be better retained in long term memory. This does not mean that putting something into short term memory hinders its retention in long term memory; it rather means that there is a kind of competition for memory inclusion, where losers in the short term memory stakes get the consolation prize of inclusion in long term memory. From the perspective of short term interests, rehearsal produces a winner in the short term; from the perspective of long term interests, rehearsal side-tracks attention to a few items, a distraction which long term memory conveniently ignores.

We can conclude generally that the short term cannot be defined simply as the first stage of the long term (the short is not a diminished long). In fact, empirically, it is difficult to know what to make of the fact that different experiments on the same phenomena elicit slightly different amounts of time before short term memory loses the ability to perform certain tasks, like reciting a word list. Might it mean that short term memories undergo continuous decay, and different experiments catch the decay at different points in the continuum? It seems that the known experimental data do not decide whether memory is continuously changing over time, or whether it exhibits variable discreteness across trials. The measure of short term memory will need a better account of the relation between continuous magnitude and discrete quanta.

As everyone knows, the whole scenario of memory decay changes when a list of words is integrated into a narrative, or into the lifetime of significant memories of the experimental subject. An individual subject's long term memory connections can have an effect on both the order and persistence of items in their short term recall of word lists.[11] Given this effect, the primary distinction is not between short term memory and long term memory but between list-memory and narrative memory. Narrative memory might decay for some other reason; but in an integrated structure, decay does not result from time passage alone. Of course, as everyone also knows, narrative integration can also introduce inaccuracies into memory, so that we remember what we expect to have remembered rather than what we actually saw; or we force our story into coherence and so erase elements that we do not know how to make fit; or we quasi-deliberately enhance our confidence level in order to appear reliable on the witness stand. It is not clear whether we should call this the long term enhancement of inaccurate memory due to narrative integration, or the substitution of narrative in the place of memory, or both. It may be that the very working process that is required even for the simplest holding memory contributes simultaneously to its longevity and to its inaccuracy. But not always—sometimes it is perception that is deceptive, and narrative rebuilding may distort perception precisely to generate a more probable picture of what happened in the world. Fortunately, for the current project, I do not need to prove that any sort of memory is truthful. The important thing is that there is one correlation between short term and decay, another correlation between long term and inaccuracy, and a further set of correlations between those two correlations. To say it differently, there are different kinds of interactions between quantity, quality, and function that all generate different types of short term memory. Some are short just in the sense of overall duration, others in the sense of intermittent activation, others by interrupted preparation, others by degree of decay (by intensive rather than extensive magnitude), others by shifting their place in order, others by incomplete integration.

Still other memories are short in the sense that they are relayed to another person. For example, there are cases of memory loss that are not exclusively part of a single person's cognition but are socially correlated with environmental situations. There are certain "I can't remember the last time I ..." situations that are especially located at certain times in history. As the study of the psycho-temporal memory weirdness arising out of the 2020 Covid lockdown heats up, we will learn more about the way people answered questions like, "When was the last time you bought toilet paper?"[12]

The De-evolution Over Time of Short Term Memory

Tetsuro Matsuzawa[13] experiments with the short term memory abilities of chimpanzees, whose recall for ordered lists of numbers is significantly better than that of humans. He hypothesizes that at an early point in human evolution, we traded off some short term memory for more semantics and syntax. It is interesting to suggest that we do not need as much short term memory for lists of discrete events if we can explain those events with meanings, but it does not seem quite right to think that language simply does with less short term memory, since after all, we need short term memory to use language. Indeed, the trope that advanced minds are better at thinking, whereas less advanced minds are better at memory, is burdened with a history of prejudice. For that matter, Matsuzawa's explanation for why we could not have developed language without having to reduce short term memory is odd: "Brain volume capacity was limited at a certain point in evolution, so we had to lose some function in order to get a new function" (Matsuzawa 2007: 102). The very idea of capacity limits is one of the definitions of short term memory, which means that Matsuzawa's explanation for the trade-off is that we had to lose some short term memory because our short term memory was not large enough to contain both short term memory and language. It would be as if short term memory were the only place we had to store any kind of cognitive capacity, as if both short term memory (for number lists) and long term memory (for language) are both stored in short term memory. Still, the idea that cognition can trade memory off for other functions is interesting, as it makes memory less an absolute function but, instead, one cognitive card among many in our cognitive hand.

Short Term Memory and the Body

I will just say a few words about neural plasticity and the physical support for short term and working memory.[14] Neuroimaging suggests that short and long term memory are correlated with different areas of the brain (Cowan 2008: 11). Even within short term memory, different parts of the brain do different jobs. Recognition of the early portions of a word list activates the hippocampal system, unlike later portions of the list. Or to take a different kind of materialist example: the Korsakoff syndrome, caused by thiamine deficiency (often brought on by alcohol), results in chronic memory loss, but has little effect on memory for short term lists.

Neuroimaging also suggests another relation between memory and perceptual delay. The part of the brain active when a subject is asked to recall a list of items in the short term, the dorsolateral region of the prefrontal cortex, is also activated when a subject is asked to delay performing a perceptual task (Aben 2012: 5–6). Short term memory thus might even be thought of as equivalent to delaying the next perception. Memory would be the "delay period of span task." This is an excellent idea, though it would take phenomenology to draw it out: memory of an event would consist in not having finished perceiving it, or in the resistance to moving on. In this operation, memory ends as soon as the delay in perception ends. It may look like chunk capacity, where memories are displaced by new perceptions, but delay resolution is a different mechanism than capacity limitation.

Women seem to be better than men at some short term memory tasks.[15] It is not clear whether the (alleged) difference is due to a difference specifically in temporal cognition or whether it has more to do with different ways of handling the relation between the familiar and the unfamiliar.

For most people, the most salient issue of embodied short term memory loss concerns Alzheimer's, sometimes described as "rapid forgetting."[16] The first symptom is typically loss of "working memory and long-term declarative memory," along with a host of other symptoms from impaired smell to sleep disturbance. Of course, short term memory loss, or the failure to process new information into short term memory, can result from many causes, including non-Alzheimer's forms of dementia, stroke, alcohol, aging, or emotional problems.

A paper by Franzen and Haut from 1991 (already citing a "logarithmic" increase of studies of memory loss beginning in 1978) sums up treatments of short term memory loss into three categories.[17] The first is neurological repair, but complete repair is rarely possible.

The second treatment for memory loss is "retraining," or in other words, "the use of spared skills in compensating for the impairment (alternate functional systems)." This is related to "brain plasticity-based training," which aims to compensate for loss of memory with other brain functions.[18] It is interesting that a non-memory function might be used to simulate memory as if something other than time might perform the function of time. The simplest way to recreate lost memories of facts would just be to learn those facts again. If a person has forgotten the names of animals, they might just learn the names again, as if learning cognition compensates for the loss of memory cognition. This seems like a circular problem for those patients who are just going to forget their new knowledge again. But it seems to work after certain brain malfunctions. The Mayo Clinic recommends it.[19]

Franzen and Haut's third treatment model for repairing short term memory loss involves "behavioral strategies to circumvent the manifest memory dysfunction (behavioral prosthetics)." As everyone knows, physical activities like jogging and sleep, mental activities like conversation and crossword puzzles, and organizational practices like list-making and taking one's meds are good for healthy memory. These are not strictly memory enhancements, but their efficacy indicates in part that short term memory takes place partly outside of memory altogether, and that short term work in non-memory areas functions as if it were memory-work. Many patients with short term memory loss compensate with behaviors that mimic memory while in conversations with others. They learn to repeat back what the other person has said, to make it look as though they remembered it themselves. Insofar as short term memory loss can be covered up with behavior, behavior could be thought of as prosthetic memory.

Naturally, much of the advice for treating Alzheimer's is addressed not to patients but to caregivers, since they will be the ones to compensate for memory loss in others. The short term memory of one person in effect becomes the working memory of the other.

While some patients undergo permanent loss of short term memory, others undergo temporary loss of long term memory. Often, this is caused by stroke or epilepsy, but the Mayo Clinic lists among other rare, but possible, causes of transient global amnesia: sexual intercourse, overwork, and sudden immersion in cold water.

Of course, not all memory loss is global; some memory loss is targeted at unbearable memories. In "dissociative identity disorder," a new term for what has been called multiple personality disorder, people who have suffered trauma, often prolonged sexual abuse as children, are able to set aside (the Mayo Clinic says, "keep at bay"[20]) otherwise debilitating memories, so that they can function in daily life. They may create a second personality to go to school, who will not remember the traumatizing experiences of the first personality. If those memories do return, they are experienced as the memories of someone else. If a person splits off a second personality at the age of ten, that personality may remain ten years old, while the school-going personality ages. If abuse continues, it may be necessary to split off another personality who remains at age twelve, and so on. The psychic phenomenon of multiple personality is based on memory compartmentalization: de-activating a subset of memories in the short term. We might call it short term non-memory. At least since Locke, personality has been described in terms of connected memories; it follows that if a person subdivides memories, they will have multiple personalities.

To conclude this chapter in general terms, the short term of short term memory is not merely a quantity of time but the interaction of different functions that sometimes compete, sometimes compensate, and sometimes produce feedback loops in each other. We can rarely, if ever, say that a short term process is a particular series that lasts a particular amount of time. The short term is a cluster of temporal functions separated off from a multiplicity of different sorts of processes undergoing other short and/or not-so-short temporal functions at the same time. The upshot of all the intriguing variations in the experimental literature on short term memory is that the short term is a machinic set of operations, interruptions, and collective displacements.

Chapter 5

SHORT TERM MEASURED BY QUANTITY
(TIME ATOMS, HEGEL)

Argument: While I have been arguing that the short term is not an exclusively quantitative concept, there are of course elements of the short term that are quantitative. This chapter argues that quantitative measures are themselves characterized by multiple measuring systems, so that, as Hegel says, when the concept of quantity becomes more complex, qualities and differential functions emerge within it. Short term temporal quantities are differential ratios, measured by a plurality of different parameters and metrics at the same time.

This chapter discusses attempts to get at the shortest time: materialist time atoms and mathematical limits. The idea of a time atom is not that there are instants of time with no duration—that is a different topic—but that there is a shortest possible time span greater than zero. Similarly, the smallest time interval in calculus is not a point in time with no interval at all, since there is no way to measure the movement across space during an amount of time that measures zero.

Short term events are often artifacts of measurement technology. Wolfgang Ernst's *Chronopoetics*[1] describes many cases of "time-critical processes and couplings between human and machine signal processing at the micro-temporal level" (Ernst 2016: 37). For example, the modern interest in short term computer memory storage is due, in part, to the fact that the vacuum tubes that were used to store information in old computers were expensive, so they could only be used for "short-term temporary storage" (Ernst 2016: 23).

Current physics defines "Planck time" as the shortest measurable amount of time. The equivalent in seconds of Planck time is 5.39×10^{-44} seconds. (It took a relatively endless 10^{-35} seconds for inflation to set in after the Big Bang.) In purely numerical terms, there is no reason not to refer to 10^{-45} seconds, which is a shorter time than Planck Time. But the Planck Time unit is physical as well as numerical; it names the shortest amount of time that it would take a physical event to occur, which means the shortest amount of time that can be physically measured, the smallest amount of time that we can give physical meaning to. A Planck Time unit is the time it takes for the fastest thing (light) to travel the shortest physical distance, namely to travel across the Planck Length. The Planck Length, in turn, is a consequence of the Uncertainty Principle in quantum physics: to measure the position of any particle, we need to observe where it is, since we need to bounce a light particle off it; but gravity, while a very small force at that level, can have a small but uncertain effect on the light particle we use to measure the position of the other particle; therefore, quantum physics implies a small margin for error of even the most accurate measurement possible; smaller than a certain length, it is impossible to measure space without uncertainty; the Planck Length is the smallest length we can measure without losing the ability to measure.[2] It is not a failure of instruments that causes the failure to measure an amount of time shorter than the Planck Time, it is the quantum nature of physical reality.

In practice, the shortest amount of time we can actually measure, given current technology, is far longer than the Planck Time. Reinhardt Dörner's team in Hamburg has measured the time it takes for light to cross a hydrogen atom: 247 zeptoseconds[3] (a zeptosecond is 10^{-21} second). Theoretically, the mean lifetime of W and Z bosons is 0.3 yoctosecond (a yoctosecond is 10^{-24} second). Even our ability to imagine instruments for measuring short times, instruments that would far surpass our current means to build them, involves times much longer than the Planck time. Physics today cannot even imagine how to measure times shorter than 10^{-33} second.[4] So, when physicists talk about the shortest time that could exist in physical terms, there is some ambiguity. They are talking about the shortest *time that can be measured* accurately, which is much shorter than the shortest *time that we can measure* accurately, or that we can even imagine being able to measure accurately. Physicists tend not to say that there can be no time shorter than the Planck Time, but rather that any time shorter than the Planck Time would violate currently known laws of physics, or in other words, that any supposedly shorter time would not function in the physical world in the way we currently understand time to function. Operationally, we would not know whether to call something shorter than Planck time shorter time, or not call it time at all. Normally, indeterminacy is described as the impossibility of measuring the velocity and the position of a particle, but since the point is that it is impossible to measure these two values of a particle at a given time, it is just as much the point in time that is indeterminate. Happily, not all philosophy of the short term is dependent on the shortest temporal measure according to physics.

The question of the shortest time has arisen from time to time in the history of philosophy. The vocabulary of "time atoms" is associated with Maimonides, though Maimonides did not believe in them himself.

Time Atoms: Maimonides and Others

According to Maimonides,[5] several of the twelve propositions of the Islamic Mutakallemim philosopher-theologians of the tenth and eleventh centuries affirm the existence of time atoms. Maimonides thinks they were wrong. In fact, it is not certain that the Mutakallemim or anyone else believed in time atoms in the first place, but we can think about them anyways. The reasoning on behalf of time atomism that Maimonides attributes to the Mutakallemim sounds rather abstract to modern ears. It is not based on anything like the technology of time measurement, or on a phenomenological description of time-consciousness, or on concepts of past, present, and future, or before and after. The reasoning on behalf of time atoms is rather that it is consistent with certain theological theses.

According to Maimonides, the first reason that time atomism is important for the Mutakallemim is that material atomism in general supports the theological thesis that "genesis and composition are identical" (First Proposition, Maimonides [1190] 1954: 120). If we did not know what the world is composed of in its basic material elements, then we also would not know how, or even whether, the world was created. It would not be so bad not to know the composition of matter, but it would be terrible not to know whether the world was created. Without positing atoms, we could not say what the material world is composed of, therefore we could not explain what it even means to say the material world was created, or that God is our creator.

Second, atomism is also required for a theory of movement, not just because the things that move are composed of material atoms (the smallest indivisible parts of matter), but because space is also composed of atoms (the smallest indivisible parts of space), and because time is composed of atoms (same again), and because even movement and rest are composed of atoms (and so on). On this model, "locomotion consists in the translation of each atom of a body from one point to the next one" (Third Proposition, Maimonides [1190] 1954: 121). Motion is the translation of one material atom across one spatial atom during one temporal atom (like a theological Planck unit). This means that in a strict sense, all motion across the same amount of space takes place in the same amount of time: that is, all motion has the same speed. What, then, accounts for the commonsense appearance that motion occurs at different speeds? "Motion that is ordinarily called quick" is really motion that "has been interrupted by fewer moments of rest" (Third Proposition, Maimonides [1190] 1954: 122). Maimonides does not quite say that the Mutakallemim believed that rest is composed of atoms, but the appeal to "moments" of rest suggests that. In some of the time atoms that exist during the translation of a material atom across spatial atoms, no translation across space occurs. We do not perceive each time atom distinctly on its own, so we are under the illusion that the material atom is moving steadily during the whole period of movement; but that must be false, since the only thing that can explain differential speed is that there are time atoms during which there is none of that movement. This seems rather odd as a description of experience (though cinematic frames-per-second is a kind of application), but it is a necessary implication of the theory of atoms, and we need to accept that theory of atoms, as we said, in order to believe that the world is created as well as composed.

The Sixth Proposition adds a third motive for the theory of time atoms, namely that it is consistent with another theologically important thesis: "No accident can have any duration" (Maimonides [1190] 1954: 124). God creates substances, which endure over time, from one time atom to the next; in contrast, accidents have no substance, and are not essentially caused by substances or forces. Therefore, accidents must be created by God moment by moment. Therefore, "accidents do not exist during two time atoms" (Maimonides [1190] 1954: 124). Indeed, since accidents can only be caused one time atom at a time, and God has the ability to act one time atom at a time, and we finite beings do not have that ability (as you personally know from experience), it follows that only God (not we) can be the cause of accidents. For example, "the cloth which according to our belief we dyed red, has not been dyed by us at all, but God created that color in the cloth when it came into contact with the red pigment" (Maimonides [1190] 1954: 124–5). Some even go farther, believing that substances too exist only one time atom at a time, which would imply that God alone can cause anything at all, or in other words, that "it must never be said that one thing is the cause of another." But Maimonides does not go so far as to say that the Mutakallemim go so far (Maimonides [1190] 1954: 125). To justify the theory of time atoms, it is enough that accidents not endure for more than the length of one time atom.

By the same principle, our knowledge of facts, which is a kind of accident in our minds, does not endure over two time atoms: "The knowledge which we have of certain things today, is not the same which we had of them yesterday; that knowledge is gone, and another like it has been created" (Maimonides [1190] 1954: 125).

That is about it for time atoms, barely enough to count as a theory, and what there is of it is only marginally focused on time atoms at all, being mostly focused on the nature of the cause of accidents. Some of the subsequent propositions have a general relation to time atoms, for example, in regarding the absence of a property as a kind of accident (as if to say, perhaps, that negations are restricted to single time atoms as well) (Seventh Proposition, Maimonides [1190] 1954: 126). Or again, the possibility that a thing could gradually become larger or smaller requires that time be composed of very small quantities (Tenth Proposition, Maimonides [1190] 1954: 128). Or again, one might see the Mutakallemim's assertion of other sorts of division into atomic components, in matter, in space, or even in concepts, as a general support for time atoms (Tenth Proposition, Maimonides [1190] 1954: 130). But except by analogy, time atoms are not much involved in these other sorts of atomism.

Maimonides has his own views of creation, accidents, causality, and time (Part 2, Chapter 13, "Three Different Theories about the Beginning of the Universe," Maimonides [1190] 1954: 171–3), but he does not actually make an effort to refute the theory of time atoms. Perhaps he thought the theory of time atoms was so preposterous that the mere attribution of it to someone else would count as a refutation of their philosophy. In fact, on almost all the occasions when the theory of time atoms has arisen in the history of philosophy, it has had this status: it is attributed to an opponent, or attributed by a commentator to a long-gone predecessor and then dis-attributed by later commentators, or attributed but then reinterpreted so that it is not really about time atoms at all. It is as if the theory of time atoms can barely last the time during which it is attributed.

Richard Sorabji[6] shows that various Ancient Greek philosophers who were thought to have believed in time atomism did not. He begins with the important point of terminology that defines time atoms as short but non-zero durations:

In Greek thought (although much Islamic thought and much fourteenth-century Western thought is different), an atom is not the same as a point or instant. Points and instants are indivisible because they have no length at all. They are not short stretches of space or time but instead are merely the count of stretches. Atoms, however, are supposed to be indivisible in spite of having a posited length, perhaps a very short one. (Sorabji 1982: 37)

Sorabji searches rarely frequented corners of ancient philosophy for an unambiguous expression of a theory of time atoms. Plato's *Parmenides*, for example, discusses the idea of the "sudden," but the sudden only implies a slice of time dividing two periods of motion, not a time atom with a duration of its own (Sorabji 1982: 49). Maybe Plato meant to posit a time atom, but if so, he does not say it clearly (Sorabji 1982: 50).

Aristotle considers the minimal amount of "time taken," which implies a maximum speed, but this is also not quite about time atoms—its focus is more about movement across space atoms (Sorabji 1982: 50).

Aristoxemus (a pupil of Aristotle) refers to "primary time" in music, the "smallest unit of measure in rhythmics" (Sorabji 1982: 77). Musical metrics are a common source of judgment in thinking about smallest times, but ancient musical theory says not much more about it.

Diodorus Cronus (d. 284 BCE) is a more promising candidate to be an advocate for time atoms, since he affirms the possibility of "something's being moved (perfect tense) in a jerk, without there ever being a stage at which it *is moving* (present tense)" (Sorabji 1982: 59). Reacting against Aristotle (Sorabji 1982: 64), Diodorus Cronus affirms the idea of "partless time," which is not an instant without duration, since by definition it "leaves room for moving" (Sorabji 1982: 62). Sorabji attributes to Diodorus two arguments for time atoms. First, if the present had multiple parts, then at least one of its parts would be in the past, and/or at least one of its parts would be in the future, which is absurd; therefore, the present must consist of a single part of time, a time atom. Second, if an object moving at the fastest speed moves through space atoms one at a time, then the time it takes to move through one space atom is by definition one time atom (Sorabji 1982: 62). This latter view is close to the view Maimonides describes. Diodorus may be the best case of a philosopher affirming time atoms, though as usual we know his texts only through the testimony of others, and it seems that in this theory, he had no followers.

Epicurus thinks that "minimal parts of time" are conceivable (Sorabji 1982: 67), and maybe even perceivable (Sorabji 1982: 69), but he does not go so far as to argue that they are real (Sorabji 1982: 67). The closest he comes is saying that from a given time, there is a "next minimal time," or a "minimal particle in the next time" (Sorabji 1982: 69). Sorabji is skeptical, but this does not sound far from time atoms to me.

Damascius (sixth century CE) has the more common anti-atom view that small jerks of time prove precisely the continuity of time, rather than the atomic segmentation of time.

Sorabji cites Nazzam (d. 846 CE), as recorded by Juwayni (d. 1085 CE), to conclude that most Islamic philosophers were trying to refute time atomism, despite what Maimonides says (Sorabji 1982: 81–2). They may have been interested in "gaps" between parts of time, or in the "fragmentation" of the route of time, or in "diagonal" movements across spatial atoms that make a process take longer than straight line movements. But Sorabji decides that they were not interested in atoms of time as such. It is possible that the interests of these Islamic philosophers is much like my own: I am not really interested in time atoms as the shortest possible pieces of time, or about their status in physical reality, or about how long they might be, but rather in gaps, fragments, and variable speeds that occur in short term events.

In his final comments, Sorabji wonders whether the classical issue of time atoms might be connected to Planck's posit of a shortest time unit.

Richard Arthur expands the oblique history of time atoms into modern philosophy.[7] Arthur is most interested in Descartes, and in the relation of time atoms to occasionalism and instantaneism. Like Sorabji, Arthur thinks that time atomism cannot be tied closely to any Ancient Greek philosopher, but Arthur thinks that it might be influenced by Gnosticism, or else by Indian Buddhist philosophies, from the first century BCE sects of Vaibhashika and Sautrantika (Arthur [2012] 2020: 6) to the first century CE Indian philosopher Kanade. Kanade offers the strange argument that without spatial atoms, all things would have the same size (and presumably, without time atoms, all events would have the same duration), since if divisibility does not end with indivisible atoms, then all things will be infinitely divisible, therefore all things will be infinitely large (and all events will be infinitely long) (Arthur [2012] 2020: 7).

Arthur's main interest is the way time atoms are related to occasionalism. If there are time atoms, then God will have to create the world anew with each time atom. (As we saw, the Mutakallemim took a different route: God only had to recreate accidents one time atom at a time; substances (and so the world qua substance) would take care of themselves after the time atom at which God created them.) Once time is divided into atoms, then time stops and starts again at the end of each time atom; it is not possible for what happens in one time atom to carry over into the next. (This is not a bad argument; maybe it ruins the Mutakallemim defense. Time segmentation (in my view) is necessary for all sorts of reasons of measurement, phenomenological description of experience, and event theory, but time atoms would be going too far in the ontology of segmentation, if they end up denying the reality of temporal continuity and even made succession impossible to understand.)

In conclusion, if there are time atoms, many unpalatable consequences follow. First, if there are time atoms, then things do not have essences, since any properties they have at one time will have to be created anew at the next time, and they have no properties that endure due to their own natures. Second, if there are time atoms, then no thing can cause any other thing to have any property at the next time atom, so only God can cause anything to happen at any time. Even our own qualities, motivations, and supposed agency can only provide the occasion for God to create what he likes. For Arthur, all of these consequences mean one thing: the theory of time atoms entails occasionalism in causality (Arthur [2012] 2020: 2–4).

Descartes is in fact an occasionalist, Arthur argues, but not a time atomist. While time atoms entail occasionalism, occasionalism does not entail time atomism. Instead of time atoms, Descartes affirms slices of time, which Arthur calls "instantaneism" (Arthur [2012] 2020: 15, citing Descartes's *Principles of Philosophy*). The relevant kind of instant, for Descartes, is an "instantaneous state of motion" (Arthur [2012] 2020: 15). The idea that motion exists in a state is already somewhat odd, as if motion is not a trajectory that takes place over time but is immanent in a single state as its "tendencies." What matters is not that time is divided into smallest atoms, but that it is possible to determine the tendencies that exist within a freeze-frame slice of time. The "balance of instantaneous tendencies at an instant" (Arthur [2012] 2020: 16) would be the state of motion.

Admittedly, theorists of time atoms, if there were any such theorists, might want to blur the difference between time atoms and time instants. If there is a clear difference, it is that time atoms need to have a duration, no matter how short, so that a plurality of tendencies of motion can exist at the same time. It does not really matter much that a very small time unit be the very smallest possible, or that it be indivisible. What is important is that it contains a plurality of impulses toward different motions, without including the differences between those motions. The function of the time atom is to get a motion started without getting to the middle or the end of that motion. A time atom would do a lot for a theory of the short term, as it would count as a process in process, without including the end of the process, or even the end of a part of the process. A time atom would thus be the paradigmatic short term. It is too bad that there is no such thing as a time atom. Our theory of the short term will have to get some of those desired results from short terms that are a bit longer.

Events

Since Planck time defines the shortest time by the fastest event over the shortest distance, we might try to define short time relative to what kinds of events there are. Conversely, we might define events in terms of the shortest amount of time during which they can take place.

Some analytic philosophers have taken this approach. Elliot Sober, appealing to Jaekwon Kim and Donald Davidson, writes: "The time at which an event occurs can be associated with the shortest time during which the object, which is the subject of the event, changes from the having of the one to the having of another, contrary property."[8] This does not mean that events are always short. It means that when we want to pick out an event from the flux of changes in the world as a whole, we isolate a particular change, and to isolate a particular change means to isolate just that amount of time in which that change takes place, and exclude from consideration the time before and after that particular change. This means that marking off the shortest amount of time during which that event can be found is what identifies and individuates that event. The cloud of changes relevant to an event may stretch into a more distant past and future, but the event per se is defined by the shortest amount of time during which it could be said to take place. If we look at a piece of time, and find the event in it, and then look at a smaller piece of time and cannot find the event in it, then the former is the shortest amount of time in which the event can be found. For example (my example, not Sober's), take the event, "Obama was elected President in 2008." We could plausibly say that his election lasted from the time he declared his candidacy to the time he was sworn in. In that sense, the event of his election took about sixteen months. But we could equally plausibly say that he was elected during the day of voting, which took about fifteen hours. Or we could equally plausibly say that the transition from the point when Obama was not president to the point where he was president consisted of Congress accepting the Electoral College votes, which usually takes just a few minutes (but sometimes takes rather longer). On the other hand, if we take the moment at which Colorado was declared for Obama, thereby putting him over the top in Electoral College votes, we could plausibly say that we do not find enough in that bit of time to count as the event of his election. To define the time of the event, we consider all the different plausible time spans of the fully defined event and take the shortest of these times. The time of the event is the shortest time in which we can find it. I am not sure this is the best account of the time of an event. In practice, it seems that there will be more fuzzy cases on this criterion than clear ones. For that matter, I am not sure in principle why the rule should be that an event takes place in the shortest amount of time in which it can be found, and not rather that an event takes place during the longest amount of time in which it can be found. Nevertheless, it is interesting to define even long events by the shortest amount of time in which they can be found. It is not quite that all events are short term, but that all events take place in the shortest amount of time possible. And insofar as this marks an event by where it is cut off, there is something right about it.

We should add one further aspect of physically short time. Shortest physical time is sometimes connected to the shortest time it takes the brain to register and to measure time. In some cases, these are not connected. We can take a long time to notice a short time, and vice versa. But there is extensive research in the neurosciences[9] about the way the (human) brain senses time duration. In some situations, we need to notice events in very short durations, and to calculate them in very short amounts of time. For example, when humans listen to someone speak, we need to notice in real time when one syllable ends and the next begins. Crickets need to evaluate pulse durations and intervals in courtship behavior. Of course, "temporal selectivity" depends not just on neurons but on learnt experience and cognitive capacities. But neurons have "time-varying synaptic properties," and the temporal "plasticity" of synapsis allows us to recognize temporal durations in real time on the scale of tens of milliseconds. "Short term synaptic plasticity as a mechanism for sensory timing" is a psychological practice of the short term.

Small Numbers and Short Times

Short material events are measured in small numbers. In turn, small numbers themselves are relevant for short terms, insofar as the construction of a small number cuts something into the shortest part. Obviously, it would be a category mistake to identify a small number with some amount of time. However, in a phenomenology of number, it may require a different sort of cognitive cutting to constitute a small number than it takes to constitute a large number. And in addition, it takes a special kind of number to represent that special kind of time interval that calculus requires, namely the time interval that is smaller than any other time interval.

Phenomenology of Small Numbers

There are competing theories about how numbers are constituted.[10] Some variation on Frege's is probably the most common, based on ordinal succession: we start with something (a mental state or whatever), which counts as one, then add another, and then another, in succession; each result is the next number.

In contrast, Dedekind's theory,[11] influential for set theory, then for Badiou, is based on the idea of a cut. (My description following is an amalgam of a number of related versions.) Here, we start with a set with some members in it. We compare it with some other set with some members. Remove one member from each of the two sets; then do that again, and again … If both sets run out of members at the same time, then they have the same number of members. What those sets have in common is a number; and what they have in common is what a number is. A set with members that do not run out when the members of another set do run out is a set with a larger number of members; a set with members that do get used up before all the other set's members are removed is a set of a smaller number of members. In Dedekind's terms, a number is a precise point at which all numbers other than it are either larger than it or smaller than it (Dedekind [1872] 1963: 5). The fact that there are discrete numbers is thus dependent on there being a continuum. A number is a discrete cutting point in the continuum of quantity. The continuum, after all, is continuous because it contains all possible larger and smaller numbers, and a number is just any place where the continuum divides into larger or smaller.

We are not focused on numbers as such. For us, it is the phenomenological act of cognizing a continuum and narrowing cognitive focus down to the thinnest cutting zone that brings us closer to the problem of the short term. Husserl, in his *Philosophy of Arithmetic*, is interested in quantitative "partition."[12] Number comes about not because we start with a unit and add other units to it (as Frege thought), nor because we start with a plurality of sets and pair off their members (as Dedekind thought), but because we start with a given quantity and subtract parts of it to see what is left over.

> To subtract a number b from a number a means that, after segregation of b units out of a, we bring together the units still remaining into a new number c ... Subtraction therefore represents the solution of the following partition problem: if a given number a can be split up into two partial numbers in such a way that b is one of the two, what is the other one? (Husserl [1891] 2003: 198)

We can break this description into two phases: (a) We distinguish individual units from a whole (turning a block whole into a composed whole), remove some of those units, group together the units remaining, and make a new whole out of these. We do not just break one whole into two wholes; we break the whole down into units, then we build those units back into two wholes. Partition is a multi-step mediation of wholes into parts and back. (b) After we break a known whole into bits, remove some, and rearrange the remaining bits, we are left with an identity question that concerns the remainder: "what is the other one"? This is a good way generally to formulate the short term remainder once it has been cut off from the known number: the problem of the short term is the problem, "What is the other one?"

Subtraction is a special case of partition (Husserl [1891] 2003: 198). It is not just the "inverse operation" of addition (Husserl [1891] 2003: 199). Husserl's thesis is that subtraction contains a temporal element, whereas addition "contains nothing of temporal succession" (Husserl [1891] 2003: 199). His reasoning is that adding 4+2 is the same as adding 2 + 4. Subtraction, in contrast, is not commutative: it matters which number we begin with. Of course, arithmetic ordering is not the same as temporal ordering (it makes no difference, for example, how long we take to carry out a subtractive operation), and Husserl does not generally emphasize the temporal structure of arithmetical thought, even in the psychology of arithmetic. But Husserl emphasizes temporality in partition, and makes a point of saying that the opposite operation, which we could call wholition, does not share an essential temporal function. In this respect, Husserl diverges from Kant, who does discuss the temporal aspect of the judgment of addition 5 + 7 = 12. For Kant, the judging subject has to add units over time in order to get to a sum—the fact that judgment is structured like counting over time is what makes it a synthetic judgment (the fact that there is no other right answer makes it a priori). Kant's idea that judgments of addition and subtraction both have a temporal component may be in part due to the way Kant presupposes partition in order to explain addition: 5 + 7 = 12 is justified by reversing the operation, by showing that the whole 12 breaks down into the smaller wholes 5 and 7 (then into units). Kant's view that addition and subtraction are inverse operations, and therefore that both judgments have a temporal structure, seems more commonsense than Husserl's view that judgments of subtraction are temporal and judgments of addition are not. But if Husserl is right, then the short term unit is temporally more determinate than long term accumulation.

Husserl is more direct about the quantification of temporal segments in his *Analyses Concerning Passive and Active Synthesis*.[13] Unlike Heidegger, Husserl has no resistance to quantifying temporal durations. Husserl asserts that every "phase" or segment of time has both "an identical temporal duration," that is, a determinate "temporal length," as well as "an identical temporal locus," that is, a determinate position that it occupies in the timeline (Husserl [1926] 2001: 189). It seems obvious that the individuation of a temporal segment is partly determined by its length. For every phase of time, and every temporal object, we can specify how long it lasts, and when its beginning and end occur. Both determinations follow from the fact that a temporal event takes place during a determinate interval.

In addition to the property of temporal identity, there is a property of "temporal uniformity" (Husserl [1926] 2001: 189) across the parts of the temporal duration. This means that a temporal phase of a certain length can be divided into equal sub-phases. The many actual notes (including the rests) in a melody (Husserl's go-to example of a timed object) may all have the same duration, or may have different durations, but in principle, the length of the melody can be divided into equal portions, and the melody can be measured by that time signature. Husserl calls this "ways of filling out, or not filling out, the temporal length," or the "temporal shape" of the length (Husserl [1926] 2001: 189).

In consequence, two or more temporal phases can be quantitatively compared—for their overall length, for the length of their parts, and for their temporal shape, that is, for the combination of the lengths of the parts that fill the overall length. Of course, two different temporal phases do not occupy the same location on the time line, but they may have the same length, in which case they can be divided into an equal number of parts of the same length. Alternatively, two temporal phases may have different lengths, but may in spite of that be measured by sub-phases of the same length. (Two melodies may be played in 4/4 time at a tempo of 120, yet one may last for four bars, another for sixteen.) In terms of their length and shape, two temporal phases can be said to be "repetitions" of one another (in the way that a melody can be repeated), whereas in terms of their location, two temporal phases cannot be repeated (which means they are "irreplaceable," Husserl [1926] 2001: 190). These seem obvious points about the quantification of the wholes and parts of temporal (or any other kind of) segments. Indeed, they ought to be obvious, since they fall under the heading of passive synthesis, structures we find in experience, which may be dynamic in their employment but which we do not have to consciously figure out or genetically construct.

Husserl's description of temporal length comparison is grounded more on cardinal numbers than ordinal, which gives it more in common with Dedekind and set theory than with Frege. For Husserl, two temporal objects have, and are experienced to have, the same length, not because we start constructing one segment with a first unit of time, then add a second, and a third, until we get to the end; then start constructing another segment and again add a series of successors, so that the two successions of ordinals end after an equal limited sequence. Equality is more like what we saw in the cutting model of set theory, and like Husserl's partition theory of subtraction: we examine two temporal segments, put them side by side, as it were, then match up one element of one with one element of the other, then match up another, and find out at the end of these one-to-one matchups whether one segment has leftover elements: "Every point of time here corresponds to a point of time there" (Husserl [1926] 2001: 189). If partition reveals no leftovers on either side, then the two segments are equal in length. The smallest temporal segment would be the one where our count of its temporal portions ends at the first portion. Commonsensically, that would define the shortest time we can experience.

This is similar to, but not quite the same as Dilthey's analysis. Dilthey does not define the shortest experience in terms of the shortest amount of time we can experience, but he does define "the smallest unit that can be called an experience" as an experience with "unitary meaning."[14] In fact, we can define the experience of shortest time in two ways, first, by the shortest experience one can have, and second, by an experience that we cannot divide into portions. As for the shortest event we can experience, cognitive science actually has several different accounts: the shortest we can experience and recognize an image is thirteen milliseconds, but we can register a flash of light in ten nanoseconds (one millisecond is 1,000,000 nanoseconds). As for an experience that we cannot break into smaller portions, a blink of an eye takes three hundred milliseconds, and for most people, a flash of color the length of the blink of an eye is too short to break into portions. We might call the first a purely quantitative shortest experience, and the second a qualitative quantitative shortest experience. Humans have experiences that match each criterion of shortest.

A bigger problem is that even if we univocally define the smallest unit of experience by the shortest amount of time passage that consciousness can notice, we still need to ask how a conscious subject experiences that two different experiences take the same small(est) amount of time. How does consciousness experience the equality of length across temporal segments? Since those segments do not have the same temporal location, they do not exist at the same time, and so cannot be compared at the same time. Bergson (in *The Immediate Givens of Consciousness*[15]) uses this difficulty of comparing the relative length of time segments at different temporal locations in order to argue that temporal segments cannot be measured at all for length. This is Bergson's provocative thesis that time is indivisible, and in that way, structurally different from space. His argument is that while we can mark off a piece of space, then cut a piece of wood (a ruler) to fit it, then move that piece of wood to another area of space, and see if the second piece of space is covered by the same piece of wood, and therefore has the same length as the first piece of space, we cannot do the same for time. We cannot mark a piece of time and make a physical object out of that length of time, then move that temporal object to another period of time, and lay it on top of the other period of time, to see if the two periods of time have the same length. To measure whether two time segments are equal, we would need to move one of those time segments to the time location of the other, and remain certain that the time segment we moved is still equal to the time segment we moved it from, but this will lead to an infinite regress. Therefore, Bergson concludes, it is meaningless to ask whether two segments of time have the same length. Bergson's conclusion is that time cannot have any quantitative properties, and cannot be partitioned into any sort of multiplicity, and cannot be quantitatively measured (though he does think temporal events have "qualitative multiplicity"). I do not think that Bergson is right about his challenge to the quantifiability of time, but I do think that in order to account for how time is quantitatively divisible, we would need to explain the act that Bergson thinks is absurd, namely the act putting two different locations of time into the same experience so as to compare their length, and determine whether, as Husserl says, "every point of time *here* corresponds to a point of time *there*." In fact, Husserl knows that the consciousness of juxtaposed temporal objects cut out of different locations on the time line is a condition for his analysis of how we measure temporal durations relative to one another. But all he says by way of explanation is that while comparing pieces of time at different times "may look like it leads to a precarious *regressus in infinitum*, I believe that a reflective analysis can overcome this difficulty perfectly well" (Husserl [1926] 2001: 192). Husserl's optimism may be open to question, but in fact, as I will consider in Chapter 9 Deleuze's spin on Bergson's co-existing memories shows how we may indeed lay one period of time over another.

Of course, a theory of short term time segments may not require that the short term be quantifiably measured at all. It is possible, for example, to say without vagueness that two events are short term without saying which one is shorter, and without measuring how short each one is. The event, and the segment of time it endures for, is short term because it is cut off at a point where it might otherwise have continued, not because there is a numerical measure for being short term, and not because it is the same length as other short term events. Even so, the idea of the short term does require that a time be cut off from the continuum, and this generates its own problem, the problem that the conception of the limit in calculus can be taken to solve.

The Limit of the Short: Calculus

The reader will be tired of hearing this, but I am not an expert in the history of calculus. I restrict myself to speculating on a few points in Carl B. Boyer's *The History of the Calculus and Its Conceptual Development*,[16] and then on some of Hegel's ideas about calculus in his *Science of Logic*.

Boyer begins with Democritus's attempts to "explain the continuous in terms of the discrete" (Boyer 1949: 26). (This is exactly how I have been presenting the general problem of short term temporal segmentation.) The problem, as Plato saw it, is that the continuous is an idea drawn from geometry, and the discrete is an idea drawn from arithmetic, and according to Plato, there is a "gulf between arithmetic and geometry" (Boyer 1949: 27), which derives from the gulf between ideal concepts and experienced space and time. The ancient mathematicians attempted to resolve the problem within geometry, to find a discrete quantum inside continuous shapes. To find a unit-part of the area of a circle, for example, would require dividing the circle into smaller and smaller sectors, until the smallest unit is arrived at. Or to say it in reverse, the idea was to try to fit an infinite number of increasingly small triangles into a circle, in order to define the circle in terms of straight lines. The ancients thus aimed to define the last term in an infinite sequence of increasingly smaller segments. Archimedes set the tone with the method of "exhaustion," in which a series of decreasing fractions is demonstrated to sum to a number neither larger nor smaller than a given limit. Problems with the image of an infinitely decreasing series remained unsolvable until the modern view began to take over, according to which the infinite sequence of smaller and smaller determinations could be represented as a discrete number having its own properties (Boyer 1949: 37). Boyer's overview is that the ancients relied too much on spatial intuition and too little on number when thinking about continua (Boyer 1949: 47). Or to put it differently, they relied too much on form and not enough on variation (Boyer 1949: 51).

For all the advances of medieval mathematics, its tendency was still to think in terms of an infinite number of infinitesimals contained in a continuum (Boyer 1949: 66). The typical problem that calculus wants to solve, namely the speed of an object at an instant, does seem like it requires something like an infinitesimally small time interval. After all, speed is calculated by the change of an object's position in space over an interval of time. You take the distance (e.g., five miles) and divide by the time (e.g., one hour). It is easy to measure the average speed of movement over a longish time in this way, but difficult to see how to measure the speed of a moving object at an instant, for example, to measure how fast the object is moving exactly ten minutes after it set off. The time of the instant cannot be zero, since there is no such thing as dividing a number (the distance) by zero (the time). (That would be like asking how many zeros it takes to add up to five; no number can be the solution to that problem.) The object's speed at a given instant seems a natural thing to want to know, but the almost-as-short-as-an-instant during which we measure speed needs to cover at least a very small time interval in order for the measurement of speed to be meaningful. As long as the time interval is larger than an instant, then we can measure the object's average speed during that interval. The so-called instant at which we measure speed needs to take up some amount of time between start and finish, but no more than the minimal amount of time, that is, not a long enough time during which the object's speed might fluctuate. Hence, the appeal of infinitesimally short durations within the continuum of time. For us, this is the interesting topic: the shortest time, the interval with the shortest term, the construction of the shortest in mathematics. There are obviously many knots one can get tied up in here (Boyer 1949: 67). It is one thing to posit the reality of indivisibles, and another to measure indivisible points.

Boyer credits Renaissance mathematics with coming close to the modern concept of limit, and for my purposes, they also come close to the metaphysics of the short term. The idea, developed by many mathematicians I had never heard of, is that "the difference [between the beginning and the end of a time interval] could, by continued subdivision, be shown to be less than any given quantity" (Boyer 1949: 100). The key phrase, "less than any given quantity," generates the positive definition of the limit. A limit is more than zero, but less than *any* given quantity. It is a quantity that is not defined as any amount, but as "less than" any amount. Yet it is still an actual quantity. It is a way of producing an infinite number of divisions that is nevertheless cut off at a finite quantity. It is the definition of the short term in an infinite universe.

Once Leibniz and Newton introduce modern definitions of calculus, almost every element is interesting from the standpoint of the short term. The idea is to stop thinking of a limit in terms of an infinite series of shorter and shorter finite lines, but instead in terms of a cut in movement itself. For example, Newton thinks of tangents not as an infinite number of straight lines composing a curve but as the direction of a moving point generated by a curve (Boyer 1949: 189). A tangent comes to a limit point not by an addition of elements but as the rate of change at a single point. Again, the goal is not to find "instantaneous motion," which is metaphysically meaningless (Boyer 1949: 193), but to measure how much continuous motion is generated at a point. Newton calls the quantity of generation at a point, a "fluent"; once we know nearby fluents, the rate of generation can be measured as a "fluxion" (Boyer 1949: 194). The conception of "dynamic" motion, opposed to the conception of infinitely small and indivisible motion, is found in Galileo's "moments," in Hobbes's "conatus," and in Newton's "fluxions" and "ratios" (Boyer 1949: 195). In general, the move is to define quantity not in terms of small parts but in terms of cuts in continuous motion.

Leibniz too defines a tangent as "a line joining two infinitely near points of the curve" (Boyer 1949: 210). Leibniz is still invested in the infinitely small, which he defines as "the vanishing or incipiency of magnitudes" (Boyer 1949: 212). But these are not "quantities already formed," they are quantities in the act of formation, so the infinitely small is closer to Newton's fluxions than to time atoms. After all, the idea is to arrive at the rate of change within a difference between two points that is smaller than any given difference. To speak of an infinitesimal is to assign a property to an "inassignable" amount of time, that is, to a segment "as small as one wishes," or again, "less than any given quantity" (Boyer 1949: 215). This, for me, is the key point. Marking a shortest term means marking a term less than any given term, drawing a cut as small as one wishes along an otherwise continuous curve. As Newton puts it: "By the ultimate ratio of evanescent quantities is to be understood the ratio of the quantities, not before they vanish, nor after, but that with which they vanish" (Boyer 1949: 216).

Everybody has introspected upon their experience of the vanishing present, and it is natural to imagine that if we divide something into smaller and smaller portions, eventually we reach the vanishing point, at which point the thing, or the time it is in, vanishes. The more technical definition of the vanishing point is that motion is quantitatively exact at a limit when the difference between two points in the infinitesimal interval, is inassignable. This leads to the odd but interesting idea that inassignable points are "qualitative zeros" (Boyer 1949: 219). Of course, the time interval measured at the limit is not quantitatively zero, not actually zero, not absolutely zero. If it were, then measurement of velocity as distance over time would again be the division of some quantity of distance by zero, $x/0$. Worse, if an object over zero amount of time is at rest, then distance as well as time would be zero, and calculus would consist of formulas with the form $0/0$. To avoid the $0/0$

consequence, the limit is conceived of as a "relative zero," an "evanescent quantity which retains the character of that which is disappearing" (Boyer 1949: 219).

If intervals are to be quantified in the mode of disappearing, if the limit is a determinate quantity that mathematics can plug into a formula without being an assignable amount, then it is natural for some theorists to speak of "equality as a particular case of inequality" (Boyer 1949: 219) or, in reverse, of an "infinitely small inequality as becoming an equality" (Boyer 1949: 219). For me, the idea of inequality "becoming-equality" might be a paradigm for the long term becoming short term. But there are obviously difficulties.

Newton introduced "fluxion" to avoid positing the infinitely short moment (Boyer 1949: 224). But this introduces an ambiguity into the idea of the short term: is it the segment that is a short term period of time, or is it the procedure for producing and changing size that captures the logic of the short term? Berkeley holds that when Newton combines flux and moment, he violates the law of non-contradiction, by treating a positive moment as a diminishing zero (Boyer 1949: 226). (A dialectician might define the idea of the short term as this very contradiction.) If all of the problems of calculus arise out of the relations between infinity, continuity, and real number, the project of post-Newtonian calculus was to avoid all the problems of fluxion and movement, inassignable and vanishing points, by replacing a geometrical account of calculus with an algebraic one, replacing motion and time with functions (Boyer 1949: 230–6).

The advance of modern calculus is that there does not have to be any analogue to physical geometry in order for the mathematics of the limit to be well defined. Hobbes's claim that a line without thickness cannot be used in geometry is outdated (Boyer 1949: 227). So is the eighteenth-century claim by James Jurin that the limit is a "fleeting" sort of being, "an increment just beginning to exist from nothing" (Boyer 1949: 228). So is Guido Grandi's eighteenth-century claim that a limit-defined number is like the Christian creation out of nothing (Boyer 1949: 241). So is Buffon's claim that since there is no last term in a sequence, the limit is a "privation" (Boyer 1949: 245). So is D'Alembert's idea of a "middle ground" between a quantity and the limit it vanishes into (Boyer 1949: 246). Indeed, the very attempt to imagine what a limit point looks like is a hindrance to its calculation.

There are interesting challenges to the idea of the short term if the mathematical limit does not represent a real or imaginable property, but is nevertheless exactly quantifiable. On the one hand, we might think that this shows precisely the difference between what mathematics tries to do with the limit in calculus and what phenomenology tries to do with the short term in ontology. Mathematics is full of quantities for which there are no images, which turn out to be useful for calculating the decay of black holes and the efficiency of solar panels. It is possible that even though calculus is commonly applied to things moving across space over time, the elements in its formulas do not represent geometrical realities like time and space but are just the right formulas to use in calculations. Still, the idea of the short term does seem to describe realities in time (historical, psychic, ontological). So it would be odd if what is good for the mathematics of small quantities turns out to be useful in descriptive ontology of time, but it would be equally odd if it turns out not to be. Calculus works best when mathematicians do not try to imagine limits as things in the environment, but if a person investigating the idea of the short term conceded that they were not even trying to deal with any short term event, it would sound fishy. Of course, fishiness is not the last word. It is not impossible that short term historical and psychic phenomena are, as in mathematics, merely functional formulas for describing history and mind, and not states of affairs that can be perceived. Perhaps short terms do not have to be imaginable, as long as a functional procedure for producing the short term is well defined. After all, short term temporal segments do have to be operationalized with procedures of various kinds (for ending therapy sessions, controlling memory loss, or grandfathering traditions). Still, operationalization in phenomenology seems a less exclusive reduction of process to function than the one that turned out to be indispensable for mathematics.

In any case, the modern solution in mathematics is to reject "vanishing infinitesimals," in favor of the "approach to a limit." It is no longer an approach to zero, but an approach to something. To take the simplest textbook formula for beginners: The limit of a function is the value of the function $f(x)$ as x approaches some number. If $f(x)$ stands for the function $3x$, then across the infinite and continuous range of numbers that x can stand for, as x approaches 2, the limit of $f(x)$ is 6. We could say that $f(x)$ approaches 6 as x approaches 2, but the point is that the *limit of $f(x)$ equals* 6 as x approaches 2. X may get closer and closer to 2 but never get there, and $f(x)$ may never get to 6, but the limit of $f(x)$ simply equals 6 when x approaches 2. This is the way calculus converts an infinite series into a plain finite number. The whole thing seemed like sophistry when it was invented, but that is mathematics, and it is exactly what we need in order to convert the idea of infinitely decreasing series into the idea of a short term.

This procedure has an analogy with the definition of number. The limit of an infinite sequence leading up to a given number is identical to the sequence itself. The sequence 0.9, 0.99, 0.999, … is the number 1. It does not make sense to ask whether this sequence ever "reaches" 1; the sequence as a whole just is the definition of 1 (Boyer 1949: 231). According to Boyer, we owe this to the mathematician Weierstrass (Husserl's PhD advisor). A convergent sequence does not "have" a limit to which it converges; "the sequence *is* the number or limit" (Boyer 1949: 286). A limit is not a process of "approaching" but the instance of an actual short term. The short term is not an ideal to strive for; the short term is a term.

The Limit of an Infinite Series Is Not a Short Cut but a Ratio: Hegel's Science of Logic

In his one hundred-page aside on calculus in his *Science of Logic*,[17] Hegel argues that calculating a limit in calculus is more like finding a ratio than like finding a determinate quantity. A ratio is a proportional relationship that holds for many different number pairs (2/4 is the same ratio as 13/26, 1,000/2,000, and so on). The ratio remains the same despite there being different quantities in the numerator and denominator positions. In other words, ratio is its own two-termed quantity and makes the particular quantities in the two positions inside each instance of that ratio irrelevant. Ratio is thus a qualitative quantity independent of particular quantities.

Hegel has the modern view of limits in calculus. He considers, but rejects, the metaphor that limits are like the vanishing of quantities (Hegel [1812] 1989: 255). He argues against the idea that the quantitative difference between a given number and the limit gets smaller and smaller until the numerical differences vanish. And he argues against the idea that as the limit is approached and the differences become extremely small, we can "neglect" them without it mattering. And he argues against the idea that infinitesimal differences resolve into zeros (Hegel [1812] 1989: 259). All of those bad theories interpret the infinitely decreasing series as an endless attempt to find the smallest interval. The bad theories recognize that the smallest interval can never be achieved, and thereby adopt what they interpret as a heuristic short cut. They think that they are justified in conceptually fudging the point, switching from small determinate numbers to a number whose determinacy has vanished, and finally treating that abstract number *as if* it were the smallest. The bad theories treat the limit as a necessary trick. It would be as if there were an infinite series of magnitudes, then *after* those magnitudes are made to vanish, there is a limit. In contrast, Hegel has the modern view that the limit is a new kind of quantity "*with which* [determinate magnitudes] vanish" (Hegel [1812] 1989: 255). What does it mean to say that there is a kind of quantity such that determinate magnitudes do not vanish after it, but with it?

While Hegel does not think that small quantities vanish as they approach zero, he does use the vocabulary of vanishing to say that determinate quantities 1, 2, 3, 4 … "vanish," that is, are irrelevant, in ratios in the form dx/dy. The particularities of the numbers do vanish, but they do not vanish into zero, they vanish into variables. In a series where quantities get smaller and smaller as they approach another quantity, and the ratio between the numbers decreases, what is important is no longer the specific numerical distance from the number arrived at so far to the number being approached. What matters is the decreasing ratio. The kind of number that matters is the ratio, the two-termed number, and not even that number, but the rule for changing that number. In other words, the numbers on the two sides of any ratio vanish in the new relational sort of quantity that pertains to the ratio (Hegel [1812] 1989: 319). This is one reason why Hegel thinks that Newton was wrong to analyze calculus in terms of motions or fluxions (Hegel [1812] 1989: 259). The idea of the approach to the limit is neither that segments always be further divisible into smaller numbers, nor that they be indivisible and get stuck at some very small number, but that the limit be a new kind of number, discontinuous with the series of determinate numbers.

Hegel's articulation is that calculus is not the sum of a series, but the repetition of a relation, the relation "for-itself." This gives Hegel the solution to the problem he had raised earlier regarding the "bad infinite." The idea of the bad infinite is that any finite thing is succeeded by, or extends itself into, or is defined by, something else, then into something else, ad infinitum. If there is a "good infinite" that can solve that problem, it cannot simply be a larger finite thing (if it were, it would have to extend itself into another again); and it could not be an infinite unit (a contradiction in terms, which at best would be separate from the finite, defined by the finite that it is not, which makes the infinite finite relative to that other thing); and it could not be an ongoing series (which is just another way of describing a bad infinite). It would have to *be* a new kind of thing, a relational thing—not a series of finite units that need to be related, but the variable relation as such. And the limit relation, as a quantity, fits the bill (up to a point). It is not an accident that Hegel discusses the "bad infinite" under the category of quality (as something that has its definition forever in alterity), and solves it with the "good infinite" precisely in the transition from quality into quantity. The number series is still a bad infinite, though a quantitative one; but relational numbers, numbering numbers, developed through the categories of ratio, to limit, to the multiple parameters of measurement, turn differences into differential equations, series into relations, bad infinites into the good infinite of being-for-self.

In sum, the interval smaller than any given interval does not refer to the arithmetical difference between points, or even to a difference becoming smaller and smaller. Nor does it have to do with the geometrical treatment of a curve as if it were really a straight line. Nor does it imply any "inexactness" that arises from leaving small differences out of account (Hegel [1812] 1989: 265). Calculations in calculus are not short cuts that cut out the infinite number of successors, so as to arrive at the limit point in less than infinite time. They are simply functions that produce a relational number by formula.

The limit is thus also separated from any sort of quasi-temporal series. In the form dx/dy, dx is not measured in relation to x but in relation to dy, and hence is not a quantitative change in a determinate quantity but a formulaic measure of a relation. This is why Hegel is modern. Mathematics for Hegel is a relation of measure in pure form, not a measure of time, space, or matter. One implication that Hegel points out is that if, like the ancients, we were to think of calculus as dealing with "parts of time," we might be tempted into a paradox. We might be led to think that over a long amount of time, motion is not uniform, whereas in infinitesimally small parts of time, it is. But this is an illusion, Hegel says, arising from empirical images of "parts of time." Calculus has nothing to do with that (Hegel [1812] 1989: 293-4).

Still, there is a subtle place where one might regard calculus as a kind of short cut in a different way. Limit is not about cutting short a series. On the contrary, limit is about converting an infinite series into a discrete result (the great discovery that Hegel attributes to Kepler) (Hegel [1812] 1989: 303). The infinite gets finished. The limit is the good infinite. The whole point of the quantitative infinite is to "resolve" continuity into a discrete magnitude. And this idea of converting continuity into discrete quantity (which might put Hegel's account of infinite quantity closer to Badiou than Badiou thinks[18]) is a kind of short cut on the grand scale—not shortening a series with a shorter series, and not cutting off the series when the changes in the series no longer matter for practical purposes, but replacing seriality with a discrete point. It is a short cut not because it makes something shorter but because it cuts out the character of seriality, and therefore carves out the topic of shortness. The limit is not shorter, or shortest. It is short.

This is the moral of the story about the quantitative short term. It ends not with the shortest time interval, either with the invisibly shortest time interval (a time atom) or with increasingly smaller intervals (the infinite decreasing series), but with what Hegel calls a transformation of the quality of the infinite into quantity, then finally, with relational and operational quantities, the transformation of the quantity of the short term back into the quality of the short term.

Chapter 6

SHORT TERM ETHICS (SOCRATES, CYRENAICS, UTILITARIANISM)

Argument: I do not argue that short term results are universally worth more than long term results. But I do argue on behalf of the ethical resources of the short term. My interest is in investigating what is meant by the short term in the context of ethics. Success in the short term typically requires preparation, which in turn means that when one chooses short term benefits, one has to value future short terms as much as present short terms.

Self-interest is sometimes associated with the short term, and community interests with the long term. But hedonism can be long term, and altruism short. Time lengths are frequently essential to ethical judgments, but in complex and interacting ways. We might have expected the history of ethical philosophy to have more to say about short and long terms. Not on every topic: if a person is trying to be good, there should be no question about how long they ought to keep it up. Yet many ethical subtopics are time sensitive: how long should punishment last and how long should we have to wait for rewards; how long should one sacrifice one's own interests for others; how long does it take to convey respect?

This chapter looks at three moments of the history of philosophical ethics in which the short term played a sharp role. The first is Socrates' dictum that it is good to keep one's speeches short, especially if one is a teacher of virtue. The second concerns the advocacy of short term pleasure attributed to the Cyrenaic philosopher Aristippus (fourth century BCE). The third is the extension of that topic in Utilitarianism.

The Ethics of Short Speech: Socrates

The ostensible topics of Plato's *Protagoras*[1] are whether virtue can be taught, whether virtue is knowledge, whether the virtues are one or many, and whether it would be smart to hire a fellow like Protagoras to teach one virtue. Running through the *Protagoras* are the categories of "short" (*brachus*) and "later" (*usteron*).

Precious little in the *Protagoras* is said about what virtue actually is or how it can be taught. Most of the dialogue is taken up by squabbling about how Simonides and Pittacus used certain words, and about what rules of order and timing Socrates and Protagoras would follow in their debate. Should they give long speeches or short?

As is typical for Socratic dialogues, the first lines hint at its eventual theme: Socrates' friend asks him how his chase after the beautiful Alcibiades is going, and Socrates, in the cringeworthy style that is his wont, says, citing Homer, that Alcibiades is in that most graceful of moments when his beard is just starting to appear. The most desirable state is just after the immature period of life, and just before the mature period, occupying a short time span that will soon be over.

The main discussion begins with a problem of timing. Hippocrates is wondering whether to hire Protagoras to teach him virtue, and Socrates praises Hippocrates for hesitating before deciding. Self-enforced hesitation is especially good when it comes to buying ideas. When you buy food, Socrates says by way of contrast, you take it home in "a separate vessel," and can later consult a doctor before eating it. But when you buy a belief from a sophist, your own mind is the vessel in which you take it home (*Protagoras* 314a-b). As soon as you hear an idea, you yourself contain it; you do not have time to think first whether to accept it. There is no time for the delay that is necessary for judging whether it is dangerous. Therefore, since it will already be too late to delay once you hear an idea, you had better delay before you hear it at all. (This theory of belief formation was the basis for the Catholic Church's *Condemnation of the Sentences* in 1277, which excommunicated people as heretics as soon as they listened to certain heretical sentences, whether they assented to them or not.[2]) Ideas about virtue are the sorts of things you should plan on getting "later": not too fast, not right away.

The same basic premise, that delayed ideas accumulate in gradations and time intervals until they can be properly appropriated, grounds Protagoras's own method of teaching. When Hippocrates asks Protagoras what benefit he will get out of his classes, Protagoras promises: "On the day you join them you will go home a better man; and on the day after, it will be the same; every day you will constantly improve more and more" (*Protagoras* 318a-b). Cognitive value is added one day at a time, continuously in sequence, not quickly in relation to a whole or an end, but serially in short improvements. We might treat this as the thesis guiding the dialogue: values are actualized sequentially in manageably short segments, delayed until the right moment, then accumulating into the distant future.

Protagoras begins his pitch with a long, peculiar speech in praise of justice (*Protagoras* 323e-324c). He narrates the old myth (the story is full of holes, so it is best not to interrupt with questions) in which Epimetheus is given the job of handing out survival traits to all the species on earth (so that no species will ever perish), but does not plan ahead very well, and so runs out just before he was to give a trait to humans. Brother Prometheus intervenes, and as consolation for humans not getting anything that can strictly be called a trait, he gives humans reason instead. Reason is weak, so humans start perishing. It is true that humans can use reason to build cities, and this helps them survive a little, but humans keep wronging each other (presumably using reason), so their cities "begin to be scattered again and to perish" (*Protagoras* 322a). Animals live long (and do not go extinct), but human life is short. Extinction for humans is a live possibility.

(The real Protagoras was known for admitting that he knew little about the gods, precisely because "human life is short."[3])

So we humans live short lives. That is not going to change. But to compensate for short life, Zeus gives to humans a second last-minute trait to help them survive: right, respect, and justice. City building is short term; justice is long term. Protagoras draws humanitarian consequences: since Zeus gives justice to the human species as a whole, not to individual humans separately, all humans are just (any person who does not claim to be just is mad); therefore, we should listen to advice on justice from everyone. (Perhaps every human can even teach virtue—Protagoras does not go that far.)

When life is short, it is important to get the timing right, and several pages of the dialogue deal with the amount of time that an education in virtue should take. Nobody wants to pay a teacher interminably. Yet Protagoras expects to get paid for a long time. His students "begin school at the earliest age and are freed from it at the latest" (*Protagoras* 326a), learning first to play the harp, later learning courage in war, and so on. And since learning is habilitation, it follows that punishment, that is, re-habilitation, should undergo the same gradual progression toward the future: we punish not to change the past, which is impossible, but to prevent wrong in the future. Given Protagoras's (possibly misleading) reputation for relativism, we might expect him to be an advocate for the short term, but in fact, he is in the teaching game for the long haul.

And this is why Socrates criticizes Protagoras. Protagoras takes too long: his overall course of study takes too long, and each of his lectures takes too long. It is too easy, Socrates says, to give long speeches, like Protagoras's speech about Prometheus. A long speech is like a bell that rings interminably after it is struck, prolonging the same monotonous note for what seems forever. It is harder, yet more educational, to break a speech up with questions and critical interruptions (*Protagoras* 329a). It is Socrates who advocates for short bursts of ideas. Of course, Socrates' questions and answers are all connected, but the point is that they are also divided, distinguished pieces of discourse, which make distinctions. Socrates' thesis is that breaking points apart analytically allows us to defeat vagueness and win the race to ideas. It is as if Zeno's division of time into pieces is precisely what gets an argument to win the race. We might wonder whether the division of dialogue into parts parallels the division of virtue itself into parts. But Socrates and Protagoras spend less time talking about virtue than they spend talking about talking.

Their bickering begins with six uses of the word "short" (*brachus*) in rapid succession:

> [Socrates]: Please bear in mind now that you have to deal with a forgetful person, and therefore cut up your answers into shorter (*brachuteras*) pieces, that I may be able to follow you.
> Well, what do you mean by short (*brachea*) answers? he [Protagoras] asked. Do you want me to make them shorter (*brachutera*) than they should be?
> Not at all, I said.

> As much otherwise than [i.e., as long as] they should be, then? he asked.
> Yes, I said.
> Then are my answers to be as much as *I* think they should be, or should my answers be as much as *you* think they should be?
> Well, I have heard that you are able, in treating one and the same subject, not only to instruct another person on it at length, if you choose, without ever being at a loss for content; or again, that you are able to speak briefly (*brachea*), indeed more briefly (*brachuterois*) than anyone. So, if you are to engage with me in dialectic, use the latter method with me, that of short speech (*brachulogia*). (*Protagoras* 334d-335a [I modify Lamb's translation slightly to preserve cognates of *brachus*])

This passage contains three arguments in favor of punctuating speech into short pieces. (1) It is good for making distinctions. (2) It is good for forcing the speaker to respond to the listeners' critiques. (3) It makes it easier for the listener to remember what has been said. Predictably, one of Socrates' friends soon shows up his little joke about having a bad memory: everyone knows that Socrates never forgets (*Protagoras* 336c).

We could find many more virtues of short forms of speech, like aphorisms, in the history of rhetoric, for example, in Francis Bacon's *Of the Proficience and Advancement of Learning* (1605)[4]:

> Writing in aphorisms hath many excellent virtues, whereto the writing in method does not approach. For first, it trieth the writer, whether he be superficial or solid: for aphorisms, except they should be ridiculous, cannot be made of the pith and heart of sciences; for discourse of illustration is cut off; recitals of examples are cut off; discourse of connexion and order is cut off; descriptions of practice are cut off. So there remaineth nothing to fill the aphorisms but some good quantity of observation; and therefore no man can suffice, nor in reason will attempt to write aphorisms, but he that is sound and grounded. (Bacon [1605] 1963): 135)

Bacon makes explicit what needs to be cut out in order to make a short speech: cut the illustrations, examples, connections, descriptions, and applications. Cut out everything that was in his day called "method." In the short format, all that a writer, or reader, can do is rely on their own observations and judgments. The shorter the writing, the more one has to contribute one's own wisdom, whereas long writings permit one to hide behind volumes of facts. Marshall McLuhan likes this passage: aphorisms are cool media (they provide less material, and so require the reader to fill in the details) whereas methodical writings are hot.

Another modern Socratic argument is found in Joyce's *Finnegan's Wake*.[5] "They ought to told you every last word first stead of trying every which way to kinder smear it out poison long" (Joyce [1939] 2021: 283). Short speech does not just take a short time to get to the end. It puts the end up front, giving away the punchline, letting the listener reap benefits from the conclusion without the slog. The speaker gets less time in the limelight, but the listener gets down to business.

How short does Socrates think a point should be? Answer: "As short as it should be." Is there such a thing as being too short (*Protagoras* 324d)? No answer. There is not really a worked out theory about time-management here, only an undertaking, in fact a command, to be short.

It is not certain whether we should draw a universal temporal ethics from the specific value of short speeches, but if we were to do so, it might look like this: An event in the present should not take up so much time that it prevents the future from becoming distinct from the present. This is especially true if the different future is an improvement, but it is still true even if the different future expresses a worse point of view than the present, as long as a still later different future is able to recognize, from the contrast, what a still better view is. To put it into a short saying: Becoming should be allowed to become. In the big picture, no doubt, permanent being is better than becoming. But no event in the sphere of becoming can be treated as if it were being itself, so it is not desirable for any event in the sphere of becoming to remain in existence over the long term without changing. A perfect world would admit long term virtue practices, but in the imperfect world, quick improvements, each lasting for the short term, until the next improvement makes things still better, is the best policy.

Protagoras does not like short speeches, but Socrates threatens to leave the conversation if Protagoras does not comply (*Protagoras* 335c). The alternative to short speech is not long speech, but even shorter speech. If Protagoras will not cut his speech into small pieces, it will be cut off entirely, it will not even start, it will be so short as to not exist. Protagoras's long speeches do not work if people go home early. Short speeches make the discussion last longer. Just as it was a joke when Socrates said he forgets easily, it is also a joke when he says he runs only short-distance races; everyone knows Socrates can keep talking all night long, that he can keep up the short run in the long run. Indeed, Socrates and Protagoras keep up this dispute over format for almost 20 percent of the dialogue, a ridiculous amount of time, as if the quarrel about the short term just cannot end in the short term.

Is Protagoras not right to hold that each speaker ought to speak the way they want to, without pressure from others? Would allowing each person their own temporal style of presentation not break things up democratically? Does the pursuit of truth allow no room for the pleasure of hearing oneself speak in one's own voice, for each person to be the measure of things for themselves? Would that not be democratic, and good? Socrates says no. The ideal of universal participation does not imply that each person does what they want, it requires a common standard of participation, a shared articulation of rights. Free participation does not allow a bully to dominate the floor. If there is truly to be dialogue, each person needs to have an equal share of speaking and listening, so there has to be give and take, with intervals short enough that the listener does not get left out of the process of discovery. Sharing has to take place one point at a time, if individual opinions are to become shared knowledge. Only speech broken up into small parts is shared. Only divided speech is unified. Only a universal rule of discourse, defined by the multiplicity of time-periods, contains a polyvocity of perspectives to be heard as a univocity of theory. Broken-up speech breaks up the tyranny of the non-critical, and progressively aims for ideals. Indeed, Protagoras himself promised that his students would not get one enormous result at the end of a superlong speech, but would get a little bit better after each day's lesson.

In our day, the payoffs of Socrates' advice are mixed. *Amazon.com* lists dozens of books with titles starting *A Brief History of ...* (Hawking's tops the list), and *A Short Treatise on ...* (from Spinoza to Badiou). There is a book series called *15 Minute Biographies*. (The most popular is about Ruth Bader Ginsburg, and it is not bad, but at sixty-three pages, the temporal advertising is blatantly false. By contrast, a biography of Mike Pence in the *30 Minute Book Series* is sixty-six pages—forty-nine not including end matter, and with larger print and less detail, so possibly true to its time promises.) Another series is called *'In Brief' Books for Busy People* (though lazy people can enjoy them too). The books in the "For Dummies" series are not short. Hegel's *Shorter Logic* is neither short nor the book's real title.

At any rate, Hippias and friends de-escalate and propose a "middle course," in which an umpire will keep watch on the "measure" (*metron*) of everyone's speeches (*Protagoras* 338a).

As seasoned readers of Plato might expect, as soon as Socrates wins the right to make short speeches, he immediately gives a very long speech (*Protagoras* 342a-349d). It centers on an interpretation of an ode by Pittacus, distinguishing *becoming* good (which is easy) from *being* good consistently (which is hard). Short term improvements (becomings) are good, as he has staked his discussion so far on proving, but there is still a long term ideal (being) somewhere in the future, even if it is in the background. The difficulty, perhaps even the impossibility, of achieving that long term state is not reason to ignore it.

Socrates' long speech includes a sarcastic story about how the muscle-bound Spartans seem to be poor at philosophy, but are not. A Spartan starts a conversation in a way that barely seems intelligent, Socrates says. But "at some fortunate moment in the discussion, he throws in a worthy logos, short (*brachu*) and compressed—a deadly (*deinos*) shot that makes his interlocutor seem like a helpless child" (*Protagoras* 342e). Socrates makes the same point two more times in quick succession. We recognize Spartan wisdom by its "short (*brachea*) memorable sayings" (*Protagoras* 343a). And again: "Why am I saying this? To show that ancient philosophy had this Laconic brevity of speech" (*brachulogia*) (*Protagoras* 343b).

Short sentences are powerful for two reasons. First, they can be deadly barbs, deflating the enemy in one fast blow. Second, they are by nature ironic. A sentence, after all, is not really deadly, or terrifying, or violent. A short sentence is rather jokey, which precisely deflates in one fast blow the enemy's violence by means of irony. The two values of short sentences are, first, violence, and second, non-violence. The second defeats the first.

Socrates is well aware that while Spartans make powerful use of short sentences, it is not really because they do what Socrates was advocating early on, namely leaving quiet gaps in speech for the listener to interject in, and being prepared to take a long time exchanging short thoughts with others. The Spartans rather try to prevent their listeners from getting a word in, and so Spartans have little chance of being virtuous. Short speeches are not ends in themselves, obviously. They are necessary conditions for virtue-creating dialogue, but to be sufficient, they need to be supplemented by a consistent, long term intent to incite a series of further relevant short considerations to follow later. In sum, the shortness of a speech does not end the matter; the short speech needs another short speech *later*. "Later" is the companion to the short term.

Short sentences appear still more important when we consider the two that Socrates names: "Know thyself," and "Nothing in excess"—the two main theses of Socratic ethics. We could rephrase these respectively as: "Virtue is knowledge," and "Interrupt with questions before it is too late." Socratic wisdom is full of short maxims: Nobody does wrong willingly; Justice is minding one's own business; The Good is thought but not seen; Philosophy rules.

In the immediate context, the short sentence at stake is "It is hard to *be* good" (*Protagoras* 343c). Socrates draws a series of quick conclusions (*Protagoras* 345b-353c): Sudden bad fortune can make a good person bad (though sudden good fortune cannot make a bad person good). Therefore, nobody can *be* good permanently. People can only become good in the short term, though if they are lucky and wise, that short term might last a long time. Therefore, good people will be of a mixed degree of goodness, not perfect. (This is a reasonable proviso to Protagoras's claim that we should take advice about virtue from everyone, since everyone has good in them. Yes, they have good in them, but not only good.) To judge which of our inclinations are truly good, knowledge is our guide. (Socrates says nothing in this dialogue about what kind of knowledge this is.)

These particular rapid-fire inferences are not really short in the good way. This is one of those Socratic passages where the interlocutor is made to interject "Yes, Socrates" over and over ("Yes" is the shortest possible speech), a rhetorical device whose effect is the opposite of critical questioning. However, there is one point where the discussion slows down a bit, and this becomes the major conclusion of the text. It hangs on the relation between pleasure, time, and measure.

In ethical terms, there are three points joined together. First, judgments should be powered by knowledge, not over-powered by ignorance. Second, knowledge should not be over-powered by pleasure, especially by "the pleasantness of food or drink or sexual acts," which drive a person to do a thing "although he knows it to be bad" (*Protagoras* 353c-d). Third, assuming that we do value pleasure somewhat, the value of pleasures in the future should not be over-powered by the immediacy of pleasures in the present (*Protagoras* 354d). We might not have expected that ignorance would be tied to present pleasures and knowledge tied to future pleasures. We might have expected that knowledge would be tied to no pleasure at all, but would operate on a purely conceptual basis. But the *Protagoras* does not operate on lofty principles of knowledge. The argument here is simply that knowledge should be used in such a way that future pleasures and pains be measured accurately relative to the short term. This type of knowledge may not suit the permanent being of the good, but it does suit the time scale of becoming good, which is the topic of the *Protagoras*.

When knowledge is focused on the measurement of short and long events over time, we finally see the connection between the "short" and the "later":

> In what sense do you call deeds bad? Is it that they produce pleasures and are themselves pleasant at the moment, but that at a later time (*hysteron chronou*) they cause diseases and poverty, and have many more such ills in store for us? (*Protagoras* 353d)

Socrates rejects the claim that pleasure is an evil in itself. As he sees it, everyone agrees: acts are bad only if they lead to "later" pain (*Protagoras* 353e). Pleasurable acts that stay pleasurable are not necessarily evil; conversely, painful acts may be good if they lead to greater pleasure later.

Most people follow this theory most of the time, for example, when they exercise. No pain no gain. Socrates' version of hedonism concludes that pleasure is always good in the end, indeed that pleasure is the only good that we can aim at, and that the job of knowledge is to determine what produces pleasure when. The problem of the ignorant is not that they act for the sake of pleasure when they know that the good is something else; their problem is that they do not know what will give more pleasure "later." Good is measured by the future, later. Knowledge is a prediction of what will happen in the future, later. The problem for knowledge is to know how much pleasure, and how much later. In current cost–benefit analysis, this is known as the Social Discount Rate: calculating the present value of a future benefit. Ethics correlates the pleasure variable with the time variable.

Ethics measures pleasure in order to see what ought to over-power what. The art of measuring pleasure should be a "science" (*episteme, Protagoras* 357c); our survival depends on it (*Protagoras* 356e). The art of measuring pleasure is thus precisely the capacity for reason that Prometheus gave to us in order that we should survive as a species. To be scientific, the variables being measured must be independent. That is, we must weigh the "greater and lesser" of certain pleasures against the greater and lesser of other pleasures (or of pains against other pains), without any other factors influencing our judgment. The problem for objectivity is that there is a factor that distorts our judgment and confuses variables. The "art of measure" (*metretike techne*) must overcome the "power of appearance" (*phainomenou dynamis*). Happily, we know what causes distortion in the art of measuring pleasure: time. "Does not the same size appear larger to your sight when near, and smaller when distant?" (*Protagoras* 356c).

This is the point that refutes the Cyrenaic claim of the following century (see below) that future pleasures have less value than present pleasures. For Socrates, it is only the distorting effect of temporal distance that makes later pleasures look smaller than present pleasures. If only we could leave time out of the equation, we would easily see the objective size of different pleasures, and correctly measure equal to equal, and excess to deficiency, so that our natural desire to choose the larger pleasure would lead to the undistorted good.

This theory could look like an argument for long term pleasure (or long term advantage) over short term, but that is not Socrates' proposal. Future pleasure has no advantage over present pleasure; they are equal once the distorting influence of time is bracketed. Nor is a single long term pleasure, extending from the present into some point in the future, inherently better than a series of different short term pleasures one after the other, covering the same duration to the same point in the future. All pleasures are measured in the short term, or better, they are measured as pleasures indifferent to time elongation. The future has no special status, other than being a "later" present. This is why, in the end, the long term is simply the short term iterated by the "later" function. The art of measure in the *Protagoras* is the short game, played for a long time. An ethics of Forms might be the long game, but the *Protagoras* is not supposed to be too idealist.

Socrates offers no rules for comparing sooner and later, no formula to compensate for how much less a future pleasure will appear to offer, and no psychological analysis of how we might predict what will give a person pleasure as she matures or declines with age. The long-distance future is generally opaque to us, with the result that we over-value short term pleasures. Because the long term is epistemically deficient, the short term appears hedonistically excessive. Increasing the epistemic long term will not make long term pleasures appear to over-power short term pleasures, it will just even them out. The principles behind these measures—measuring the size of pleasures according to their temporal distance from the present, and knowing what one will value in the future—Nothing in excess, and Know thyself—are the two things that an education in virtue was supposed to provide. Socrates seems to have come around to Protagoras's original position that virtue can be taught, and that virtue is a kind of knowledge, yet the dialogue ends aporetically, with the feeling that we have no idea yet how to get that knowledge. For a more detailed (though still skeptical) account of the time variable in our evaluation of future pleasures, we have to look at the Cyrenaics.

Before we move to Aristippus, we might take a moment to offset Socrates' ironic defense of short speeches, and consider an ironic criticism of short speeches in Shakespeare's *Love's Labour's Lost*.[6] While this play has its share of long speeches, it mostly consists of vulgar one-liners and stand-alone punchlines. Almost every character plays the game of short witty insults, most of which criticize the other characters for their short witty way of speaking. As the Princess of France says: "Such short-lived wits do wither as they grow" (Act 2, Scene 1, 540). To make a thesis statement out of this witty saying: short-lived things are pathetic, and what is worse, they do not last long. The short word "wit" in this witty line is lengthened into "wither," which is what wit does if one spends too long thinking about it. In fact, the line could have been shortened without much loss into "Some wits are short-lived." The predicate "wither as they grow" basically means the same "short-lived," so the short subject term of the line is made into a longer line only by adding a redundant predicate. The line that complains about short things should itself have been shorter than it is. And this is one of the paradoxes of short speeches: they can never be short enough to satisfy the lovers of the short. Yet if a person truly loves the short, they cannot get enough of it, and end up repeating the short ad nauseam. The paradox is that if one wants to criticize short speech, the most incisive way to do it is with a short speech. Speech about the short gets longer, and speech about the long gets shorter: long stories short, and short stories long.

Most of us will go on blending short speeches with long as we always have. Johann Martin Chladenius's wit-free *Introduction to the Correct Interpretation of Reasonable Discourses and Writings* (1742) gives good, sound, vague, advice: "It is not reasonable to write nothing but glosses [i.e., comments with few words], nor is it a good idea to write a commentary which consists solely of long passages. A reasonable interpretation will consist of both glosses and lengthy annotations."[7]

And then there is Kwame Gyekye's interpretation[8] of the Akan proverb, "If a problem lasts for a long time, wisdom comes to it": a wise person should take a long time to ponder a problem, then present the insight in a short proverb. It needs a lot of time to think of a short speech.

The Measure of Future Pleasures: Aristippus the Cyrenaic

The fourth century BCE Cyrenaics assign a low value to future pleasures, and a high value to the short term. Socrates would judge them victims of time distortion. Right or wrong, they are the first real theorists of the time–pleasure correlation.

There is little extant writing of Aristippus of Cyrene (and his grandson, also named Aristippus), but commentary has developed around ideas we think they had. I discuss the texts, then two commentators: Tim O'Keefe[9] and Voula Tsouna.[10]

Diogenes Laertius's *Lives of the Eminent Philosophers*[11] (third century BCE) reports on Aristippus's love of food and money, and his preference for present pleasure over future pleasure. "He derived pleasure from what was present (*parousia*), and did not toil to procure the enjoyment of something not present" (Diogenes 1959: II, 66). This is not the same as what analytic philosophers today call "presentism," the view that the only part of time that exists is the present. Aristippus is not skeptical about whether pleasures will exist in the future. Rather, he makes the ethical judgment that present pleasures are more valuable. All pleasures are pleasurable, but pleasures in the present are more desirable.

Happiness is defined as "the sum total of all particular pleasures, in which are included both past and future pleasures" (Tsouna 1998: 217). One might think that this makes a lifetime of happiness the goal by which all particular pleasures, present and future, are judged. But for Aristippus, the fact that happiness includes both present and future is exactly what makes happiness suspect. In practical terms, the job of "accumulating" pleasures so that they add up to happiness is itself an "irksome business," not pleasurable at all. Having pleasure is nice, but reasoning out a balance sheet of pleasures and working hard to get them is not. Pleasures, he says, are desirable for their own sake, whereas happiness is at best desirable only insofar as it is made up of particular pleasures. Pleasures in the present are immediately valuable, whereas pleasures in the future, which have no face value in direct experience, would need to be calculated based on theories and narratives. It is not only that future pleasures are less certain to arrive, but that imagining future pleasures is less pleasant than having them, and having pleasures is possible only in the present.

> Further, they [Cyrenaics] do not think pleasure is achieved by memory or expectation of goods, as Epicurus believed. For they think the movement of the soul is worn out by time... they think that though pleasure is choice-worthy in itself, the disturbing things that produce certain pleasures are often of the contrary sort. And so it appears to them that the accumulation (*hathroismos*) of pleasures that produce happiness is most disagreeable. (Diogenes 1959: II, 89–90)

Athenaeus's *The Deipnosophists* (third century CE)[12] leads us to the short term:

> Aristippus welcomed the experience of pleasure (*hedupatheia*), and said it is the end, and that happiness is founded on it. And he said that it was for a single time only (*monochronos*). Like prodigal people, he thought that neither the memory of past gratifications nor the expectation of future ones was anything to him, but he discerned the good by the single present time alone. He regarded having been gratified and being about to be gratified as nothing to him, on the grounds that the one no longer is and the other is not yet and is unclear—just like what happens to self-indulgent people, who suppose that only what is present benefits them. (Athenaeus 2021: XII, 544a)

"Monochronic" could mean, first, an experience that one has only once; second, an experience that exists only in the present; third, an experience that lasts only for the short term. We might have expected Epicurians to be the clearest defenders of short term happiness, pleasures, and interests. But mainstream Epicureanism recommends foregoing some short term pleasures in exchange for greater long term pleasures. Moreover, Epicureans allow, against the Cyrenaics, that "the expectation of future pleasures can itself be pleasant" (O'Keefe 2002: 405). As Tim O'Keefe argues, the Cyrenaics more consistently value pleasures limited to the short term present. The premise is that all pleasures end; the conclusion is that we should enjoy them before they end.

One of O'Keefe's arguments on behalf of the Cyrenaics is that happiness does not have a general structure. Each happiness-producing activity is independent and different, so there is no single sense of happiness that could last a lifetime. Therefore, the only kind of happiness one can deliberate about or choose is short term. The Cyrenaics articulate these individual happiness procedures as events in the "present," "now" (O'Keefe 2002: 395).

What the Cyrenaics do not account for is that the short term is not the same as the "now." Even a short term pleasure, even a "present" one—an evening of wine tasting, or a spending spree at Place Vendôme—involves internal sequencing over an interval of time, predicting, planning, pursuing, acceptance of delay, gradual fulfillment with pauses and brief interruptions, even some short amount of "future concern"—albeit less of these than the long term requires. O'Keefe's counter-Cyrenaic example is that gambling might be fun in the present but not good policy for a person who values pleasure. Indeed, O'Keefe's evaluation is that blowing one's savings in Vegas "seems like a good strategy for leading an *unpleasant* life" (O'Keefe 2002: 396). "Prudent hedonism" has to have a little bit of future concern: indeed, one cannot even enjoy current pleasures if "one has no care about anything that extends beyond the present temporal point that one inhabits" (O'Keefe 2002: 396). Even reaching for a nice-looking drink on the table right here requires thinking "a few seconds hence" (O'Keefe 2002: 396). In sum, hedonism is not compatible with strict presentism (O'Keefe 2002: 397). The Cyrenaics needed a more concrete phenomenology of the short term.

Now, when the Cyrenaics appeal to "monochronic" time, they might not mean "instantaneous present time" but "a single time." "Single time" could simply mean that each pleasure experience is quantitatively distinct. But "single time" could also mean that the experience has a short, but non-instantaneous, relatively autonomous time-zone in which it takes place, with a beginning, middle, and end, all positioned within a limited time segment, so that its beginning cannot be traced back further into the causal history of that pleasure, and its end cannot be retained longer in the persistent glow of pleasure. A person may remember that he once had that time of pleasure, but he does not prolong it past the border of its one time duration. The "single time" in this way covers a genuine short term.

One way to prioritize the short term over the long term is with the practical maxim "not to worry about the future" (O'Keefe 2002: 396), though this is not easy for humans. A second way is by accepting the mathematical impasse: if we have as yet no evidence by which to quantify future pleasures (which does not seem to be an entirely plausible premise), then there are no grounds to defer to them. A third, more conceptual way of rejecting long term future pleasures is to reject the idea of a continuous self over time (O'Keefe 2002: 398). If the self I will have become at the time of a future pleasure is not the self I am now, then it is not in my interest to defer my own pleasure for the sake of that other future person's pleasure. It seems to me, though, that if I am truly going to become that other self, perhaps it *is* in my interest to help out that other person who I will by then have become.

A fourth strategy to explain the "lack of future-concern" (O'Keefe 2002: 404) is to say that what the Cyrenaics most despise is "*planning* for the future." If the future is uncertain, then planning is pointless, and we might as well enjoy the pleasures "at hand." When the Cyrenaics believe that we should not worry about "long term consequences," it means not so much that we should not worry about the length of time a pleasure will last, or the length of time a plan will aim at, but that we should not worry about the consequences of our actions. Either way, whether we focus on length of time, or consequences, the point is not to worry about what comes "next."

A fifth argument is that because the future is "unclear," we should never trade present pleasure for future pleasure. Uncertainty might be mitigated if we could know probabilities about the future (O'Keefe 2002: 405)—it may make sense to forego present pleasure in order to avoid an 80 percent chance of pain. But as Humeans say, we cannot know whether an 80 percent binge-to-hangover pain rate we experienced in the past entails that there will be an 80 percent pain rate in the future, so probabilities are no more certain in the future than certainties are certain in the future.

O'Keefe contrasts what he calls the "radical interpretation" of the Cyrenaics, namely the position that does not care anything about the future, with his own "conservative interpretation" (O'Keefe 2002: 408), according to which one might care about future pleasures as long as one does not compare them with present pleasures. A person might not think a future pleasure benefits them now, but that a future pleasure will benefit them in the future, that is, when it later becomes present. But does the fact that a future pleasure will benefit a person entail that it already does benefit them? This puzzle is just what makes Cyrenaics devalue future pleasures at the time when present pleasures are indisputably pleasant. A conservative Cyrenaic might concede that a person might in principle be happier if she deferred some pleasures until later, but might nevertheless hold empirically that most people prefer to sit back and enjoy present pleasures (O'Keefe 2002: 409). As a matter of psychological fact, O'Keefe concedes David Gauthier's utilitarian thesis: "Practical reason takes its standpoint in the present."[13]

O'Keefe's final concession to the Cyrenaics is less about grounding the evaluation of pleasures in the present, and more about basing happiness on individual "episodes" (O'Keefe 2002: 413). The short term would be more about the lack of the whole, than the lack of the long. Yet it is not enough to define mono-chronicity by saying that it is a part of time rather than the whole, that it is different from maxi-chronicity, summa-chronicity, or totum-chronicity. We need to say more about what makes a short amount of time hang together as one piece, about how pleasure fills up one short but extended event. What marks off that one segment of time?

Voula Tsouna offers a different translation of *monochronos*, not as "short lived," "short duration," or "momentary," but as "unitemporal" (Tsouna 1998: 15). After all, she says, even a Cyrenaic ought not to deny that some headaches last longer than others, or that it is nice to wear comfortable shoes all day long. Monochronic pleasures exist only in the present, but they last through an "extended present" (Tsouna 1998: 15). For Tsouna, the Cyrenaic point is that one pleasure persists during "one time unit," however long or short. The time unit of the present is self-contained, and indifferent to "prospective or retrospective values" (Tsouna 1998: 16). The present is a segmentary, non-porous, time extension. It is short in the sense that it is unitemporal, but it does not impose more shortness than the pleasure is good for.

For Tsouna, the Cyrenaic's main point is that a present pleasure can neither anticipate nor re-present a future or past pleasure. The soul's "movement" (*kinema*) cannot repeat a past experience, since the experience "dies away with [the past]" (Tsouna 1998: 16). Experiences at different times can be similar, but one can only step into each experience once. And if a present experience cannot be repeated by another, it cannot be revived by another, or be reinforced by a future experience. It is logically possible that a future experience *will be* pleasurable; but the future pleasure cannot be pleasurable in the present. Nor (Bergson would agree) is there any current way of measuring whether future pleasures are stronger or weaker than pleasures in the present. The science that Socrates envisages for measuring the relative strength of present and future pleasures cannot exist. Such a comparative science would presuppose that we can take two events from different times and compare them at the same time. For the Cyrenaics, every pleasure is singular, beyond comparison, even beyond increase and decrease over time. Eating BBQ is complete pleasure while we are eating BBQ; Socratic debate is complete pleasure while we are debating. Each singularity is its qualitative and quantitative monochronicity. Indeed, fullness of pleasure during its period is effectively the measure of the time segment. A time segment is as long as the quality of the experience lasts. The quantitative measure of the time period begins when the pleasure (or pain) begins, and ends when it ends. The time of the event is short and unitary because its quality is uniform, however many minutes it lasts. That is what we value.

However, it is not always right to measure a short term event by the persistence of a uniform quality. A triathlon is short (relative to a marathon), but is composed of three qualitatively different events. It may be natural to think of the pleasure of eating as short term because it does the same thing for a while and then tapers off due to its nature. It is less clear whether the pleasure of spending money, a particular interest of Aristippus, naturally cuts out, as long as one keeps earning more money to spend. Spending money won in gambling is a different matter: easy come easy go. Examples are mixed. Not all short terms are short by monochronicity defined by the constancy of a fragile quality while it lasts, but some are.

The reflection that one should stop wasting time and act now, for the good of the now, can be found also, though with a different moral, in Seneca's *On the Shortness of Life*.[14] Most people allow "time to seep out through the chinks and holes of the mind" (Seneca [49CE] 2018: 25), and worse, they let other people steal their time. In a surprising way, this supports Kierkegaard's sense that time itself is not in the final analysis scarce, but rather that "there is so much of it that we waste an obscene amount" (Seneca [49CE] 2018: 7). Seneca's explanation of the discrepancy between the abundance of time in itself and its scarcity, for most of us, follows the Cyrenaic maxim that "the greatest obstacle to living a full life is having expectations, delaying gratification based on what might happen tomorrow which squanders today ... Live Now!" (Seneca [49CE] 2018: 22). And that in turn leads Seneca to share with speed junkies of all ages the commandment that "you must compete with time's haste in the speed of using it" (Seneca [49CE] 2018: 22). The problem is that it is not clear what Seneca thinks counts as a valuable use of time, the kind of life that gives us enough time to live well in. He names many things that he thinks are a waste of time: wealth, sex, food (things Aristippus likes), honor, power, prayer, planning and worrying, knowledge for its own sake (things Aristippus does not like), relaxing, and chess. Spending time with friends who live the right sort of life may be the most now-enhancing way to live the right sort of life ("Any man can spend time with them day or night," Seneca [49CE] 2018: 32), but obviously that begs the question of what we and our friends would actually do during the right sort of life. Perhaps the overall absence of desire is sufficient to make life feel long enough. But with that conclusion, Seneca is clearly no Cyrenaic.

What is the point in acting for the now if there is nothing much one desires to do now or ever? We are unlikely to devote our energy to time-management in the field of pleasure if we do not want much of it.

Conservative Cyrenaics might wish that Protagoras would give advice on how long to keep up this or that pleasure. How long should we wait for an event, and how long should it last? How long a time should there be between now and the beginning of the event, and how long a time should there be between the beginning of the event and its end? How long do events of different types remain pleasurable (taking into account their different curves of increase and decrease)? Non-hedonist ethicists too might like advice from experts: how long is one responsible for shoveling a neighbor's sidewalk, sympathizing with an alcoholic, or delaying marriage to care for an elder? How long should a person be punished for a given crime? We expect utilitarians to have much more to say about this.

Propinquity: Bentham

Surprisingly, there is not a lot of discussion about short term pleasures or duties in utilitarianism. We would not expect virtue ethics or idealist ethics to care that much about finite temporality, but we would have expected utilitarianism to be more interested in pragmatic timing. Typical utilitarian slogans prioritize long term happiness (for ourselves and others) over short term kicks that give us a headache. The criterion of the greatest happiness for the greatest number values accumulation: the more happy consequences an action has, no matter how long it takes before they are added to the ledger, the better the action is. But how do we measure whether long-lasting pleasures are more pleasurable than short-lasting pleasures, and whether pleasures soon are better than pleasures later?

Bentham's *Principles of Morals and Legislation*[15] offers four parameters for measuring whether a pleasure is greater or lesser. The first three are the intensity, the duration, and the degree of certainty of a pleasure. The fourth, which interests us here, is the "propinquity or remoteness" of the pleasure (Bentham [1789] 1963: 29). Duration measures how short or long the pleasure is from the time it begins to the time it ends; propinquity measures how short or long a time there will be between the time the pleasure is represented in the mind as possible, and the time it is expected to begin.

There are other parameters too for measuring the value of a pleasure that also raise temporal issues, for example, the "fecundity," or "profit" of the pleasure, which concerns "the value of each pleasure which appears to be produced by it *after* the first" (Bentham [1789] 1963: 30–1), that is, the pleasures that it produces after one or more intermediate steps. Such cases include "emolument," defined as "the cause or instrument of distant pleasure" (Bentham [1789] 1963: 31). The problem is that it is not clear how long afterward we have to wait before we can measure the value of a given pleasure. It is tantamount to Aristotle's odd but persuasive claim that we can only know if a person is happy after they have died, since only then do we know what the actions in their lives led to, and how those actions have contributed to the sum of the person's happiness, especially to the important state of happiness in their last moments, not to mention the happiness of the loved ones they left behind. In any case, distant pleasures raise the issue of propinquity.

Propinquity is useful for cases like the ownership of land, where there is no great pleasure in ownership as such, but where ownership makes it likely that the owner will get some pleasure out of it in due course, such as the pleasure of eating fresh apples next Fall, or spending rent money paid by sharecroppers.

> The value of such an article of property is universally understood to rise or fall according to the length or shortness of the time which a man has in it: the certainty or uncertainty of its coming into possession: and the nearness or remoteness of the time at which, if at all, it is to come into possession. (Bentham [1789] 1963: 32)

The capitalist's excuse is a twist on this: they deserve to enjoy profits earned from investing in somebody else's company, not because they labored for the company whose profits they benefit from, but because they could have enjoyed their money right away but instead let someone else use it while they waited. Lenders lend not just money, they lend pleasurable time.

If we were actually going to quantify the pleasure of owning a given article (a plot of land, a pair of cufflinks, a political favor), we would have to analyze the rise and fall of value over time, as we do with stock market holdings. Articles do not have fixed value depending on how long they are held before sale, like bonds are supposed to. Future value fluctuates, it takes a random walk, it depends on the psychology of a large number of investors, it goes through boom and crisis periods, it can become an object of gamesmanship (like GameStop at the time of this writing), and during a financial crisis may lose its value altogether (see the "if at all" clause in the passage above). Portfolio management is a quagmire.[16] Furthermore, both the level of certainty about the future and the future event's distance from the present depend on decisions of persons other than the person who is trying to measure the value of their own future pleasure. And to add yet another complication, contrary to what the Cyrenaics believed, there are expectations for the future that themselves give pleasure in the present: "The pleasures of expectation are the pleasures that result from the contemplation of any sort of pleasure, referred to time *future,* and accompanied with the sentiment of *belief*" (Bentham [1789] 1963: 37).

But the greatest complication for measuring propinquity is the logic of disjunction that enters into all decisional futures.[17] Agents often aim to achieve different results relative to "*present, past,* or *future*" (Bentham [1789] 1963: 90). Bentham spends several pages on the case of Sir Walter Tyrrel, who killed King William II of England in the year 1100. Tyrrel's intent was to shoot the king in either the hand or the leg, but not both, so as to maim him; but as it turned out, the wound was mortal. Tyrrel's "intention" was "disjunctive" (Bentham [1789] 1963: 87), and disjunction is a crucial property of the agent's "consciousness" (Bentham chapter 10, "On Consciousness"). The knotty problem is that Tyrell "knew not of the probability" that his arrow would reach the king (Bentham [1789] 1963: 91). This is true of virtually all intentions. A person thinks: I will shoot an arrow; it might land in many different places; two of the places it might land will lead to the king's injury (if it succeeds in this result, there will be another disjunctive branch: the king's physicians may cure him quickly, or slowly, or not at all); some places the arrow might land will lead to the king's death; other places it might land will lead to nothing relevant. Some possibilities will lead to short term consequences, some to long term, some to none at all. The same decision leads to many possible actions, each with many possible durations.

To make things worse, Tyrrel did not know that somebody else had dipped his arrow in poison, which made his act "unadvised with respect to the existence of a *past* circumstance" (Bentham [1789] 1963: 91). The act was thus premised on a "*mis-supposal* of a *preventative* circumstance" (Bentham [1789] 1963: 91). Worse still, "at the very instant that Tyrrel drew the bow, the king, being screened from his view by the foliage of some bushes, was riding furiously, in such manner as to meet the arrow in a direct line: which circumstance was also more than Tyrrel knew of. In this case the act was unadvised, with respect of a *present* circumstance" (Bentham [1789] 1963: 91). And triply worse, "The king being at a distance from court, could get nobody to dress his wound till the next day; of which circumstance Tyrrel was not aware. In this case the act was unadvised, with respect to what was then a *future* circumstance" (Bentham [1789] 1963: 91). If the whole time-series—past, present, and future—is compromised with mis-supposals, then the measurement of propinquity is not really going to be possible. There will in fact be future pleasures and pains, and they will be at some determinate nearness or remoteness, but measuring them is entangled in branching disjunctions, probabilities, contingencies, the consciousnesses of other people, mis-advisedness, mis-intention, and mis-supposition.

Of course, once we know what happened to the king after the fact, we can say whether it took a long time for the king to die or a short time, so one might conclude that all these intriguing details have little effect on short or long durations. But the point is that decisions about what to do in the world that does not yet exist, about what future states of affairs to give value to, about how long we need to take to arrive at them and how long we should try to keep them going, about how long we should take to figure them out before passing to act are exactly the concrete problems of disjunction that characterize the ethics of temporal measure. If Tyrrel could have known every little detail about the world, like Laplace's ideal scientist, then he could have managed his time properly. But disjunctive complexity is intractable.

The morass of exceptions and disjunctions in the propinquity calculation can lead to casuistry, which in turn can lead to conspiracy theories, like it does in JFK conspiracy theorist Jim Garrison's 1967 memo, "Time and Propinquity."[18] Garrison's idea was that if two JFK-related episodes occurred within a short amount of time or space, they constitute a pattern, and therefore evidence of conspiracy. So, for example, the fact that Layton Martens, who was anti-Castro, had two uncles who lived a block away from Lee Harvey Oswald makes a pattern. Similarly, David

Ferry, who worked for the Cuban Liberation Front, listed someone named Bruce Nolan as a contact in case of emergency; the phone book lists D. H. Nolan (no relation to Bruce Nolan) as an employee at the phone company; John C. Oswald Jr. (no relation to Lee Harvey Oswald) worked at the same phone company at the same time: ... pattern ... conspiracy. Far be it from me to express an opinion as to the real killer, but it is worth noticing that propinquity is not always a mark of epistemic or value relevance.

But our conclusion is that propinquity, as problematic as it makes temporal ethics, does play out in branching alternative futures, which multiply considerations about what happened, what to do, and how to measure time frames. The Cyrenaic alternative of restricting ethical judgment to the immediate short term is not feasible. Ethical agents need to take into account the fact that arrows do go astray, poisons do spread through the body, kings do turn their horses unexpectedly, conspirators do assassinate leaders. As uncertain as they are, these are just the kinds of semi-informed guesses that ethical decisions are about. Even the principle of acting in the present is meaningless if people do not know what is happening in their surroundings, who touched their arrows last, or how to locate a moving horse ten seconds from now. This is another way of saying that the short term present contains things are happening, have happened, and will happen.

To some readers' eyes, this motivates ethical skepticism, but it is not so different from game theoretical ethics, with its probabilistic, multi-step look-ahead and back-propagation to probabilistic valuations under conditions of sometimes very large but still incomplete data. Like reinforcement learning algorithms, valuation is more accurate with more sampling of distant outcomes. Of course, sooner does not always mean higher probability; the probability of winning at roulette one minute from now is lower than the probability of a rainy day one millennium from now. Still, it is easier to predict the weather tomorrow than a year from now. So if higher probability results are more desirable than low, and short term results are higher probability than long, why would calculation ethics like utilitarianism hold in general that it is better to choose long term aims over short? Perhaps it is because long term means more time to reap the same advantage: ten days of vacation are better than five. Or perhaps there is a puritanical bias that anything we get easily cannot be very good. Or perhaps utilitarianism does not in fact favor long term goals in general, but only makes room for them on those occasions where the long term pleasure is especially good and demonstrably likely.

In the final analysis, utilitarianism should restrict itself to calculating better and worse actions based solely on what people in fact take pleasure in, and choose to value. An ethical dogmatist might argue that humans ought to take pleasure in certain results, long term results for example, or the more stable "higher" pleasures, but that is not the job of utilitarianism. Utilitarianism is allowed to encourage people to examine their pleasures more carefully so as not to make mistakes about what they really like, and to imagine what they might like in the future, and to be rational about pursuing those desires consistently. And it requires individuals to count other peoples' pleasures. But if people in fact do not desire long term results, or future pleasure, it is not up to utilitarianism or game theory to tell people they should. For David Gauthier (1986: 13), if one person desires to save for the future and benefit one's later self (e.g., to insulate their house against the cold while it is still summer, when it is less expensive), it is rational for that person to satisfy that desire. However, if someone else prefers present pleasure instead, so be it. From this pluralistic perspective, neither utilitarianism nor any other ethical theory ought to posit any normative value hierarchy for short or long term pleasures.

How Much Time Does Moral Calculation Take? J. S. Mill

Mill's concept of expediency in *Utilitarianism*[19] might sound like it means expeditious, or speedy. And there are times when the act that produces the most happiness is the act that does so most quickly. But not always. When Mill discusses justice and expediency in Chapter 5, the only question of timing that comes up is the right to a speedy trial. "Few hurts which human beings can sustain are greater, and none wound more, than when that on which they habitually and with full assurance relied fails them in the hour of need" (Mill [1861] 2001: 61). Justice must be done before the end of the "hour of need." The value of justice being done in the short term, not delayed, is central to jurisprudence. Courts need good case flow management. Civil suits should not allow wealthy defendants to delay trials with trivial motions, or delay paying up when decisions go against them. Governments should not put off decisions with endless commissions of enquiry. Death penalty cases are the exception to the value of speedy judgment, since there is no future time at which a wrong judgment can be reversed; if its reversal is by definition too late, its enactment is by definition too hasty.

While Mill rarely considers time duration as a parameter in calculating good and bad consequences, he does consider the value of making a decision within a relatively short time frame. Of the (by my count) eight objections to utilitarianism he sets out in Chapter 2, the seventh is this: "that there is not time, previous to action, for calculating and weighing the effects of any line of conduct on the general happiness" (Mill [1861] 2001: 23). If utilitarian decisions take too long to make, then utilitarianism will not satisfy utility and will not be a good moral theory. Mill offers (by my count) four responses to this (seventh) objection.

Mill's first is the "You too" response: every moral theory shares the same time problem. Christian morality, for example, will not be a usable moral theory if a person has to read through the whole of scripture whenever they make a decision (Mill [1861] 2001: 23). This first response is not satisfying. Utilitarianism more than other moral theories prides itself on taking a lot of factors into account, and that takes time, maybe too much time to be good.

Mill's second response is more to the point, and makes an interesting switch. "The answer to the objection is that there has been ample time, namely, the whole past duration of the human species" (Mill [1861] 2001: 23). Calculation does take a long time, but human civilizations have been taking their time for thousands of years, and the basic calculations are now done. Socrates took the trouble to calculate the relative happiness of rational conversation vs wallowing in the mud, so the next time a person has to make that calculation, they can look it up. Assuming that that wisdom "has been taught to the young" (Mill [1861] 2001: 24), the long term of the past permits action in the short term of the present. We make decisions in time to be useful, not because we make them in a short amount of time but because we make them in a long amount of time, most of which is past time. Socrates envisaged a moral science that would start now and evaluate future pleasures; Mill envisages that that moral science has already passed down the largest portion of those evaluations. Measured from the present, we do calculate in the short term; but measured from the time we started calculating, we do so over a long term. It is a mistake when "people talk as if the commencement of this course of experience had hitherto been put off, and as if, at the moment when some man feels tempted to meddle with the property or life of another, he had to begin considering for the first time whether murder and theft are injurious to human happiness" (Mill [1861] 2001: 24). Humans did not "put off" moral judgment; they jumped on it as soon as they were able. The starting point for action is back-dated to the beginning of human thought. It is just that the end of that long time has to be a short time from now.

After making this not unconvincing point, Mill takes another direction for his third response. Even if we could not rely on the long history of calculation, we would still not usually overthink decisions endlessly, since "universal idiocy" is not the human condition (Mill [1861] 2001: 24). Hmm. In my experience, even in apparently simple matters involving "meddling in the property of others," it is not easy to determine whether private ownership generates more or less happiness than some alternative. Universal non-idiocy is not enough to guarantee good results in a timely manner.

Mill's fourth response is more subtle. A regular person, or a philosopher, can make decent calculations, as long as they act on those conclusions only "until they have succeeded in finding better" (Mill [1861] 2001: 24). The "until" proviso is crucial. The best way to manage the short time limit on calculations is to take steps one at a time, knowing that the next time might give a different result and require revision. "Given the progressive state of the human mind, their improvement is perpetually going on" (Mill [1861] 2001: 24). The short term does not mean the term up to a single end point; it means a series of provisional limit points, after each of which there will be other points, at which the decision will be remade. All calculation is incomplete, but incomplete calculation is still calculation. Decisions remain urgent, and bad calculation at any point might be disastrous, but the fact that the perfect calculation will not be made at any single time is not a reason not to do one's best each time. This is a moral truism, but it is one we accept in many contexts: "Nobody argues that the art of navigation is not founded on astronomy because sailors cannot wait to calculate the Nautical Almanac" (Mill [1861] 2001: 24–5).

The conclusion of this fourth counter-objection is that the short term preserves flexibility in the form of revisions after it ends. As Mill puts it, "to inform a traveler respecting the place of his ultimate destination is not to forbid the use of landmarks and direction-posts on the way" (Mill [1861] 2001: 24). Starting instructions only provide the first temporal phase of planning. A point in time is not a slice of time, it is a direction-post that points to the next direction-post. Similarly, the time limit on decision-making is not the end of the decision-making process, it is just one landmark in a series of ending points that do not end. A person calculates for one hour today, and finds that an action he will perform tomorrow will have a certain benefit after one year. The decision starts now (leaving aside the part that has been taking place throughout human history) and ends in one hour; the action begins early tomorrow and ends late tomorrow; the benefits start accruing late tomorrow and end in a year; at any point between now and a year from now (and beyond), there are more beginning and end points for decision revisions, and for new benefits to arise. Events do take place at times, and every interval between one time and another is limited. But in the context of ongoing time, where humans improve, there is no such thing as one short term, there are only many short terms.

A person educated in morality is thus educated in the flexible use of time scales. "Enlightened" self- (and other-)interest does not mean interest for people with short attention spans, nor does it mean only long term interest. It is as foolish to delay all one's pleasures as it is to gulp down all one's pleasures right away. Enlightenment means knowing how to use all temporal resources in combination, short and long.

It would be easier for ethics if earlier were always better than later (or vice versa) simply on the grounds that it is better to be happy sooner, to live closer to the moment, or because near time is morally and eudaimonistically better time than distant time. I would make that argument if I could. But policy analysis has to balance short and long term goals: providing the best health care in the short run without undermining the long term, reducing taxes in the short term without running too high a deficit, maintaining peace today without giving enemies time to become a greater threat.

Existential Escape from Time Constraint

Levinas criticizes the Cyrenaics both for misunderstanding time passage and for not trying to escape temporal constraints[20]:

> Aristippus's hedonism is chimerical because he allows for an indivisible present, possessed in pleasure. But it is precisely the instant that is split up in pleasure ... Pleasure appears as it develops. It is neither there as a whole nor does it happen all at once ... This is a movement that does not tend toward a goal, for it has no end. (Levinas [1935] 2003: 61)

As a state of mind, pleasure is not the sort of thing that either will or will not be fulfilled in a final moment. I think I know an exception to Levinas's generalization, but even so, he is right that every pleasure undergoes a history, grows and diminishes, cycles and changes focus, transfers from figure to background and back. Perhaps the pleasure in listening to music has this sort of world-escaping autonomy while it lasts. Having a history does not entirely embed a given pleasure in history; on the contrary, during its period of time, it has its own autonomous rhythm, relatively independent of the rest of world history.

If this is true, then pleasure is in itself neither long nor short term relative to the rest of time. It is a term that expands and shrinks in a temporal sphere that belongs to it alone, depending on how we attend to it, nourish it, or suppress it. The existential context for Levinas's remarks is his idea that we need to separate ourselves from the present-at-hand. We thus need to separate ourselves from beings, and then to separate ourselves from our selves as well. Any experience that abandons the usual commitment to entities, and to the length of time they normally last, is satisfying for the achievement of this existential need. Pleasure is one way of escaping from the present-at-hand. Existential pleasure, he thinks, is the antidote to materialistic desire, which asks for future guarantees and urges us to calculate on time-to-pleasure scales (Levinas [1935] 2003: 50). Materialist pleasures are short term in a factical sense, because they claim to give us something of certain value in the short term that mitigates against the uncertainties of the future. Escapist pleasures, in contrast, do not try to solve the uncertainty of the future, they abandon the concern with both present and future in order to bypass normal time. In that sense, existential pleasures are short term in a different way, because they take pleasure in risk. They are short not by staying in the present but by dissociating from temporal sequentiality. They are short by inserting an autonomous historical thread inside the normal sequence of cause and effect.

One might also see political possibilities in this different sort of short term, defined by history-evasion rather than by historical quantity. Hardened realists presume that revolutionary ideas will always be co-opted over time, that disruptions will be smoothed over by systems, that experiments will be assessed by future effects, that social structures ride the long wave of time. Depending on one's values, one might find this heartening, or discouraging, or exciting. But as a fourth alternative, Bifo's "post-futurism" is a Levinas-inspired politics for the existential short term.[21] If the hope of progress toward a future age defines "futurism," then "post-futurism" values the autonomous time flow inside a singular event-sequence. Bifo's argument against futurist politics is drawn both from environmental exhaustion (the power source for future progress is running out) and from political crises (like the First Iraq War), whose triumphalism put us on the "brink of disaster." Bifo does not advocate short term politics as such, as much as the value of the "autonomy" of temporal segments. Nevertheless, there is a link between Levinas's existential spin on the Cyrenaic present, the complexity of disjunctive propinquity, and the politics of temporary autonomous temporality zones. To pursue the temporal effects of existentially short term events, we look later at Deleuze's account of May 68. For the moment, we might say that the ethical value of short term activities is not just that they enhance longer term processes (conversation, happiness, decision-making, social welfare), but that they can monochronically constitute a good time within the limits of their time alone.

Chapter 7

SHORT TERM IN PRACTICE (PSYCHOTHERAPY, INVESTMENT, POLITICS, MISSIONS, AND ROMANCE)

Argument: Each of these fields of practice has developed conceptual and operational definitions of the short term that would not be apparent without a study of the concrete. I do not in general either advocate or disdain short term practices in these fields (tempting though it is). Rather, my goal is to understand the nature of both the short and long term, so that we can direct a combination of temporal resources toward best temporal practices. I choose these five fields for this chapter because when one Googles "short term," the most common search results pertain to short term psychotherapy, short term investment, short termist politics, short term missionary work, and short term romance.

My method is to observe short term processes and structures in context, to turn some of those practices into concepts that we would not have thought of otherwise. Of course, the fact that certain short term procedures take place in practice does not automatically make them reasonable, effective, or good. Most short term practices are controversial among practitioners themselves. Some are based on greed, laziness, and thoughtlessness; others arise from noble motives but underestimate unintended consequences; others are brilliant conceptual finds.

I am not a professional in any of these fields. There was a time between 2007 and 2014 when I commuted between Canada and the United States for work, and after some years, I fancied that I had discerned a pattern whereby currency exchange rates quickly followed stock market fluctuations. I thought then of playing the currency exchange, but never did, which was just as well, since the correlation I imagined did not hold up during the Trump years. Which is to say that I am not advising the reader on how to conduct, or avoid, any short term activity. I merely draw conceptual possibilities of short term structure from quick study in a few directions.

Each applied short term field has its own determination of what time scale counts as short; its own subdivision of the short term into beginning, middle, and end; its own projection of pre- and post-short term extensions; its own motives, strategies, crisis interventions, fads, and compromises.

One motive that short term therapy, short term investment, and short term missionary work have in common is that participants would like to achieve benefits in time for they and others to enjoy their results. Of course, some people enjoy for its own sake the self-reflection of therapy, the thrill of investment, or the satisfaction of mission. But others want to get healthy, rich, or worthy, and then enjoy life (or afterlife). Many (not all) want their diets, military service, and education to be over and done with. Some people want their youth to be short.

Short Term Psychotherapy

It is easy to take a skeptical attitude toward short therapy. But clearly it is desirable to get results. Doing something in a short time is not inherently anti-time, anti-humanist, anti-scientific, or unethical, and for that matter, short term activity is dialectically interwoven with the long term.

How Long Is Short?

Freud declared the Wolf Man cured after only four years, and analyzed Judge Schreber without ever even meeting him. Lacan made use of "what they call our short sessions" (*ce qu'on appelle nos séances courtes*), by which he meant sessions shorter than one hour.[1] In part, this was to keep sessions flexible, in part so that each session would deal with just one question, and in part so that the clock would not artificially overextend the process. A short "chipped stone" is not always a "cornerstone," but sometimes it is. Lacan believed, for example, that the shortness of a certain session helped him to discover the male fantasy of anal pregnancy. He would sometimes dismiss patients without warning after just ten minutes.[2] A wealthy patient arrived with a gift; Lacan accepted it, asked for his regular payment, and announced the session was over.[3] This seems more like a Zen koan than psychoanalytic technique, but maybe it helped. Some patients complained that he kept sessions short to increase profit, or that he was too impatient to listen to their problems; but he accused them of being jealous of other patients.[4] Lacan does not discuss short session at length; American psychotherapists of the 1980s say a lot more.

What counts as short term therapy is complex and disputed. We are interested here in "brief therapy," not "time-limited therapy": time-limited therapy may be limited to five years, for example, which is not so brief (De Geest and Meganck, 2019: 207).[5] There are also back-end questions about how long results of short term therapy last, but let us begin with how long it takes.

The American Psychological Association (2017)[6] summarizes "recovery" results: 50 percent of patients recover after fifteen to twenty sessions, with sessions held once a week. This is regarded as "moderate" treatment length. Other patients require twenty to thirty sessions spread over six months or longer. Some patients never recover. Brief therapy is defined as fewer than fifteen sessions: this is enough time for a minority of patients to recover, though the data are mixed.

A collection of papers from 1990, edited by Richard Wells and Vincent Giannetti, *Handbook of the Brief Psychotherapies*,[7] is a treasure of useful material. Wells and Phillip Phelps[8] offer more detail on length criteria than the APA website. Short term therapy aims for six to eight sessions (normally of one-hour duration), with results expected within six months (though in extreme cases, short term therapy may last only a single session, and the eight sessions might be covered in eight days). Happily, these time scales match what many patients imagine is an appropriately short amount of time (Wells and Phelps 1990: 9). A "dose-effect" study in 1986 found that 50 percent of patients improve over eight sessions (different from the APA's assessment), whereas 75 percent improve over twenty-six sessions (De Geest and Meganck 2019: 207). A 2002 study found that only 20 percent improve over five sessions. A 2009 study found that even briefer therapies show some results. (Perhaps shorter therapies lead to smaller scale but faster improvement.) Studies since 2003 show that improvement is somewhat accelerated when therapy is limited to sixteen sessions but not when limited to eight (De Geest and Meganck 2019: 214). However, these calculations are often based on what patients say in a questionnaire when the sessions end, and exit questionnaires are not a good way to assess outcomes, due to a bias called the "hello goodbye effect" (De Geest and Meganck 2019: 214). A 2001 study found that dropout rates are lower for short term therapies, which could be a sign of effectiveness, but might simply be because there is less time in brief therapy for dropouts to occur (De Geest and Meganck 2019: 216). For that matter, dropout might not be a sign of failure, it may just further shorten the already short. A 2005 study recommends "intermittent psychotherapy," distributing short sequences of sessions over a long time (De Geest and Meganck 2019: 220).

Unfortunately, few therapists run control groups, which makes it difficult even for therapists to judge whether short term therapy actually works (De Geest and Meganck 2019: 209). Studies of whether patients feel comfortable (which is not the same as whether they improve) with brief therapy are also inconclusive (De Geest and Meganck 2019: 213). Seventy-nine percent of therapists in 1990 believed that "managed care" (where time limits are imposed by insurance plans) has a negative influence on results (De Geest and Meganck 2019: 211). In 1990, 20–30 percent of therapy in the United States was short term. Skepticism in the profession seemed at the time likely to keep the numbers limited, but it has grown since then (Wells and Phelps 1990: 22).

Measuring the length of short term therapy can mean either (a) the total time from first session to last, which might last months (in an extreme case, a single one-hour session each year for ten years); or (b) the total amount of time spent in sessions, for example, fifteen hours in total (whether distributed across fifteen one-hour sessions once a week or all in one fifteen-hour marathon session); or (c) the length of each session (sessions are typically fifty minutes long, but shorter sessions are easier for shift workers). Hoyt distinguishes "prolonged brief therapy from brief prolonged therapy" (one week of sixteen-hour daily sessions sounds like a cult) (Hoyt 1990: 122). Even saying that a one-hour session lasts for one hour is misleading, since (some) therapists take notes afterward and review them before the next session. Calculating time spent is decided by administration as much as by clock.

Motives for the Short Term

Wells and Giannetti[9] present a number of motivations for limiting therapy to the short term. (1) It is beneficial for client morale and optimism about treatment (though optimism might or might not be conducive to improvement). The American Institute of Short-Term Dynamic Psychotherapy promotes the benefit of short therapy in overcoming patients' resistance to therapy. Michael Hoyt[10] recommends starting each session by asking the client: "Are you ready to change today?" (Hoyt 1990: 125). (2) It wards off the temptation of both clients and therapists to linger past the point of diminishing returns. (3) It is cost efficient. (4) It motivates efficiency in technique—no time for mistakes. (5) It prefers action-oriented over insight-oriented therapy. (6) It allows therapists to help more clients. (7) It is easier for student therapists to observe a full course of treatment (Imber and Evanczuk 1990: 578).[11] (8) It is a stop-gap when long term therapy is unavailable (Imber and Evanczuk 1990: 575).

If some advantages of short term therapy are counter-intuitive, so are some of its disadvantages. One might have thought that it would be easier for therapist and patient to maintain commitment when therapy is shorter. But given that the shorter period is more intensive, it might actually be more difficult (Imber and Evanczuk 1990: 579). (Does some marital therapy end in separation just because the high level of commitment over an intense period of time makes the participants anxious?) The main risk of short term therapy is that it allows less time to correct errors (Imber and Evanczuk 1990: 579).

Some cases are especially suited for short term therapy: (1) Crisis intervention, where a solution must be found quickly to avert disaster. We might have thought that mild cases are most suitable for brief therapy, but crisis management suggests the opposite. (2) Age-specific problems around adolescence or retirement, where the patient needs help with a situation that will last a relatively short time. (3) Marital therapy is often treated as the best candidate for short term therapy. (4) Behavior therapy aims at eliminating a symptom rather than the underlying source, so it can be cut off as soon as the symptom is relieved. (5) If a client's problem is procrastination in making decisions or commitments, or the paralysis of "not until" (not being able to get married until …), then the whole point is that they need therapy to manage the short term.

In contrast, there are cases where short term therapy is not advisable, as in the case of narcissism, which resists intervention by others (De Geest and Meganck 1990: 217). Jason Worchel[12] recommends brief therapy only for those patients who are non-resistant (Worchel 1990: 196). Counter-transference may lead some therapists themselves to exaggerate their self-importance and opt for too-long therapies (Hoyt 1990: 123). The short term is only right for the right patients and the right therapists. Time makes the person.

The general motto for brief therapy is that short work is good work. Without a short term goal, therapy might extend indefinitely due to sheer momentum, just because the client's sessions are penciled into the schedule, or because "work expands or contracts to fill the time available for it" (Parkinson's Law) (Hoyt

1990: 129). Efficiency is pragmatic in health as in business, so shortness is a selling point, which means that it should be explicit up front. Of course, the goal is to make short term therapy into a science, not just to end the therapy when the patient runs out of insurance or runs away, or if the therapist retires. It is true that knowing that there is only a little time left in therapy may heighten anxiety and hinder the remainder. But on the opposite side of the ledger, there are times when long term therapy gets "stuck," and forcing the remainder into a short term limit can unstick it.[13]

Beginning the Short Term Before It Starts

The beginning, middle, and end of a short term have different structures. The patient in short term therapy is typically informed in advance of the term limit. This creates an "expectancy effect" for both therapist and client to keep things moving (or else) (De Geest and Meganck 1990: 206). Therapy almost always has some preparatory lead-in; it is rare to find oneself in therapy all of a sudden. It can take a fair amount of time before a short term can begin.

The Middle—How Long and How Segmented, and What Happens Meanwhile

It is difficult to organize long therapy into beginning, middle, and end phases, since the participants may not know what should count as the end until they get close to it. Deliberate short term therapy, in contrast, has to map out in advance the sequential pattern of its beginning, middle, and end.[14] Each session should result in an identifiable outcome (Wells and Phelps 1990: 12). Short term therapy should empower the patient at each stage in the process, as stakeholder and contract signatory.

Therapy may number how many sessions belong to the beginning, middle, and end phases. The different phases may start and end punctually, or phase in and out. And internal to each phase, there is a sub-sequence, since the beginning has a beginning, middle, and end; the middle has a beginning, middle, and end; and the end has a beginning, middle, and end (Hoyt 1990: 118). This may seem artificial, but the short term is already artificial, and artificiality is its advantage: solutions are forced to emerge in the time allotted. Brevity is the mother of invention. Obviously, sessions will have to begin on time, and sessions cannot be either "squandered" or "squeezed" (Hoyt 1990: 119).

Wells and Giannetti suggest three desiderata. First, the therapist must have the discipline not to allow digressions, even when they seem relevant. Second, the therapist must intervene more than in long term therapy. Third, the client can be given homework between sessions; the therapist monitors compliance, making the client responsible for articulating and advancing toward outcomes. Techniques should not just be short, they should cause shortness.

This last point introduces a different kind of middle: the "meanwhile" sense, or multi-tasking. If a person can do two therapeutic activities over the same time, they can achieve two results in less time. This uses the interstices between sessions to pack more therapeutic events into a day. Middle time, formerly dead time, makes therapy denser. The denser the time, the less of it we need. Measured by client hours per week, this doubled-up therapy would make the short term longer; measured by weeks of therapy, it is just as short, despite having a second time line squeezed into the same overall time, which shows again that durations of complex activities have to be measured in several ways at once.

Another way to make the same amount of time more dense is group therapy (typically five to twelve members), where different peoples' processes overlap interactively over the same time. Group therapy is time-saving, whether it ends after a short time or not, because it allows several patients to be treated simultaneously. It also reduces waiting lists, which is a non-trivial time saver. Ideally, patients share discoveries that speed the process for others (Garvin 1990: 518).[15] On the downside, regression, hospitalization, or a crisis episode of one member of the group, or turnover of participants and therapists (Imber and Evanczuk 1990: 571–3), may slow down the rest of the patients (Kanas 1990: 561).[16] Groups also tend to need extra preparation, including group decisions about its composition (Garvin 1990: 521). If there are several therapists in the group, time must be added before and after sessions for communication (Imber and Evanczuk 1990: 573). A short term group therapist is not likely to know each patient in detail, and so may treat the patients together as one "universal" (Imber and Evanczuk 1990: 577).[17] While the short term sounds like it picks out a subset of the whole, there are thus situations where the short term is more generic than the larger whole.

This is the nature of the middle of the short term: it segments sequentially; interposes "meanwhile" procedures in the gaps between segments; multiplies co-existing processes into a dense temporal field; and intensifies, for better and for worse, the status of incompleteness.

The End, and the Aftermath, of the Short Term

The image of a long time sounds like it extends all the way, and the image of a short time sounds like it just gets started and then cuts out before getting anywhere. But the point is that the short is short because it ends. It can happen that the short gets there suddenly, whereas the long may never get past the point where it began.

Marital therapy is often presented as the obvious candidate for short term therapy. R. Taylor Segraves's[18] suggestion to end therapy as soon as "destructive discord [in the marriage] has ended" and "the couple have had the experience of a safe and pleasurable bonding" (Segraves 1990: 456) sounds naïve. Determining the end of marital therapy is not so obvious.

No evidence-based theory wants the talk-show model of instant therapy to lead to clients shopping for the fastest therapist, or therapists competing for the most cures (Wells and Phelps 1990: 17–18). Therapy should end "on a positive note," "at the right time," not just a short time (Reid 1990: 64).[19] Obviously, it is also possible that therapy will end "when the client has had enough" or becomes a "no show" (Reid 1990: 65) or, though advocates of brief therapy do not emphasize this, when it "goes nowhere" (Reid 1990: 66).

Termination criteria can take the form of "twelve sessions," or "end on November 7," or "end on the wedding day." What is important is that the end must take place as scheduled, otherwise the whole process is undermined (and future patients will not buy it). The patient should not be permitted to extend the therapy after the time is up. In rare cases, follow-up sessions might be allowed, or the termination date corrected, or a second round of short term therapy begin. (Wells and Phelps propose that any further sessions should be free of charge (1990: 16).) There are exceptions: in cases where success is defined by a specific outcome, like the return of a child from foster care, administrative delays in the child's release may require that the child's therapy continue for a further short period (Reid 1990: 65). Still, extensions must be limited, otherwise therapy is short term in name only (Reid 1990: 66). The principle is to "conduct therapy as if time really mattered" (Welles and Giannetti 1990: 512).

Yet the concept of the end is complicated, simply due to the fact that when a short process is cut off, time continues. The therapist needs to be honest that the patient's problems will not absolutely end when the patient leaves the last session. The assumption is rather that patients can be trained in a short time to continue after-work on their own, applying the techniques they remember (though patient memory is problematic) (Rosenbaum 1990: 183). The last session of a short therapy regime should include a discussion about "next steps" and long term goals (Garvin 1990: 532). Ideally, patients in short term therapy learn to handle future challenges better than patients in long term therapy do, where they remain dependent on the therapist.

There is one kind of therapy that is not just short in process but is also short in content: some people make decisions in a way that is too influenced by the way they were trained in childhood. "Redecision therapy" (Hoyt 1990: 135–7) re-trains patients to make decisions that do not take too much of their past into account, to increase the separation of present and past, to get patients to accept influences only from a recent amount of past time. Of course, it is not always a good idea for decisions to draw only from the recent past. But if shortening psychic attention leads to positive outcomes, do it. This is what we expect: long term durations are not inherently better or worse than short term, whether in ontology, epistemology, morality, or psychic health. We need to know how both work, so we can use them in situations that work best.

Short or Instant?

No therapist promises instantaneous outcomes. But some short term therapies do appeal to sudden insights at "decisive moments of life" (Rosenbaum 1990: 165).[20] Rosenbaum looks for even faster than usual results, namely in single-session therapy. Even fast treatment should avoid "rushing," and therapists should resist the temptation "to be brilliant" (Rosenbaum 1990: 175). There are no magical results. (Sadly, Rosenbaum uses the metaphor of "magic" on his last page, Rosenbaum 1990: 186.) Rather, it relies on the therapist's long years of learning how to "pivot" at a moment's notice (Rosenbaum 1990: 180) (see Mill's second answer to objections in the previous chapter).

Hoyt makes a similar half-serious appeal to instantaneous transformation. On the one hand, "change can occur *in the moment*" (Hoyt 1990: 115). "In the moment" sounds like "here and now" therapy from the 1960s. On the other hand, Hoyt rejects "instant cures" and "instant society" (Hoyt 1990: 119). No therapy is so brief that it has no sessions at all. More important than any particular quantity is that it be "as short as possible" (Hoyt 1990: 120).

The case calling for the fastest therapy is crisis intervention, where "a person faces an obstacle to important life-long goals that is, for a time, insurmountable through the utilization of customary methods of problem solving" (Imber and Evanczuk 1990: 566).[21] Such a short term problem is an obstacle to long term goals. Indeed, the whole idea of crisis assumes that the long term is the norm. Something short prevents a person from living the long way, and therapy has to act in the short term to end the short term crisis and return the person to the healthy long. I am not sure I would define short term events as interruptions rather than as pieces of life with their own value. Nor is it clear whether an impasse is temporary or long term while it is taking place. But people do face crises, typically arising from sudden loss.

Charles Patrick Ewing describes many forms of quick proto-therapy: calls to a hotline, emergency room counseling, police intervention in domestic violence, pharmacists confronting patients who are not taking their medications, and grief counseling immediately after a death (Ewing 1990: 277).[22] In practice, patients in "acute crisis," and with top priority, may wait months for treatment, and during the interim before even short term therapy can begin, some even shorter stop-gap therapy may be better than nothing. Prevention of disaster needs to be "fast-paced" (Imber and Evanczuk 1990: 570), just as emergency medicine stabilizes a patient so they can receive longer term care. Needless to say, it should be well funded.

In a broad sense, anyone who comes to a therapist is in crisis. One can ask any new patient: " 'Why now?'; 'What has led you to seek help at this particular time?' " (Ewing 1990: 285). "Why now" is inherently a short term factor.

Conclusion to Brief Psychotherapy

Time measure is essential to the whole idea of therapy: the persistence of past effects in the present, and the measured direction toward future outcomes (Hoyt 1990: 116). Nobody can turn back time, and too much desire for the future can be counterproductive in the present (Hoyt 1990: 116). Temporal figuration applies in every sort of therapy, from treatment of anxiety toward death ("the horror of time") (Hoyt 1990: 130) to schizophrenic "disturbances of time-consciousness,"[23] down to the way a patient "looks at his watch" during a session (Hoyt 1990: 132).[24] Depression makes short time intervals seem even shorter, whereas manic states overestimate time passage. A whole range of "problems with time and the personal future" ("time disorientation, time disintegration of sequences, rate and rhythm problems, temporal perspective problems, and desynchronized transactions") call for psycho-temporal treatment to repair rifts in the short term/long term dynamic (Hoyt 1990: 133). The point is that time-relations can be problematized, manipulated, and reconstructed like any other psychic element. The sciences of time-consciousness make the range of practical temporal resources available to us users.

Short Term Investing

MagicCredit.ca offers "short term loans" of $500 to $2,000. Getting something extra fast is magic, or to be more direct, a con.

Short and Long Term Investment

Some financial advisors weight portfolios with long term investments in high value stocks that distribute dividends, designed to generate income as the company invents and sells more good products, and its value increases. Other advisors recommend short term speculation, designed to make money by selling stocks at a higher price shortly after they are purchased. The difference is not just how long one keeps the stock; the difference is between company value and share price. I am not advising my reader to invest one way or the other. It seems counter-intuitive that short term investing could be good either for humanity or for investors. But if a short term investment in solar energy looks good, how do I know that that is ethically wrong, or historically bad, or a bad bet? My concern, as usual, is to understand what is meant by short term in the context of investment, and to see what resources that offers us to manage time-consciousness and temporal reality.

Some investment funds, like college tuition funds, have short term purposes. Retirement funds are generally opposite: one may start saving fifty years in advance, or one year (a sixty-four-year-old planning to retire the following year is investing short term), but nobody wants their pension funds to terminate before they do. The time-range of investment is vast, from agricultural futures that pay according to how the cows winter, to savings accounts that can be liquidated in seconds at the ATM, to complicated instruments that few people understand. Short term trading may offer advantages, but potential for damage is high. Short often means volatile, but not always.

A "short" investment can mean five years, or 180 days, or same-day. In algorithm-driven "high-frequency" trading (remember the "Flash Crash" of 2021), which accounts for 10–40 percent of stock trading today, the plan is to buy and sell stocks within micro-seconds (a few millionths of a second). The large volume of trades means that even if each trade only captures a fraction of a cent in profit, they add up.

One simple measure can be found at *Investopedia.com*: "Accountants define short term as current, so a current asset equals cash or an asset that will be converted into cash within a year."[25] The classical purpose of short term investment was to park a portion of one's investment capital in a short term corporate or government bond, or even a bank account, while one considers where to invest in the long term. Maybe one has won a lottery, or has sold a large investment, or maybe the stock market is on its way down, and one wants to wait a while before making a long term investment. Classically, one only puts money into short term investments for a short term. In contrast, a long term strategy of investing only in short term projects is non-classical.

Victoria Ivashina and Josh Lerner (professors at Harvard Business School) offer a recent defense of long term investing.[26] Their time scale (longer than *Investopedia*'s, but shorter than others') is that holding a stock for under five years counts as short term. In 1976, five years was the average length of time that stocks were held; by 2016, the average was six months (Ivashina and Lerner 2019: 7). The social value of long term investment, they say, is that it encourages innovative products, like the early Apple products, or pharmaceuticals, which take time to develop (Ivashina and Lerner 2019: 8–10). In fact, this is a paradox. We might think that long term attitudes favor products that remain stable in the long term, but allowing time for innovation means that long term investment is precisely what encourages novelty, that long term investment can thus cut short, in a good way, the length of time a product remains on the market. Long term investment can thus favor short term products (Ivashina and Lerner 2019: 9).

Examples of economic fails caused by too much attention to short term gain are easy to find and enjoyable to ridicule, like the "ghost airports" in Spain, and like the failure of capital so far to develop universal solar energy (Ivashina and Lerner 2019: 1). In the first case, short term obsession caused massive investment in a huge useless thing; in the second, it is causing a failure to invest in a huge great thing.

Needless to say, risk-positive techniques in the context of private venture capital can lead to bad judgments, dishonest fund managers, illusory growth, and criminal temptation (Ivashina and Lerner 2019: 126). The increased use of "leverage" in the 1970s, incurring large debts and deferring debt repayment (Ivashina and Lerner 2019: 111), as well as the normalized boom-and-bust cycles in the 1990s tolerated situations in the short term that would be intolerable in the long term. It comes to the same thing to underestimate short term problems in expectation of long term benefits and to indulge in short term enthusiasm by not worrying about long term effects.

Long term investment does not generate either stability or novelty if it is stop-and-start. We expect long term investment to have ups and downs, and investors are told to stay level-headed. But that is difficult to do, even for investors like university endowments used to gradual compensation, now that it is so easy to follow one's investments online minute by minute (Ivashina and Lerner 2019: 26). Until 2000, pension funds were restricted to low risk investments under the "prudent man rule," but no longer (Ivashina and Lerner 2019: 40). Temporality-defective investment rationality, as predicted by behavioral economics, is caused as much by new technology as by archaic psychology.

Psychologically, it is hard to avoid over-valuing the short term, whether one's intent is to give more value to the short term or to the long term. It is a trope that activist shareholders pressure companies to show increased profits in quarterly reports. But even investors who think of themselves as backing long term projects still imagine that the long term will be covered quickly, that somehow years' worth of product development will pay off in the near future, in what high-tech companies have for years called "warp speed."

Of course, in one sense, it is right to use short term actions to chip away at the long term, since even the long term has a limited time span. For example, long term investment does not imply always re-investing in the same things over time. An investment that shows good results in one quarter does have a high probability of performing well the next quarter, but no more than average probability two quarters later (a phenomenon called "alpha extinction," Ivashina and Lerner 2019: 61).

Long term investment also does not imply that the same person in an investment fund should keep making the decisions (by "grandfather rights," Ivashina and Lerner 2019: 62). On the other hand, the fact that CEOs today have less job security than they used to may result in shorter term vision. Younger investors find short term investing more fun and more empowering. Yet on the other side of the short–long balance sheet, the fact that TIAA-CREF's reports are so boring may increase the number of investors who want to just leave their money in the hole from now until retirement.

In short, some choose each. Some choose some of each. Some of each are better than others of each. As capitalists rather than philosophers, Ivashina and Lerner are not interested in the long term for its own sake, but only when they make profit from it.

Short Windows of Decision

Aside from the amount of time one invests for, there is the question of how long one has to decide whether to invest. When a relatively sudden event occurs, like the acquisition (or rumor of an acquisition) of one company by another, the market responds as soon as it can. This is called a "short-window event."[27] "Event studies" in business management theory defines the short window as briefly as a "snapshot," a day, six months, or up to three years (Oler 2008: 154).

Profits following a corporate acquisition turn out to be short-lived. Derek Oler suggests re-evaluating investments in newly acquired corporations after several different time-periods—after three days, again after 360 days, and so on (Oler 2008: 173). The paradox is that quick judgments are bad at handling uncertainties, yet situations calling for quick judgment tend to be the situations with the most uncertainties (Oler 2008: 153). Sometimes an over-optimistic investment after an acquisition will itself cause the stock price to rise, which in the short run will make investor's over-optimism into a self-fulfilling prophesy. The short term event that generates short term investment has short term success. So (though Oler does not raise this effect), other investors, watching these over-confident investors, might decide to bet against them, over the long term. The same event has short term consequences, due to short term thinking, but third-party thinkers, who see the long term perspective on the short term, see straighter. The long term is not just longer than the short term, the long is the meta-perspective of the short. Or in reverse, the short is not just the micro of the long, the short is the narcissism of the long.

On the other side of temporal misadventure, there are some cases in which the investment economy seems oblivious to daily events, to respond to events with a curiously long time lag. In late May 2020, for example, the US economy was starting to reopen after lockdowns designed to slow the spread of the coronavirus. Medical experts predicted that without a vaccine and without adequate testing, reopening so early would lead to long term worsening of the economy. The markets nevertheless rose, which suggests short termism and disregard for long term risk. On the other side, in June 2020, there were consecutive days of increasing protests in the United States condemning police brutality, along with looting by white supremacist groups, and hence a further shutdown of the consumer economy, followed by Trump's threat that he would "dominate" US cities with an active military, matched by isolation of the United States by world leaders. And yet, the Dow Jones rose by 527 points on June 3, 2020. Of course, day-by-day fluctuations in the stock market are often unrelated to the real world, but even so, there are times when it seems the market is unable to take into consideration the events of the day.

Many investors today believe they can generally ignore short term crises, on the grounds that the economy has in recent times bounced back quickly from crises. This is disputed, but if an investor has this bounce-back perspective, the dangers of short term investment will appear to have an acceptably short impact. As long as the bad effects of short term vision are themselves short, one can afford short term risks in the long run.

In the end, even though long term does not mean the same as high profit (the ultimate criterion), and does not mean the same as low risk, and does not mean the same as wise social policy, and does not mean the same as honest brokerage, Ivashina and Lerner conclude that all of these desirable outcomes are on average met better with long term investment than short term. But then how are investors supposed to respond quickly to events? I wish I knew.

Short Term Financial Operations: Short Selling, Overnight Commercial Paper, Day Trading, Payday Loans

Many short term financial phenomena are problematic, even when they are unavoidable or valuable.

(a) "Short selling" is in the news again (January 2021). Large investors were shorting GameStop, and some clever Reddit users started buying up GameStop shares, raising the price of their shares, and defeating the short sell. This quick build-up of share prices had nothing to do with the value of the GameStop company, whose brick-and-mortar stores sell video games on discs, a recipe for going Blockbuster bust. As I write, both short sellers and Reddit pranksters are under investigation, and nobody knows how it will turn out, other than that GameStop itself still has no future. For our purposes, it matters less who will win, and who is worse, but that a short term David took on a short term Goliath.

Short selling is notorious. You borrow someone else's stocks. (The person lending them to you charges you a certain amount to borrow them.) You then sell those stocks, believing that they are going to go down in price. When they do go down, you buy them again, for less than you sold them for. You now have the same stocks you started with, and you also have the surplus in cash that came from having sold them for more than you bought them for. Then you give them back to the person you borrowed them from. If the cost of borrowing was less than the surplus you got from selling and re-purchasing, then you made a profit. The problem for an economic system is that it may ruin otherwise viable companies if large investors drive stock prices down in order to short them. Short selling was blamed in part for the 1929 Great Depression. The 2008 Great Recession can in part be blamed on Credit Default Swaps, whereby large investors bet in a different way on company failures. The difference is that short selling is dependent on the short turnover sale and re-purchase of stocks, whereas someone who bets on another company's failure may be willing to wait years.

(b) "Short term paper" or "commercial paper" is pervasive in modern finance (though to most people invisible).

> Commercial paper is a commonly used type of unsecured, short-term debt instrument issued by corporations, typically used for the financing of payroll, accounts payable and inventories, and meeting other short-term liabilities. Maturities on commercial paper typically last several days, and rarely range longer than 270 days ... The commercial paper market played a big role in the financial crisis that began in 2007 (*Investopedia*).[28]

In brief, large financial companies, like banks, borrow money for very short periods, sometimes literally overnight, to finance their payroll and inventory. If the lenders, which are also large financial companies, do not trust a bank to repay the loan the next day, they will not issue it such loans. The borrower, whose daily business depends on these short term loans, will thus have a liquidity crisis, will not be able to pay its daily obligations, and may be ruined, as Lehman Brothers was in 2008.[29]

A compounding problem in 2008 was that overnight paper is supposed to be backed by assets, to ensure that the borrower will be able to pay off the debt the next day. But in 2008, those assets were allowed to be "off balance sheet." The borrower could claim assets, but did not have to demonstrate their value, and many banks' assets turned out to be untenable mortgage-based securities. Only when mortgages began to fail did lenders realize that most of the large, well-known borrowers were high credit risks. Worse, those mortgage assets, which backed the short term loans, were long term investments, so there was a "maturity mismatch" between the long term toxic assets and the short term paper loans they were supposed to guarantee (Kacperczyk and Schnabl 2010: 33). This had a snowball effect. When banks could not get short term loans, they declined to lend to other private enterprises, large and small, which in turn led to failures in the productive economy.

There are interesting short term elements in all the contributing factors that led to the 2008 financial crisis: loan financing, Securities and Exchange Commission regulations, the international Basel Accords on assets and capital risk for banks, accounting tricks used to game the Bond Ratings Agencies, Collateralized Debt Obligations (CDOs), derivatives, and tranches. What is important for us is that without massive short term fund transfers at the less-than-a-day time frame, the international banking system collapses.

(c) There are potential disasters for individuals who, whether by need, fun, or addiction, try their hand at day trading. NADEX (North America Derivatives Exchange) is a company that allows individuals to participate: "Make volatility work for you."[30] *Investopedia* defines day trading as "intraday"[31]: a person buys a stock and sells it before the end of the day. When investments are held overnight, or for a few days, it is called "swing trading." "Scalping ... attempts to make numerous small profits on small price changes throughout the day." "High-frequency trading" uses neural network algorithms to "exploit small or short term market inefficiencies." Unfortunately, most people who do it do not know enough to guess which direction stocks are going, or are too late to catch the wave that large investors have already ridden to completion. Without access to AI, day trading does not work.[32]

(d) Payday Loans.[33] Optimism is expressed in investment, anxiety in debt. In the United States, low-income people (disproportionately African Americans and military personnel) can use their upcoming employment check as collateral to take out a short term "payday" loan with companies like *Cashadvance.com*, at an annual interest rate of 390 percent. In 2016, 11,000,000 Americans took a payday loan. One in five who took a payday loan to buy a car eventually had the car repossessed. By 2018, twelve states had prohibited this business, following "Truth in Lending" complaints, but Trump reversed them.[34]

Some argue that the fact that high interest loans are unappealing, and low interest loans are unavailable, leads to the beneficial result that low-income people are less likely to go into debt. Still, high interest loans lead to an increase not only of bankruptcy in conditions of racial disparity but also of alcoholism, obesity, and sexual disorders. Some of these effects are stereotypically associated with doing things too quickly: fast food leads to obesity, short deadlines lead to anxiety, rushed sex leads to performance anxiety. Hasty things are not always bad, but some are.

(e) Short term employment. This does not always help employers, since those with more short term employees end up with lower productivity (especially when employees have special skills),[35] yet employers are doing more of it. Short term employees lose out in terms of income level, unemployment insurance, and pension. Some humans prefer commitment-free employment, but they take on risk in terms of mental health, alcoholism, and family planning, not to mention anxiety.[36] Short term employment exacerbates discrimination based on age, gender, and ethnicity. Pressures on short term employees are lessened if they are treated in the workplace the same way as their long term counterparts, which shows again that the quality of being short term is not just temporal but also social.

Short term full-time work (like temp teaching), which can be a life-long career path, is different from long term part-time work (a few hours per day, or one season each year). Temporary part-time work can be the worst, as double-short term employment. However, if a person prefers long term part-time work, it might not feel short. Some permanent jobs begin with a trial period: these are long term jobs in principle that become long term in actuality after a (relatively) short initial segment, as in tenure-track employment, which begins with a six-year "short" probation, after which the job lasts forever (or so we thought). Of course, the short term is not always bad, in employment or anything else. For some employees, it is at the moment they are granted tenure that they want to quit then and there, like people whose marriage ceremony is exactly what makes them want a divorce. Longtermphobia is not for everyone, but it is not temporally superficial.

Fads and Trends

Some commodities only exist in the short term. Jewelry dealer Mark Schneider distinguishes "fads" and "trends."[37] Overall, there are three time frames. (1) A "classical" design has heirloom status "forever." (2) A "trend" is a variation on classical design, and merits five years shelf space. (3) A "fad" is "short-lived," and lasts a "season." A "season" can mean the length of time until the weather changes, so that a fad in winter boots lasts until Spring and will not be available next winter; or it could last less than a month. (Schneider does not go into this, but a micro-seasonal fad might last the length of an advertising cycle, or until social media chatter dies down.) A fad may thus be defined by three parameters: chronometrically by season; psychometrically by attention span; or by desire transiency (let us call that a "craze"). Some fads eat up a lot of cash before consumers realize it is a fad and not a trend. Predictably, the advice of a jewelry seller is that one should spend less money on fads than trends.

It is difficult to distinguish fads from trends while they are in play. For example, there is debate over whether zombie movies today are a fad, a trend, or a classic. Some good trends, like gluten-free diet, are dismissed as fads. Critics of modernity say that modernity trends away from classical values, but this criticism could itself be a fad.

There are complex interactions across time scales within the same phenomenon. Companies in the fad business have a long term business formula by which they market pet rocks one year and silly bands the next. Other companies have a short term business model for selling a short term product: fly-by-night companies selling subprime long term mortgages in 2006 had the intent to vanish into that night once the pyramid collapsed.

A fad is different from an impulse buy. A person might buy an heirloom, or a home, on impulse. The short term character of the desire to buy does not mean that the thing one desires to buy is a fad commodity. In contrast, there are fads that buyers get stuck with for a long time, like shag carpets.

Marketers have an incentive to distinguish accurately between fads and trends, but may not have a complete perspective. Jerker Denrell and Balázs Kovács discuss selection bias around this distinction.[38] Researchers into fads find it easiest to study fads that are popular. Unpopular fads may or may not exhibit the same longevity curve as popular fads—researchers do not know.

Socio-statistically, fads arise when popularity breeds more popularity, and this produces a predictable rise and fall of purchases along a timeline. A short term fad can thus be analyzed purely in terms of its temporal dynamic, the momentum by which a consumer item, a political idea, a name in the news ("Lewinsky" or "Napster"), or financial jargon (the authors use the example of "Total Quality Management") becomes a short term fad. Before they are fads, they are strictly neither short nor long term phenomena; they would have to be called sporadic, or even non-phenomena. Similarly, one can study the drop-off by which fads stop having short term significance and decay into long term insignificance.

Planned obsolescence is a manufacturer's way of overriding the length of a commodity's use value. Cosima Dannoritzer's documentary, *Prêt-à-jeter* (2010), tells the story of the incandescent light bulb. Invented in the 1870s, bulbs lasted 2,500 hours. In 1924, the "Pheobus Cartel" met in Geneva to de-engineer the light bulb for added fragility, to last only 1,000 hours. The cartel fined any participating company that refused to lower longevity. By the 1950s, this was called "death dating." Though the United States sued in 1942, and won a decision (after only eleven years in court) requiring GE not to deliberately shorten the life of their bulbs, that life never did increase over 1,000 hours until LED lights increased bulb life twentyfold (invented in 1962, they became popular around 2008). There are many such stories. Nylon stockings could last for years, but the nylon is deliberately altered to weaken when exposed to sunlight; computer printers are built with a computer chip to count the number of pages printed and then shut off for good. Everyone knows about Apple batteries. Engineers writing in *Design News* in the 1950s were uncomfortable about hiring engineers to make products worse, but Engineering Schools today teach just these "product life cycles" for "frequent repeat purchase." *Printer's Ink* magazine, 1928: "An article that refuses to wear out is a tragedy of business." Real estate broker Bernard London's pamphlet *Ending the Depression through Planned Obsolescence* (1932)[39] argued on ethical grounds for short-lived commodities as a way of increasing employment. We know now that the throwaway economy is disastrous for a finite planet, in terms of landfill, toxicity, and climate. As always, a short term is not just a quantity of time but entails qualities of space and health.

Planned obsolescence can shorten the life of commodities either by making the product break or by enticing the consumer to want a new one even though the last still works. But when products are made to be obsolete, secondary markets extend their life. For example, when a short term product lasts longer than the short term desire for it, the market for second-hand goods takes up the slack; when the short term desire lasts longer than the short term product, the repair industry extends product life; when short term desire exceeds income, the credit industry permits premature purchases. The whole economy is called into action to make short term production work systematically.

There are three kinds of solutions to short term commodities, each of which has a different implication for the relation between short and long term. One is to make commodities last longer, to make the short longer. A second is to repair things as they break, to take one short-lived part out of a machine and replace it with a different short-lived part. The third is "cradle to cradle" production, where producers pay the hidden costs of recycling, so that products, when they do stop working, become "nutrients," not waste. Here, neither the whole nor the part needs to last very long, as long as the series of short term things feed back into a sustainable order of short term things. On this third model, ecology makes the circle of life out of the short term.

Short Term Political Economics and the Criticism of "Short Termism"

Complaints against "short termism" argue that, like short term investors, short term political actors put both social policy and the economy at risk. Decisions made primarily for short term benefit tend to primarily benefit the decision-makers. The claim is that the short term favors profit over ethics.

A 2015 paper by William Galston is typical: "Against Short-Termism: The rise of quarterly capitalism has been good for Wall Street—but bad for everyone else."[40] Galston's examples include companies returning 80–90 percent of earnings to stockholders in the form of dividends and stock buybacks, which leaves less investment capital for long term projects. Managers receive "performance based pay" for short term decisions, which suppress hiring, reduce innovation, and ignore aging infrastructure.

Felwine Sarr[41] shows how short term analysis can make a political/economic investment look either too dangerous or too rosy. For example, when international bankers consider investing in Africa, they tend to see only a current lack of development, and fail to appreciate long range potential. Sarr calls this "short term analysis, or more precisely, what I call thought from the trough of the wave" (Sarr 2019: 28). Furthermore, the failure to see a long term future is tied to a failure to see the "longer term economic history of the African continent" (Sarr 2019: 29). The long future can only be seen with reference to the long past, that is, to the many previous periods of time when African economies were thriving. The long past allows the short term present to be assessed accurately.

The situation is obviously not as simple as saying that profit goals are short term while ethical principles are long term. Some ethical goals are short term, like flattening the curve of a virus. So the critique against short termism is not against every possible short term. One complex case of mixed long and short term is "reverse innovation"[42]: reviving past technologies to solve current problems. During Covid, this means, for example, recognizing that African practices of limiting contagion, developed during earlier Ebola outbreaks, can be more effective in social distancing and curtailing misinformation than newer technologies. "Trickle-up innovation" reverses the short term into a backward turn from a distance to a previous short term crisis and its solution.

Misreading the subtle interactions of long and short terms can lead politicians to self-injury. On June 22, 2020, Trump held a rally in Tulsa, Oklahoma, the first of the 2020 campaign, intended to brag, prematurely, that the Coronavirus pandemic in America was over.[43] He assumed that his supporters would attend in large numbers, in spite of the fact that the virus was increasing in Oklahoma at the time. He announced that over 1,000,000 people had requested seats. Due in part to the disconnect between the long term of the virus and the short term of Trump's planning, and in part to quickly semi-organized dirty tricks in which teenagers on *TikTok* registered en masse for rally tickets they had no intention of using, only 6,200 people came to the 19,000 seat stadium. *Washington Post* columnist Philip Bump: "In short order, he [Trump] set himself up for disaster."

Predictably, the complaint that corporations over-emphasize the short term is disputed. Corporate lawyer Lizanne Thomas argues that companies invest more than enough on the long term.[44] Charles Nathan and Kai Goldberg, authors of "The Short-Termism Thesis: Dogma vs. Reality,"[45] who work for a public relations company that advises financial services companies, argue that stock buybacks do not limit capital available for long term investment, since companies take on extra debt to cover those investments. (This is an odd argument—that debt deferral, which postpones debt reduction for a very long time in order to keep up short term profits, actually shows the companies' long term values.) Further, they argue that short term investment is good in the long term. They make the ad hominem claim that the only people who complain about corporate short termism are politicians and reporters who want a juicy but fake story that makes them popular in the short term. Complainers are Luddites, they say, like those fools who used to oppose automation merely on the grounds that it would cause unemployment. In any case, they say, it is shareholders who should decide how companies act, and the fact that shareholders vote for lots of short term profit is proof that the short term is a good target. Most of this is public relations rhetoric, but there may be some ways in which short term advantage can contribute to long term success.

Some corporate board members, like Dambisa Moyo, turn the criticism of corporations on its head and blame democracy and its voters for short termism instead. Since voters do not back politicians who promote long term policies, "democratic systems encourage short-termism."[46] She cites America's failing infrastructure and complains that elected bodies too quickly overturn laws, treaties, and executive orders passed by their predecessors. However, the connection she asserts between democracy and short termism is clearly not general. It is just as likely for non-democratic systems to be short termist, since authoritarians can always use the military to avoid consequences if things go bad, just as non-democratic corporations like Enron imagine that they can squeeze wealth out of a nation and flee. Conversely, longer terms for political office-holders, which Moyo advocates as a way to mitigate voter irrationality, carry their own dangers. And she has the terrible idea that people should be allowed to run for office only if they have "real-world" job experience (she says she would not restrict candidates to businesspeople, but that is her paradigm). Opposition to the short term is sometimes code for opposition to democracy.

The solution, easy to articulate but difficult to coordinate, would be to balance short and long term political thinking. Jonathan Boston, professor of Public Policy, recommends "intertemporal tradeoffs" (Boston 2014: 10).[47] Decision-makers should get "incentives" to make longer term decisions (Boston 2014: 26) and should be "insulated" from short term pressures (Boston 2014: 15). "Insulation" is not the best term for Boston's intention to get the long term "coupled with day-to-day policy-making" (Boston 2014: 18)—at least to allow warning signs to temper "adroit" short term decisions. A few countries have made half-hearted attempts. In 1993, Finland created a "Parliamentary Committee for the Future" (Boston 2014: 19); in 1977, US President Carter commissioned a "Global 2000" report, though President Reagan ignored it only three years later in 1980 (Boston 2014: 21). Boston ends his article with the suggestion that Christian faith is good for long term decision-makers (Boston 2014: 27). To my mind, while religion obviously takes the long view, it is a mistake to over-connect temporal and other ontological commitments.

Iconio Garrì[48] highlights a surprising difficulty in intertemporal trade-offs. In Italy, it turns out that corrupt politicians support capital expenditures on infrastructure that are good for society long term, just because those expenditures enable them to take larger bribes short term (Garrì 2010: 197). On the other hand, their desire for re-election leads them to allocate short term public expenditures, where the visibility of results (hence voter approval) is greatest. When there is a hard choice, they tend toward the short term, but each short term win by a bribe-desiring politician gives them opportunities to make long term bribe-rich allocations for the public good. Corrupt short termism benefits long termism. Garrì says that in Italy, voters understand that it is a "bad sign" if a politician explicitly aims at the long term. So when a politician does do long term good, they would be prudent not to leave signs of it. In the end, Garrì suggests that more decisions should be made by referendum. Voters asked to decide for themselves whether to make long term allocations may say yes more often than they will support politicians who make the same allocations (Garrì 2010: 208).

Intertemporal trade-offs need to be played out with variations depending on the hand one is dealt. It is often said that democratic governments are at a disadvantage in international diplomacy, since they have only a few years before an election replaces them, whereas governments not dependent on elections can afford to play the long game. It is said, for example, that the Taliban has an advantage in being able to wait out the short attention span of American voters. The ability to wait it out may sound like an advantage. But it is not as though governments-in-waiting generally have an awesome track record. Waiting the other out is frequently poor strategy, whether in diplomacy or romance. For that matter, the truism that governments facing frequent elections do less waiting-out than governments without temporal checks does not seem likely either. Short two-year election cycles (as in the US House of Representatives), for example, tend to bunch up long term decisions in the first year of the cycle and scale the short term decisions during the second, when fundraising takes over. Election cycling creates unique rhythms of long and short term bundling, but does not in principle favor the short over the long. Every person and every society has both short and long term resources and limitations. The point is to invest in temporal combinatories.

Short Term Missionary Work

Short Term Religious Missions

Christian missionaries used to travel for years, but in recent times, short term missionary work, in formats from eight weeks to as short as a day, has become the norm. The number of Americans involved in short term missions (religious and/or medical) grew from 22,000 in 1979 to 1,600,000 in 2007.[49] Most missionaries work in a country less wealthy than their own, and wealth and technological inequality deserve more intertemporal analysis. I am not going to consider here whether religious conversion is good or bad in the long term or the short. I am just going to consider the temporality of short and long term missionary effects.

Evidence for long term effects on the missionaries themselves is mixed. LiErin Probasco[50] finds that high school students, who do "brief but intense" missionary work, do more volunteer work than the average person for years afterward. But in contrast, Kurt Alan Ver Beek's 2006 study of an American Christian mission to construct houses in Honduras[51] finds that short term missionaries do not show increased charitable giving afterward, nor do they pray more than other Christians upon returning. This study also compares houses built by missionaries, which cost $30,000 each (including the cost of the missionary's travel), with houses built by local Honduran Christians, at $2,000 each. The quality of houses was about the same, as was the level of happiness of the new homeowners. This study indicates that short term missionaries rarely speak local languages, rarely build lasting personal relationships with the people they come to assist, provide fewer long term benefits than local aid agencies, take jobs from local providers (nurses, homebuilders), and do insufficient follow-up to find out whether they have helped in the long term. Better to send money.

There is greater long term impact for both the missionary's education and the missioned's benefits when there is more follow-up reporting shortly after the end of the short term mission. The short term thus has more effect if there is also more long term activity—but there is only a short window during which the long term can get properly started.

There is much discussion about how long religious conversion, sometimes called "religious switching," lasts before converts start to undergo "deconversion,"[52] or switching back, or switching again to another religion, or switching from religion to the absence of religion, known as "secular exit." It is not easy to find statistics on this. How many people does a missionary have to try to convert in order to convert one? Some converts speak of being overcome suddenly; some converters patiently recommend that people take their time before converting.

The media overworks the phrase "fastest growing religion" to describe Islam. It is not easy to find evidence about which religion is the fastest for a person to convert to, but there is much discussion of online missionary work in Islam. Rahman et al.[53] discuss the relatively quick success that Islam has had in gaining adherents online in Malaysia. As one would expect, people with a positive attitude toward the internet (younger users) are more likely to convert online. Successful recruitment cultivates major personal commitment out of small initial acts done quickly: asking subscribers to send greeting cards for religious holidays, making small charitable contributions, and attending short meetings. Online cult-generation in white supremacy cyberspace engages with equally short time scales.

Short Term Medical Missions

Similar issues are found in non-religious short term medical missions, which likewise increased dramatically around 2000.[54] More people will volunteer for shorter missions, and short health care can be better than none, especially after a natural disaster or disease outbreak, where the need is temporary. But it is an unsolved question whether many short visits are better than fewer longer visits, or better than sending aid to local providers, given that short term medical care alleviates symptoms and averts crises but rarely solves underlying conditions.

Short term medical trips tend to "report outputs rather than outcomes." Kevin Sykes (2014: e38) cites a mission that reported how many cleft palate surgeries they did, but did not assess how much better their patients' speech became in the months afterward. Long term patient morbidity is not well known. Providers rarely know how long medical equipment left behind after the trip remains in good repair, and rarely know the extent to which patients have the resources and motivation to continue taking prescribed medications (assuming those medications are locally available or affordable) and to continue physical therapy.

Janice Hawkins[55] summarizes problems with short term missions:

— Lack of knowledge of individual patient histories
— Inability to communicate, or to label medication containers, in the patients' language
— Disruption of the care the patient had been receiving from local health providers
— Increased risk of drug overdose, accidental ingestion of drugs by children, lack of familiarity of those drugs by local pharmacists and poison centers, as well as the short shelf life of medications left behind
— Health care providers practicing areas of medicine they are not licensed for at home
— Depriving local practitioners of the chance to learn how to solve local problems

The concern that the short term is bad for cross-cultural understanding is similar to Braudel's idea that short term social science can "ensnare the observer in a hurry—the ethnologist who spends three months with a small Polynesian people, the industrial sociologist who offers us the clichés of his latest survey, or who thinks that, with a clever questionnaire and cross-tabulations using perforated cards [hmm] he can capture perfectly a social mechanism" (Braudel [1960] 2009: 185–6). Will the age of big data solve the data collection limitations of the short term?

One way to mitigate the risks of short term medical missions, while retaining the format of short visits, would be to make repeated short term trips with the same personnel to the same communities (just as recurring short terms improve brief psychotherapy, and just as part replacement mitigates planned obsolescence). An interrupted but patterned sequence of short terms might mimic the long term when the continuous long term is not available.

Short Term Relationships

Many books listed on *Amazon* have titles like *15-Minute Marriage Makeover* and *The 15-Minute Relationship Fix*. Fifteen is a common number for promises of short term results: how to find purpose in your life, how to draw, cook diet dinners, win a nuclear war. Some teach skills in sessions of five minutes, a few in one minute, very few in under twenty-nine seconds. There is a limit, after all.

"Short term marriage," a term used to calculate alimony, usually refers to a marriage that ends after one or two years. Of course, there are cultural differences. The average marriage in Rome is eighteen years; in Ottawa, fourteen; in Doha, Qatar, five.[56] The mean duration of cohabitation in 2006 was 2.6 years in the United States, but four to six years in most European countries.[57] A relationship deemed short in Europe would thus seem relatively long in North America. There is a stereotype that everything is done in a shorter time in North America, but short term is measured one practice at a time. A train trip covering three hundred miles in two hours will seem very short to an American traveling in Europe, but average to a European.

Many popular websites give advice on how to either turn a one-night stand into a long term relationship, or to prevent it. Some people find dating a bother, and hope that they only have to do it short term, after which they will transition into marriage. Others enjoy it for its own sake while it lasts. That makes it different from short term therapy, investment, or mission, which, whether one does them for a brief or a long time, are not typically ends in themselves but aim at future consequences.

Paul Eastwick's study[58] (a disproportionate number of respondents were white middle-class Americans, and only two-person relationships were considered) finds that short and long term relationships are largely indistinguishable in their early stages (flirting, initial romance, first sex) and differ only in later periods (caregiving, etc.) (Eastwick 2018: 747). It was a surprise to the researchers that short and long term relationships do not differ more from the start, and that people generally do not know what they want or what they are doing when they start a relationship.

People therefore know only in hindsight whether they are in a short or long term, casual or serious, relationship (Eastwick 2018: 750). One sign that people are in a long term relationship is that they re-write history in a different way: they "shift the beginning of time backward" (Eastwick 2018: 751). That is, when people in a relationship are asked when their relationship began, some will date the beginning from the first time they met, and others will date the beginning from the first declaration of affection. The former group backdates the beginning into a longer term, and this is the first sign that they are actually in a long term relationship. Long term and short term relationships are thus not defined by how long into the future they proceed, but by how far back into the past they are historicized.

There are no doubt more relationship categories besides those that this study offers respondents: "fling, one-night stand, brief affair, etc." It asks respondents to measure stages of their relationship according to an "interest scale" from 0 to 100, but not all respondents will interpret that scale in the same way. Nor are the fifty event-types they give respondents to plot into their relationship history part of every relationship (first coffee, first oral sex, first meeting with the parents, first feeling of clinginess, etc.) (Eastwick 2018: 752–3). Despite these problems, the data are interesting. For example, when respondents were asked to date "events" in their relationship so far, short and long term relationships began to diverge around the time of the fifteenth event (whichever event was the fifteenth on a given respondent's series). Also, the longer the term of the relationship, the longer the time intervals between remark-worthy events. That is, most people remember many relationship-defining events over the first ten days of a relationship, but few around day forty-six (Eastwick 2018: 756). The decline in frequency over time of relationship-changing events means that we might define the short term as the dense term and the long as the sparse term.

Another statistical oddity is that only 23 percent of respondents in a relationship reported that they were in a short term one (Eastwick 2018: 759). It seems that many people who think they are in a long term relationship are really not. They only discover that fact when it is over. Because of this, there is some uncertainty about how to interpret their other responses, like their current level of sexual interest, which may in reality be lower than they report.

This study is neutral as to the moral values and eudaimological desirability of short vs long term relationships. Social standards tend to prefer the long term, but not always. Mary Sokol, for example, defends Bentham's argument from the 1780s in favor of short term relationships[59] and notes precedents, like Olympe de Gouges's *Déclaration des Droits de la Femme et de la Citoyenne* in 1791. (De Gouges was guillotined in 1793.) At that time, marriage laws did not yet specify minimum age, applicability to non-Christians, or adultery provisions. Bentham accepts some constraints on sexuality, but he is sympathetic to homosexuality, bastards and prostitutes, cohabitation outside of marriage, and "wives against bad husbands" (Sokol 2009: 9–11). His support for legal divorce recognizes that some marriages only function well for a limited time. If marriage contracts could specify a termination date in advance, it would render divorce unnecessary (Sokol 2009: 13). It is too bad that one-night marriages (including prostitution) are felt to be shameful, he thinks. Since almost all temporary cohabitations in Bentham's time consisted of a man with a mistress who was his social inferior, treating short term relationships with honor would have protected all genders and classes.

There might be utilitarian reasons to keep a marriage short, either for appetite or variety, or to provide time for a person to have relationships while they complete their studies (Sokol 2009: 13), taking propinquity into account. As we have seen in short term therapy, short term investment, short termist politics, and short term missions, greater happiness gained in the short term is not a complete justification for acting short term, but neither is pleasure irrelevant to justifying the short term.

Conclusion

Analyzing the concept of the short term using the sharp definitions that practitioners are forced to think through and organizing eidetic variations on the model of the short term allow us to use the resources of the temporal combinatory to best effect. I come down on the side of variation.

Chapter 8

SHORT TERM AESTHETICS (EPHEMERAL ART AND THE FREE USE OF TEMPORAL CONSTRAINTS)

Argument: The art of controlling time, both freeing and constraining, consists of inventing and layering temporal patterns, and creating new perceptual faculties capable of perceiving more temporal variation.

The short term is explored in performance art, poetry, cinema, and even in the least temporal of arts, painting. As always, a short temporal segment makes use of short and long time-periods before, during, and after the segment itself: preparation time, runtime, and memorial time. And within each short segment are shorter and longer sub-segments. A short performance may follow long rehearsals; a long performance may be started with no rehearsal but follow long years of practice; the memory of it may last long afterward but begin the instant the piece begins.

Performance Art: The Ephemeral

Ephemeral art is art that only lasts for a short amount of time. There are many forms of ephemeral art, from sculpture to performance, but the term is usually used to describe a work of art that only occurs once, like a happening, and cannot be embodied in any lasting object to be shown in a museum or gallery. Ephemeral art first came to prominence in the 1960s with the Fluxus group, when artists like Joseph Beuys were interested in creating works of art that existed outside the gallery and museum structure and had no financial worth. Happenings, performances, and sound sculptures were all part of ephemeral art, as were flyers and cheap mass-produced items that carried subversive messages out into the world (Tate Gallery).[1]

In ephemeral art, the short term (even if some performances last an uncomfortably long time) is connected to outdoor (or site-specific[2]) space, low cost, and subversive politics. It challenges the tradition that art has lasting value, upheld not only by collectors and speculators but also by people who just want to enjoy great works of the past again and again.

Of course, a happening can be filmed and watched again later. Collections manager Katrina Windon compromises between the "cultural interest" of art lovers and the artwork's "right to decay with dignity."[3] The recording of an ephemeral performance will not have the shock-value of the happening, but it makes possible a much larger audience. Rigorous ephemerists, who value the transience of time more than beauty, will not want to allow recordings, even on spectators' cellphones. (Phone videos function somewhere between conservation and ephemera.) They do not allow us to step into the same art space twice (or spend much time there when we step into it once). This is not very nice. But neither is the short term.

Some ephemeral art, limited by an occasion, is "low" art, like butter sculptures at a state fair, or piñatas at birthday parties. But some ephemerality has religious significance: Tibetan Buddhist sand mandalas have as their theme the impermanence of all things, the ultimate short term cosmology. At a Kalachakra, a multi-day meditation practice, a mandala, several feet across, of complex traditional design is meticulously constructed (from the center out toward the periphery) a few grains of sand at a time, over dozens of hours. Within a few hours after the intricate multi-colored image is completed, it is swept away in a few minutes. Sweeping away the mandala at the end of the short term takes a bit of time to accomplish. The mandala is a short term religio-aesthetic object that ends in an act of termination that is itself a distinct short term process. It could have been ended instantly, with one blast of wind, but the ceremony deliberately takes a few minutes, as if to emphasize that the time interval it takes to exhibit the impermanence of the mandala occupies an (impermanent) amount of time on its own. The end of the short term begins with bell ringing and chanting; then, monks (dressed appropriately) with brushes (or with fingers or a *dorje*) sweep the sand (not too precisely) into a pile, beginning at the outside and sweeping inward to the center, where blessings are captured, as the colors mix together.[4] Sometimes, they sweep toward the center in a spiral pattern, which makes impermanence into an aesthetic of its own. Some of the sand may then be scooped into a small gold cup. Sometimes the sand is later thrown into a river. When a monk explains that mandalas are destroyed after the meditation rituals are over, he laughs. These rituals raise an odd question: how long does it take a performance to become ephemeral? We might think that if it is ephemeral, it is so right away. But in the case of the mandala, impermanence is itself a kind of becoming, one that takes time to accomplish, though not very much time. (One might imagine a ceremony in which a mandala is destroyed as slowly as it was made, a few grains at a time, until it was finally gone. Such a practice might even intensify the sense of impermanence. But the tradition went a different way.)

In fact, it is not easy to make something ephemeral. Performance art events by Marina Abramovic, known for decades for the bodily and emotional risks she takes in public, which seemed to put them in the only-she-could-have-done-that category, were reprised by other performers during her 2010 retrospective at MOMA.[5] Reprised ephemera suggest a positive aesthetic answer to the ontological question of whether a segment of lived time can be extracted, moved, then reinserted into the temporal continuum at a later date. Indeed, it is not clear if events in an age of reproduction can ever be ephemeral again. Perhaps they never were. Socrates must have known that his live-only words were destined for posterity the instant they left his mouth.[6] Rabbi Nachman of Breslov burned his books for spiritual motives, but burning a book may be just the ticket for keeping its thoughts alive.[7] Gregory Arkadin faked amnesia to avoid prosecution, then murdered all the witnesses to his past life, then, finally, faked—or did he?—his death (*Mr. Arkadin*, Orson Welles, 1955). In the Anthropocene age of reproducible ephemera, it is not clear whether it is more difficult (or more moral, or more aesthetically pleasing) to establish a lasting legacy, or to erase one's footprints.

Structural Short Term: Ending—Endings—Unending/Short—Long—Short: In Writing (Short Story (Eichenbaum)), Music (Cadence (Barthes)), and Painting (Frame (Derrida))

Since a short term temporal segment is cut off at the end, whereas time is continuous, it follows that if a process ends after a short term, it is because time is understood to be cut. In this way, framing in the plastic arts (like painting) is analogous to ending in the temporal arts (like poetry and music). *Ut pictura poesis.*

There are literary forms named specifically for their shortness, like the ancient "epyllion" (the diminutive of "epic"), and the short story. Italo Calvino cites the "economy of expression" in folk tales.[8] As we have found generally, shortness is as much structural as quantitative. And structures are defined by variations.

The Russian formalist Boris Eichenbaum, in "O. Henry and the Theory of the Short Story,"[9] offers a quantity–quality definition of the short story, distinguishing it both from the longer novel and the still shorter "sketch." Quantitatively, the short story, the "small form," is defined simply by its "small size" (Eichenbaum [1925] 1971: 232). Eichenbaum agrees with Edgar Allen Poe's "The Philosophy of Composition" (1846): a rhymed poem should be readable in one hour, a prose tale in two (Eichenbaum [1925] 1971: 234). The qualitative definition of shortness in a story is a different matter, involving "the impact of plot on the ending" (Eichenbaum [1925] 1971: 232). Unlike novels, which mix together descriptions, sentimental reflections, and plot digressions, a short story is defined by the fact that none of its parts does anything other than lead toward the end. This is what makes its read-time short. In contrast, a novel needs multiple ending scenarios for its multiple characters, each with their own back-story to fulfill. Novels therefore extend outward into epilogical post-stories (*Nachgeschichte*). Eichenbaum speculates that the taste for short and fast stories belongs especially to 1920s America, illustrated by O. Henry's sharp endings. Of course, there are exceptions. Eichenbaum analyzes elements in O. Henry himself that are not so focused on plot-ending, like his ironic self-referential comments on the art of story writing inserted into many of the stories. For that matter, O. Henry's endings (the ending of "The Gift of the Magi" is a cliché everyone knows) are anti-climactic as much as climactic, more trick than surprise. Even so, Eichenbaum's paradigm is a good one: "By its very essence, the story, just as the anecdote, assesses its whole weight toward the ending. Like a bomb dropped from an airplane, it must speed downward so as to strike with its warhead full-force on the target" (Eichenbaum [1925] 1971: 231). For a story to have an end that makes it count as short, it has to not only end, it has to accelerate toward that end. The end has to have been the drive behind the story from the beginning and throughout. The end has to be coming quickly and inevitably, yet it has to arrive in a strike of unexpected violence. Its shortness is both gradual and sudden, both continuous and discrete magnitude.

So far, this seems straightforward. The one-point ending makes a story short, whereas delayed distributed endings make a story long. But there is a third option besides single ending (all-ending) and plural endings (some-endings), namely no-ending. One might have thought that if the single ending is short, and the plural ending is longer, the unending would be longest. But it turns out that only some-ending is long; both all-ending and none-ending are short, though in different ways.

Let us assume that the closing cadence in a piece of music is analogous to the plot closure of a short story. In defining short format music, Roland Barthes uses the opposite element from the one that Eichenbaum used to define short format story writing.[10]

> The man who has best understood and practiced the aesthetic of the fragment (before Webern) is perhaps Schumann; he called the fragment an "intermezzo"; he increased the intermezzi within his works as he went on composing; everything he produced was ultimately intercalated: but between what and what? What is the meaning of a pure series of interruptions? ... Webern's small pieces: no cadence, with what sovereignty he *turns short*. (Barthes [1975] 1977: 94–5)

Where Eichenbaum said that the one-point ending makes a story (whatever its word length) short, Barthes says that it is precisely the absence of a clear ending that makes a piece of music (however long it takes to play it) short. Barthes's criterion is that if a piece of music ends with a cadence, it is not short but full. But if it stops without a cadence, and so does not announce its ending with a flourish, it consists, by definition, of fragments, intermezzi, and interruptions without termination points, which means that it "turns short." "Turning short," like "stopping short" or "cutting short," ends without the flourish of resolution. It ends without a signal of ending. It does end, but does not refer to an ending. It ends before it gets to the official ending. Non-ending is shortened.

But the point is not just that it ends before it says it ends, the point is that it is made of pieces that are inherently fragmentary, and in that way, it could go on indefinitely. A piece with an ending cadence might have an extra bit stuck on after that ending, in which case it will seem to overstay its welcome. But a piece with no such ending can keep going without prejudice. Quantitatively, it has no natural limit, and so can be long. But structurally, it bypasses the criterion by which length is defined by waiting for a cadence, so it is not long on that criterion. We do not need to conclude that since it is not long, it is therefore short, but we can say that it "turns short."

In sum, Eichenbaum points to the way that a short term piece terminates at a discrete point that is natural to its content; Barthes points to the way that a short term piece terminates before some other point could have brought it to a close more naturally. Ultimately, these two opposite definitions of short format art are not contradictory, but instead point to two different aspects of the short term. Short processes have to have both sorts of terminating qualities: they end, and they could have gone on. It is this double feature of ending without an end that we have been using to define the short term throughout this work. This same double feature of the short can produce opposite phenomena: either classical resolutions or fragmentary intermezzi.

This is the structural conclusion: there are two opposite kinds of short term: the kind with one ending, and the kind with no ending. There is just one kind of long term: the kind with some endings. Singularity is short, plurality is long, infinite multiplicity is short. This is the paradox of the infinite, from Anaximander to Hegel to Badiou: an infinite compilation never reaches a singular substance, and an infinite sequence never counts as a singular event. The infinite is less than the one; the one thing the infinite sequence leaves out is the whole, and this constitutes its ontological shortage.

This implication stages Derrida's discussion of painting. The edge of a painting or a photo, where the frame goes, cuts the scene from its surroundings. No matter how the within-frame is sutured to the out-of-frame, the enframing cut gives the picture its content by taking it out of context. Indeed, seeing the beauty in an object already separates the object from its natural function. Its beauty becomes an end in itself; its beauty is endless, but extends only to the limit of the frame and no further. This is Derrida's point in "Parergon,"[11] his essay in *The Truth in Painting* devoted to Kant's *Critique of Judgment*.

> The wild tulip is, then, seen as exemplary of this finality without end, of this useless organization, without goal, gratuitous, out of use. But we must insist on this: the being cut off from the goal only becomes beautiful if everything in it is straining toward the end. Only this absolute interruption ... produces the feeling of beauty. If this cut were not pure, if it could be prolonged, completed, supplemented, there would be no beauty. (Derrida [1978] 1987: 87)

Kant's theory is that we experience an object, like a flower, as beautiful when we experience it *as if* it had been designed for our pleasure, that is, as if it had been designed to stimulate our free play of imagination and understanding.[12] But we know that there is no actual teleology in nature. We thus experience beauty when we begin speculating in teleological terms, but then cut that thinking off before we start believing in it. Beauty arises when we strain toward a teleological end but do not let that end even seem like it could be fulfilled.

Beauty thus arises in a three-step procedure: we introduce a continuing goal; we cut the goal off in mid-stream; then imagination plays at the "edge of this cut" (Derrida [1978] 1987: 88). Had there been no goal in the first place, no ideal beyond nature, then there would be no feeling of beauty, just a factual perception of the flower's sensory qualities. On the other hand, had the goal not been cut off, there would be no feeling of beauty, just a judgment of the flower's purpose. It is only when the end is posited, then cut, that at the threshold of the cut, there is a distinctive sort of experience, namely aesthetics.

For Kant, this kind of short cut is uniquely about beauty. Experiencing an object in its real purposiveness prolongs the object into the long term, where it either will or will not come to fruition. It is not morally, technologically, or epistemologically useful to cut objects short from their long results in this way. In contrast, when the purpose of the object is cut out of the picture, perception of it becomes a short term experience and does not project the object beyond the time it is perceived. Only aesthetic perceptions are short term in this way.

Purposiveness without a purpose does not at first sound temporal. But the removal of the farthest-time end point is the same structure that allows near-time temporal segmentation. It is just because an event does not need to be understood to go all the way to the end that it can be understood in the confines of a relatively autonomous period. Derrida's conceit is that when Kant's frame creates a "cut out sector" (Derrida [1978] 1987: 42), it does not just put an outer bound on a picture but cuts a missing space out of its inside. The cut both draws a shape with a line and smudges what is inside the line with the emptiness of what is outside, extending the ambiguity of the line indefinitely outward. For us, the issue is not the frame of painting per se but the cut. As always, the question is how a cut is possible in a field that we know expands beyond its outer line. Since Derrida is all about the passage beyond the line, this is the general problem of deconstruction: are there cuts, really?

When, for deconstruction, is a cut not a cut? (a) When what has been cut off survives. The outside has been cut off, but it is still there. The top segment of a Rothko painting cuts off the lower segment, which is there anyways; an author passes away, and Derrida mourns him by writing a text for him addressed to the beyond (*Living On/Borderlines, for Blanchot*); the specter of an outdated philosophy remains "hauntology" (*Spectres of Marx*). The event is short term, but does not terminate. (b) When what has been cut off multiplies, proliferates, dehisces, metastasizes, contaminates, and communicates effects into what comes after. This always happens: there is no short term. But the opposite also happens.

When *is* a cut a cut, and a frame a frame? When does an individual (or a divisible one, a dividual) live, and in what part of the world? When it has an unconstrainable tendency to keep moving, but no end to get to. It does not get all the way, and in that sense, it is cut short. But it is cut short precisely because there is nothing at the end that cuts it off. Paradoxically, the cut shortens the term by refusing to end it. By cutting out the end, cutting out the one thing that could cut it off, cutting out the cut-out mold, it keeps its limit. It is short not because it is not long but because it does not get to the end. Insofar as it is not complete, the short term is longer than the long term. The distinction here is not between short term and long term but between the short term and defined term.

If we lived in the standpoint of the totality of space and time, cuts would be irrational. We would never see episodes without their results. But since we live in the standpoint of finite places of space and time, we see finite episodes in short term segments. The anomalous objects of aesthetics, objects cut off from their futures, are in this way the paradigmatic super-topic of the lifeworld. In cinema, and the many media in which we screen and scroll through moving pictures, we experience these cuts as a matter of course.

Short Cut and Fast Montage: Cinema

Some films are just plain short. Watch the four-second *YouTube* video with the tag "The Shortest Movie Ever."[13] The shortest Oscar-nominated film is *Fresh Guacamole* (PES 2012), coming in at 1:35 not including titles.[14] If the Lumière Brothers' *Arrival of a Train at La Ciotat* (1894) had become the paradigm, the average film would last under a minute, not including intermissions and commercial breaks. Accelerated projection can make long events into short films, for example, by recording clouds drifting by at 1,000 frames/second, and playing the footage back at the usual frame rate of twenty-four: this is short term via forced temporal perspective. But more important than the shortness of the film is the way shortness functions in cuts.

The cut of a frame in space and a cinematic shot in time lift part-objects out of context. But when things are cut free from their natural contexts, neighbors, and histories, they come into contact with other things at a distance that they were not naturally connected to, and assemble into hybrids. Until a thing is cut from its neighbor, it connects only to that neighbor. Once it is cut, it can connect to anything.

This is a temporal analogue to Dziga Vertov's[15] 1920s theory of the "camera eye," which sees more, and differently, than the organic eye stuck in our biological bodies. The camera eye can see things farther away than our bio eyes can see, and closer up. It can be sent inside private rooms that our bodies are not allowed into. And engineers will improve the camera eye still further in times to come, much faster than medicine will improve the eyes in our heads. Vertov mentions that there is also a "radio-ear" and a "kinok-editor." By cutting and splicing, the editor-eye can see two events that happen a long time apart, and show them to the viewer one immediately after the other. In his inimitable hyperbolic way ("I am kino-eye, I create a man more perfect than Adam," Vertov [1923] 1985: 17), Vertov proclaims, "You're walking down a Chicago street today in 1923, but I made you greet Comrade Volodarsky, walking down a Petrograd Street in 1918, and he returns your greeting" (Vertov [1923] 1985: 16–17). The time-eye does not only piece small separated segments of time together into a continuous sequence, it also makes events across those intervals interact immediately, as if the persons living in those two times are present simultaneously. This is montage: to control time passage by controlling time intervals, "organizing the minutes of the life-structure" (Vertov [1923] 1985: 21).

Film editors have many views on how to cut and paste.[16] Some value themes and others stories; some value images and others style; some want their editing to be invisible to the viewer, others want it to be a work of art on its own. In all cases, film editing is a craft of the short term. In *Cinema 1*,[17] Deleuze takes to heart

Godard's reflection that "The problem with cinema seems to me more and more when and why to start a shot and when and why to end it."[18]

Even beginners at filmmaking have experienced the challenge of making each shot exactly the right length, starting with a rough cut and refining it by trimming single frames. Whether viewers can tell whether a single frame has been cut or added is difficult to say, but it means the world to editors. The average feature film today consists of over 1,000 shots spliced together. In typical filmmaking, every single shot (a shot is defined as anything the camera captures between the moment the record button is pressed and the moment it is stopped) will need to be shortened. The reason the director says "camera … action" is so that the camera will start rolling a couple of seconds before the actors do anything—the last thing one wants is for the actors to do something worth seeing and not have the camera on. Similarly at the end of the shot. So even if the shot was great, it still needs to be cut at the beginning and the end, to make different beginning and end points than those that were captured by the recording, that is, to make it shorter. The experience of short term cinematic events thus means something different for the viewer and for the editor. For the viewer, a shot is a (relatively) short event in the sense that it ends before the next shot begins. It is short in the sense that the last frame of it is present at a certain moment. For the editor, the shot is short because there were more frames than the last frame that is going to be in the movie. The subsequent frames still exist on the cutting room floor (or in a digital file) but are cut out of the timeline. For the editor, the event is short not because it ends, that is, because it has a last present, but because it has been shortened from something longer, that is, because in the past, it had a successor that made it longer, but that successor is omitted.

This dual definition of the cinematic short term is inherent in all short terms: a time segment is short both because it has a last moment and because there is an extra moment after the last moment, which is not included when measuring its length. This is analogous to the definition of a finite number. On the one hand, a number is finite if it is the last member of a set of ordinal numbers. The set (1, 2, 3, 4, 5, 6) ends with the number 6, and 6 has no successor in the set, so 6 is a finite number. Of course, there is a successor to 6, it is just not a member of this particular ordinal set, so 6 is a finite number because it has a successor which is not a member of the set that ends with 6. Likewise for the set of frames in a shot.

Raymond Bellour divides films into "segments" (along with "super-segments," "sub-segments," and "micro-segments") (Bellour [1976] 2001: 198–202)[19] (comparable to Christian Metz's "syntagms"). Most segments consist of a relatively short sequence of images, which is relatively uninterrupted for its duration, and "punctuated" when it ends, for example, once there is a turn in the plot or a new character enters the frame (Bellour [1976] 2001: 195–8). However, a segment is not ultimately defined as an autonomous sequence, as if it might have counted as a short film of its own; a segment is rather defined by the way it fits into the *grande syntagmatique* of a film. It only becomes a segment, with its own meaning, when it has an effect on other segments. That is, a segment is not a one-unit piece that lasts a certain small amount of time on screen. Rather, a segment is defined by its ability to "rhyme" with other segments, which are usually not contiguous with it in time. For example, a segment where characters A and B enter a café together is a segment precisely when paired with another segment where A and C enter a café later in the film. Though a segment is cut at both ends, it is inherently conjoined with rhyming terms at a distance. It is cut off, or shortened, not by a quick cut to its immediate successor, that is, not by immediate continuations before and after, but by a long passage to the distant series, which it will only eventually be succeeded by. Any shot is a short term segment relative to the whole film; but its length is aesthetically indeterminate until it "echoes" in, and is measured alongside, its pair, that is, until it has "differential and repetition effects" (Bellour [1976] 2001: 197). A short piece of something is in this way not just a single piece but is, in addition, a shorter piece of a still short, but not as short, assemblage. The increasing divisibility of segments in their minor effects is part of the theory of segments. A cut within a cut is the temporal analogue of a frame within a frame: both are strategies built on cutting style: *découpage*. A frame does not just have smaller frames inside of it; a frame is cut *to* another frame.

To develop his theory of time-images in cinema, Deleuze activates Hölderlin's account of the caesura implied in the cut (Deleuze [1968] 1994: 87, [1983] 1986: 33). Hölderlin says that the caesura in Sophocles's plays cuts the drama into two unequal parts: the part before the gods reveal themselves, during which narrative expectation makes sense, and the part after, when the narrative is no longer worth pursuing due to the tragic collapse. There is no continuity across the cut: "Each twist of the spiral, or segment, divides up in its turn into two unequal opposing parts" (Deleuze [1983] 1986: 33). In some sense, every cut is a "jump cut" (Deleuze [1983] 1986: 35), a "qualitative leap" (Deleuze [1983] 1986: 37). Montage is not just about changing points of view but about the "intervals" of time that each one captures before it suddenly moves on to the next (Deleuze [1983] 1986: 37). Here, the segment is not about how soon it can end but about how long it can be prolonged before it cannot be prolonged any further.

Let us survey five innovations in film editing, to see how filmmakers' creations of short term events can be turned into concepts.

The first clip I recommend the reader look at now comes from an Indian movie, *Vettaiyaadu Vilaiyaadu* (*The Hunter Hunted*, Gautham Menon, 2006), starring heartthrob Kamal Hassan. The language of the film is Telugu, hence "Tollywood." Early in the film, there is a jump cut. Before Godard made jump cuts acceptable in the 1960s, a cut was supposed to do one of two things: (a) A cut could transition between two perspectives without interrupting the action: from a camera outside a house, we see a person turning the door handle, and without a gap in time, we switch to a camera inside the house showing the person step in. Many short shots may be strung together in a long scene, and as long as the cuts are edited continuously, like the short fast camera cuts of the short fast knife cuts in the shower scene in Hitchcock's *Psycho*, the scene as a whole may last a long time. (b) A cut could exit one scene and move to another scene at a distance: we see a person leave home, then suddenly we see them arrive at the office. What was not supposed to happen was (c) A person is walking down the sidewalk and, after a cut, is suddenly three steps further along. It was fine to cut across different angles in a continuous movement, and fine to move to another place discontinuous in space, but wrong to make a small jump in a continuous movement. That never happens in real life, and it makes no sense. Only an incompetent editor would do it. But Godard introduced jump cuts to have exactly this effect, to break the continuity while remaining inside a continuous action, to cut a person's actions in the middle and pick them up again for no obvious reason after a second's interruption, as if we had missed something. By now, fifty years after Godard, jump cuts have become an everyday tool in the filmmaker's repertoire. Viewers hardly notice them. We might even find that we do in fact experience such jumps in real life. But even an unobtrusive case like the one in *Vettaiyaadu Vilaiyaadu* has interesting implications. (Please watch it now. The hero and the heroine are riding on a motorcycle, their first romantic song together is beginning. We see them riding across the screen for a second—they start about sixty feet away from the camera (i.e., from us) and continuously approach us until they are about fifty feet away; then there is a jump cut and we suddenly see them forty feet away, ten feet closer to us than an instant ago; then we see them ride for a second as they continuously move from forty feet away from us to thirty; then another jump cut; we suddenly see them at twenty feet; and for the next second, they move continuously to ten feet away. End of scene.)

Without the cuts, the scene might have taken five seconds; with the cuts, it takes about three seconds. Normally, the whole ride from sixty feet away from us to ten would be one continuous shot with a cut at the end. Here, there are two additional cuts, with missing bits, inside the shot before the cut at its end. The shot subterminates before it really terminates. What is cut out in the jump is a tiny amount of time during which the motorcycle will have moved over a relatively small amount of space. The shot as a whole is short, and the cuts that make it shorter are themselves short; the shortening is itself short. It is not atomism, since we are not reduced to individual frames; it is not in stop motion. The shots are shorter than would be natural, but they are not the minimum. The short term is not perfected in the shortest, just in the shorter. In any case, the value of these cuts is not really to make the shot shorter, since they only save a second or so, and we are not that pressed for time. And to make the jumping device more useless, the shot is in slow motion. If it were played at full speed, it would already have only taken a second for the motorcycle to get from sixty to ten feet away. Directors use slow motion precisely so that we can spend time watching something of interest that would otherwise go by too quickly. The odd feature of this scene is that the shot is slowed so we can spend more time on it, but then, in compensation, it is jumped, so it will not be quite so long as all that. But the calculation of total time is not the game here. The jumps have added shortness value on their own, independent of the longer thing that they make shorter. Shortness is more a strategy of articulation than a quantity of time, even though quantity is where that strategy intervenes. This particular application of short term cutting does not, to my mind, make the scene more romantic, or more exciting. Maybe it is, finally, bad editing, but maybe all the same it is good short term.

The second clip I suggest you watch is by Godard, who in *Made in U.S.A.* (1966) experimented with jump cuts in sound.[20] Godard takes familiar melodies whose momentum makes us almost feel we can hear the continuation already, and cuts them short in the middle of a bar. Beethoven's Opus 49 piano sonata is cut short, then we hear a few notes of Beethoven's Symphony 5, which is cut short as well, and repeat. Either of these melodies cut short by itself would have been plenty irritating, but together, they suggest that a short thing is not only short in relation to its own long form but also in relation to a different thing's long form. J-cuts are a classic tool in editing, where the sound is cut at a different moment that the visual is cut; two people are in conversation, and the camera switches from one person's face to the other's while the first person is still talking. Non-synchronous parallelism is a general theme of Godard, expressed in the titles of several of his films: *Six fois deux, Numéro deux, 2 ou 3 choses que je sais d'elle, One P.M.* ("*One Parallel Movie*"). In the counter-cut jump, the jump across jumps, every cut, every short term event, is an intercut across two series. A series only ends short insofar as another series continues it, only to be cut short in turn. A single line cannot strictly speaking be cut short (a line on its own continues forever), but two lines can cut across one another in such a way that one or both are cut short at the cross-point. One or both lines may continue on the other side of the cross-point, and the shortness of the term of a line is even intensified when the line does continue on the other side. The short line is less emphatically short if it simply stops participating in the shapes to come, and more emphatically short if its longer form becomes present too, so that the short form is underlined by contrast. There may even be a way to make secondary use of a shortened line after it has been cut off and left behind (as in the game of Go).

While jump cuts interrupt continuity, one almost never wonders what happened between the two shots. We feel as if we virtually saw the intervening movements. The in-between is unimportant simply by virtue of having been skipped over. In fact, many acts of human seeing could have been shorter than they were, without loss of informational content. Many human experiences go on too long to be worth it. It is not that we do things too fast. Both slow and fast can be too long. And this is because often, not much happens in the middle period of events. I do not remember all the details of my drive to work yesterday, and if I had to write my autobiography including everything that happened to me last year, I would not know what to say about the majority of the moments. I am not sure whether to say that the last year of my life could have been shorter, lived in jump cuts, or if it is just that memory is retained in a montage of privileged instants. It may rather be that the length of experience is fine to endure in the event but that much of it is boring to recount later on. In Chapter 4, we mentioned experiments in which subjects provided with just a few facts remember them as a narrative that includes facts not in evidence; the converse is that a full narrative life could just as well be represented in a shortlist of its best representative experiences. In this respect, the short term is made possible by the natural phenomenological condensation of long continuities into experiential part-objects whose intermediating connections can be omitted without much bother.

This is not a manifesto for short experiences, since the same synthetic process that allows contraction into the short also allows expansion into the long. But rather than blandly concluding that some events are short and some long, I would like to try out the thesis that the long is a subcategory of the short. Look next at Marie Menken's abstract experimental film, *Eye Music in Red Major* (1961). You do not need to watch all six minutes, but watch enough to feel that it is a tad long for what it is. Its images are abstract, and there is no soundtrack, so by definition it is not fit to the length of any event, hence it cannot count as either longer or shorter than it should be. It is not that it feels long because it is a pain to watch—it is a pleasure to watch. It is a long experience derivative from a short time.

In contrast, now watch the Stargate sequence from Kubrick's 2001 (1968)—watch enough to feel the long term. Not much happens—astronaut Dave is plummeting toward the mysterious planet—and there is no dialogue, only amorphous music by Ligeti. Again, the scene is not fit to the length of some known event, so it cannot be either longer or shorter than it would take in real life. It cannot be measured in relation to an appropriate length, it is pure length. But this is just the sense in which the long is a special, stretched out case of the short, rather than the short being a defective case of the long. The long shot whose final cut is not motivated by objectivity is all in. When it eventually ends, it leaves nothing on the table to be continued. No remainders leak out the back end, no resources remain untapped. If a shot is just a little bit too long, its end just a bit delayed, then when it is cut short, the cut is not absolute, as there remains more to have been continued. In contrast, if the long is just plain long, until it goes away, then although of course it could have gone on indefinitely and we could still be watching hours of red major, or Stargate, on a loop until the wee hours, still, it cannot go on forever. When the long form ends, it is good and done. The terminating long term is absolutely short, whether or not it is relatively short.

Finally, watch a few minutes (13:00 to 17:00) of a brilliant ultra-low budget movie called *Who Killed Captain Alex?* (2010) by Isaac Nabwana. It was made in Kampala, capital of Uganda, in a neighborhood called Wakaliga, hence "Wakaliwood." Nabwana's VJ (video jockey) voice-over creates many novel interventions in the film, and you will hear the multi-tasking effects he gets. I do not know of any other movie where the director yells "What the Heck?" in the middle of his own film, as if he did not know what was going to happen, even though he has just warned us that it was going to happen. Some of his voice-over describes the action, some gives context ("Everybody in Uganda knows Kung Fu"), some advertises the sequel, some advertises the very movie we are watching (certain scenes within the movie function as short trailers for itself), in some, the VJ praises his own VJ work. We might call such voice-overs audio intertitles; they do not interrupt the visuals the way the intertitles in silent films did, but they have a similar effect in re-initializing the movie with announcements direct to the viewer. Watch also Nabwana's voice commentary over Buster Keaton's otherwise silent movie *The General*, in the Wakaliwood series "Supa Commandos of Film History," which yields a simultaneity-movie in the spirit of Woody Allen's *What's Up Tiger Lily?* (1966). The VJ's call in *Captain Alex*, "And now, Wakaliwood the

Musical" reboots a movie-within-the-movie into another genre. The first splash of blood (as Godard said when critics complained that his *Pierrot le fou* was too bloody, "It's not blood, it's red"; Godard might have said, "in the key of red") is like a *Wizard of Oz* turn from black and white to color, except that *Captain Alex* was already in color. Nabwana's peculiar mode of short term segmentation is to divide without resorting to division, to create short terms without the usual procedures for shortening. It is procedural short term, of course, giving away and bragging about its tricks the moment he uses them. Bragging is even the key trick, the self-reference that, more than the voice-over, colorizing, and genre-bending, breaks into the events with a second level, like the color commentary over a hockey game, an ironical commentary in an unironical tone.

Many directors break the fourth wall when a character speaks directly to the viewer (some directors hate that). I am not focused on aesthetic judgment, just as I am not focused on whether short term events are ethically good or bad, or whether short term perceptions are true or false. I am interested in how the short term can be constructed and, in particular, whether the short term can be constructed without divisions into discontinuous pieces. Film editing provides a procedural paradigm for thinking the short term given that time is indivisible. Even though it is now possible to construct a film without cuts (with digital cameras), the possibility of the cut is a formal constraint on the whole art form. Like all formal constraints, and like all limits that are surpassed the instant they are reached, and so like all temporal segments some part of which exceeds their end, the formal constraint of cutting short is as much a kind of freedom as it is a limit.

Shortness Constraints: Oulipo Poetics

The difference between a long text and a short one is complicated by Raymond Queneau's *A Hundred Thousand Billion Poems*.[21] This book contains ten sonnets. Each line of each sonnet is printed on a separate strip of paper. The sonnets are designed so that each of the fourteen lines in each sonnet can be substituted for its counterpart in each of the other sonnets, making a total of 1.1×10^{16} different poems. Is this book short or long? Because of transformation rules like this, converting short texts to long and vice versa, shortness cannot be defined as the simple extent of the text but as the possibility of constraining a text on parameters of extension. Something becomes short or long because a second, intervening mechanism makes it so. Lengths are plural in their root construction.

The short term can equally be the result of constraint, or of freedom. This is true for everything short, from historical processes, to how many hours I will sleep tonight. I use Oulipo to discuss short term by constraint, and I use prospective poetry to discuss short term by spontaneity. Oulipo is the *Ouvroir de la littérature potentiel*, founded in 1960 by mathematician François le Lionnais and poet Raymond Queneau. Its early members include Duchamp and Calvino; then later, Georges Perec, Jacques Roubaud, Harry Mathews, Michelle Grangaud, Jacques

Jouet, Hervé Le Tellier, and others. You are invited to a live reading once a month at the *Bibliotèque Nationale* in Paris. Le Lionnais wrote the manifesto:

> Every literary work is built on inspiration (at least, that is what its author wants you to believe), which must accommodate itself, for better or worse, to a series of constraints and procedures that are embedded inside one another like Russian dolls. Constraints of vocabulary and grammar, such as the constraints of the rules of a novel (division into chapters, etc.), or of classical tragedy (the rule of the three unities), constraints of general versification, constraints of the "fixed forms" (as in the case of the rondeau or of the sonnet), etc.[22]

The project of Oulipo is to stop pretending that inspiration precedes the constraints of technical procedures, and instead to analyze and invent constraints, and to use them to produce literature that will satisfy all of our usual expectations, and then some. The whole project might have resulted in gimmicks had Oulipo authors not been able to draw the most intense feelings out of harsh constraints. Before discussing temporal constraints, I mention a few amazing productions.

1. *La Disparition*, Georges Perec's 1969 book-length lipogramme, written without the letter "e," a touching novel about the disappearance of a loved one, along with the disappearance of the beloved letter "e." (See also Gilbert Adair's unbelievable translation into English, still without "e.")
2. "What a Man!" (a French text with an English title), Perec's 1980 two-page monovocalism whose only vowel is "a," and Jacques Jouet's amazing translation of this text, still in French, into "o."
3. S + 7: choose a text, and choose a dictionary. For each substantive in the text, count down seven substantives in that dictionary, and replace. Try it with, "In the beginning was the word," and make the substitutions, using several different dictionaries. The result, surprisingly, is theology.
4. The baobob, deploying sounds of words within other words. If the target sounds are "*vrai*" and "*faux*," when a poet reads aloud some line about how I loved you "*dans la forêt*," she will leave the syllable "*fo*" to be read by her nearby confederate, who will shout "*faux*" in its place, a loud yet silent commentary on the vagaries of love.

Oulipo has not experimented with as many purely temporal formal constraints as one might like. Perec's *Je me souviens* is a list of hundreds of small local memories, recording the ephemeral. Jacques Jouet's "Metro Poems" is a more direct case of temporal constraint:

>> What is a subway poem?
> From time to time, I write subway poems. This poem being an example.
>> Do you want to know what a subway poem consists of? Let's suppose you do. Here, then, is what a subway poem consists of.
>> A subway poem is a poem composed during a journey in the subway.

> There are as many lines in a subway poem as there are stations in your journey, minus one.
> The first line is composed mentally between the first two stations of your journey (counting the station you got on at).
> It is then written down when the train stops at the second station.
> The second line is composed mentally between the second and the third stations of your journey.
> It is then written down when the train stops at the third station. And so on.
> You must not write anything down when the train is moving.
> You must not compose when the train has stopped.
> The poem's last line is written down on the platform of the last station.
> If your journey necessitates one or more changes of line, the poem will then have two or more stanzas.
> An unscheduled stop between two stations is always an awkward moment in the writing of a subway poem.[23]

This temporal constraint is both rigorous (the line in the poem must be written between the time the subway leaves one station and arrives at the next; and every such time interval must be represented by one line of the poem) and yet uncontrolled, since the exact amount of time between stations depends on traffic. There is a limited amount of time to perform the writing act, and one knows only roughly when that limit will arrive.

One might imagine other temporal constraints: an order to complete a poem in an amount of time too short to accomplish it, so that the poem will end before it has been fully written; or an order to leave a long time lag between the time one part of the poem may be written and the time the next may be written, so that the poem will show gaps; or an order that poetry readings must be short, so that the audience will spend more time traveling to the venue than listening to the poems.

Oliver Pierre Bray uses Jouet's model to create an improvised performance within six minutes.

> The 30-minute performance was separated into five intervals of six minutes, my version of Jouet's metro stops as it were. These six-minute intervals had a major impact on the shape and tone of the performance. I spent many hours listening to an interval timer set to six minutes in order to understand that duration. I did this in an effort to comprehend the "shape" of that time, to be able to visualize the quantity of content and the kinds of narrative that could fit within in. Because the performance material wasn't fixed, and so there was no content to learn, this understanding of time was crucial—it was one of the constants available to me in terms of my understanding of the work—time was one of the few things that didn't shift. The six-minute sections gave the performances a pacey, urgent quality.[24]

Bray habituated himself over many hours to feeling exactly when a six-minute segment ends. Precise short terms are possible objects of experience, but not easy to attain.

Nesting stories within stories does not at first appear as a specifically temporal constraint, but there is a relation between short term and layering, for example, in the algorithms Calvino invented to compose *If on a Winter's Night a Traveller*, and in Queneau's overlapping histories in *Les fleurs bleus*.

Speaking of interlocking histories, philosophers know Raymond Queneau from another context, as the editor of Alexandre Kojève's 1930s lectures, *Introduction à la lecture de Hegel*.[25] According to Kojève, the foundation of Hegel's *Phenomenology*, speaking of embedded stories, is the intersubjectivity of desire:

> Human desire must relate to another desire. In order that there be human desire, there must first exist a plurality of (animal) desires, so that self-consciousness may be born out of self-feeling ... this reality must be essentially multiple. A human can only appear on earth inside a herd. (Kojève 1947: 13)

Feelings become conscious when one person's story is embedded in another's. Indeed, Queneau edited Kojève's text in such a way that Kojève's comments are embedded in parentheses inside Hegel's own text.

> {Hegel:} This evolution (of self-consciousness) will first manifest the inequality of the two self-consciousnesses. [{Kojève:} which is to say, of the two humans who confront one another in respect of recognition]. {H:} Or in other words, it makes evident the expansion of the middle term. [{K:} which is mutual and reciprocal recognition] {H:} in the two extremity points [{K:} who are the two who confront one another]. (Kojève 1947: 16)

Kojève/Queneau's text reads like an Oulipo event in which each member continues the previous member's story, with the advantage that Kojève's text also provides the dialectical proof that all human self-consciousness, society, writing, and planetary existence presuppose inter-nested layers. Inter-nesting is a necessary, and possibly sufficient, condition for evolution. Mutual recognition has a long impact, but it changes perspective suddenly, cutting across different subjective identities.

In fact, in addition to inventing interlocking subjectivity, Hegel invents just the relation between formal constraint and feeling that accounts for Oulipo's success.

Vibration, Digression, Improvisation: Hegel on Music

Pius Servien describes rhythm as "perceived periodicity" extracted from "the habitual flow of time."[26] Its elements are the long and the short.

The short form of music is the note. Its quantity is its "value." The large form of music, though still time-limited, is the performance. Whether rehearsed or improvised, performance has the now-or-never, time-has-come, no-second-chance constraint (which it shares with war and dating). It is not clear which performance is more risky and anxiety-producing: not to know what one is supposed to perform next, or to know what one is supposed to perform exactly without error. It is not clear which is more short term: a unique happening without a type, or a singular enactment of a type. The former sense of short term means "only once"; the latter means "each moment must be perfect."

Short term notes "vibrate" into short and long combinations. In the *Encyclopedia Philosophy of Mind*,[27] Hegel analyzes the "feeling soul" (*die fühlende Seele*), by analogy with music, in terms of its internal vibration. Whereas a purely monadic individual would be self-enclosed, and would feel nothing,

> the true self [must be] a different subject from [the monadic individual]—a subject which may even exist as another individual. By the selfhood of the [second individual] … [the first] is then set in vibration (*durchzittert*). (Hegel [1830] 1969: s. 405)

What a feeling soul feels is the presence of the other individual inside it. In this way, "the mother is the genius of the child" (Hegel [1830] 1969: s. 405). Following a digression into mind-reading, Hegel notes the dangers and benefits of a soul with "two different personalities," where new bodily feelings are added into the soul without overwhelming it (Hegel [1830] 1969: s. 409). The solution is not to cancel the plurality of feelings but to constrain them in a measured way. To control feelings, the soul makes its body "into an instrument, so that when a conception (e.g., a series of musical notes) is in me, then without resistance and with ease, the body gives them correct utterance" (Hegel [1830] 1969: s. 410). To put it differently, short term novelties enter into habitual fields—not to cancel but to measure them. In Hegel's *Aesthetics*,[28] the name for multiple insertions into a musical field is again "vibration."

Hegel likes music because it is so abstract. Painting tries to abstract too, by reducing space to two dimensions, or by extracting color from objects in the world. But space can only be fully abstract when it

> turns to movement, and so vibrates in itself that every part of the cohering body not only changes its place but also struggles to replace itself in its former position. The result of this oscillating vibration (*schwingenden Zitterns*) is sound or a note, the material of music. (Hegel [1829] 1966: 261/[1829] 1975: 890)

We do not hear a note externally but as an "inner vibration (*inneren Erzitterns*) of the body" (Hegel [1829] 1966: 261/[1829] 1975: 890). Musical vibrations are therefore not about nature or culture or emotion; music is free of meaning, and "expresses only the element of feeling" (Hegel [1829] 1966: 264/[1829] 1975: 894). Hence, differences in music are only differences in vibrations, in the laws of rhythm and harmony, in short and long time-quantities and the proportions among them. We could of course find a "theme" in a composition, but the theme is stated in a few seconds, and the rest of the piece would be superfluous if meaning were its substance. The form of music is flight and return (Hegel [1829] 1975: 897), repetition and elaboration, "eurhythmics" (Hegel [1829] 1975: 894). This brings us to the point that connects Hegel with Oulipo: formal constraint and freedom from content.

> A composer of a piece of music has liberty generally either to execute it within strict constraints (*gehaltener*) and to observe, so to say, a plastic unity, or, with subjective liveliness, to let himself go at will in greater or lesser digressions (*Abschweifungen*) from every point, or similarly to rock (*wiegen*) to and fro, stop capriciously, make this or that interrupt his course or rustle forward again in a flooding stream. (Hegel [1829] 1966: 267–8/[1829] 1975: 897–8)

To condense, there are three forms within composition: constraint, digression, and rock.

Hegel sometimes thinks of art as a way of constraining feeling. Interjections of cries and laughter, "the 'och' and 'oh' of the heart (*Gemüts*)" may express feeling, but until art turns them into "cadenced interjections," coordinating the "ensemble of differences" into structured "harmonies, oppositions, contradictions and modulations" (Hegel [1829] 1966: 273/[1829] 1975: 903), feelings like rage and joy remain "unbridled" (Hegel [1829] 1975: 939). His argument is not just that without "prohibitions" of form, the freedom to feel is capricious and vulgar (Hegel [1829] 1975: 929), though Hegel does sometimes say this. Nor is his argument just that harmony "restricts" what can be done within a key (Hegel [1829] 1975: 931), though Hegel says this too. The important argument is that calibrating the vibrations of the music to the feelings of a certain person, in relation to another certain person, and in a certain context, is precisely what keeps feelings from being abstract and empty. The mathematics of rhythm, harmony, and melody are what "gets hold of *this* man," making this person sing and dance or that one's restaurant experience appetizing (Hegel [1829] 1975: 905–7). The rules of musical form are not experienced as "dry numerical relations" or "general ideas" but as the body's trembling (Hegel [1829] 1975: 924), the "intensity" (Hegel [1829] 1975: 941) of one's own rage and joy (Hegel [1829] 1975: 933). Rossini, for example, makes our bodies become-joyous, Hegel says. In short, constraints channel feeling-vibrations into the intersubjective body. Hegel is the genius of Oulipo.

Most important are the constraints that call for digressions. Counting four beats in a bar already implies returning to the first beat in the next bar, renewing the vibrating power after an interruption (Hegel [1929] 1975: 915, Victor Zuckerkandl[29] shows how complex asynchronies are embedded even in common metrics). For Hegel, uniform motion implies heterogeneity and syncopation (Hegel [1929] 1975: 917); harmony implies drama and dialogue (Hegel [1929] 1975: 923); consonance tarries with dissonance (Hegel [1929] 1975: 929). To be sure, dissonance demands resolution—opposites are not going to resolve *themselves* after all (Hegel [1929] 1975: 928)—but there is no harmony until there are several voices simultaneously (Hegel [1929] 1975: 932), and consonance is only heard as a response to "transgression" (Hegel [1929] 1975: 933).

Hegel insists on the constraint that moves beyond limit and digression to rock. Constraint is the "battle *between* freedom and necessity" (Hegel [1829] 1975: 932). Librettos, for example, may appear to subsume musical variety in narrative coherence, but in recitative and declamation, what we hear are "unexpected accentuations, less mediated transitions, sudden changes and conclusions," fragments and pauses, disturbances and counter-flashes (Hegel [1829] 1975: 942–43), even irony and vaudeville (Hegel [1829] 1975: 951), even "caprice" and "ingenious freaks" (Hegel [1829] 1975: 955), even "improvisation" (Hegel [1829] 1975: 957) and the "grotesque" (*Barocke*) (Hegel [1829] 1966: 326/ [1929] 1975: 958). Formal constraint does not reduce, but produces, the effects of multiple layering, packing multiplicity into a single short term event.[30]

Hegel admits that "a well-founded treatment of the subject would require a more exact knowledge of the rules of composition ... than I possess" (Hegel [1829] 1975: 930). Imagine: Hegel admitting he needs other people to help him philosophize. But after all, that is the constraint of music itself, the multiplication of voices and instruments (Hegel [1829] 1975: 936), to feel the other's vibrations move one from within.

Of course, not all Oulipian constraints have this intersubjective effect. Some involve years of solitary work with jigsaw puzzles. But the whole idea of substitution rules and eidetic variation could be thought of as a logic of vibration, generating neighbors and classes, trills and mordents, plagiarists, genius mothers, and competitors.

In a Queneau story called "*Panique*," written in 1934, the second year of Kojève's lectures, a prospective tenant asks the landlady if he can count on the place being quiet: "*Elle rit pour bien montrer que c'était evident, comme si l'evidence faisait rire*" ("She laughs in order to show that it was evident, as if evidence made one laugh").[31] The burst of laughter, the noisy neighbors, the vicissitudes of inference, all locked into one short "as if."

Short Term Poetry without Constraint: Charles Olson's Projective Verse

The constraint of the premature ending may come from outside a process (when police break up a demonstration) or from an agent inside the process (when a poet decides to stop declaiming at midnight). Poetic cut-off may express the freedom of the short term rather than the constraint of it.

Charles Olson advocates speed. While his three-volume *Maximus* is a massive poetic investigation of Gloucester Massachusetts in the 1600s, which in the American context counts as a very long book about very long term history (the poems linger for hundreds of pages at every little turn in those old country roads), it is also a work of the very modern 1950s, some call it postmodern, cutting edge. Olson's *Special View of History* includes the rule: "Know the new facts early," which became the heart of Ed Sanders's political beat poetry.[32] Olson turns the long term field into the recency of new expression.

Olson's essay "Projective Verse"[33] rejects the primacy of form in favor of "OPEN verse" (Olson [1950] 1966: 15). He proposes four explanations. The first appeals to energy:

> Okay. Then the poem itself must, at all points, be a high energy-construct and, at all points, an energy-discharge (Olson [1950] 1966: 16). [Interjections, CAPITALS, parentheses, stuttering, and commas are Olson's.]

His second explanation appeals to quickness:

> ONE PERCEPTION MUST IMMEDIATELY AND DIRECTLY LEAD TO A FURTHER PERCEPTION. It means exactly what it says, is a matter of, at *all* points (even, as I should say, of our management of daily reality as of the daily work) get on with it, keep moving, keep in, speed, the nerves, their speed, the perceptions, theirs, the acts, the split second acts, the whole business, keep it moving as fast as you can, citizen. And if you also set up as a poet, USE USE USE the process at all points, in any given poem always, always one perception must must must MOVE, INSTANTER, ON ANOTHER! (Olson [1950] 1966: 16)

Get on with those "split second" acts, citizen. It is not clear why formal constraint could not say to do the same thing. Nor is it clear why quick replacement of one perception by another is more open, whereas leaving time before the successor is more closed. But Olson's point here is less about form vs no-form, and more about keeping each act short in order to keep moving. The important thing is that poetry not lag behind its next bit. Our concern is with Olson's invention of poetic short term.

The third explanation is temporal-stylistic: Olson is best known for breathers between lines:

> If a contemporary poet leaves a space as long as the phrase before it, he means that space to be held, by the breath, an equal length of time. If he suspends a word or syllable at the end of a line (this was Cummings' addition), he means that time to pass that it takes the eye—that hair of time suspended—to pick up the next line. If he wishes a pause so light it hardly separates the words, yet does not want a comma—which is an interruption of the meaning rather than the sounding of the line—follow him when he uses a symbol the typewriter has ready to hand:
>   "What does not change / is the will to change." (Olson [1950] 1966: 23)

Mobilize "that hair of time," the "pause so light" before the pickup that ends the pause and moves on. Speed is carried less by the density of perceptions than by the shortness of the interval between them. It is a separation (though "hardly separated"), not literally "immediate," as Olson had suggested before. But it is a separation whose shortness emphasizes the closeness of elements before and after. The short bits of time may need to be contrasted with longer breathing pauses, but when it is time for a short time, even a comma takes too long. The typed " / " is faster.

Olson's fourth explanation is explicitly temporal:

> Do not tenses, must they not also be kicked around anew, in order that time, that other governing absolute, may be kept, as must the space-tensions of a poem, immediate contemporary to the acting-on-you of the poem? (Olson [1950] 1966: 21)

Olson combines his critique of grammatical form with his advocacy of free action, in order to generalize about the time tensions of poetry. There is no grammatical intermediary, like verb tense, through which one perception connects to the next. However long the breath might take to get to it, it gets there without syntactical intermediaries, and in that sense, gets to the next straightaway. This need not always mean that there is only a short quantity of time between one point and the next, though Olson does like that; it means that there is nothing other than time (no formal mechanism) between one point and the next.

It may be that Olson's preferences around typography and breathing are not so different from Oulipo's constraints, except for the final idea, namely that for Olson, there is nothing other than time (no subway) that separates things in time. Moving through short lengths of time is for humans the art thing to do.

Chapter 9

"HAVE SHORT IDEAS" (DELEUZE AND GUATTARI): A GENERAL THEORY OF TEMPORAL SEGMENTATION

Argument: This chapter develops a general theory of temporal segmentation, and suggests further resolutions of outstanding problems from previous chapters dealing with short term memory, short term history, short term politics, short term aesthetics, short term phenomenology, and short term temporal ontology.

I have divided this chapter into two parts: Part 1: Short Term Events, and Part 2: A General Theory of Temporal Segmentation. Part 1 adds Deleuzian solutions to the problems of short term history and epistemology developed in Chapters 1, 3, 4, and 6. Part 2 repurposes Deleuze and Guattari's theory of micropolitical segmentation into a theory of temporal segmentation, and this functions as the conclusion to my own analysis of short term ontology.

Part 1: Short Term Events

At the end of "Rhizomes," Deleuze and Guattari recommend: "Have short ideas," "*Ayez des idées courtes*" (Deleuze 1980: 36/1987: 25).[1] Brian Massumi translates this as "short-term ideas." Eugene Holland connects short ideas with Deleuze and Guattari's stated preference a few pages earlier for "short term memory" (*mémoire courte*, Deleuze 1980: 24/1987: 16).[2] In "The Smooth and the Striated" Plateau, Deleuze and Guattari say that short term memory produces free and spontaneous connections, whereas long term memory makes things appear coherent after the fact. The worst kind of memory is "integrative memory," "the memory of an Oedipal childhood," which identifies, circumscribes, and represses.[3] When, instead, memory multiplies the rememberer and their pasts, as "molecular memory," as short term memory, it can be part of productive becoming.

Artists, say Deleuze and Guattari, create in the short term, making immediate use of their perceptions, whereas people who look at the art afterward do so from a long term perspective: "A painting is done at close range (*de près*), even if it is seen from a distance (*de loin*). Similarly, it is said that composers do not hear: they have close-range hearing (*rapprochée*), whereas listeners hear from a distance (*de loin*). Even writers write with short-term memory (*mémoire courte*), whereas readers are assumed to be endowed with long-term memory" (*mémoire longue*, Deleuze

1980: 615/1987: 493). Deleuze and Guattari's pairings do not always line up with the facts, since there are long-winded writers and short-tempered readers. But the point is that short term memory is not defined primarily by the quantity of temporal distance between perception and recollection. It is defined by practices of cutting perceptual horizons into pieces by multiplication. Past a certain point in a perceptual production, reproduction takes over, as the writing act passes over into the reading act. Perception and its repetition depend on localization, the interruption between what is inside and what is outside a temporal horizon, and the production of a new series on the other side of the cut.

The phrase "Memories of …" appears in many of the subtitles of the "Becoming-Intense" Plateau, but at a certain point, Deleuze and Guattari backtrack on their preference for short term memory: "Wherever we used the word 'memories' (*souvenir*) in the preceding pages, we were wrong to do so; we meant to say 'becoming', we were saying becoming" (Deleuze 1980: 361/1987: 294).

Whether short ideas are analogous to short term memories or not, we still need to know what short ideas are.

Subtraction

The simplest interpretation of the recommendation to have short ideas is that we should have ideas only for brief amounts of time. But on Deleuze and Guattari's assemblage model of ideas, where ideas connect and divide ad infinitum, it does not seem like ideas could remain short for long. Assemblage seems to extend the range of ideas, not to shorten it. Furthermore, Deleuze and Guattari recommend short ideas as examples of rhizomes, and they say (three times) that rhizomes neither begin nor end. Normally, what we mean by short term is precisely that the ending occurs shortly after the beginning. How can ideas that do not begin or end be short term?

But if assemblage seems to lengthen ideas, there is a proviso. The condition for assemblage begins with subtraction, not with +1 but with −1, because it begins by detaching things and ideas from their natural contexts. Just as a property detaches from its thing, the way the green of a leaf rubs off on one's pants, so also ideas detach from their context, after which they can re-attach to other ideas. In this sense, *idée courte* may refer to rhizomatic idea fragments more than to ideas that only last a short amount of time.

But perhaps there are still ways to construe short ideas temporally. First, the exhortation to short ideas might mean that as reality changes, prudence requires adaptation to new concepts. This sounds plausible, but the problem is that ideas, for Deleuze, do not represent states of affairs that change in chronological time but create problems that recur in different contexts. So short term changes in a state of affairs should not mean that ideas become passé, and only endure for the short term. The old saw that the only truth in the long term is that all truths are short term is not true. Or that a long journey is made up of short steps—also not true. Even if reality changes, having ideas that are relevant only until the next change is not a recipe for thinking across those changes.

A second pragmatic value of short ideas might be that since there are so many great ideas to be had, it would be imprudent to stick with any one for too long. A third value is that since different people (and animals) have different ideas, we should relay ideas frequently. But these are all pragmatic values of the short term, rather than immanent forces that divide time into short terms. A fourth possibility is that there is something inherent to time that imposes time limits on ideation. This is the strongest and most interesting reading, but it brings us back to the onto-phenomenological problem: if time is continuous, how can it be segmented into short terms? And even if it is possible, why do it?

Relative Short and Long Terms vs Absolute Short and Long Terms

I am going to distinguish relative and absolute short terms. Deleuze does not explicitly draw this distinction, but it fits his distinction between two (or three) structures of time, and also fits the distinction between relative and absolute deterritorialization.

Deleuze distinguishes successive, chronological time (called "chronos" in *Logic of Sense*, and "the first synthesis of time" or "the synthesis of the present" in *Difference and Repetition*) from co-existing layers of time (called "aion," and "the second synthesis of time" or "the synthesis of the pure past" in the same two texts). The former describes events insofar as they are embedded in temporal and social context, connected by causal relations to precedents and successors. The latter describes events as paradigms or diagrams, extractable from their contexts, virtually repeatable in different ways at various times and social contexts. It is not that the latter are non-temporal, but they are temporal in a different sense. Chronological events are temporal in the sense that they are positioned in an unbroken timeline of passing phenomena (an ongoing lived present), whereas virtual events are temporal in the sense that their repeatability (with differences) persists, in a set of virtual possibilities that co-exists with all periods of chronological time.

Sometimes, the properties of the two kinds of time are not what one might expect. For example, we might have expected that chronological events would be dated, but Deleuze and Guattari say in the "Postulates of Linguistics" Plateau that it is a mark of virtual, repeatable, events[4] to be dated "down to the hour, minute, and second" (Deleuze 1980: 103/1987: 81). Chronological states of affairs are certainly positioned in a longer context of measurable time, and that is of course a kind of dating. But marking an event with a date, like "January 1," "Juneteenth," "May 68," "Eighteenth Brumaire," "1776," "Earth Day," or "*le dimanche de la vie*," lifts it out of context and makes celebrations of it repeatable on schedule. '68, for example, has a status quite separate from that of 1967 and 1969; the events of '68 have a date all their own. This kind of evental intrusion into chronological time is precisely not a continuous division of time, it is an interruption of one kind of time (the chronological kind) with another kind of time (the virtual kind).

Dating enunciations that cut the before from the after, like Lenin's announcement that the revolution has begun, or like an announcement that devalues a nation's currency, seem to mark instantaneous divisions in time. They seem to be cutting instants rather than short durations. But in practice, devaluing the Deutschmark on a certain day in 1922 lasts for a certain short amount of time, until the next revaluation. For that matter, instant and duration are not always mutually exclusive. The instant, as Bachelard, the instant philosopher, implies, is the inauguration of a duration to come; and duration, as Bergson, the duration philosopher, says, is the continuity between qualitatively differential instantiations. In sum, the temporal concept of a date has two meanings, depending on whether we are talking about chronological time or virtual time.

There are other properties of time too, besides dating, that require two independent explanations, due to the fact that there are two independent, equally real, time structures. For example, the concepts of slow and fast require different definitions, depending on whether we are talking about chronological events or virtual events. A chronological event is slowly changing if each of its stages requires a quantitatively long interval to come to an end once it has begun; a virtual event is slowly changing if its repeatability is relevant to many qualitatively different contexts at a distance. Similarly, novelty and predictability are defined differently for chronological and virtual time. The point for us is that the concept of the short term depends on which of these two structures of time is at issue.[5]

Each of the two kinds of time—chronological-relative and aionic-absolute—has a justifiable way of dividing segments into short and long. And to add another complication, *Difference and Repetition* distinguishes not two but three syntheses of time: one described by retentions and protentions in the passing present (like chronological time in *Logic of Sense*); one described by co-existing repeatable events (like aionic time in *Logic of Sense*); and one described as the empty but determinable future (with no counterpart in *Logic of Sense*). Each of the three structures of time provides its own way of cutting time into segments: the first cuts the continuity of time by expanding and contracting temporal attention to longer and shorter portions during the lived present; the second cuts time into segments by differentiating repeatable events, some rare and some common; the third diverges at caesura-points into a plurality of possible futures none of which has happened yet. Each of these three functions—contraction into the up-until-now present (limits), de-contextualizing an episode for subsequent re-deployment (modules), and diverging into exceptional futures (precursors and drop-offs)—is a genuine way of generating and measuring temporal segments.

Deleuze is best known for the second kind of time, so I focus on the conception of the short term implied therein.

A Bit of Time in the Pure State

In *Proust and Signs*,[6] Deleuze connects pure time with "little bits of time." Proust describes a certain recurring melodic phrase, as "a bit of time in the pure state": "*un peu de temps à l'état pure*" (Deleuze 1964: 76). For Deleuze, time in a pure state does not mean eternity in general or as a whole[7]; it means that a series of elements (in this case, a series of musical notes) is repeatable, relayed into different conditions, returning each time the same but with a difference. *Qua series*, a melody consists of an initial tone prolonged into a limited number of pitches for a relatively short amount of chronological time, after which some other musical events happen. But *qua bit* of pure time, that singular series is repeatable, like a syntagm, either within the same composition as a theme or as the source point for variations by other composers. It may get stuck in a listener's head involuntarily. It may become a symbol for jealousy or a motif for a shark. In this way, though it seems strange to say, pure time is always instantiated in a "bit of time," as a short term series.

If we choose in this way to call pure time eternal, it will follow that eternity appears only in short term segments. In two passages, Deleuze uses the connector "that is to say" (*c'est à dire*) to define "a bit of time in the pure state": in the first passage, he defines a bit of time in the pure state as "the essence of localized time" (*l'essence du temps localisée*, Deleuze 1964: 76); in the second, he defines it as "a piece" or "a morsel" of time (*un morceau*, Deleuze 1964: 148). The second definition says that a series is only repeatable if it is limited to a portion of time. Time as a whole is all the time there is, so the whole of time cannot happen twice. Only a portion of time can happen twice. Only a segment of time can appear at a later time. Only small amounts of time are virtual. The first definition says that since it is a portion of time, its first appearance is a dated episode, that is, localizable in time. If its first appearance is then de-localized, so that as a virtual model, or an abstract machine, it can appear again later, then it is its second appearance that is localized (in Deleuze's later vocabulary, "reterritorialized"). This is the nature of any time segment: cut out of its individual context, it becomes a virtual model; once virtual, it can be put into a different individual context; a time segment is necessarily short, then unhinged from chronology, therefore potentially short again. Deleuze is interested in the political implications.

Short Term Politics: "Postscript on Control Societies"

Deleuze is interested in political events that arise suddenly and are over quickly, like the events of May 68. Short term events like this often have the longest term effects.

In the opening section of "Postscript on Control Societies,"[8] subtitled "Historical," Deleuze starts with Foucault's idea that institutions like prisons, which emerged in the seventeenth century, are "short-lived" (*brièveté*) (Deleuze 1990: 240/1995: 177). Their administrative solutions to social problems are situational and contingent, and will not last forever. But it does not follow that institutions take hold suddenly; on the contrary, they "took place gradually." Likewise, the breakdown of these institutions in the twentieth century results from "slowly moving" forces (Deleuze 1990: 241/1995: 178). At first, this seems paradoxical: new social forms arise slowly, but their life is short. In fact, there are two different time scales, depending on whether we are talking about how slowly they took hold, or how long they are expected to remain. To say that prisons, hospitals, school systems, and so on arose slowly means that they arose over the course of fifty years or more. To say they are short term historical phenomena is to say we expect them to last for a while longer, and then eventually to be replaced by other social forms. They have lasted since about 1750 (270 years). They might collapse a few years from now, or may last a few more centuries, but they are not likely to last 1,000 years. There is no contradiction in the juxtaposition of (relatively) slow origins and (relatively) short time spans.

However, it still seems conceptually paradoxical that slow-moving histories do not last longer than fast-moving ones. But Deleuze suggests a more ontological mechanism that limits slow-moving changes to a shorter term, and extends fast-moving changes into a longer term. A fast-arising event like May 68, which seems to be both short and fast, and seems to have a short life precisely because it burns so bright, is nevertheless long-lasting in the virtual way, precisely because its speed, its ability to get from inception to termination so quickly, gives it the power to instantiate itself repeatedly again and again.

For this point, we need to make use of the difference between relative and absolute short and long terms. Relative short and long terms are chronological, measuring a shorter or longer time scale between an event's beginning and end—defining beginnings and ends relative to predecessors and successors, measuring from the last point in time when the event was not yet, to the first point in time when the event will no longer be. In contrast, absolute short and long term pertain not to chronological time but to virtual events extracted from the temporal whole so that they can be put again into play at any given time. In that form, all events are short term, in that they have beginnings and ends that are not extended indefinitely into predecessors and successors. Yet in that form, all events are also long term in a different sense, in that they can re-enter the time line at any point in the future (in the way that short term working memories can be placed into an active memory buffer at any point in a person's lifetime). In this sense, absolute short term events are relative long term events. To put it simply, they are short by length and long by application.

In sum, the power of administrative institutions like the prison system is gained and lost slowly, and lasts a relatively short time (a few hundred years). But after the age of institutions, Foucault and Deleuze assert, a new kind of power system has emerged, one which controls the desire of individuals without large-scale, centrally organized, administrative institutions. This new form of power, the "society of control," promotes and distributes privately chosen niche desires (bio-power), consumption, point-to-point near-simultaneous communication, and lifestyle multiplication. I am not going to analyze this social theory here; the point in Deleuze I want to focus on is that this form of power arises and spreads more rapidly than large planned institutions do.

The temporal puzzle is that Deleuze says that the slow gains of institutional power were short term events, whereas the fast gains of control over desire is long term. Why is the slow not long, and the fast not short? The basic idea is that slow changes in big systems are made one step at a time, building up into results that are expressed by their successors—we have called those procedures relatively short and long, short pieces building into something longer. When gradual, they may be relatively long, but they are always made of relatively shorter pieces. In contrast, fast changes are made more suddenly, creating new desires for hurried gratification—we have called those procedures absolutely short. Since they are repeatable at any point in the future, not just for the duration of any stable institution, they are also absolutely long. This pattern allows Deleuze to say that slow history is short term and fast history is long term.

Deleuze says (citing Virilio) that after the Second World War, society has been changing with "ultrarapid advances" (Deleuze 1990: 241/1995: 178). On the surface, the transition from slow to fast changes in social forms is accelerationism. However, there is another paradox here, in that the old form departs more slowly than the new form arrives. In the way that Althusser and Balibar describe staggered social change,[9] anachronistic features of past ages persist in new forms, and futuristic elements prematurely arise in old ones. The same transitional event is fast in some places and slow in others, short term in some places and long term in others. This creates a double articulation of temporal cuts. From the standpoint of the earlier temporal segment, the cut is made gradually, as the past social form degrades over time. Yet from the standpoint of the later temporal segment, which is attached to the end of the first by succession, time-fullness does not arrive slowly but rapidly. The new social form replaces the old while the old is largely still there. For a certain amount of time, a time segment is filled to more than 100 percent fullness (which Kant's "Anticipations of Perception" would have said was impossible). The spliced-off end of the first segment covers a different amount of time than the spliced-on beginning of the second. One side of the cut is long term while the other side of the same cut is short term.

It is not that every single change is long in its old form and short in its new form. Only when events are accelerating is this true. As long as events progress at a constant rate of change, the old and the new segments are measured by a common standard. But the old and the new segments of accelerating events are measured by different standards. In this sense, the very idea of events accelerating from a standing position is equivocal; the first segment of the acceleration is not accelerating at all—that is the key to acceleration. Only the second segment accelerates, relative to the first. Such a historical development is not a sequence of slow*er* becoming fast*er* (that can happen too, but it is not what happened at the beginning of the current stage of history) but of slow becoming fast*er*. The point is that the two periods of social history operate on different time scales across the threshold of the change.

Indeed, this paradoxical form of continuation is precisely what is meant by short term. A time segment is short precisely in comparison with the long segment that hangs onto its backside.

After having discussed the transitions between socio-historical models, the second section of Deleuze's essay, entitled "Logic," treats the temporal procedures within each: "In disciplinary [institutional] societies, you were always starting all over again (as you went from school to barracks, from barracks to factory), while in control societies [this is us], you never finish anything" (Deleuze 1990: 243/1995: 179). In institutional societies, we used to repeat a series of procedures in one institution until we completed them, then we started a cycle in another institution. (School, then work.) In contrast, today, we undergo "*endless postponement* in (constantly changing) control societies" (Deleuze 1990: 243/1995: 179), crisscrossing overlapping structures without passing through customs. (Continuing education, permanent debt.) To be sure, Deleuze says, current society "vacillates" across both models at once (Deleuze 1990: 243/1995: 179). But the two models have "very different ways of doing things" (Deleuze 1990: 243/1995: 179) over time. Describing the change of temporal models across social changes will help us to explain why slowly changing events are overall chronologically shorter than fast-changing events.

Changing Directions and "Short Term Semiotics": Guattari

With every change in social direction, there is a change in temporal scheme. This is the basis of Guattari's "short term semiotics" in "*La causalité, la subjectivité, et l'histoire.*"[10]

According to Guattari, there are specific temporal codes for each region of politics (a temporal code for revolution, a code for getting old, etc.) (Guattari [1966–7] 2003: 174). Since political regions further subdivide, "time explodes into a thousand temporalities" (Guattari [1966–7] 2003: 174). Just as the same phrase, for example, "Bonjour, mon pote" (Guattari [1966–7] 2003: 178, which we might translate as "Hey, fella") does not signify in the same way when one bicycles past a friend on the street, as when one has just killed the Czar (Guattari [1966–7] 2003: 178), so also a date signifies differently for the Valley of the Kings and Silicon Valley. So when there is interplay among temporal signifiers of political regions within the same society, they produce zones of temporal ambiguity. "This is the Althusser operation: You are given as many temporalities as you want, but it is up to you to figure out how to rediscover some synchrony. You will never rediscover that" (Guattari [1966–7] 2003: 174).

The only way a set of signifiers can be univocal and systematic, temporally or otherwise, is at moments in history when no radical changes are taking place. Codes are recognizable only as long as a society is not undergoing history, that is, when no subjective decisions are being made, so that the system of meanings is in equilibrium. In contrast, where there is active history, there are no reliable codes. "History has nothing to do with the signifier. It is when it [history] swings into non-sense that the problem of the subject is posed, i.e., with the production of a representative of the subjective cut, starting with a 'supplementary' deployment in the order of the signifier" (Guattari [1966–7] 2003: 176).

In other words, when a historical period shifts, "the signifying chains lose control, and events are inscribed 'directly onto reality' according to a short term semiotic (*sémiotique à court terme*), which is incoherent and absurd, while waiting for the restructuring of a plane of reference 'structured like a language'" (Guattari [1966–7] 2003: 178).

The idea is not that a short term semiotic is a signifying system that only lasts for a short time. On the contrary, a short term semiotic is not a signifying system at all (admittedly, this is a provocative use of the term "semiotic"); a short term semiotic describes the period of confusion in significations during the historical transition between historically determinate signifying systems. A short term semiotic is precisely the moment at which the event of a changing situation is met head-on, in all its equivocations, without there being signifiers capable of describing it. At some point, a new set of signifiers will (probably) emerge to describe the new situation, and even possibly to describe the period of uncertainty between situations. But in the meantime, during the becoming, in the gap between signifying regimes, there is a different sort of semiotic, a short term semiotic. In this picture, the short term is not the contrary of the long term; the short term is the contrary of the signifying. It is the vague period of transition between measurable time-periods.

Short Term Control and Lack of Control

Guattari's idea of short term periods where signifiers lose control fits into the transition between Foucault's two kinds of social power. "Disciplinary" social power, which large institutions work with, insert individuals into functional positions. "Control" power incites each person to follow their own desires, to make their desires known so subjects can be sold whatever commodities and ideologies they enjoy. Disciplinary power is most suitable during stable periods of synchronic social systems, whereas the more individuated power of control suits interim periods of short term unorganized semiotics.

Deleuze's difficult formula is that "Control is short-term (*à courte terme*) and rapidly shifting, but at the same time continuous and unbounded, whereas discipline was long-term (*de longue durée*), infinite, and discontinuous" (Deleuze 1990: 246/1995: 181). Why would Deleuze say, contrary to the usual correspondences, that shifting short terms are continuous, and that the long term is discontinuous? The idea behind these attributions is that a term is made long because there is always a new separate stage adding to its length, whereas a short term shifts continually.[11] A long term event builds up by sticking on accretions and appendices, the way Gothic architecture adds more and more spires to a cathedral over the centuries, or the way that a person who perseveres in a bureaucracy is promoted into new jobs. The long term gets long by splicing together discontinuous segments. It is true that in order for discontinuous additions to make something long, the pieces have to count as stages of a single whole—not necessarily a continuous whole but a valuable whole. Long-term institutional power, which is designed to last, passes people along from stage to stage in what they think of as one enduring goal of self-improvement. Its unity is ideationally, though not materially, continuous. Institutional totalization, like that of an educational system organized by independent streams, levels, and grades, is thus dependent on an Enlightenment attitude, according to which people believe in universals that interpret diverse stages under a common concept of progress. Only in the Enlightenment do we believe in, and actualize, long term historical processes of this form. In the history of humanity, the Enlightenment period is rather short, but this short phase is a phase that constructs particularly long term processes. It is designed for modern humanity (organizable, docile, expressive, self-interested, progressive, and perseverant). Since this image will not last forever, the Enlightenment, and its way of measuring historical segments, has a built-in social term limit. The long term social form lasts only for the short time that this human type lasts.

In contrast, the modality of control in today's societies comes from each person's individual desires being reflected back to them. If an individual desires tradition, that is what they are sold; if they desire novelty, the same political system's open market provides it to them. The resilience of the control that reaches into individual desires is precisely constructed out of the short-term shifting of those desires.

This is the conclusion: short term shifters keep themselves going longer than long term institutions, because they adapt quickly to micro-changes. Of course, the short term is not necessarily more free, as we know. Sometimes large-scale power centers give us the governmental power to do good in society the way we choose to. Large-scale power centers also sometimes have the advantage of being too big to notice exceptions, leaving brief interstices in which their commands are delayed, and dissenters go unpunished. By the same token, shifting small-scale power can sometimes be all the more constraining. While it does not impose constraints from above, it is sometimes able to constrain freedom by inserting itself into molecular times in between larger time scales. Long and short term power models thus each have their ways of both adding to and subtracting from freedom, but their procedures are different. Freedom requires understanding the mechanisms of, and the resources for, both deploying and resisting, both time scales.

Let us summarize. (1) Relative short term events are extended across less chronological time, but absolute short term events are not merely extensions between the periods before and after. Absolute short term events are also absolute long term events, namely events that are repeatable at various times thereafter. (2) While everyday usage associates fast events with short term events, and slow with long, there is another sense in which fast events are extended into the long term. This is because fast sudden events without preparation are absolute short term events, that is, repeatable in segments, and absolute short term events are therefore also absolute long term events. This is not merely playing with words; it is a practical consequence of the capacity to shift social activities and contexts. Plastic, flexible, and variable strategies re-set as conceptual frameworks change, better than stable strategies that depend on specific conditions. (3) While everyday usage associates the slow and the continuous, it is the quickly changing that is continuous. The fast is long not because it is continuously the same but because it is continuously adapting.

Deleuze's essay "Postscript on Control Societies" ends with a hint of a different future, modern in the sense that it is relayed in short terms, yet not dominated by micro-political bio-power control: "Can one already glimpse the outlines of future forms of resistance?" (Deleuze 1990: 247/1995: 182). In economic terms, Deleuze would like to see the fluxes of capitalism used against capitalism. Can some emancipatory aspect of the short term be used against the politics of desire that otherwise keeps the short term under control? Can intensities of the short term relay resistance over the long term?

May 68: Why Did It Not Last? Did It Not Last?

Deleuze and Guattari's essay "*Mai 68 n'a pas eu lieu*"[12] suggests a possibility. Its guiding idea is that the only thing that can be eternal is what is brand new, and that it is just those events that are dated that cannot go out of date.

Events like May 68 are "unstable states that open a new field of possibles" (Deleuze [1984] 2003: 215). Revolutionary events—not necessarily the kind that change governments, but the kind that change desires—propagate themselves by putting small differences into resonance "inside individuals," across divergent states of affairs. In this way, an event "does not let itself become outdated" (*dépasser*)." When social phenomena are defined by small differences and fluctuations, they cannot die out, just because almost anything will prolong them in existence (as in the May 68 slogan, "*Début d'une lutte prolongée*"). Only a reactionary (*renégat*) would ever say an event like 68 is passé.

> There were many agitations, words, stupidities, and illusions in 68, but that is not what counts. What counts is that … a society saw with a single shock (*tout un coup*) that it contained something intolerable and also saw the possibility of something else. It is a collective phenomenon in the form: "let there be something possible, or I'll suffocate" … The event creates a new existence, a new subjectivity (new relations with the body, with time …). (Deleuze [1984] 2003: 215–16)

Of course, in order for an event to bring about a positive mutation, a society has to desire it (Deleuze [1984] 2003: 216). Deleuze and Guattari think that in the case of the American New Deal, it did. But the case of France 68 was mixed. Those in power preferred that it "settle down" (*ça se tasserait*) (Deleuze [1984] 2003: 216), and to a large extent, they got their wish. The crises that France is undergoing today (writing in 1984), on both the left and the right, are the "direct implication of the incapacity of French society to assimilate May 68 … Each time, the possible has been closed back down" (Deleuze [1984] 2003: 216). If revolutionary desire does not connect to people's desires, there is no guarantee that it will last beyond the moment of shock.

And yet, even if the event becomes dated in the eyes of contemporary subjects, the event itself escapes the place where it becomes outdated. The event as such is a permanent virtual possibility. The being of an event does not exist in the place where the outdated thing exists; the event itself "did not take place" in the chronological sense. It insists in the little shorter places whenever anyone remembers it with enthusiasm. It is not exhaustively described in the clichéd media pronouncements that May 68 belongs to the past, that it was naïve, that its good ideas have already been instituted anyways. Even if those media truisms have a bit of truth in them, that has nothing to do with the "possibles" of the event. (This is the way Sartre speaks.) The event as such persists in little divergences today between what (some) people desire and what society offers them, and these are the very same kinds of divergences that it introduced back in 68. It renews itself in every little question and refusal and wishful thinking and exceptional self-affirmation that does not fit the times. This kind of short term is not a small piece of control, but a repeatable moment of exception. Ultra-short in this way, it becomes virtual, and thereby is prolonged into the long term.

We can generally contrast the short term in politics and in memory. May 68 is *functional because it is virtual*; it works as a short term in the long term because it does not essentially take place. In contrast, short term memory, as working memory, repeats as long as it functions. It is *virtual because it is functional*. Short term memory and short term politics are both virtual and functional, but in opposite ways.

Combining the virtual with the functional, what might a general theory of short term temporal segments look like?

Part 2: A General Theory of Temporal Segmentarity

My speculative plan is to repurpose Deleuze and Guattari's theory of socio-political segmentation in the "Micropolitics and Segmentarity" Plateau into a theory of temporal segmentation. In some passages, Deleuze and Guattari make this easy; in others, I have to stretch.

The "Micropolitics and Segmentarity" Plateau starts with a tripartite version of the history of social forms we saw earlier. Premodern segmented societies have relatively independent power centers and distinct codes binding its different social groups. Modern institutional societies extend an over-coded power by relays throughout their territory. Today's control societies (sometimes called postmodern) insert themselves into individual desires, whose byproduct is that schizo-nomads can pursue lines of flight. As the Plateau continues, we find that these distinctions become fuzzy, since all societies have some segmentation, as well as some flows across segments. At first, premodern molecular, sectional segmentation seems more supple, and seems to allow more difference, than big modern molar segments. But in other ways, centralized societies can allow for more upward mobility within a shared framework. And fascist society raises another paradoxical combination in which an extreme central authority encourages out-of-control power frenzy at the local level. The distinctions between the segmented and the continuous thus undergo several revisions in the course of the Plateau. As I read it, differently structured societies destabilize and intercut each other, reshuffle each other's procedures, and operate most powerfully in the zones of indiscernibility at their porous borders. As a result, the segmented lines that define the structure of a society (or of anything else, including time) are both causes and effects of the flows between those segments. "Segmentarity is not grasped as something separate from a segmentation-in-progress operating by outgrowths, detachments, and mergings" (Deleuze 1980: 255/1987: 209). So to take a few examples, an economy is described both by the segmented line-items of a budget as well as by the flow of capital across sectors; a church both segments morality by categorizing sins and also wipes them away by a return to conscience;

statistics are both positivist quantities and waves of data-packs. Segmentation and counter-segmentation are part of the same process. The same holds for temporal segmentation.

What interests me is what happens when a temporal segment not only breaks off but at the same time "steers and emits flows (pilote les flux à quanta ... émet de nouveaux quantas)" (Deleuze 1980: 273/1987: 223). Wherever a segment (material, social, spatial, or temporal) ends, it emits a flow, out of which a next segment may begin. A segment is bunched up at its borders and limits, where it begins a difference. This makes for an odd theory of time, with time segments bunched up at pressure points. Strange as it is, that is how time flows in a segmented world.

As we have seen throughout, the ontological dilemma for a theory of temporal segments is that almost any process could be continued. True, a person can only drink until the wine runs out, but one can always change the substance. One can only live on November 25 until midnight, but living on November 25 is not really the name of a process that is cut short at midnight, it is the artificially named cut in the middle of a continuing process of living. A hard temporal exit would have to deterritorialize a part of time from the temporal whole, and to preserve the limits of that segment in the face of continued time passage. A temporal exit would have to reterritorialize on, or as, a different layer of time. What is a temporal segment?

Point Interruptions

"A machine may be defined as a system of interruptions or breaks" (Deleuze [1972] 1983: 36).

The most straightforward sense of a temporal segment is that exactly when one segment ends, the next begins. "Micropolitics and Segmentarity" begins this way, with processes found in institutional societies: "We are segmented in a *linear* fashion, along a straight line or a number of straight lines, each of which represents an episode or a 'proceeding': we have just finished one proceeding when we begin another" (Deleuze 1980: 254/1987: 209).[13] The first example is again: home, school, work. "School tells us 'You're not at home anymore'" (Deleuze 1980: 254/1987: 209). After finishing school, people go to work—I didn't, but lots of people do. So what does it mean to pass the end of a segment?

In *Anti-Oedipus*,[14] Deleuze and Guattari first describe technical machines, like batteries and socks, which obey the logic of "until": they work until their work is finished, or until they wear out, after which they do not (Deleuze 1972: 38/[1972] 1983: 31). They then sketch a classification system for different types of breaks (*coupures*): (a) "detachment breaks" (*coupures-détachements*), (b) "slicing-off breaks" (*coupures-prélèvements*, or lifting-off, or skimming-off breaks), and (c) "residual breaks" (*coupures-reste*) (Deleuze 1972: 47/[1972] 1983: 39–40). Detachment breaks happen in broken chains (like a half-built border wall). They include brain lesions and sentence fragments, and they include the phallus as a detached object (Deleuze [1972] 1983: 73), as well as capital detached from land ownership (Deleuze [1972] 1983: 245). Sometimes not just material bricks but time itself is cut into "bricks and blocks," a term Deleuze and Guattari borrow from the

Monakow-Mourge bio-neurology of the 1920s to describe the brain's "chronogenic" system, by which different stages of mental growth emerge in different parts of the brain at different times. This is the simplest kind of interrupted flow, and it is the case of interruption most easily applied to temporal segmentation. A chain is broken off, and at the broken end, some other process is located.

Other break-types include "hiatuses and ruptures, breakdowns and failures, stalling and short-circuits, distances and fragments" (Deleuze [1972] 1983: 42). Whenever something is segmented, it is broken off by an interruption, but the interruption is a combination that extends the series in a different way. We might draw paradigms from the way stages of a rocket separate, or the way cells divide.

Ultimately, however, successively starting and stopping the stages of processes at different times turns out to not be what Deleuze and Guattari mean by short term, because the only kind of machines that that kind of detachment describes are technical machines. The other sorts of machines are desiring machines, and the latter do not break into segments only when their function comes to an end, they break apart precisely when they are working best: "desiring machines work only by continually breaking down" (Deleuze [1972] 1983: 8). When desiring machines break down, that is how they keep going. They work precisely because they do not function in a proper, continuous way. A desire functions just by converting our nightmares into filmscripts, or by contriving for us against all odds to love somebody, by getting a technical machine to short circuit, to disengage the car's muffler to make it macho, or to emote with emojis. (Deleuze and Guattari appeal to Dali's clocks.) Interruptions in this second form are not two-stage events, where one process ends before the next begins. These interruptions are rather connectives (Deleuze [1972] 1983: 5), so that at a certain point, a process becomes itself "and," simultaneously, another process (Deleuze [1972] 1983: 14). A schizo takes shape not because a person changes qualities or becomes a different person instead of the person they were, but because another person gets added on top without erasing the first at all. For a schizo, when a process stops, it does not really stop. In this case, Deleuze and Guattari ask, "What is meant here by 'succeeding'? The two [predecessor and successor states or persons] co-exist" (Deleuze [1972] 1983: 11). It is not that one proposition describes a schizo in the short term until another truth holds; each truth short circuits the one before by grafting onto it and overcharging it. Repulsion, paranoia, detachment, and castration are not about getting rid of something but about preserving something in a way that wanders about as a part-object. The schizo violates the tense logic of "until." For the schizo, layering staggered continuations are the source of a new kind of short term, a short term not structured by detachment but by overlap.

All these desiring machines of interruption have one thing in common, namely that what constitutes a short term episode between one break and the next is inseparable from the flows within and between those periods. Temporal segmentation is just what makes time flow.

To put it slightly differently, interruption "draws off part of a flow" (Deleuze [1972] 1983: 5). Desire pulls part-objects out of a flow of experience, making them fragmentary and temporally segmentary; it also "constantly couples continuous flows" across those fragments. A detached part-object is desired wherever and whenever one goes. The relation between a flow and an interruption, a continuity and a fragment, is reciprocal: "Every 'object' presupposes the continuity of a flow; every flow the fragmentation of the object" (Deleuze [1972] 1983: 6). Flows and individuation, deterritorialized continuities and territorial segments, production and anti-production, are equal players in the schizoanalysis of anything. True, it may often seem that Deleuze and Guattari are saying that the flow is the real, and the cut just an appearance that results from failure to see the bigger flow. If that were the situation, any apparent short term event would be illusory. But Deleuze and Guattari do not treat interruption as an error of interpretation. On the contrary, fluidity depends on interruption (Deleuze [1972] 1983: 8). Even though interruptions are precisely not irreparable divisions in the long run, they constitute a real sense of the short run. This requires, as is usually the case with Deleuze and Guattari, an inversion of the usual conceptual associations. Usually, we think of undifferentiated flow as the long term, and fixed identities that emerge out of the flow as short term phenomena. But if we instead focus on the way that fixed identities, or substances, are introduced into ontology precisely to explain how certain things endure over time in spite of accidental changes, we could then say that it is identity that plays the role of the long term, and it is the flow without identity, which changes not just by quality but by substance, over time, that plays the role of short term fluctuations.

This means that segmentarity, and temporal segmentarity most of all, while an artifact of interruption, is not ontologically spurious. As we saw, while "activity is continuous, segmentarity is not something separate from a segmentarity-in-progress operating by outgrowths, detachments, and mergings" (Deleuze 1980: 255/[1980] 1987: 209). In other words, while continuities and cuts seem like opposites, they are both effects of the same merger. Or to say it differently, there is never just one long or short magnitude; numbers are always numbering and numbered by other numbers, or in Hegel's terms, quantities are ratios. If segments are provisionally divisible, they are also accumulating; distances in time are both nearer and farther away than they appear; and a temporal cut that contains one episode whole also contains part of another. It is not merely that short term segments are in the eye of the interpreter, but that there are many temporal terminators emerging and demerging at all points along a duration. On the one hand, "each segment has its own unit of measure" (Deleuze 1980: 257/[1980] 1987: 211): while in school, there are indeed fifty-minute segments of class time, on vacation, there are no such segments. But on the other hand, "there is [sometimes] a translatability between units" (Deleuze 1980: 257/[1980] 1987: 211). This is obvious if we focus on activities like speaking while eating, which overlap over time and have different units of measure. And it is true of time itself. Time does not run along a single line of equal units, but rather in a bundle of threads, like a nodal line, with knots of different accelerations and delays, where time passage occasionally leaps or hesitates around localizable zones of indiscernibility.

Even with these complications around the measurability of commensurable time segments, the point of all segments, whether rigid or supple, is to describe sequences that go from point to point, where different series diverge at the point of a point. The logic of transition is that "*each* point continues to emit independent sequences" (Deleuze 1980: 257/[1980] 1987: 211).

Point Emissions and Temporal Leakage

After the problem of the provisional cut, the next essential element for a theory of time segments is thus the problem of point emission. A time segment does not end time for good; there is no conflagration of worlds at the end of each time segment, and no cycle of eternal return that starts with each new segment. Yet the next point after the last point in a segment is not just an extension of the same segment either. A time segment does not simply end, and it does not simply not end. The character of a time segment is that a temporal turning point occurs at its threshold. The last point of a segment is a different sort of time element than the point before it. A terminating point is not only a time marker; it is also a time emitter. For an amount of time to be short, it does not really matter how much time there had been before the last point comes, what matters is that the last point of a segment emits a point that that segment does not contain, but the new segment does.

This pattern has many variations. There are microsegments too short to notice when we have left them behind, like single pulses. Other thresholds look like the edge of a cliff, which leave us too short-sighted to imagine getting past them (as Mark Fisher says about the difficulty of imagining past the end of capitalism[15]). Some time segments seem like too much of a squeeze even to contain their own points, the temporal equivalents of the cramped rooms that Kafka's clerks work in (Deleuze 1980: 275/[1980] 1987: 225).[16] Others are segments whose successors are not contiguous but "skip from point to point" (as Deleuze and Guattari say of fascism).[17] Michel Serres suggests that time be thought not just as passage but as *pissoir*, a "sieve" or "filter."[18]

These labyrinthine patterns on the time line raise the general problem of "where to draw the line" of beginnings and ends of segments (Deleuze 1980: 265/[1980] 1987: 217). When did I start to get hungry, when did I begin composing this sentence, did I start composing the sentence before or after I got hungry? Ambiguities at beginning and end points reveal that leakages between temporal segments are zones of indiscernability.

The leakage between segments brings us closer to the second and third types of interruption: "skimming-off breaks" and "residual breaks" (Deleuze [1972] 1983: 39–40). Deleuze and Guattari begin with kitchen utensils that slice ham, which break a contiguous solid in order to pile up separated slices of the same thing. But they are more interested in inserting a bi-valve nozzle into a thing, so that different fluids flow out of it—to use their example, the way the penis alternates emitting urine and semen (Deleuze [1972] 1983: 36). Once a solid has multiple exits for extrudate to pass through, there are lots of resources for using, or not using, inflows and outflows. Deleuze and Guattari cite the way that closing one's eyes can intensify certain pleasures (Deleuze [1972] 1983: 37). Of course, just because a cut will almost always release a flow does not mean we want to cut everything we see without delay. (Let the roast rest for ten minutes out of the oven; if you cut into it right away, the juices will leak out prematurely and your dinner party will be dry.) The question for us is whether and how diagrams of cuts and flows might describe the flow of time. Many philosophers are for good reason skeptical about the metaphor of "time flow," just as others are for good reason skeptical about the alternative metaphor of the "block universe of time." But the metaphor of flow is complex and resilient, since flow is not merely the succession of one damn thing after another but the passage of extrudate from the inside of one block, though a series of tubes and valves, to the outside of that block, into the open space around, and into nearby recipients, if any. If there is such a thing as the flow of time, it will look like that.

The vocabulary of "flow," and "leak," as in *fuite d'eau* (water leak), is the same as the vocabulary of "flight" in *ligne de fuite* ("line of flight"). This is how Deleuze and Guattari define a line of flight: as a line that "leaks out between segments and escapes" ("*Comme si une ligne de fuite … coulait entre les segments et s'échappait …*," Deleuze 1980: 263/[1980] 1987: 216).[19] In this way, even though "temporal leakage" makes use of the metaphor of time "flow," its function is almost the opposite. A time leak precisely escapes the time flow. Or to say it in reverse, time flow depends on escaping from time passage. The valve at the threshold of a temporal segment literally allows two time-series to exit from a single point, at the same time, in staggered co-existence. To test this in practical experience, try boxing, or film editing, or listening to philosophy in a language one barely speaks, or playing the game of Go.

Leakage is different from implication. In a "rigid" system of interactions, one process leads to another process taking over; a more "supple" system includes "knots" at which divergent ideas begin, not by inference or by natural necessity but because excess is produced that at some point risks overflowing the container. "There is always some line that flows or flees, that escapes the binary organizations" (Deleuze 1980: 263/[1980] 1987: 216). It is not obvious whether lines of flight are best described with the vocabulary of segmentation and leakage, and Deleuze and Guattari even consider the possibility that "the words 'line' and 'segment' should be reserved for binary and molar organization, and other, more suitable words should be sought for molecular composition," for example, words like "quantum flow" (Deleuze 1980: 264/[1980] 1987: 217). But if we ask whether we ought to call a line of flight a segment of its own type (it is obviously not binary, and since it leaks, it has no definite end, but it may have an end point of a different kind), perhaps the best way to use the vocabulary of segmentation is to answer yes. Just as, temporally, there is one kind of short term for chronological time and another for virtual time, so ontologically, there will be one kind of short term for molar segments and another, more fluid kind, for molecular flows.[20]

In other Plateaus, Deleuze and Guattari offer musical examples of temporal leakage. The first is improvisation, which they describe as finding what is there in front of one: "To improvise is to join with the World, or meld with it. One ventures from home on the thread of a tune" (Deleuze 1980: 382/[1980] 1987: 311, "On the Refrain"). This differs from switching to a new theme or key signature.

Improvisation does move on from the previous line, but uses the last as the first of what was not yet there when the last was there, to venture away in such a way that what used to be home becomes retroactively what was already leaking. Deleuze and Guattari's second musical example of temporal leakage is rubato, which they describe as "freeing non-pulsed time" (Deleuze 1980: 329/[1980] 1987: 269, "Becoming-Intense"). Rubato markings leave it to the performer how much time to rob from some notes to give to others, to experiment with tempo trade-offs across different series in the same composition. It is not here the pitch of one note that leaks into the next (as when a pianist holds a note with the sustaining pedal while touching the next); it is speed itself that leaks between time segments. There are several different tempos at work simultaneously, which a given phrase accelerates or decelerates into, catching up with or zooming ahead of the speed that it leaves behind. "It is as though an immense plane of consistency of variable speed were forever sweeping up forms and functions, forms and subjects, extracting from the particles and affects. A clock keeping a whole assortment of times" (Deleuze 1980: 332/[1980] 1987: 271). It is not a change in tempo, a new tempo after the last, but leaking tempos pulling leftover speed that had not been used up.

This allows Deleuze and Guattari to say about fast and slow what we have been saying about short and long, namely that "Speed and slowness are not quantitative degrees of movement, but rather two types of qualified movement" (Deleuze 1980: 460/[1980] 1987: 371, "Nomadology"). Faster and slower may in some cases simply be degrees of quantity, but becoming-faster and becoming-slower in leaking phenomena like rubato are also qualitatively different: leaking-forward and leaking-backward.

The point is that whenever there is a stop and a new start, there is a leak between them. This might sound atomistic, as though the time between two marked positions is made up of temporal particles that leak from one to the other, as though a sub-piece of the previous time segment detaches from that amount of time, and slides over into the next amount of time, and the transport of that piece of time is what continuity is. I do not want to get caught in a Lucretius cartoon, but what is at stake is that a single time segment is machinic, with differentiated working time-parts: one time-part to emit a flow, one to cut into its forward edge, one to float on ahead, and so on. A line of flight is leaked temporal free matter. ("Free matters" is a term Hegel adopts from eighteenth-century chemistry.[21]) When leaked matter is found in the next segment, then "segments are like reterritorializations" (Deleuze 1980: 268/[1980] 1987: 219). But in its own right, temporal leakage is temporal deterritorialization.

As sometimes happens, Deleuze's theory of time becomes the opposite of Bergson's. Bergson's argument for the unquantifiability of time is the apparently obvious thesis that whereas in space we can move a yardstick from one place to another, and thereby measure one segment of space by re-positioning it to overlay another segment of space, we cannot move an amount of time from one time to another, and therefore cannot measure whether two amounts of time are the same length. Deleuze and Guattari's thesis that something leaks from one time segment to the next surprisingly suggests that in fact we can move one segment of time to the time of another time, and that that very oddity accounts for how time is segmented in the first place and, conversely, how it is continuous.

As a bonus, temporal leakage explains "the difference between macro-history and micro-history" (Deleuze 1980: 270/[1980] 1987: 221). Deleuze and Guattari hold that this latter distinction "has nothing to do with the length (*longeur*) of the durations, long or short (*le grand et le petit* [here they do not say *courte*])." Short term history does not mean short duration, it means that "the flow continues beneath the line, forever mutant" (Deleuze 1980: 270/[1980] 1987: 221). On my take, this metaphor of the flow beneath the line is not as good, not as machinic, as the earlier metaphor of leakages between lines. I think that as a matter of reality, time is relayed as one time segment off-gasses into a successor, and is not a measureless substrate "beneath" the line. But both metaphors (the wavy ocean and the leaky pipes) express one idea in common, namely that something short is not short because of its length, but because it emits the thing that will make something else become long. No doubt, there are time segments that simply are short on duration. But on the leaky principle, every bit of time is both too tight and too loose (life is short but the day is long); a short term could be either short or long, or both, or have no length at all. The short term is rather the procedure for passing back and forth between segments of any sort. As a time-experiencer, I do not have to do anything special to get time segments to shorten, leak, and move aside. To get the time segment when I am writing to you here to overlap with the times we will each be eating later, it is enough that time itself is already leaking on its own.

Plugging the Leaks Disjunctively

The general procedure of flow is: escape, shape, reshuffle. It is true that some segments are relatively rigid, but the processes that cut and paste segments into the montage of time trend against rigidity: "Where just before we saw end points of clear-cut (*bien tranchées*) segments, now there are indistinct fringes, encroachments, overlappings, migrations, acts of segmentation that no longer coincide with the rigid segmentarity" (Deleuze 1980: 278/[1980] 1987: 228). Segments with indistinct fringes (with no precise end points) overlap and migrate in fluxes. This is the supple in-between in all segmentation.

Since segments are not natural divisions, but are cut into shape by something like a decision, a segment is always merely the territorial contour of deterritorialized matter. Indeed, the more deterritorializable matter is, the more it is segmentable in different ways—and time is the most deterritorializable matter of all. This is why deterritorialization is so powerful, because it can order flows in a manner that flows. Deterritorialized flows can thus overflow, and over-power, rigid forms. "The most deterritorialized flow determines the dominant segment; thus the dollar segment dominates currency, the bourgeoisie dominate capitalism, etc." (Deleuze 1980: 276/[1980] 1987: 226). Trade overpowers monetary policy, consumer psychology surprises portfolio management, and swarm robotics is more efficient than classical artificial intelligence. "Segments, then, are themselves governed by an abstract machine" (Deleuze 1980: 276/[1980] 1987: 226).

Finally, after temporal interruptions and temporal emissions, we have to say something about temporal plugs. When a segment emits a flow, and the flow is reterritorialized, the flow becomes a segment (again) (Deleuze 1980: 268/[1980] 1987: 219). In such a situation, the flows "conjugate." They undergo a "relative stoppage, like a point of accumulation that plugs or seals (*bouche ou colmate*) the lines of flight" (Deleuze 1980: 269/[1980] 1987: 269/220). But a plug is not a binary on/off switch. In fact, the question of whether or not there is a stoppage between segments is answered only in the form of an inclusive disjunction: "We could also put it this way: lines of flight are primary, or [*ou* is in italics] the already-rigid segments are, and supple segmentations oscillate between the two" (Deleuze 1980: 271/[1980] 1987: 222). Bergson uses disjunctions in this way also: "I call two flows simultaneous when they are equally one *or* two."[22] Time is not linear, and it is not cyclical either. Time is disjunctive.

Deleuze and Guattari do not say that "neither" flows nor segments are primary, and they do not say that "both" are primary; rather, they say that one "*or*" the other is primary, and that the thing that swings between the two keeps their disjunction real (Deleuze [1972] 1983: 12). A "point of disjunction" is not a point where an alternative is decided and selected against the others, it is a point where "an entire network of new syntheses is now woven into a body" (Deleuze [1972] 1983: 12). Their sociological example involves migrant barbarians, who swing between "coming and going" on the one hand and, on the other hand, "assigning themselves a segment of the empire" (Deleuze 1980: 272/[1980] 1987: 223). There is a pragmatist element in this description, which makes the nomadic short term not a definite property but a challenge "to translate as best they can flow quanta into line segments" (Deleuze 1980: 274/[1980] 1987: 225). Pragmatism does not mean taking the best guess, it is a strategy of disjunction, a laying up of rhythmic resources. Precisely when there is disjunction, where there is "one or several (*une ou des*) ..., there is a war machine" (Deleuze 1980: 271/[1980] 1987: 222). The temporal analogue is that a short term is always a swing away from the long term, but in addition, which is to say, *or*, a short term only hypothetically makes a cut in the long term continuum.

This combination of a quasi-plug with a definite emission explains how there can be ontologically real and pragmatically buildable short term segments in continuous time. A breakdown is less like a single machine stopping, and more like one machine permeating and corrupting its pair. This is what we expect from temporal deterritorialization: a non-symmetrical intersection in discontinuous vectors and broken chains, where every cut is a cross-cut, pluralizing a line, and forcing a temporal encounter with its own difference. The practical consequence is that, as we have seen with many concrete examples, it is not always obvious whether a given idea is short or long. A state of affairs in itself is neither short nor long, it sways into short or long by the segments it emits. Deterritorialization is a short term-making machine: a short term machine breaks a long term machine into other short term machines.[23]

The downside of letting flows into segments and vice versa is that each cell might be infused with too much of the intensity of the flow that gushed into it: viral memes, not to mention viral viruses, paranoia, microfascisms, that sinking feeling. Happily, the solution to emitting sick flows and connecting to segments better left in the fuzzy past—in fact, the solution to all the dangers of a too unsegmented flow—is to connect with still more other lines. The solution both to segments and to flows is to connect segments. The solution both to short term enthusiasm and long term redundancy is to emit the short term again.

General Conclusion, Short Version: Free Use of the Resources of Both Short and Long Term Temporalities

Short and long term are complicated and interactive concepts, schematized by interlocking variations, dialectically coming to be in a pluralized network of continuous and discrete magnitudes. The concept of the short term is not only quantitative but also qualitative and functional, and understanding the highly varied operations of the short term gives us resources for managing the temporal properties of a vast range of ethical, political, aesthetic, cognitive, conceptual, and ontological spheres.

We have used a wide range of operations in analyzing the phenomenon of the short term: variability along multiple parameters of temporal measure (Introduction); cuts and the surpassing of limits in time-consciousness (Chapter 1); existential finality and its remainder (Chapter 2); short and long events and trends (Chapter 3); the relation between quantity and function in short term memory (Chapter 4); the quantification (and qualification) of short terms in physics and mathematics (Chapter 5); the value of the short term according to a variety of ethical systems (Chapter 6); the innovative use of short term resources in practical activities (Chapter 7); the control of short term creation in several art forms (Chapter 8); the short term escape from fixed social norms (Chapter 9 Part 1); and a general theory of temporal segmentation (Chapter 9, Part 2). In one way, these are all elements in the same problem of temporal segmentation: its measures and operations, cuts and overflows, blockages and extensions, interlayering and cross-cuts, anticipations and productions, images and interventions. Phenomenology, dialectics, multiplicities, arts and sciences, ideals and practices all contribute to the schematic conceptualization of temporal control and temporal freedom. But in another way, different short term forms are distinct temporal formations, only possible in their own fields of expression, which converge conceptually but diverge structurally when they encounter other short term forms at some moment in time. Short term crossover situations, however long they may last, arise whenever short term events are defined as short term in relation to other short term events. The pattern of temporality is never simple succession. It is the multi-layered crosscutting of variable mobile segmentation.

NOTES

Introduction

1. Some authors hyphenate short-term and long-term, and some do not. I do not hyphenate when writing my own sentences, but when I quote other authors, I retain their spelling.
2. Vladimir Mayakovsky, *How Are Verses Made?*, trans. G. M. Hyde (London: Jonathan Cape, [1926] 1970), 37.
3. Jay Lampert, "Husserl and Hegel on the Logic of Subjectivity," *Man and World* 21 (1988): 363–93; Jay Lampert, "Limit, Ground, Judgement ... Syllogism: Hegel, Deleuze, Hegel, and Deleuze," in *Hegel and Deleuze*, ed. James Vernon and Karen Houle (Evanston, IL: Northwestern University Press, 2013), 183–203.
4. Jean-Paul Sartre, *L'Age de raison* (Paris: Gallimard, 1966), 315.
5. Fredric Jameson, *The Prison-House of Language* (Princeton, NJ: Princeton University Press, 1972), 72.
6. Michael Fowler, "Graduate Classical Mechanics Lecture Notes," https://galileoandeinstein.phys.virginia.edu/7010/home.html (accessed March 2021).
7. Marshall McLuhan, *Understanding Media* (New York: Signet Books, 1964), 57–70.
8. Émile Benveniste, "*Le langage et l'expérience humaine*," in *Problèmes de linguistique générale, 2* (Paris: Gallimard, 1974), 67–78.
9. Alain Badiou, *The Century*, trans. Alberto Toscano (Cambridge: Polity Press, 2007), 12–13.
10. Gunter Nitschke, "*MA*: Place, Space, Void," *Kyoto Journal*, May 2018, https://kyotojournal.org/culture-arts/ma-place-space-void/ (accessed March 2021). Based on a talk at Cornell University in 1976.
11. Michael Kramer, *Manifestation and Revelation of Psyche: A Phenomenological Study of the Sense of Psychedelic Experience in Its Aesthetic and Noetic Dimensions*, PhD Diss. in progress, Duquesne University, Pittsburgh.
12. Paul Morand, *The Man in a Hurry*, trans. Euan Cameron (London: Pushkin Press, [1941] 2015), 14.
13. Ibid., 30.
14. Laszlo Krasznahorkai, *Baron Wenckheim's Homecoming*, trans. Ottilie Mulzet (New York: New Directions, 2019), 291.
15. Jay Lampert, *Simultaneity and Delay* (London: Bloomsbury, 2006).
16. Frantz Fanon, *The Wretched of the Earth*, trans. Constance Farrington (New York: Grove Weidenfeld, [1961] 1963), 68.
17. Steven Pinker, *Enlightenment Now: The Case for Reason, Science, Humanism, and Progress* (New York: Penguin Books, 2019).
18. Gilles Deleuze and Félix Guattari, *A Thousand Plateaus*, trans. Brian Massumi (Minneapolis: University of Minnesota Press, 1987), 367.
19. "Ideal" sciences like geometry employ only exact essences, but "morphological" sciences, which analyze "sensuously intuitable shapes" (which I take to include shapes

of time-consciousness), employ vague essences: "The *vagueness* of such concepts, the circumstance that their spheres of application are fluid, does not make them defective; for in the spheres of knowledge where they are used, they are absolutely indispensable, or in those spheres, they are the only legitimate concepts." Edmund Husserl, *Ideas Pertaining to a Pure Phenomenology and to a Phenomenological Philosophy, First Book*, trans. F. Kersten (The Hague: Martinus Nijhoff, [1913] 1983), section 74, 166.

20 Alexander Humez et al., *Short Cuts: A Guide to Oaths, Ring Tones, Ransom Notes, Famous Last Words, and Other Forms of Minimalist Communication* (Oxford: Oxford University Press, 2010).

21 Thomas De Quincey, "The English Mail Coach," in *Selected Writings*, ed. Philip Van Doren Stern (New York: Random House, [1849] 1937), 915.

22 Ibid., 934–5.

23 David L. Weimer and Ellie Karls, "Negotiating Values: Implementing Rubric Change in Transplant Organ Allocation," presented at the Conference of the American Political Science Association, 2022.

24 Gérard Genette, *Narrative Discourse: An Essay in Method*, trans. Jane E. Lewin (Ithaca, NY: Cornell University Press, [1972] 1980), 106, 127.

25 James Chen, "Short Term Paper," *Investopedia*, https://www.investopedia.com/terms/s/short-term-note.asp (accessed March 2021). James Chen, "Commercial Paper." *Investopedia*, https://www.investopedia.com/terms/c/commercialpaper.asp (accessed March 2021).

26 Bonnie Lambourn, "Capturing the Ephemeral: Altars, Mandalas, and Time Capsules: Similarities in Ritual—Depictions of a Culture," *Houston Teachers Institute*, 2006, https://uh.edu/honors/Programs-Minors/honors-and-the-schools/houston-teachers-institute/curriculum-units/pdfs/2006/photography/lambourn-06-photography.pdf (accessed February 2021).

27 Enrique Vila-Matas, *A Brief History of Portable Literature*, trans. Anne McLean and Thomas Bunstead (New York: New Directions Books, 1985), 4.

28 Franz Kafka, "The Cares of a Family Man," trans. Willa and Edwin Muir, in *Collected Stories*, ed. Gabriel Josipovici (New York: Alfred A. Knopf, [1919] 1993), 183–5.

29 "Quick," *Online Etymology Dictionary*, https://www.etymonline.com/word/quick (accessed February 2021).

30 Robert Walser, *Microscripts*, trans. Susan Bernofsky (New York: New Directions Books, 2012).

31 Valentin Goranko, "Temporal Logic," *Stanford Encyclopedia of Philosophy*, 1999, revised 2020, 4.2 "Adding Since and Until," https://plato.stanford.edu/entries/logic-temporal/ (accessed March 2021).

32 John Mbiti, *African Religions and Philosophy* (New York: Anchor Books, 1970), 19–36.

33 Not all African philosophers agree with Mbiti. See Kwame Gyekye, *An Essay on African Philosophical Thought: The Akan Conceptual Scheme* (Philadelphia, PA: Temple University Press, 1987), 169–77.

34 Macedonio Fernandez, *The Museum of Eterna's Novel (The First Good Novel)*, trans. Margaret Schwartz (Rochester, NY: Open Letter Press, 2010), 43.

35 "Granger causality," *Wikipedia*, https://en.wikipedia.org/wiki/Granger_causality (accessed December 2020).

36 Rachel Carsons, *Silent Spring* (Boston, MA: Houghton-Mifflin, [1962] 2002), 6–7.

37 Slavoj Zizek, "Series Forward," MIT Press "Short Circuits" series (Cambridge, MA: MIT Press, 2009).

38 Marshall McLuhan, "The Motorcar: The Mechanical Bride," in *Understanding Media* (Cambridge, MA: MIT Press, [1964] 1994).
39 Mathias Nilges, *Right Wing Culture in Contemporary Capitalism: Regression and Hope in a Time without Future* (London: Bloomsbury Academic, 2019), 1. See https://longnow.org/clock/ (accessed December 2022).
40 "The Immortality of Writers," in *Ancient Egyptian Literature: The New Kingdom*, ed. Miriam Lichtheim (Berkeley: University of California Press, [circa 1200 BCE] 1976), 177.

Chapter 1

1 Maurice Merleau-Ponty, *Phenomenology of Perception*, trans. Colin Smith (New York: The Humanities Press, [1945] 1994), 420–1.
2 Immanuel Kant, *Critique of Pure Reason*, trans. Norman Kemp Smith (New York: St. Martin's Press, [1781] 1929); *Kritik der reinen Vernunft* (Hamburg: Felix Meiner Verlag, [1781] 1990).
3 G. W. F. Hegel, *Philosophy of Nature*, trans. A. V. Miller (Oxford: Clarendon Press, [1842] 2004); *Enzyklopädie der philosophischen Wissenschaften II, Werke 9* (Frankfurt am Main: Suhrkamp Verlag, [1842] 1970).
4 Ernst Pöppel, "Lost in Time: A Historical Frame, Elementary Processing Units, and the 3-Second Window," *Acta Neurobiologiae Experimentalis* 64 (2004): 295–301.
5 Edmund Husserl, *The Phenomenology of Internal Time-Consciousness*, trans. James S. Churchill (Bloomington: Indiana University Press, 1964), section 10, 48. See my *Simultaneity and Delay* (London: Bloomsbury Academic, 2012), 21–30.
6 Nicolas de Warren, *Husserl and the Promise of Time: Subjectivity in Transcendental Philosophy* (Cambridge: Cambridge University Press, 2009).
7 James Dodd, "Reading Husserl's Time-Diagrams from 1917/18," *Husserl Studies* 21 (2005): 111–37, especially 113.
8 Edmund Husserl, *Logical Investigations*, 2 vols., trans. J. N. Findlay (New York: Routledge, [1900] 2001).
9 Salomé Jacob, "Husserl's Model of Time-Consciousness and the Phenomenology of Rhythm," in *The Philosophy of Rhythm: Aesthetics, Music, Poetics*, ed. Peter Cheyne et al. (Oxford: Oxford University Press, 2019), 291–306.
10 Edmund Husserl, *The Crisis of European Sciences and Transcendental Phenomenology*, trans. David Carr (Evanston, IL: Northwestern University Press, [1936] 1970).
11 G. W. F. Hegel, *The Science of Logic*, trans. A. V. Miller (Atlantic Highlands, NJ: Humanities Press International, [1812] 1989).
12 Segun Gbadegesin, "Yoruba Philosophy: Individuality, Community, and the Moral Order," in *African Philosophy: Traditional Yoruba Philosophy and Contemporary African Realities* (Bern: Peter Lang, 1996).
13 Jay Lampert, *Synthesis and Backward Reference in Husserl's Logical Investigations* (The Hague: Kluwer Academic, 1995).

Chapter 2

1 Blake Victor Kent et al., "Forgiveness, Attachment to God, and Mental Health Outcomes in Older U.S. Adults: A Longitudinal Study," *Research on Aging* (2017): 1–24.

2. Sheena M. Horning et al., "Atheistic, Agnostic, and Religious Older Adults on Well-Being and Coping Behaviors," *Journal of Aging Studies* 25(2) (2011): 177–88.
3. Roman Jakobson, "On a Generation That Squandered Its Poets," trans. Edward J. Brown, in *Verbal Art, Verbal Sign, Verbal Time*, ed. Krystyna Pomorska and Stephen Rudy (Minneapolis: University of Minnesota Press, 1985), 111–32, especially 123.
4. T. R. Simon, A. C Swann, K. E. Powell, L. B. Potter, M. J. Kresnow, and P. W. O'Carroll, "Characteristics of Impulsive Suicide Attempts and Attempters," *Suicide and Life Threatening Behavior* 32(suppl.) (2001): 49–59.
5. Carol Parrot, "Death with Dignity as an End of Life Option," *Death with Dignity*, https://www.deathwithdignity.org/faqs/ (accessed January 2021).
6. Akira Kurosawa, *Ikiru* (Japan: Toho, 1952). Lyndall Hobbs, *Dead on Time* (Great Britain: Michael White Productions, 1983).
7. Søren Kierkegaard, "At a Graveside," in *Three Discourses on Imagined Occasions*, ed. and trans. Howard V. Hong and Edna H. Hong (Princeton, NJ: Princeton University Press, [1845] 1993), 69–102. I thank Dan Cook for this reference.
8. Sensodyne, https://www.youtube.com/watch?v=28TJpDHKljU (accessed October 2021). Brush twice daily.
9. Cosmo Sheldrake, "Eggs and Soldiers," from the CD, *The Much Much How How and I* (London: Transgressive, 2018). I thank Hector Lampert-Bates for this reference.
10. Simone de Beauvoir, *The Coming of Age*, trans. Patrick O'Brian (New York: W. W. Norton, [1970] 1996).
11. Velimir Khlebnikov, "The Trumpet of the Martians," in *The King of Time: Selected Writings of the Russian Futurian*, trans. Paul Schmidt (Cambridge, MA: Harvard University Press, [1913] 1985), 126–9.
12. She seems to be referring to Bachelard's *La formation de l'esprit scientifique* (Paris: J. Vrin, [1938] 2011).
13. Arthur Schopenhauer, "Additional Remarks on the Doctrine of the Vanity of Existence," in *Parerga and Paralipomena*, Volume 2, trans. E. F. J. Payne (Oxford: Oxford University Press, [1851] 1974), 283–90.
14. Walter Benjamin, "Moscow," in *Walter Benjamin: Selected Writings*, Volume 2, Part 1, 1927–30, ed. Michael W. Jennings et al. (Cambridge, MA: Harvard University Press, [1927] 1999), 22–46.
15. Theodor W. Adorno, "Free Time," in *The Culture Industry* (London: Routledge, [1972] 1991), 187–97.
16. Elie Metchnicoff, *The Prolongation of Life: Optimistic Studies* (1908), trans. Peter Chalmers Mitchell) (Delhi, India: Lector House Books, [1908] 2019). I owe this reference to Enrique Vila-Matas' novel, *Never Any End to Paris*, trans. Anne McLean (New York: New Directions Books, 2011), a book whose title refers to a different long term phenomenon, namely the unending effects of having spent a year of one's youth in Paris.
17. See Yuri Dolgushin's fiction, "Rays of Life" (1939), based on the work of biologist Porfirii Bakhmetyev, in *Red Star Tales: A Century of Russian and Soviet Science Fiction*, ed. Yvonne Howell (Moscow: Russian Information Services [1939] 2015), 181–95.
18. *2045 Strategic Social Initiative*, http://2045.com (accessed January 2021).
19. Dmitry Itskov, "Want to Be Immortal? Act!," http://www.immortal.me (accessed January 2021).
20. Illah Reza Nourbakhsh (Professor of Robotics, Carnegie Mellon University), "The Coming Robot Dystopia: All Too Human," *Foreign Affairs* (2015), https://www.foreignaffairs.com/articles/2015-06-16/coming-robot-dystopia (accessed January 2021).

Chapter 3

1. Paul Ricoeur, *Time and Narrative*, Volume 1, trans. Kathleen McLaughlin and David Pellauer (Chicago: University of Chicago Press, [1983] 1984). Volume 2 ([1984] 1985). Volume 3 ([1985] 1988). My references in the text cite volume as well as page number.
2. Ricoeur cites many philosophers and historians. With the exception of Braudel and Simiand, I omit their names.
3. Martin Heidegger, *Contributions to Philosophy (From Enowning)*, trans. Parvis Emad and Kenneth Maly (Bloomington: Indiana University Press, [1938] 1999).
4. Matthias Fritsch, *Taking Turns with the Earth: Phenomenology, Deconstruction, and Intergenerational Justice* (Stanford, CA: Stanford University Press, 2018), 159–62. Also Tristana Martin-Rubio, *Becoming Otherwise: A Critical Phenomenology of Aging*, PhD Diss., Duquesne University, in progress.
5. Jean-Paul Sartre, *Critique of Dialectical Reason Volume 1*, trans. Alan Sheridan-Smith (London: Verso, 2004).
6. Jean-Paul Sartre, *Cahiers pour une morale* (Paris: Éditions Gallimard, 1983).
7. "10 Historical Events That Were Much Shorter Than You Thought," *Listverse*, https://listverse.com/2015/08/20/10-historical-events-that-were-much-shorter-than-you-thought/ (accessed December 2020).
8. See my discussion of branching tense logic in *The Many Futures of a Decision* (London: Bloomsbury Academic, 2018).
9. Because it is mapped by divergences rather than by trends, the historical long term is very different from a historical whole. See Manuel De Landa, *A Thousand Years of Nonlinear History* (New York: Swerve Editions, 1997), on Braudel's long term and Deleuze's microsegmentarity.
10. Fernand Braudel, "History and the Social Sciences: The *Longue Durée*," trans. Immanuel Wallerstein, *Review (Fernand Braudel Center)* 32(2) ([1960] 2009): 171–203.
11. The idea that the long term is an antidote to specialization remains prevalent. Jo Guldi and David Armitage, *The History Manifesto* (Cambridge: Cambridge University Press, 2014).
12. Étienne Balibar, "Sur les concepts fondamentaux du matérialisme historique," in Louis Althusser et al., *Lire le Capital* (Paris: Presses Universitaires de France, 1996), 419–568. See also my "Theory of Delay in Balibar, Freud and Deleuze: *Retard, Nachträglichkeit, Décalage*," in *Deleuze and History*, ed. Jeffrey A. Bell and Claire Colebrook (Edinburgh: Edinburgh University Press, 2009), 72–91.
13. Robert Rollinger, Julian Degen, and Michael Gehler (eds.), *Short-term Empires in World History* (New York: Springer, 2020).
14. Alfred Jarry, *Exploits and Opinions of Dr. Faustroll, Pataphysician*, trans. Simon Watson Taylor (Boston, MA: Exact Change, 1996), 21.
15. Carl Schmitt, *Political Theology*, trans. George Schwab (Chicago: University of Chicago Press, 1985), 5.
16. Michel de Certeau, *The Practice of Everyday Life*, trans. Steven Rendall (Berkeley: University of California Press, [1974] 1984), 77–90.
17. Pierre Bourdieu, *The Logic of Practice*, trans. Richard Nice (Stanford, CA: Stanford University Press, [1980] 1990), 99–100.

18 François Simiand, "*La psychologie sociale des crises et les fluctuations économiques de courte durée*" (*Annales sociologiques, Série D, Sociologie économique, Fasc. 2*, 1937): 3–32. (Based on lectures given at the Collège de France in 1934–5.)
19 Nassim Nicholas Taleb, *The Black Swan: The Impact of the Highly Improbable* (New York: Random House, 2010).
20 Friedrich Nietzsche, *Human, All Too Human*, trans. R. J. Hollingdale (Cambridge: Cambridge University Press, 1997), 12–13.
21 G. W. F. Hegel, *Philosophy of History*, trans. J. Sibree (New York: The Colonial Press, [1837] 1900).
22 See my "Dates and Destiny: Deleuze and Hegel," *Journal of the British Society for Phenomenology* 33(2) (2002): 206–20.
23 Stefan Skrimshire, "The End of the Future: Hegel and the Political Economy of Deep Time," *International Social Science Journal* 62(205–6) (2011): 325–38.
24 Ricoeur's account of variable beginnings, middles, and ends is similar to Noël Carroll's in *The Philosophy of Motion Pictures* (London: Wiley-Blackwell, 2007).
25 Ricoeur refers to Deleuze's book *Proust et les signes* (Paris: Presses Universitaires de France, 1964) on the relation of time to truth (Ricoeur 1985: 3:131). Ricoeur describes Vinteuil's little musical phrase as a case of associative memory, but not as "a bit of time in its pure state," which is Deleuze's focus.
26 Walter Abish, *Minds Meet* (New York: New Directions, 1975).
27 Karlheinz Stockhausen, "… how time passes …," *Die Reihe* (1956): 10–40.
28 See my discussion of musical time in *Simultaneity and Delay* (London: Bloomsbury, 2006).
29 See Ralph Stephenson and J. R. Debrix, *The Cinema as Art* (Harmondsworth: Penguin Books, 1965), chapter 4. Also, Gregory Currie, *Image and Mind: Film, Philosophy, and Cognitive Science* (Cambridge: Cambridge University Press, 2008), chapter 7.
30 Italo Calvino, "How I Wrote One of My Books," trans. Iain White, in *Oulipo Laboratory* (London: Atlas Press, 1996), 1–20.

Chapter 4

1 Edmund Husserl, *The Phenomenology of Internal Time-Consciousness*, trans. James S. Churchill (Bloomington: Indiana University Press, [1928] 1964).
2 Roman Jakobson and Krystyna Pomorska, "Dialogue on Time in Language and Literature," in *Verbal Art, Verbal Sign, Verbal Time*, ed. Krystyna Pomorska and Stephen Rudy (Minneapolis: University of Minnesota Press, [1980] 1985), 11–27, especially 20.
3 Nelson Cowan, "What Are the Differences between Long-Term, Short-Term, and Working Memory?," *Progress in Brain Research* 169 (2008): 323–38. Page references are to the online text at https://www.ncbi.nlm.nih.gov/pmc/articles/PMC2657600/ (accessed March 2019).
4 Bart Aben, Sven Stapert, and Arjan Blokland, "About the Distinction between Working Memory and Short-Term Memory," *Frontiers in Psychology* 3, Article 301 (2012): 1–9, www.frontiersin.org (accessed March 2019).
5 K. A. Ericsson and W. Kintsch, "Long Term Working Memory," *APA Psychological Review* 102(2) (1995): 211–45.

6 Brandon Rohre, "Recurrent Neural Networks (RNN) and Long Short-Term Memory (LSTM)," https://www.youtube.com/watch?v=WCUNPb-5EYI (accessed August 2018).
7 Gray Umbach, Pranish Kantak, Joshua Jacobs, Michael Kahana, Brad E. Pfeiffer, Michael Sperling, and Bradley Lega, "Time Cells in the Human Hippocampus and Entorhinal Cortex Support Episodic Memory," *PNAS* (*Proceedings of the National Academy of Sciences*) 117(45) (October 27, 2020): 28463–74.
8 Daniel L. Greenberg and Mieke Verfaellie, "Interdependence of Episodic and Semantic Memory: Evidence from Neuropsychology," *Journal of the International Neuropsychological Society* 16(5) (2010): 748–53.
9 Wolfgang Ernst, *Chronopoetics: The Temporal Being and Operativity of Technological Media* (London: Rowman and Littlefield, 2016).
10 Dennis Morris, "Short-Term Memory and Long-Term Memory Are Still Different," *APA Psychological Bulletin* 143(9) (2017): 992–1009.
11 Jean Saint-Aubin and Marie Poirier, "The Influence of Long-term Memory Factors on Immediate Serial Recall: An Item and Order Analysis," *International Journal of Psychology* 34(5–6) (1999): 347–52.
12 Fielding Cage, "Why Time Feels So Weird in 2020," https://graphics.reuters.com/HEALTH-CORONAVIRUS/TIME/gjnvwwjegvw/ (accessed January 2021).
13 Tetsuro Matsuzawa, "Comparative Cognitive Development," *Developmental Science* 10(1) (2007): 97–103. (I owe this reference to Hector Lampert-Bates.)
14 Jesse J. Langille and Richard E. Brown, "The Synaptic Theory of Memory: A Historical Survey and Reconciliation of Recent Opposition," *Frontiers in Systems Neuroscience* 12(52) (2018), https://doi.org/10.3389/fnsys.2018.00052 (accessed March 2021). Memories may survive in spite of synapse destruction, and short term memories may resurface later due to long term plasticity and neural networking. See Catherine Malabou, *What Should We Do with Our Brain?*, trans. Sebastian Rand (New York: Fordham University Press, 2008).
15 Margarita Kaushanskaya et al., "Gender Differences in Adult Word Learning," *Acta Psychologica* 137(1) (2011): 24–35.
16 Holger Jahn, "Memory Loss in Alzheimer's Disease," *Dialogues in Clinical Neuroscience* 15(4) (2013): 445–54.
17 Michael D. Franzen and Hout, "The Psychological Treatment of Memory Impairment: A Review of Empirical Studies," *Neuropsychology Review* 2(1) (1991): 29–63.
18 Henry W. Mahncke et al., "Memory Enhancements in Healthy Older Adults Using a Brain Plasticity-Based Training Program: A Randomized, Controlled Study," *Proceedings of the National Academy of Sciences* 103(33) (2006): 12523–8.
19 Mayo Clinic, "Amnesia," https://www.mayoclinic.org/diseases-conditions/amnesia/diagnosis-treatment/drc-20353366 (accessed May 2019).
20 Mayo Clinic, "Dissociative Disorders," https://www.mayoclinic.org/diseases-conditions/dissociative-disorders/symptoms-causes/syc-20355215 (accessed January 2021).

Chapter 5

1 Wolfgang Ernst, *Chronopoetics: The Temporal Being and Operativity of Technological Media* (London: Rowman and Littlefield, 2016).

2. *Fermilab Today*, "Planck Length, Minimal Length?," https://www.fnal.gov/pub/today/archive/archive_2013/today13-11-01_NutshellReadMore.html (accessed March 2021).
3. Goethe University Frankfurt am Main, "Zeptoseconds: New World Record in Short Time Measurement," *PhysOrg* (October 16, 2020), https://phys.org/news/2020-10-zeptoseconds-world-short.amp (accessed March 2021).
4. Bob Yirka, "Theorists Calculate Upper Limit for Possible Quantization of Time," *PhysOrg* (June 26, 2020), https://phys.org/news/2020-06-theorists-upper-limit-quantization.html (accessed March 2021).
5. Moses Maimonides, *The Guide for the Perplexed*, trans. M. Friedländer (New York: Dover, [1190] 1954), I, 73, "Twelve Propositions of the Kalam," 120–33.
6. Richard Sorabji, "Time and Time Atoms," in *Infinity and Continuity in Ancient and Medieval Thought*, ed. Norman Kretzmann (Ithaca, NY: Cornell University Press, 1982), 37–86.
7. Richard T. W. Arthur, "Time Atomism and the Ash'Arite Origins for Cartesian Occasionalism Revisited," in *Asia, Europe, and the Emergence of Modern Science*, ed. Arun Bala (London: Palgrave Macmillan, 2012), 73–92. Page references according to https://www.humanities.mcmaster.ca/~rarthur/papers/AshariteOrigins.pdf (accessed February 2020).
8. Elliot Sober, "Event Theory," in *A Companion to Metaphysics, Second Edition*, ed. Jaekwon Kim et al. (Oxford: Wiley-Blackwell, 2009), 236.
9. Helen Motanis et al., "Short-Term Synaptic Plasticity as a Mechanism for Sensory Timing," *Trends in Neurosciences* 41(10) (2018): 701–11, https://doi.org/10.1016/j.tins.2018.08.001 (accessed March 2021).
10. Alain Badiou, *Number and Numbers*, trans. Robin Mackay (Cambridge: Polity Press, [1990] 2008).
11. Richard Dedekind, "Continuity and Irrational Numbers," trans. Wooster Woodruff Beman, in *Essays on the Theory of Numbers* (New York: Dover, [1972] 1963), 1–27.
12. Edmund Husserl, *Philosophy of Arithmetic*, trans. Dallas Willard (Dordrecht: Kluwer Academic, [1891] 2003).
13. Edmund Husserl, *Analyses Concerning Passive and Active Synthesis*, section 30, "Individuation in Succession and Coexistence," trans. Anthony J. Steinbock (Dordrecht: Kluwer Academic, [1918–26] 2001), 189–92.
14. Wilhelm Dilthey, "Draft for a Critique of Historical Reason," trans. H. P. Rickman, in *The Hermeneutics Reader*, ed. Kurt Mueller-Vollmer (New York: Continuum, [1907] 1989), 150.
15. Henri Bergson, *Essai sur les données immédiates sur la conscience* (Paris: Flammarion, [1889] 2013).
16. Carl B. Boyer, *The History of the Calculus and Its Conceptual Development* (New York: Dover, [1949] 1959).
17. G. W. F. Hegel, *Science of Logic*, trans. A. V. Miller (New York: Humanity Books, [1812] 1991). See Alain Lacroix, "The Mathematical Infinite in Hegel," *Philosophical Forum* 31(3–4) (2000): 298–327.
18. Alain Badiou, *L'être et l'événement* (Paris: Éditions du Seuil, 1988), 181–90.

Chapter 6

1 Plato, *Protagoras*, trans. W. R. M. Lamb, Loeb Edition, Volume 2 (Cambridge, MA: Harvard University Press, 1977), 85–259.
2 Hans Thijssen, "Condemnation of 1277," in *The Stanford Encyclopedia of Philosophy* (Winter 2018), ed. Edward N. Zalta, https://plato.stanford.edu/archives/win2018/entries/condemnation/ (accessed January 2021).
3 Protagoras, *Concerning the Gods* (fragment of the lost work), trans. Hermann Diels and Walther Kranz, *Die Fragmente der Vorsokratiker*, Band 2 (Hildesheim, Germany: Weidmannsche Verlagsbuchhandlung, 1992), DK 80 B4.
4 Francis Bacon, *Of the Proficience and Advancement of Learning* (London: Parker, Son, and Bourn, [1605] 1863).
5 James Joyce, *Finnegan's Wake* (London: Wordsworth, 2021).
6 William Shakespeare, *Love's Labour's Lost*, in *The Norton Shakespeare*, ed. Stephen Greenblatt et al. (New York: W. W. Norton, 2015).
7 Johann Martin Chladenius, *Introduction to the Correct Interpretation of Reasonable Discourses and* Writings, trans. Carrie Asman-Schneider, in *The Hermeneutics Reader*, ed. Kurt Mueller-Vollmer (New York: Continuum, [1742] 1989), 62.
8 Kwame Gyekye, *An Essay on African Philosophical Thought: The Akan Conceptual Scheme* (Cambridge: Cambridge University Press, 1987), 64–5.
9 Tim O'Keefe, "The Cyrenaics on Pleasure, Happiness, and Future Concern," *Phronesis* 47(4) (2002): 395–416.
10 Voula Tsouna, *The Epistemology of the Cyrenaic School* (Cambridge: Cambridge University Press, 1998), 15–18.
11 Diogenes Laertius, *Lives of the Eminent Philosophers*, trans. R. D. Hicks, Volume 1, "Aristippus" (Cambridge, MA: Harvard University Press, 1959), 194–233.
12 Athenaeus, *Deipnosophists*, trans. C. B. Gulick, http://www.attalus.org/info/athenaeus.html (accessed January 2021).
13 David Gauthier, *Morals by Agreement* (Oxford: Oxford University Press, 1986), 38.
14 Lucius Annaeus Seneca, *On the Shortness of Life*, trans. Damian Stevenson (Scotts Valley, CA: CreateSpace, [49 CE] 2018).
15 Jeremy Bentham, *The Principles of Morals and Legislation* (New York: Hafner, 1963), Chapter 4: "Value of a Lot of Pleasure or Pain, How to Be Measured," 29–32. (I thank Martin Fitzgerald for this reference.)
16 Daniel Peris, *The Strategic Dividend Investor* (New York: McGraw-Hill, 2011).
17 Jay Lampert, *The Many Futures of a Decision* (London: Bloomsbury Academic Books, 2016).
18 Jim Garrison, "Time and Propinquity," https://www.onthetrailofdelusion.com/post/garrison-s-weird-investigative-technique-the-theory-of-propinquity (accessed January 2022). This website is authored by Fred Litwin, a one-time fervent JFK conspiracy proponent who became a fervent anti-conspiracy proponent.
19 John Stuart Mill, *Utilitarianism* (Indianapolis: Hackett, [1861] 2001).
20 Emmanuel Levinas, *On Escape*, trans. Bettina Bergo (Stanford, CA: Stanford University Press, [1935] 2003).
21 Franco Bernardi ("Bifo"), *After the Future*, ed. Gary Genosko and Nicholas Thoburn (Edinburgh: AK Press, 2011).

Chapter 7

1. Jacques Lacan, "The Function and Field of Speech and Language in Psychoanalysis," trans. Bruce Fink, in *Écrits* (New York: W. W. Norton, [1953] 2006), 259, 268n.
2. Elisabeth Roudinesco, *Jacques Lacan and Company: A History of Psychoanalysis in France, 1925–85* (Chicago: University of Chicago Press, 1990), 229.
3. Jean Allouch, *Les impromptus de Lacan* (Paris: EPEL, 1998), 54. Discussed in Owen Hewitson, "The Short Session," *LacanOnline.com* (July 4, 2010), https://www.lacanonline.com/2010/07/the-short-session/ (accessed March 2021). Pierre-Gilles Guégen, "The Short Session and the Question Concerning Technique with Lacan," *The Symptom* 10 (2009), https://www.lacan.com/symptom10a/the-short.html (accessed March 2021).
4. Bruce Fink, *A Clinical Introduction to Lacanian Psychoanalysis: Theory and Technique* (Cambridge, MA: Harvard University Press, 1999), 139.
5. Rosa Maria De Geest and Reitske Meganck, "How Do Time Limits Affect Our Therapies: A Literature Review," *Psychologica Belgica* 59(1) (2019): 206–26.
6. American Psychological Association, "How Long Will It Take for Treatment to Work?" https://www.apa.org/ptsd-guideline/patients-and-families/length-treatment (accessed May 2020).
7. Richard A. Wells and Vincent J. Giannetti, ed. *Handbook of the Brief Psychotherapies* (New York: Plenum Press, 1990).
8. Richard A. Wells and Phillip A. Phelps, "The Brief Psychotherapies: A Selective Overview," in *Handbook of the Brief Psychotherapies*, 3–26.
9. Richard A. Wells and Vincent J. Giannetti, "'Preface' and 'Introductions' to Parts 1–5," in *Handbook of the Brief Psychotherapies*, xi–xii, 1–2, 91–2, 191–2, 295–6, 511–12.
10. Michael F. Hoyt, "On Time in Brief Therapy," in *Handbook of the Brief Psychotherapies*, 115-43.
11. Stanley D. Imber and Karen J. Evanczuk, "Brief Crisis Therapy Groups," in *Handbook of the Brief Psychotherapies*, 564–82.
12. Jason Worchel, "Short-Term Dynamic Psychotherapy," in *Handbook of the Brief Psychotherapies*, 193–216.
13. Jose Szapocznik et al., "Innovations in Family Therapy: Strategies for Overcoming Resistance to Treatment," in *Handbook of the Brief Psychotherapies*, 93–114.
14. Michael F. Hoyt, "On Time in Brief Therapy," in *Handbook of the Brief Psychotherapies*, 115-43.
15. Charles D. Garvin, "Short-Term Group Therapy," in *Handbook of the Brief Psychotherapies*, 513–36.
16. Nick Kanas, "Short-Term Therapy Groups for Schizophrenics," in *Handbook of the Brief Psychotherapies*, 551–64.
17. Stanley D. Imber and Karen J. Evanczuk, "Brief Crisis Therapy Groups," in *Handbook of the Brief Psychotherapies*, 564–82.
18. R. Taylor Segraves, "Short-Term Marital Therapy," in *Handbook of the Brief Psychotherapies*, 437–59.
19. William J. Reid, "An Integrative Model for Short-Term Treatment," in *Handbook of the Brief Psychotherapies*, 55–77.
20. Robert Rosenbaum et al., "The Challenge of Single-Session Therapies: Creating Pivotal Moments," in *Handbook of the Brief Psychotherapies*, 165–89.

21 They draw their definition of "crisis" from Gerald Caplan's *An Approach to Community Mental Health* (New York: Grune and Stratton, 1961).
22 Charles Patrick Ewing, "Crisis Intervention as Brief Psychotherapy," in *Handbook of the Brief Psychotherapies*, 277–94.
23 Kai Vogeley and Christian Kupke, "Disturbances of Time Consciousness from a Phenomenological and a Neuroscientific Perspective," *Schizophrenia Bulletin* 33(1) (2007): 157–65, https://www.ncbi.nlm.nih.gov/pmc/articles/PMC2632289/ (accessed June 2020).
24 Hoyt cites F. T. Melges, *Time and the Inner Future: A Temporal Approach to Psychiatric Disorders* (New York: Wiley, 1982).
25 *Investopedia*, "Short Term Assets," https://www.investopedia.com/terms/s/shortterm.asp (accessed July 2017). *Investopedia* is regarded as a credible online source, run by a holding company called IAC, based on compilations of scholarly articles.
26 Victoria Ivashina and Josh Lerner, *Patient Capital: The Challenges and Promises of Long-Term Investing* (Princeton, NJ: Princeton University Press, 2019). Daniel Peris, *Getting Back to Business: Why Modern Portfolio Theory Fails Investors and How You Can Bring Common Sense to Your Portfolio* (New York: McGraw-Hill, 2018).
27 Derek K. Oler et al., "The Danger of Interpreting Short-Window Event Study Findings in strategic Management Research: An Empirical Illustration Using Horizontal Acquisitions," *Strategic Organization* 6(2) (2008): 151–84.
28 *Investopedia*, "What Is Commercial Paper?," https://www.investopedia.com/terms/c/commercialpaper.asp (accessed February 2021).
29 Marcin Kacperczyk and Philipp Schnabl, "When Safe Proved Risky: Commercial Paper during the Financial Crisis of 2007–2009," *Journal of Economic Perspectives* 24(1) (2010): 29–50.
30 *NADEX*, "Your Home for Short-Term Trading," https://join.nadex.com/offer-nadex-general/?CHID=1&QPID=239744197&gclid= Cj0KCQiAyJOBBhDCARIsAJG2h5fE9GUudsEA6e7UJs1zpZymiO3Tyvb BpP0KZLT5tgdn4w7Jmhqnh SEaAmIPEALw_wcB&gclsrc=aw.ds (accessed June 2020).
31 *Investopedia*, "Day Trading: An Introduction," https://www.investopedia.com/articles/trading/05/011705.asp (accessed January 2021).
32 David Byrd et al., "Intra-Day Equity Price Prediction Using Deep Learning as a Measure of Market Efficiency," https://arxiv.org/pdf/1908.08168.pdf (accessed February 2021).
33 David Trilling, "Do Payday Loans Exploit Poor People? Research Review," *Journalists' Research: Harvard Kennedy School, Shorenstein Center for Media, Politics, and Public Society*, September 19, 2016, https://journalistsresource.org/studies/economics/personal-finance/payday-loans-exploit-poor-people-research/ (accessed June 2020).
34 Elizabeth Sweet et al., "Short-Term Lending: Payday Loans as Risk Factors for Anxiety, Inflammation, and Poor Health," *SSM (Social Science and Medicine): Population Health* 7(5) (2018): 114–21.
35 Domenico Lisi and Miguel A. Malo, "The Impact of Temporary Employment on Productivity," *Journal of Labour Market Research* 50 (2017): 91–112.
36 Moshe Krausz, "Effects of Short- and Long-Term Preference for Temporary Work upon Psychological Outcomes," *International Journal of Manpower* 21(8) (2000): 635–47.
37 Mark Schneider, "Fad, Trend, or Classic: What's the Difference," https://www.markschneiderdesign.com/blogs/jewelry-blog/fad-trend-or-classic-what-s-the-difference (accessed July 2020).

38 Jerker Denrell and Balázs Kovács, "The Effect of Selection Bias in Studies of Fads and Fashions," *PLoS One (Public Library of Science, US National Library of Medicine, National Institutes of Health)* 10(4) (2015), doi: 10.1371/journal.pone.0123471 https://www.ncbi.nlm.nih.gov/pmc/articles/PMC4401772/ (accessed August 2020).

39 Bernard London, *Ending the Depression through Planned Obsolescence* (New York: Self-published, 1932).

40 William Galston, "Against Short-Termism: The Rise of Quarterly Capitalism Has Been Good for Wall Street—but Bad for Everyone Else," *Democracy: A Journal of Ideas* 38 (2015), https://democracyjournal.org/magazine/38/against-short-termism/ (accessed June 2020).

41 Felwine Sarr, *Afrotopia*, trans. Drew S. Burk and Sarah Jones-Boardman (Minneapolis: University of Minnesota Press, 2019).

42 Ravi Ramamurti, "Using Reverse Innovation to Fight Covid-19," *Harvard Business Review* (June 17, 2020), https://hbr.org/2020/06/using-reverse-innovation-to-fight-covid-19 (accessed July 2020). Jeffrey R. Immelt et al., "How GE Is Disrupting Itself," *Harvard Business Review* (October 2009), https://hbr.org/2009/10/how-ge-is-disrupting-itself (accessed July 2020).

43 Philip Bump, "Trump's Desire for Short-Term Good News Led Him to Break a Cardinal Rule of Political Campaigning, Not to Mention the Crux of His Strategy," *Washington Post* (June 22, 2020).

44 Lizanne Thomas, "Stop Panicking about Corporate Short-Termism," *Harvard Business Review* (June 28, 2019), https://hbr.org/2019/06/stop-panicking-about-corporate-short-termism (accessed June 2020).

45 Charles Nathan and Kai Goldberg, "The Short-Termism Thesis: Dogma vs. Reality," *Harvard Law School Forum on Corporate Governance* (March 8, 2019), https://corpgov.law.harvard.edu/2019/03/18/the-short-termism-thesis-dogma-vs-reality/ (accessed June 2020).

46 Dambisa Moyo, "Why Democracy Doesn't Deliver: Endless Elections, Unqualified Leaders, Uninformed Voters, and Short-Term Thinking Are Impeding Economic Growth," *FP (Foreign Policy)* (April 26, 2018), https://foreignpolicy.com/2018/04/26/why-democracy-doesnt-deliver/ (accessed June 2020).

47 Jonathan Boston, "Governing for the Future: How to Bring the Long-Term into Short-Term Political Focus," Seminar at the Center for Environmental Policy, School of Public Affairs, American University, Washington, DC (November 5, 2014): 1–42, https://www.american.edu/spa/cep/upload/jonathan-boston-lecture-american-university.pdf (accessed June 2020).

48 Iconio Garrì, "Political Short-Termism: A Possible Explanation," *Public Choice* 145 (2010): 197–211.

49 Janice Hawkins, "Potential Pitfalls of Short-Term Medical Missions," *Journal of Christian Nursing Online Extra* 30 (4) (2013): e1–e6.

50 LiErin Probasco, "Giving Time, Not Money: Long-term Impacts of Short-Term Mission Trips," *Missiology: An International Review*, 2013, https://doi.org/10.1177/0091829612475166 (accessed June 2020).

51 Kurt Alan Ver Beek, "The Impact of Short-Term Missions: A Case Study of House Construction in Honduras after Hurricane Mitch," *Missiology: An International Review* 34(4) (2006): 477–95.

52 John D. Barbour, *Versions of Deconversion: Autobiography and the Loss of Faith* (Charlottesville: University of Virginia Press, 1994). Paul Di Giorgio, *The Phenomenology of Conversion*, PhD Diss., Duquesne University (2021), 38–44. J.

Patrick Hornbeck II, "Deconversion from Roman Catholicism: Mapping a Fertile Field," *American Catholic Studies* 122(2) (Summer 2011): 1–29.
53 Azimaton Abdul Rahman et al., "Muslims in Cyberspace: Exploring Factors Influencing Online Religious Engagements in Malaysia," *Media Asia* 42(1–2) (2015): 61–73.
54 Kevin J. Sykes, "Short-Term Medical Service Trips: A Systematic Review of the Evidence," *American Journal of Public Health* 104(7) (2014): e38–e48.
55 Janice Hawkins, "Potential Pitfalls of Short-Term Medical Missions," *Journal of Christian Nursing Online Extra* 30 (4) (2013): e1–e6.
56 *Hopes&Fears*, "How Long Does an Average Marriage Last Around the World?," http://www.hopesandfears.com/hopes/city/city_index/214133-city-index-marriage-lengths (accessed April 2021).
57 Jaap Dronkers, "Cohabitation, Marriage, and Union Instability in Europe," *Institute for Family Studies* (2016), https://ifstudies.org/blog/cohabitation-marriage-and-union-instability-in-europe (accessed April 2021).
58 Paul W. Eastwick et al., "What Do Short-Term and Long-Term Relationships Look Like? Building the Relationship Coordination and Strategic Timing (ReCAST) Model," *Journal of Experimental Psychology: General* 147(5) (2018): 747–81.
59 Mary Sokol, "Jeremy Bentham on Love and Marriage: A Utilitarian Proposal for Short-Term Marriage," *Journal of Legal History* 30(1) (2009): 1–21.

Chapter 8

1 "Ephemeral Art," Tate Gallery, https://www.tate.org.uk/art/art-terms/e/ephemeral-art (accessed February 2021).
2 Rachel Elliot, "Risking the Habit Body through Immersive Resonance: Jen Reimer and Max Stein's Site-Specific Improvisation," Duquesne Women in Philosophy Conference, Pittsburgh, April 2018.
3 Katrina Windon, "The Right to Decay with Dignity: Documentation and the Negotiation between an Artist's Sanction and the Cultural Interest," *Art Documentation: Journal of the Art Libraries Society of North America* 31(2) (2012): 142–57.
4 A two-minute example, with the Dalai Lama presiding at a ceremony at Princeton University in 2014, can be seen at https://www.youtube.com/watch?v=xNu5zdEIhr0 (accessed March 2021). For another example, in Columbus Ohio, https://www.youtube.com/watch?v=_au5RCor55M (accessed March 2021).
5 Matthew Akers and Jeff Dupre, dirs *Marina Abramovic: The Artist Is Present* (Show of Force Productions, 2012).
6 Jacques Derrida, *The Post Card: From Socrates to Freud and Beyond*, trans. Alan Bass (Chicago: University of Chicago Press, [1980] 1987).
7 Marc-Alain Ouaknin, *Le livre brulé: Philosophie du Talmud* (Paris: Points, 2016).
8 Italo Calvino, *Six Memos for the Next Millennium* (Cambridge, MA: Harvard University Press, 1988), Memo 2, "Quickness," 37.
9 Boris M. Ejxenbaum, "O. Henry and the Theory of the Short Story," trans. I. R. Titunik, in *Readings in Russian Poetics*, ed. Ladislav Matejka and Krystyna Pomorska (Cambridge, MA: MIT Press, [1925] 1971), 227–70.

10 Roland Barthes, *Roland Barthes by Roland Barthes*, trans. Richard Howard (New York: Farrar, Straus and Giroux, [1975] 1977).
11 Jacques Derrida, *The Truth in Painting*, trans. Geoff Bennington and Ian McLeod (Chicago: University of Chicago Press, [1978] 1987).
12 Immanuel Kant, *Critique of Judgment*, trans. Werner S. Pluhar (Indianapolis: Hackett, [1790] 1987), 84–91.
13 Mark24, *The Shortest Movie Ever* (2013), https://www.youtube.com/watch?v=8KLVPrODZu4 (accessed February 2020).
14 PES, *Fresh Guacamole* (2012), https://www.youtube.com/watch?v=dNJdJIwCF_Y (accessed February 2020).
15 Dziga Vertov, "The Council of Three," in *Kino-Eye: The Writings of Dziga Vertov*, trans. Kevin O'Brien (Los Angeles: University of California Press, [1923] 1985), 14–21.
16 Karen Pearlman, *Cutting Rhythms: Shaping the Film Edit* (Burlington, MA: Focal Press, 2009).
17 Gilles Deleuze, *Cinema 1: The Movement Image*, trans. Hugh Tomlinson (Minneapolis: University of Minnesota Press, [1983] 1986), 37. Gilles Deleuze, *Difference and Repetition*, trans. Paul Patton (New York: Columbia University Press, [1968] 1995).
18 Jean-Luc Godard, interview about his film *Pierrot le fou*, in *Godard on Godard*, trans. Tom Milne (New York: Da Capo Press, [1965] 1986), 214.
19 Raymond Bellour, "To Segment/To Analyze (on *Gigi*)," trans. Diana Matias, in *The Analysis of Film*, ed. Constance Penley (Bloomington: Indiana University Press, [1976] 2001), 193–215.
20 Jean-Luc Godard, *Made in U. S. A.* (1966), https://www.youtube.com/watch?v=_q0G0PI_zMw (accessed March 2021).
21 Raymond Queneau, *Cent mille milliards de poèmes* (Paris: Gallimard, 1961).
22 François Le Lionnais, "La LiPo: Le premier Manifeste," in *Oulipo: La littérature potentielle* (Paris: Éditions Gallimard, 1973), 16.
23 Jacques Jouet, "Subway Poems," trans. Ian Monk, *SubStance* 30(3) (2001): 64–70.
24 Oliver Pierre Bray, *Exercises in Constraint: The Poetics of OuLiPo in Performance*, PhD Diss., University of Leeds, 2018.
25 Alexandre Kojève, *Introduction à la lecture de Hegel*, ed. Raymond Queneau (Paris: Gallimard, 1947).
26 Pius Servien, *Essai sur les rhythmes toniques du Français* (Paris: Les Presses Universitaires de France, 1925), 37.
27 G. W. F. Hegel, *Enzyklopädie der Philosophischen Wissenschaften* (Hamburg: Felix Meiner Verlag, [1830] 1969).
28 G. W. F. Hegel, *Asthetik, Band II* (Frankfurt am Main: Europäische Verlagsanhalt GmbH, [1829] 1966). G. W. F. Hegel, *Hegel's Aesthetics*, Volume 2, trans. T. M. Knox (Oxford: Clarendon Press, [1929] 1975). When I refer to the German, I cite both German and English texts; otherwise, I cite only the English translation.
29 Victor Zuckerkandl, *Sound and Symbol: Music and the External World* (Princeton, NJ: Princeton University Press, 1969).
30 Andrea Peloso, a Toronto singer-songwriter, pointed out to me in conversation that a "song" has a big impact in a short time. The composer processes ideas that the listener does not have time for.
31 Raymond Queneau, *Contes et propos* (Paris: Gallimard, 1981), 50.
32 Edward Sanders, *The Z-D Generation* (New York: Station Hill Press, 1981), 1.

33 Charles Olson, "Projective Verse," in *Selected Writings*, ed. Robert Creeley (New York: New Directions Books, [1950] 1966), 15–26.

Chapter 9

1 Gilles Deleuze and Félix Guattari, *Mille Plateaux* (Paris: Les Éditions de Minuit, 1980); *A Thousand Plateaus*, trans. Brian Massumi (Minneapolis: University of Minnesota Press, 1987). When I cite the French, I refer to page numbers in the form French/English, as in Deleuze 1980: 36/[1980] 1987: 25.
   I thank Dan Smith for referring me to the anti-hippie phrase popular in France in the 1960s: "long hair and short ideas" (*cheveux longs et idées courtes*). And I thank Brent Adkins for realizing that this comes from a 1966 song title by Johnny Hallyday, who asserts that long hair is not sufficient to fight injustice. Hallyday had short hair at the time, but by 1968, his hair was long. (There are websites that claim that the phrase comes from one of Schopenhauer's insults to women, but I think this is inaccurate.) Jacques Sternberg, cranky pataphysician, accuses *Cahiers du Cinéma* of "idées courtes," in his 1972 pamphlet, *Lettre aux gens malheureux et qui ont bien raison de l'être* (Paris: Le Terrain Vague), 21. The fact that Deleuze and Guattari's phrase borrows from satire does not make it less serious.
2 Eugene W. Holland, *Deleuze and Guattari's "A Thousand Plateaus": A Reader's Guide* (London: Bloomsbury, 2013), 41. "Short-term memory is thoroughly rhizomatic, and so Deleuze and Guattari advocate writing a book using short-term memory and what they call 'short-term ideas.'"
   Thomas Nail, *Returning to Revolution: Deleuze, Guattari, and Zapatismo* (Edinburgh: Edinburgh University Press, 2012), 125. Deleuze and Guattari characterize "the aims of the revolution in the short term, mid term, and long term."
3 Gilles Deleuze and Félix Guattari, *Kafka: Toward a Minor Literature*, trans. Dana Polan (Minneapolis: University of Minnesota Press, [1975] 1986), 4.
4 "Postulates of Linguistics" Plateau. See my *Deleuze and Guattari's Philosophy of History* (London: Continuum Books, 1995), Chapter 5.
5 Julia Kristeva gives a similar double description of short term time in "The Novel as Polylogue," trans. Thomas Gora et al., in *Desire in Language: A Semiotic Approach to Literature and Art*, ed. Leon S. Roudiez (New York: Columbia University Press, [1974] 1980), 159–209.
6 Gilles Deleuze, *Proust et les signes* (Paris: Quadrige, 1964).
7 Though in some sense, one can call it eternity. Brenton Ables, *A Deleuzian Theory of Eternity*, PhD Diss., University of Guelph, Canada, 2019.
8 Gilles Deleuze, "Post-scriptum sur les sociétés de contrôle," in *Pourparlers: 1972–1990* (Paris: Les Éditions de Minuit, 1990), 240–7. "Postscript on Control Societies," in *Negotiations: 1972–1990*, trans. Martin Joughin (New York: Columbia University Press, 1995), 177–82.
9 See my *Simultaneity and Delay* (London; Bloomsbury Academic, 2006).
10 Félix Guattari, "La causalité, la subjectivité, et l'histoire" (1966–7), in *Psychanalyse et transversalité: Essais d'analyse institutionnelle* (Paris: La Découverte, 2003), 178.
11 Deleuze's terms for "term" are different: *courte terme* for short term, but *longue durée* for long term. The short literally has a term and the long does not.

12 Gilles Deleuze, "Mai 68 n'a pas eu lieu (avec Félix Guattari)," in *Deux régimes de fou*, ed. David Lapoujade (Paris: Les Éditions de minuit, [1984] 2003), 215–17.
13 Biographies build up out of "finite linear proceedings, one of which ends before the next begins" (Deleuze 1980: 167/[1980] 1987: 133, "On Several Regimes of Signs").
14 Gilles Deleuze and Félix Guattari, *L'Anti-Oedipe* (Paris: Les Éditions de Minuit, 1972); *Anti-Oedipus*, trans. Robert Hurley, Mark Seem, and Helen R. Lane (Minneapolis: University of Minnesota Press, 1983).
15 Mark Fisher, *Capitalist Realism: Is There No Alternative?* (Winchester: Zero Books, 2009).
16 "*L'étoitesse de la ruelle*"; Massumi's translation reads: "there is so little room."
17 The fascist impulse always finds itself elsewhere (science fiction writers say "elsewhen").
18 Michel Serres and Bruno Latour, *Conversations on Science, Culture, and Time*, trans. Roxanne Lapidus (Ann Arbor: University of Michigan Press, 1995), 58.
19 I follow Massumi's translation of *couler* as "leak." It could have been "run," or even "flow" (if *fuite* didn't already mean "flow"). The combination "*couler et s'échapper*" justifies "leak."
20 Processes can thus take shape even though the conditions for them had not been prepared; this undermines the "leftist" excuse that "'conditions' are not yet not ripe"; every point can rotate into a revolution (Deleuze 1980: 264/[1980] 1987: 216).
21 G. W. F. Hegel, *Science of Logic*, trans. A. V. Miller (Atlantic Highlands, NJ: Humanities Press International, [1812] 1969), 494.
22 Henri Bergson, *Duration and Simultaneity*, trans. Herbert Dingle (Indianapolis, IN: Bobbs-Merrill, [1922] 1965), 51. See my *Simultaneity and* Delay, 127–30.
23 Short term segments are not individuals, but dividuals. Gerald Raunig, *Dividuum: Machinic Capitalism and Molecular Revolution* (South Pasadena, CA: Semiotext(e), 2016).

REFERENCES

"10 Historical Events That Were Much Shorter Than You Thought," *Listverse*. Available online: https://listverse.com/2015/08/20/10-historical-events-that-were-much-shorter-than-you-thought/ (accessed December 2020).

2045 Strategic Social Initiative. Available online: http://2045.com (accessed January 2021).

Aben, Bart, Sven Stapert, and Arjan Blokland (2012), "About the Distinction between Working Memory and Short-term Memory," *Frontiers in Psychology*, 3(301): 1–9.

Abish, Walter (1975), *Minds Meet*, New York: New Directions.

Ables, Brenton (2019), "A Deleuzian Theory of Eternity," PhD Diss., University of Guelph, Canada.

Adorno, Theodor ([1963] 1992), "Berg's Discoveries in Compositional Technique," in *Quasi una fantasia: Essays on Modern Music*, trans. Rodney Livingstone, London: Verso, 179–200.

Adorno, Theodor ([1972] 1991), "Free Time," in J. M. Bernstein (ed.), *The Culture Industry*, London: Routledge, 187–97.

Allouch, Jean (1998), *Les impromptus de Lacan*, Paris: EPEL.

American Psychological Association, "How Long Will It Take for Treatment to Work?" Available online: https://www.apa.org/ptsd-guideline/patients-and-families/length-treatment (accessed May 2020).

"Amnesia," *Mayo Clinic*. Available online: https://www.mayoclinic.org/diseases-conditions/amnesia/diagnosis-treatment/drc-20353366 (accessed May 2019).

Arthur, Richard T. W. (2012), "Time Atomism and the Ash'Arite Origins for Cartesian Occasionalism Revisited," in Arun Bala (ed.), *Asia, Europe, and the Emergence of Modern Science*, London: Palgrave Macmillan, 73–92.

Athenaeus ([third century CE] 1930), *Deipnosophists*, trans. C. B. Gulick. Available online: http://www.attalus.org/info/athenaeus.html (accessed January 2021).

Bacon, Francis ([1605] 1863), *Of the Proficience and Advancement of Learning*, London: Parker, Son, and Bourn.

Badiou, Alain (1988), *L'être et l'événement*, Paris: Éditions du Seuil.

Badiou, Alain ([1990] 2008), *Number and Numbers*, trans. Robin Mackay, Cambridge: Polity Press.

Badiou, Alain ([2005] 2007), *The Century*, trans. Alberto Toscano, Cambridge: Polity Press.

Balibar, Étienne ([1965] 1996), "Sur les concepts fondamentaux du matérialisme historique," in Étienne Balibar, Louis Althusser, Roger Establet, Pierre Macherey, Jacques Rancière, *Lire le Capital*, Paris: Presses Universitaires de France, 419–568.

Barbour, John D. (1994), *Versions of Deconversion: Autobiography and the Loss of Faith*, Charlottesville: University of Virginia Press.

Barthes, Roland ([1975] 1977), *Roland Barthes by Roland Barthes*, trans. Richard Howard, New York: Farrar, Straus and Giroux.

Bellour, Raymond ([1976] 2001), "To Analyze, to Segment," trans. Diana Matias, in Constance Penley (ed.), *The Analysis of Film*, Bloomington: Indiana University Press, 193–216.

Benjamin, Walter ([1927] 1999), "Moscow," trans. Edmund Jephcott, in Michael W. Jennings, Howard Eiland, and Gary Smith (eds.), *Walter Benjamin: Selected Writings*, Volume 2, Part 1, 1927–30, Cambridge, MA: Harvard University Press, 22–46.

Bentham, Jeremy ([1789] 1963), *The Principles of Morals and Legislation*, New York: Hafner.

Benveniste, Émile (1974), "Le langage et l'expérience humaine," in *Problèmes de linguistique générale, 2*, Paris: Gallimard, 67–78.

Bergson, Henri ([1889] 2013), *Essai sur les données immédiates de la conscience*, Paris: Flammarion.

Bergson, Henri ([1922] 1965), *Duration and Simultaneity*, trans. Herbert Dingle, Indianapolis, IN: Bobbs-Merrill.

Bernardi, Franco ("Bifo") (2011), *After the Future*, ed. Gary Genosko and Nicholas Thoburn, Edinburgh: AK Press.

Boston, Jonathan (2014), "Governing for the Future: How to Bring the Long-Term into Short-Term Political Focus," Seminar at the Center for Environmental Policy, School of Public Affairs, American University, Washington, DC, November 5, 2014. Available online: https://www.american.edu/spa/cep/upload/jonathan-boston-lecture-american-university.pdf (accessed June 2020).

Bourdieu, Pierre ([1980] 1990), *The Logic of Practice*, trans. Richard Nice, Stanford, CA: Stanford University Press.

Boyer, Carl B. ([1949] 1959), *The History of the Calculus and Its Conceptual Development*, New York: Dover.

Braudel, Fernand ([1960] 2009), "History and the Social Sciences: The *Longue Durée*," trans. Immanuel Wallerstein, *Review (Fernand Braudel Center)*, 32(2): 171–203.

Bray, Oliver Pierre (2018), "Exercises in Constraint: The Poetics of OuLiPo in Performance." PhD Diss., School of Performance and Cultural Industries, University of Leeds.

Bump, Philip (2020), "Trump's Desire for Short-Term Good News Led Him to Break a Cardinal Rule of Political Campaigning, Not to Mention the Crux of His Strategy," *Washington Post*, June 22.

Byrd, David, and Tucker Hybinette Balch (2019), "Intra-Day Equity Price Prediction Using Deep Learning as a Measure of Market Efficiency." Available online: https://arxiv.org/pdf/1908.08168.pdf (accessed February 2021).

Cage, Fielding, "Why Time Feels So Weird in 2020." Available online: https://graphics.reuters.com/HEALTH-CORONAVIRUS/TIME/gjnvwwjegvw/ (accessed January 2021).

Calvino, Italo (1988), *Six Memos for the Next Millennium*, Cambridge, MA: Harvard University Press.

Calvino, Italo (1996), "How I Wrote One of My Books," trans. Iain White, in *Oulipo Laboratory*. London: Atlas Press.

Caplan, Gerald (1961), *An Approach to Community Mental Health*, New York: Grune and Stratton.

Carroll, Noël (2007), *The Philosophy of Motion Pictures*, London: Wiley-Blackwell.

Carsons, Rachel ([1962] 2002) *Silent Spring*, Boston, MA: Houghton-Mifflin, 2002.

Chen, James, "Short Term Paper," *Investopedia*. Available online: https://www.investopedia.com/terms/s/short-term-note.asp (accessed March 2021).

Chen, James, "Commercial Paper," *Investopedia*. Available online: https://www.investopedia.com/terms/c/commercialpaper.asp (accessed March 2021).

Chladenius, Johann Martin ([1742] 1989), "Introduction to the Correct Interpretation of Reasonable Discourses and Writings," trans. Carrie Asman-Schneider, in Kurt Mueller-Vollmer (ed.), *The Hermeneutics Reader*, New York: Continuum, 54–71.

Cowan, Nelson (2008), "What Are the Differences between Long-Term, Short-Term, and Working Memory?" *Progress in Brain Research*, 169: 323–38.

Currie, Gregory (2008), *Image and Mind: Film, Philosophy, and Cognitive Science*, Cambridge: Cambridge University Press.

"Day Trading: An Introduction," *Investopedia*. Available online: https://www.investopedia.com/articles/trading/05/011705.asp (accessed January 2021).

Dead on Time (1983). Dir. Lyndall Hobbs, Great Britain: Michael White Productions.

De Beauvoir, Simone ([1970] 1996), *The Coming of Age*, trans. Patrick O'Brian, New York: W. W. Norton.

De Certeau, Michel ([1974] 1984), *The Practice of Everyday Life*, trans. Steven Rendall, Berkeley: University of California Press.

De Geest, Rosa Maria, and Reitske Meganck (2019), "How Do Time Limits Affect Our Therapies: A Literature Review," *Psychologica Belgica*, 59(1): 206–26.

De Landa, Manuel (1997), *A Thousand Years of Nonlinear History*, New York: Swerve Editions.

De Quincey, Thomas ([1849] 1937), "The English Mail Coach," in Philip Van Doren Stern (ed.), *Selected Writings*, New York: Random House, 913–81.

De Warren, Nicolas (2009), *Husserl and the Promise of Time: Subjectivity in Transcendental Philosophy*, Cambridge: Cambridge University Press.

Dedekind, Richard ([1872] 1963), "Continuity and Irrational Numbers," trans. Wooster Woodruff Beman, in *Essays on the Theory of Numbers*, New York: Dover, 1–27.

Deleuze, Gilles (1964), *Proust et les signes*, Paris: Presses Universitaires de France.

Deleuze, Gilles ([1968] 1994), *Difference and Repetition*, trans. Paul Patton, New York: Columbia University Press.

Deleuze, Gilles (1983), *Cinema 1: The Movement Image*, trans. Hugh Tomlinson, Minneapolis: University of Minnesota Press.

Deleuze, Gilles (1990), "Post-scriptum sur les sociétés de contrôle," in *Pourparlers: 1972–1990*, Paris: Les Éditions de Minuit, 240–7. "Postscript on Control Societies" (1995) in *Negotiations: 1972–1990*, trans. Martin Joughin, New York: Columbia University Press, 177–82.

Deleuze, Gilles, and Félix Guattari (1972) *L'Anti-Oedipe*, Paris: Les Éditions de Minuit. *Anti-Oedipus* (1983), trans. Robert Hurley, Mark Seem, and Helen R. Lane, Minneapolis: University of Minnesota Press.

Deleuze, Gilles, and Félix Guattari ([1975] 1986), *Kafka: Toward a Minor Literature*, trans. Dana Polan, Minneapolis: University of Minnesota Press.

Deleuze, Gilles, and Félix Guattari (1980), *Mille Plateaux*, Paris: Les Éditions de Minuit. *A Thousand Plateaus* (1987), trans. Brian Massumi, Minneapolis: University of Minnesota Press.

Deleuze, Gilles, and Félix Guattari ([1984] 2003), "Mai 68 n'a pas eu lieu," in *Deux régimes de fou*, ed. David Lapoujade, Paris: Les *Éditions de minuit*, 215–17.

Denrell, Jerker, and Balázs Kovács (2015), "The Effect of Selection Bias in Studies of Fads and Fashions," *PLoS One (Public Library of Science, US National Library of Medicine, National Institutes of Health)*, 10(4). Available online: doi: 10.1371/journal.

pone.0123471 https://www.ncbi.nlm.nih.gov/pmc/articles/PMC4401772/ (accessed August 2020).

Derrida, Jacques ([1978] 1987), *The Truth in Painting*, trans. Geoff Bennington and Ian McLeod, Chicago: University of Chicago Press.

Derrida, Jacques ([1980] 1987), *The Post Card: From Socrates to Freud and Beyond*, trans. Alan Bass, Chicago: University of Chicago Press.

Di Giorgio, Paul (2021), "The Phenomenology of Conversion," PhD Diss., Duquesne University.

Dilthey, Wilhelm ([1907] 1989), "Draft for a Critique of Historical Reason," trans. H. P. Rickman, in Kurt Mueller-Vollmer (ed.), *The Hermeneutics Reader*, New York: Continuum, 148–64.

Diogenes Laertius ([third century CE] 1959), *Lives of the Eminent Philosophers*, trans. R. D. Hicks, Volume 1, "Aristippus," Cambridge, MA: Harvard University Press, 194–233.

"Dissociative Disorders," *Mayo Clinic*. Available online: https://www.mayoclinic.org/diseases-conditions/dissociative-disorders/symptoms-causes/syc-20355215 (accessed January 2021).

Dodd, James (2005), "Reading Husserl's Time-Diagrams from 1917/18," *Husserl Studies*, 2005(21): 111–37.

Dolgushin, Yuri ([1939] 2015), "Rays of Life," in Yvonne Howell (ed.), *Red Star Tales: A Century of Russian and Soviet Science Fiction*, Moscow: Russian Information Services, 181–95.

Dronkers, Jaap (2016), "Cohabitation, Marriage, and Union Instability in Europe," *Institute for Family Studies*. Available online: https://ifstudies.org/blog/cohabitation-marriage-and-union-instability-in-europe (accessed April 2021).

Eastwick, Paul W. et al. (2018), "What Do Short-Term and Long-Term Relationships Look Like? Building the Relationship Coordination and Strategic Timing (ReCAST) Model," *Journal of Experimental Psychology: General*, 147(5): 747–81.

Eco, Umberto (1986), *Semiotics and the Philosophy of Language*, Bloomington: Indiana University Press.

Ejxenbaum, Boris M. ([1925] 1971), "O. Henry and the Theory of the Short Story," trans. I. R. Titunik, in Ladislav Matejka, and Krystyna Pomorska (eds.), *Readings in Russian Poetics*, Cambridge, MA: MIT Press, 227–70.

Elliot, Rachel (2018), "Risking the Habit Body through Immersive Resonance: Jen Reimer and Max Stein's Site-Specific Improvisation," Duquesne Women in Philosophy Conference, Pittsburgh.

"Ephemeral Art," *Tate Gallery*. Available online: https://www.tate.org.uk/art/art-terms/e/ephemeral-art (accessed February 2021).

Ericsson, K. A and W. Kintsch (1995), "Long Term Working Memory," *APA Psychological Review*, 102(2): 211–45.

Ernst, Wolfgang (2016), *Chronopoetics: The Temporal Being and Operativity of Technological Media*, London: Rowman and Littlefield.

Eye Music in Red Major (1961). Marie Menken, USA: [No Producer].

Fanon, Frantz ([1961] 1963), *The Wretched of the Earth*, trans. Constance Farrington, New York: Grove Weidenfeld.

Fernandez, Macedonio ([1967] 2010), *The Museum of Eterna's Novel (The First Good Novel)*, trans. Margaret Schwartz, Rochester, NY: Open Letter Press.

Fink, Bruce (1999), *A Clinical Introduction to Lacanian Psychoanalysis: Theory and Technique*, Cambridge, MA: Harvard University Press.

Fisher, Mark (2009), *Capitalist Realism: Is There No Alternative?* Winchester: Zero Books.

Fowler, Michael, "Graduate Classical Mechanics Lecture Notes." Available online: https://galileoandeinstein.phys.virginia.edu/7010/home.html (accessed March 2021).

Franzen, Michael D., and Marc W. Haut (1991), "The Psychological Treatment of Memory Impairment: A Review of Empirical Studies," *Neuropsychology Review*, 2(1): 29–63.

Fresh Guacamole (2012). Dir. PES, USA: PES Productions.

Fritsch, Matthias (2018), *Taking Turns with the Earth: Phenomenology, Deconstruction, and Intergenerational Justice*, Stanford, CA: Stanford University Press.

Galston, William (2015), "Against Short-Termism: The Rise of Quarterly Capitalism Has Been Good for Wall Street—but Bad for Everyone Else." *Democracy: A Journal of Ideas*, 38. Available online: https://democracyjournal.org/magazine/38/against-short-termism/ (accessed June 2020).

Garrì, Iconio (2010), "Political Short-Termism: A Possible Explanation," *Public Choice*, 145: 197–211.

Garrison, Jim (1967), "Time and Propinquity." Available online: https://www.onthetrailofdelusion.com/post/garrison-s-weird-investigative-technique-the-theory-of-propinquity (accessed January 2022).

Garvin, Charles D (1990), "Short-Term Group Therapy," in Richard A. Wells and Vincent J. Giannetti (eds.), *Handbook of the Brief Psychotherapies*, New York: Plenum Press, 513–36.

Gauthier, David (1986), *Morals by Agreement*, Oxford: Oxford University Press.

Gbadegesin, Segun (1996), "Yoruba Philosophy: Individuality, Community, and the Moral Order," in *African Philosophy: Traditional Yoruba Philosophy and Contemporary African Realities*, Bern: Peter Lang, 61–104.

Genette, Gérard ([1972] 1980), *Narrative Discourse: An Essay in Method*, trans. Jane E. Lewin, Ithaca, NY: Cornell University Press.

Godard, Jean-Luc (1986), *Godard on Godard*, trans. and ed. Tom Milne, New York: Da Capo Press.

Goethe University Frankfurt am Main (2020), "Zeptoseconds: New World Record in Short Time Measurement," *PhysOrg*. Available online: https://phys.org/news/2020-10-zeptoseconds-world-short.amp (accessed March 2021).

Goranko, Valentin (1999, revised 2020), "Temporal Logic," *Stanford Encyclopedia of Philosophy*, 4.2 "Adding Since and Until." Available online: https://plato.stanford.edu/entries/logic-temporal/ (accessed March 2021).

"Granger causality," *Wikipedia*. Available online: https://en.wikipedia.org/wiki/Granger_causality (accessed December 2020).

Greenberg, Daniel L., and Mieke Verfaellie (2010), "Interdependence of Episodic and Semantic Memory: Evidence from Neuropsychology," *Journal of the International Neuropsychological Society*, 16(5): 748–53.

Guattari, Félix ([1967] 2003), "La causalité, la subjectivité, et l'histoire," in *Psychanalyse et transversalité: Essais d'analyse institutionnelle*, Paris: La Découverte, 173–209.

Guégen, Pierre-Gilles (2009), "The Short Session and the Question Concerning Technique with Lacan," *The Symptom*, 10. Available online: https://www.lacan.com/symptom10a/the-short.html (accessed March 2021).

Guldi, Jo, and David Armitage (2014), *The History Manifesto*, Cambridge: Cambridge University Press.

Gyekye, Kwame (1987), *An Essay on African Philosophical Thought: The Akan Conceptual Scheme*, Philadelphia, PA: Temple University Press.

Hawkins, Janice (2013), "Potential Pitfalls of Short-Term Medical Missions," *Journal of Christian Nursing Online Extra*, e1–e6.
Hegel, G. W. F. ([1812] 1989), *The Science of Logic*, trans. A. V. Miller, Atlantic Highlands, NJ: Humanities Press International.
Hegel, G. W. F. ([1829] 1966), *Ästhetik, Band II*, Frankfurt am Main: Europäische Verlagsanhalt GmbH. *Hegel's Aesthetics* ([1829] 1975), Volume 2, trans. T. M. Knox, Oxford: Clarendon Press.
Hegel, G. W. F. ([1830] 1969), *Enzyklopädie der Philosophischen Wissenschaften I*, Hamburg: Felix Meiner Verlag.
Hegel, G. W. F. ([1830] 1970), *Enzyklopädie der philosophischen Wissenschaften II, Werke 9*, Frankfurt am Main: Suhrkamp Verlag. *Philosophy of Nature* ([1830] 2004), trans. A. V. Miller, Oxford: Clarendon Press.
Hegel, G. W. F. ([1830] 1900), *Philosophy of History*, trans. J. Sibree, New York: The Colonial Press.
Heidegger, Martin ([1938] 1999), *Contributions to Philosophy (From Enowning)*, trans. Parvis Emad and Kenneth Maly, Bloomington: Indiana University Press.
Hewitson, Owen (2010), "The Short Session," *LacanOnline.com*. Available online: https://www.lacanonline.com/2010/07/the-short-session/ (accessed March 2021).
Holland, Eugene W. (2013), *Deleuze and Guattari's "A Thousand Plateaus": A Reader's Guide*, London: Bloomsbury.
Hornbeck II, J. Patrick (2011), "Deconversion from Roman Catholicism: Mapping a Fertile Field," *American Catholic Studies*, 122(2): 1–29.
Horning, Sheena M. et al. (2011), "Atheistic, Agnostic, and Religious Older Adults on Well-Being and Coping Behaviors," *Journal of Aging Studies*, 25(2): 177–88.
"How Long Does an Average Marriage Last around the World?" *Hopes&Fears*. Available online: http://www.hopesandfears.com/hopes/city/city_index/214133-city-index-marriage-lengths (accessed April 2021).
Hoyt, Michael F. (1990), "On Time in Brief Therapy," in Richard A. Wells and Vincent J. Giannetti (eds.), *Handbook of the Brief Psychotherapies*, New York: Plenum Press, 115–43.
Humez, Alexander et al. (2010), *Short Cuts: A Guide to Oaths, Ring Tones, Ransom Notes, Famous Last Words, and Other Forms of Minimalist Communication*, Oxford: Oxford University Press.
Husserl, Edmund ([1891] 2003), *Philosophy of Arithmetic*, trans. Dallas Willard, Dordrecht: Kluwer Academic.
Husserl, Edmund ([1900] 2001), *Logical Investigations*, 2 volumes, trans. J. N. Findlay, New York: Routledge.
Husserl, Edmund ([1913] 1983), *Ideas Pertaining to a Pure Phenomenology and to a Phenomenological Philosophy, First Book*, trans. F. Kersten, The Hague: Martinus Nijhoff.
Husserl, Edmund ([1918–26] 2001), *Analyses Concerning Passive and Active Synthesis*, trans. Anthony J. Steinbock, Dordrecht: Kluwer Academic.
Husserl, Edmund ([1928] 1964), *The Phenomenology of Internal Time-Consciousness*, trans. James S. Churchill, Bloomington: Indiana University Press.
Husserl, Edmund ([1936] 1970), *The Crisis of European Sciences and Transcendental Phenomenology*, trans. David Carr, Evanston, IL: Northwestern University Press.
Ikiru (1952). Dir. Akira Kurosawa, Japan: Toho Company.

Imber, Stanley D., and Karen J. Evanczuk (1990), "Brief Crisis Therapy Groups," in Richard A. Wells and Vincent J. Giannetti (eds.), *Handbook of the Brief Psychotherapies*, New York: Plenum Press, 564–82.
Immelt, Jeffrey R. et al. (2009), "How GE Is Disrupting Itself," *Harvard Business Review*. Available online: https://hbr.org/2009/10/how-ge-is-disrupting-itself (accessed July 2020).
"The Immortality of Writers" ([c. 1200 BCE] 1976), in Mirian Lichtheim (ed.), *Ancient Egyptian Literature: The New Kingdom*, Berkeley: University of California Press.
Itskov, Dmitry, "Want to Be Immortal? Act!" Available online: http://www.immortal.me (accessed January 2021).
Ivashina, Victoria, and Josh Lerner (2019), *Patient Capital: The Challenges and Promises of Long-Term Investing*, Princeton, NJ: Princeton University Press.
Jacob, Salomé (2019), "Husserl's Model of Time-Consciousness and the Phenomenology of Rhythm," in Peter Cheyne et al. (eds), *The Philosophy of Rhythm: Aesthetics, Music, Poetics*, Oxford: Oxford University Press, 291–306.
Jahn, Holger (2013), "Memory Loss in Alzheimer's Disease," *Dialogues in Clinical Neuroscience*, 15(4): 445–54.
Jakobson, Roman ([1930] 1985), "On a Generation That Squandered Its Poets," trans. Edward J. Brown, in Krystyna Pomorska, and Stephen Rudy (eds.), *Verbal Art, Verbal Sign, Verbal Time*, Minneapolis: University of Minnesota Press, 111–32.
Jakobson, Roman, and Krystyna Pomorska ([1980] 1985), "Dialogue on Time in Language and Literature," in Krystyna Pomorska and Stephen Rudy (eds.), *Verbal Art, Verbal Sign, Verbal Time*, Minneapolis: University of Minnesota Press, 11–27.
Jameson, Fredric (1972), *The Prison-House of Language*, Princeton, NJ: Princeton University Press.
Jarry, Alfred ([1911] 1996), *Exploits and Opinions of Dr. Faustroll, Pataphysician*, trans. Simon Watson Taylor, Boston, MA: Exact Change.
Jouet, Jacques (2001), "Subway Poems," trans. Ian Monk, *SubStance*, 30(3): 64–70.
Joyce, James ([1939] 2021), *Finnegan's Wake*, London: Wordsworth.
Kacperczyk, Marcin, and Philipp Schnabl (2010), "When Safe Proved Risky: Commercial Paper during the Financial Crisis of 2007–2009," *Journal of Economic Perspectives*, 24(1): 29–50.
Kafka, Franz ([1919] 1993), "The Cares of a Family Man," trans. Willa and Edwin Muir, from *A Country Doctor*, in Gabriel Josipovici (ed.), *Collected Stories*, New York: Alfred A. Knopf, 183–5.
Kanas, Nick (1990), "Short-Term Therapy Groups for Schizophrenics," in Richard A. Wells and Vincent J. Giannetti (eds.), *Handbook of the Brief Psychotherapies*, New York: Plenum Press, 551–64.
Kant, Immanuel ([1781] 1990), *Kritik der reinen Vernunft*, Hamburg: Felix Meiner Verlag. *Critique of Pure Reason* ([1781] 1929), trans. Norman Kemp Smith, New York: St. Martin's Press.
Kant, Immanuel ([1790] 1987), *Critique of Judgment*, trans. Werner S. Pluhar, Indianapolis, IN: Hackett.
Kaushanskaya, Margarita et al. (2011), "Gender Differences in Adult Word Learning," *Acta Psychologica*, 137(1): 24–35.
Kent, Blake Victor et al. (2017), "Forgiveness, Attachment to God, and Mental Health Outcomes in Older U.S. Adults: A Longitudinal Study," *Research on Aging*, 40(5): 1–24.

Khlebnikov, Velimir ([1913] 1985), "The Trumpet of the Martians," in Charlotte Douglas (ed.), *The King of Time: Selected Writings of the Russian Futurian*, trans. Paul Schmidt, Cambridge, MA: Harvard University Press, 126–9.

Kierkegaard, Søren ([1845] 1993), "At a Graveside," in *Three Discourses on Imagined Occasions*, ed. and trans. Howard V. Hong and Edna H. Hong, Princeton, NJ: Princeton University Press, 69–102.

Kojève, Alexandre (1947), *Introduction à la lecture de Hegel*, ed. Raymond Queneau, Paris: Gallimard.

Kramer, Michael (forthcoming), "Manifestation and Revelation of Psyche: A Phenomenological Study of the Sense of Psychedelic Experience in Its Aesthetic and Noetic Dimensions," PhD Diss., Duquesne University.

Krasznahorkai, Laszlo (2019), *Baron Wenckheim's Homecoming*, trans. Ottilie Mulzet, New York: New Directions.

Krausz, Moshe (2000), "Effects of Short- and Long-Term Preference for Temporary Work upon Psychological Outcomes," *International Journal of Manpower*, 21(8): 635–47.

Kristeva, Julia ([1974] 1980), "The Novel as Polylogue," trans. Thomas Gora et al., in Leon S. Roudiez (ed.), *Desire in Language: A Semiotic Approach to Literature and Art*, New York: Columbia University Press, 159–209.

L'arrivée d'un train à La Ciotat (1896). Dir. Louis Lumière and Auguste Lumière, France: Lumière.

Lacan, Jacques ([1953] 2006), "The Function and Field of Speech and Language in Psychoanalysis," trans. Bruce Fink, in *Écrits*, New York: W. W. Norton, 197–268.

Lacroix, Alain (2000), "The Mathematical Infinite in Hegel," *Philosophical Forum*, 31(3–4): 298–327.

Lambourn, Bonnie (2006), "Capturing the Ephemeral: Altars, Mandalas, and Time Capsules: Similarities in Ritual – Depictions of a Culture," *Houston Teachers Institute*. Available online: https://uh.edu/honors/Programs-Minors/honors-and-the-schools/houston-teachers-institute/curriculum-units/pdfs/2006/photography/lambourn-06-photography.pdf (accessed February 2021).

Lampert, Jay (1988), "Hegel and Husserl on the Logic of Subjectivity," *Man and World*, 21, 363–93.

Lampert, Jay (1995), *Synthesis and Backward Reference in Husserl's Logical Investigations*, The Hague: Kluwer Academic.

Lampert, Jay (2002), "Dates and Destiny: Deleuze and Hegel," *Journal of the British Society for Phenomenology*, 33(2): 206–20.

Lampert, Jay (2006), *Deleuze and Guattari's Philosophy of History*, London: Bloomsbury Academic.

Lampert, Jay (2009), "Theory of Delay in Balibar, Freud and Deleuze: Retard, Nachträglichkeit, Décalage," in Jeffrey A. Bell and Clair Colebrook (eds.), *Deleuze and History*, Edinburgh: Edinburgh University Press, 72–91.

Lampert, Jay (2012), *Simultaneity and Delay*, London: Bloomsbury Academic.

Lampert, Jay (2013), "Limit, Ground, Judgement … Syllogism: Hegel, Deleuze, Hegel, and Deleuze," in James Vernon and Karen Houle (eds.), *Hegel and Deleuze: Together Again for the First Time*, Evanston, IL: Northwestern University Press, 183–203.

Lampert, Jay (2018), *The Many Futures of a Decision*, London: Bloomsbury Academic.

Langille, Jesse J., and Richard E. Brown (2018), "The Synaptic Theory of Memory: A Historical Survey and Reconciliation of Recent Opposition," *Frontiers in Systems*

Neuroscience, 12(52): 1–15. Available online: https://doi.org/10.3389/fnsys.2018.00052 (accessed March 2021).

Le Lionnais, François ([1963] 1973), "La LiPo: Le premier Manifeste," in *Oulipo: La littérature potentielle*, Paris: Éditions Gallimard, 15–18.

Levinas, Emmanuel ([1935] 2003), *On Escape*, trans. Bettina Bergo, Stanford, CA: Stanford University Press.

Lisi, Dominico, and Miguel A. Malo (2017), "The Impact of Temporary Employment on Productivity," *Journal of Labour Market Research*, 50: 91–112.

London, Bernard (1932), *Ending the Depression through Planned Obsolescence*, New York: Self-published.

Made in U.S.A. (1966). Dir. Jean-Luc Godard, France: Anouchka Films.

Mahncke, Henry W. et al. (2006), "Memory Enhancements in Healthy Older Adults Using a brain Plasticity-Based Training Program: A Randomized, Controlled Study," *Proceedings of the National Academy of Sciences*, 103(33): 12523–8.

Maimonides, Moses ([1190] 1954), *The Guide for the Perplexed*, trans. M. Friedländer, New York: Dover.

Malabou, Catherine ([2004] 2008), *What Should We Do with Our Brain?*, trans. Sebastian Rand, New York: Fordham University Press.

Marina Abramovic: The Artist Is Present (2012). Dir. Matthew Akers and Matthew and Jeff Dupre, USA: Museum of Modern Art, New York.

Martin-Rubio, Tristana (forthcoming), "Becoming Otherwise: A Critical Phenomenology of Aging," PhD Diss., Duquesne University.

Matsuzawa, Tetsuro (2007), "Comparative Cognitive Development," *Developmental Science*, 10(1): 97–103.

Mayakovsky, Vladimir ([1926] 1970), *How are Verses Made?* trans. G. M. Hyde, London: Jonathan Cape.

Mbiti, John (1970), *African Religions and Philosophy*, New York: Anchor Books.

McLuhan, Marshall (1964), *Understanding Media*, New York: Signet Books.

Melges, F. T. (1982), *Time and the Inner Future: A Temporal Approach to Psychiatric Disorders*, New York: Wiley.

Merleau-Ponty, Maurice ([1945] 1994), *Phenomenology of Perception*, trans. Colin Smith, NJ: Humanities Press.

Metchnicoff, Elie ([1908] 2019), *The Prolongation of Life: Optimistic Studies*, trans. Peter Chalmers Mitchell, Delhi, India: Lector House Books.

Mill, John Stuart ([1861] 2001), *Utilitarianism*, Indianapolis, IN: Hackett.

Morand, Paul ([1941] 2015), *The Man in a Hurry*, trans. Euan Cameron, London: Pushkin Press.

Morris, Dennis (2017), "Short-Term Memory and Long-Term Memory Are Still Different," *APA Psychological Bulletin*, 143(9): 992–1009.

Motanis, Helen et al. (2018), "Short-Term Synaptic Plasticity as a Mechanism for Sensory Timing," *Trends in Neurosciences*, 41(10): 701–11.

Moyo, Dambisa (2018), "Why Democracy Doesn't Deliver: Endless Elections, Unqualified Leaders, Uninformed Voters, and Short-Term Thinking Are Impeding Economic Growth," *FP* (*Foreign Policy*). Available online: https://foreignpolicy.com/2018/04/26/why-democracy-doesnt-deliver/ (accessed June 2020).

Mr. Arkadin (aka *Confidential Report*) (1955). Dir. Orson Welles, USA: Filmorsa.

Nail, Thomas (2012), *Returning to Revolution: Deleuze, Guattari, and Zapatismo*, Edinburgh: Edinburgh University Press.

Nathan, Charles, and Kai Goldberg (2019), "The Short-Termism Thesis: Dogma vs. Reality," *Harvard Law School Forum on Corporate Governance*, March 8, 2019. Available online: https://corpgov.law.harvard.edu/2019/03/18/the-short-termism-thesis-dogma-vs-reality/ (accessed June 2020).

Nietzsche, Friedrich ([1878] 1997), *Human, All Too Human*, trans. R. J. Hollingdale, Cambridge: Cambridge University Press.

Nilges, Mathias (2019), *Right Wing Culture in Contemporary Capitalism: Regression and Hope in a Time without Future*, London: Bloomsbury Academic.

Nitschke, Gunter (2018), "MA: 'Place, Space, Void'," *Kyoto Journal*. Available online: https://kyotojournal.org/culture-arts/ma-place-space-void/ (accessed March 2021).

Nourbakhsh, Illah Reza (2015), "The Coming Robot Dystopia: All Too Human," *Foreign Affairs*. Available online: https://www.foreignaffairs.com/articles/2015-06-16/coming-robot-dystopia (accessed January 2021).

O'Keefe, Tim (2002), "The Cyrenaics on Pleasure, Happiness, and Future Concern," *Phronesis*, 47(4): 395–416.

Oler, Derek K. et al. (2008), "The Danger of interpreting Short-Window Event Study Findings in Strategic Management Research: An Empirical Illustration Using Horizontal Acquisitions," *Strategic Organization*, 6(2): 151–84.

Olson, Charles ([1950] 1966), "Projective Verse," in Robert Creeley (ed.), *Selected Writings*, New York: New Directions Books, 15–26.

Ouaknin, Marc-Alain ([1986] 2016), *Le livre brulé: Philosophie du Talmud*, Paris: Points.

Parrot, Carol (n.d.), "Death with Dignity as an End of Life Option," *Death with Dignity*. Available online: https://www.deathwithdignity.org/faqs/ (accessed January 2021).

Pearlman, Karen (2009), *Cutting Rhythms: Shaping the Film Edit*, Burlington, MA: Focal Press.

Peris, Daniel (2011), *The Strategic Dividend Investor*, New York: McGraw-Hill.

Peris, Daniel (2018), *Getting Back to Business: Why Modern Portfolio Theory Fails Investors and How You Can Bring Common Sense to Your Portfolio*, New York: McGraw-Hill.

Pierrot le fou (1965). Dir. Jean-Luc Godard, France: Films Georges de Beauregard.

Pinker, Steven (2019), *Enlightenment Now: The Case for Reason, Science, Humanism, and Progress*, New York: Penguin Books.

"Planck Length, Minimal Length?" (2013), *Fermilab Today*. Available online: https://www.fnal.gov/pub/today/archive/archive_2013/today13-11-01_NutshellReadMore.html (accessed March 2021).

Plato, *Protagoras* ([fourth century BCE] 1977), trans. W. R. M. Lamb, Loeb Classical Library, Volume 2, Cambridge, MA: Harvard University Press, 85–259.

Pöppel, Ernst (2004), "Lost in Time: A Historical Frame, Elementary Processing Units, and the 3-Second Window," *Acta Neurobiologiae Experimentalis*, 64: 295–301.

Prêt-à-jeter (2010). Dir. Cosima Dannoritzer, France: ARTE.

Probasco, LiErin (2013), "Giving Time, Not Money: Long-term Impacts of Short-term Mission Trips," *Missiology: An International Review*, 41(2), 202–24. Available online: https://doi.org/10.1177/0091829612475166 (accessed June 2020).

Protagoras, *Concerning the Gods* ([fifth century BCE] 1992), in Hermann Diels and Walther Kranz (eds.), *Die Fragmente der Vorsokratiker*, Band 2, Weidmannsche Verlagsbuchhandlung, DK 80 B4.

Psycho (1960). Dir. Alfred Hitchcock, USA: Universal Studios.

Queneau, Raymond (1961), *Cent mille milliards de poèmes*, Paris: Gallimard.

Queneau, Raymond (1981), *Contes et propos*, Paris: Gallimard.

"Quick," *Online Etymology Dictionary*. Available online: https://www.etymonline.com/word/quick (accessed February 2021).

Rahman, Azimaton Abdul et al. (2015), "Muslims in Cyberspace: Exploring Factors Influencing Online Religious Engagements in Malaysia," *Media Asia*, 42(1–2): 61–73.

Ramamurti, Ravi (2020), "Using Reverse Innovation to Fight Covid-19," *Harvard Business Review*, June 17, 2020. Available online: https://hbr.org/2020/06/using-reverse-innovation-to-fight-covid-19 (accessed July 2020).

Raunig, Gerald (2016), *Dividuum: Machinic Capitalism and Molecular Revolution*, South Pasadena, CA: Semiotext(e).

Reid, William J. (1990), "An Integrative Model for Short-Term Treatment," in Richard A. Wells and Vincent J. Giannetti (eds.), *Handbook of the Brief Psychotherapies*, New York: Plenum Press, 55–77.

Ricoeur, Paul ([1983] 1984), *Time and Narrative*, Volume 1, trans. Kathleen McLaughlin and David Pellauer, Chicago: University of Chicago Press.

Ricoeur, Paul ([1984] 1985), *Time and Narrative*, Volume 2, trans. Kathleen McLaughlin and David Pellauer, Chicago: University of Chicago Press.

Ricoeur, Paul ([1985] 1988), *Time and Narrative*, Volume 3, trans. Kathleen McLaughlin and David Pellauer, Chicago: University of Chicago Press.

Rocky (1976). Dir. John G. Avildsen, USA: Chartoff-Winkler Productions.

Rohrer, Brandon (2018), "Recurrent Neural Networks (RNN) and Long Short-term Memory (LSTM)." Available online: https://www.youtube.com/watch?v=WCUNPb-5EYI (accessed August 2018).

Rollinger, Robert, Julian Degen, and Michael Gehler (eds.) (2020), *Short-term Empires in World History*, New York: Springer, 2020.

Rosenbaum, Robert et al. (1990), "The Challenge of Single-Session Therapies: Creating Pivotal Moments," in Richard A. Wells and Vincent J. Giannetti (eds.), *Handbook of the Brief Psychotherapies*, New York: Plenum Press, 165–89.

Roudinesco Elisabeth (1990), *Jacques Lacan and Company: A History of Psychoanalysis in France, 1925–85*, Chicago: University of Chicago Press.

Saint-Aubin, Jean, and Marie Poirier (1999), "The Influence of Long-Term Memory Factors on Immediate Serial Recall: An Item and Order Analysis," *International Journal of Psychology*, 34(5–6): 347–52.

Sanders, Edward (1981), *The Z-D Generation*, New York: Station Hill Press.

Sarr, Felwine (2019), *Afrotopia*, trans. Drew S. Burk and Sarah Jones-Boardman, Minneapolis: University of Minnesota Press.

Sartre, Jean-Paul ([1945] 1966) *L'Age de raison*, Paris: Gallimard.

Sartre, Jean-Paul ([1960] 2004), *Critique of Dialectical Reason*, Volume 1, trans. Alan Sheridan-Smith, London: Verso.

Sartre, Jean-Paul (1983), *Cahiers pour une morale*, Paris: Éditions Gallimard.

Schmitt, Carl ([1934] 1985), *Political Theology*, trans. George Schwab, Chicago: University of Chicago Press.

Schneider, Mark (2020), "Fad, Trend, or Classic: What's the Difference." Available online: https://www.markschneiderdesign.com/blogs/jewelry-blog/fad-trend-or-classic-what-s-the-difference (accessed July 2020).

Schopenhauer, Arthur ([1851] 1974), "Additional Remarks on the Doctrine of the Vanity of Existence," trans. E. F. J. Payne, in *Parerga and Paralipomena*, Volume 2, Oxford: Oxford University Press, 283–90.

Segraves, R. Taylor (1990), "Short-Term Marital Therapy," in Richard A. Wells and Vincent J. Giannetti (eds.), *Handbook of the Brief Psychotherapies*, New York: Plenum Press, 437–59.

Seneca, Lucius Annaeus ([49 CE] 2018), *On the Shortness of Life*, trans. Damian Stevenson, Scotts Valley, CA: CreateSpace.

Serres, Michel, and Bruno Latour (1995), *Conversations on Science, Culture, and Time*, trans. Roxanne Lapidus, Ann Arbor: University of Michigan Press.

Servien, Pius (1925), *Essai sur les rhythmes toniques du Français*, Paris: Les Presses Universitaires de France.

Shakespeare, William ([1595] 2015), *Love's Labour's Lost*, in Stephen Greenblatt et al. (eds.), *The Norton Shakespeare*, third edition, New York: W. W. Norton, 799–870.

Sheldrake, Cosmo (2018), "Eggs and Soldiers" (audio), from the CD, *The Much Much How How and I*, London: Transgressive Records.

"Short term assets," *Investopedia*. Available online: https://www.investopedia.com/terms/s/shortterm.asp (accessed July 2017).

Simiand, François (1937), "La psychologie sociale des crises et les fluctuations économiques de courte durée," *Annales sociologiques, Série D, Sociologie économique, Fasc. 2*, 3–32.

Simon, T. R. et al. (2001), "Characteristics of Impulsive Suicide Attempts and Attempters," *Suicide and Life Threatening Behavior*, 32(suppl.): 49–59.

Skrimshire, Stefan (2011), "The End of the Future: Hegel and the Political Economy of Deep Time," *International Social Science Journal*, 62(205–6): 325–38.

Sober, Elliot (2009) "Event Theory," in Jaekwon Kim et al. (eds.), *A Companion to Metaphysics*, second edition, Oxford: Wiley-Blackwell, 235–8.

Sokol, Mary (2009), "Jeremy Bentham on Love and Marriage: A Utilitarian Proposal for Short-Term Marriage," *Journal of Legal History*, 30(1): 1–21.

Sorabji, Richard (1982), "Time and Time Atoms," in Norman Kretzmann (ed.), *Infinity and Continuity in Ancient and Medieval Thought*, Ithaca, NY: Cornell University Press, 37–86.

St. Benny the Dip (1951). Dir. Edgar G. Ulmer, USA: Benny Productions.

Stephenson, Ralph, and J. R. Debrix (1965), *The Cinema as Art*, Harmondsworth: Penguin Books.

Sternberg, Jacques (1972), *Lettre aux gens malheureux et qui ont bien raison de l'être*, Paris: Le Terrain Vague.

Stockhausen, Karlhein (1956), "… How Time Passes …," *Die Reihe*, 10–40.

Sweet, Elizabeth et al. (2018), "Short-Term Lending: Payday Loans as Risk Factors for Anxiety, Inflammation, and Poor Health," *SSM (Social Science and Medicine): Population Health*, 114–21.

Szapocznik, Jose et al. (1990), "Innovations in Family Therapy: Strategies for Overcoming Resistance to Treatment," in Richard A. Wells and Vincent J. Giannetti (eds.), *Handbook of the Brief Psychotherapies*, New York: Plenum Press, 93–114.

Sykes, Kevin J. (2014), "Short-Term Medical Service Trips: A Systematic Review of the Evidence," *American Journal of Public Health*, 104(7): e38–e48.

Taleb, Nassim Nicholas (2010), *The Black Swan: The Impact of the Highly Improbable*, second edition, New York: Random House.

Thijssen, Hans (2018), "Condemnation of 1277," *The Stanford Encyclopedia of Philosophy* (Winter 2018). Available online: https://plato.stanford.edu/archives/win2018/entries/condemnation/ (accessed January 2021).

Thomas, Lizanne (2019), "Stop Panicking about Corporate Short-Termism," *Harvard Business Review*. June 28, 2019. Available online: https://hbr.org/2019/06/stop-panicking-about-corporate-short-termism (accessed June 2020).

Trilling, David (2016), "Do Payday Loans Exploit Poor People? Research Review," *Journalists' Research: Harvard Kennedy School, Shorenstein Center for Media, Politics, and Public Society*. September 19, 2016. Available online: https://journalistsresource.org/studies/economics/personal-finance/payday-loans-exploit-poor-people-research/ (accessed June 2020).

Tsouna, Voula (1998), *The Epistemology of the Cyrenaic School*, Cambridge: Cambridge University Press.

2001: A Space Odyssey (1968). Dir. Stanley Kubrick, USA: MGM.

Umbach, Gray, et al. (2020), "Time Cells in the Human Hippocampus and Entorhinal Cortex Support Episodic Memory," *PNAS (Proceedings of the National Academy of Sciences)*, 117(45): 28463–74.

Ver Beek, Kurt Alan (2006), "The Impact of Short-Term Missions: A Case Study of House Construction in Honduras after Hurricane Mitch," *Missiology: An International Review*, 34(4): 477–95.

Vertov, Dziga ([1923] 1985), "The Council of Three," in *Kino-Eye: The Writings of Dziga Vertov*, trans. Kevin O'Brien, Los Angeles: University of California Press, 14–21.

Vettaiyaadu Vilaiyaadu (2006). Dir. Gautham Vasudev Menon, India: Photon Factory.

Vila-Matas, Enrique (1985), *A Brief History of Portable Literature*, trans. Anne McLean and Thomas Bunstead, New York: New Directions Books.

Vila-Matas, Enrique ([2003] 2011), *Never Any End to Paris*, trans. Anne McLean, New York: New Directions Books.

Vogeley, Kai, and Christian Kupke (2007), "Disturbances of Time Consciousness from a Phenomenological and a Neuroscientific Perspective," *Schizophrenia Bulletin*, 33(1): 157–65.

Walser, Robert ([1933] 2012), *Microscripts*, trans. Susan Bernofsky, New York: New Directions Books.

Weimer, David L., and Ellie Karls (2022), "Negotiating Values: Implementing Rubric Change in Transplant Organ Allocation," presented at the Conference of the American Political Science Association.

Wells, Richard A., and Vincent J. Giannetti (eds.) (1990). *Handbook of the Brief Psychotherapies*, New York: Plenum Press.

Wells, Richard A., and Phillip A. Phelps (1990), *Handbook of the Brief Psychotherapies*, ed. Richard A. Wells and Vincent J. Giannetti, New York: Plenum Press, 3–26.

"What Is Commercial Paper?" *Investopedia*. Available online: https://www.investopedia.com/terms/c/commercialpaper.asp (accessed February 2021).

Who Killed Captain Alex? (2010). Dir. I. G. G. Nabwana, Uganda: Ramon Film Productions.

Windon, Katrina (2012), "The Right to Decay with Dignity: Documentation and the Negotiation between an Artist's Sanction and the Cultural Interest," *Art Documentation: Journal of the Art Libraries Society of North America*, 31(2): 142–57.

Worchel, Jason (1990), "Short-Term Dynamic Psychotherapy," in Richard A. Wells and Vincent J. Giannetti (eds.), *Handbook of the Brief Psychotherapies*, New York: Plenum Press, 193–216.

X-Men: Days of Future Past (2014). Dir. Bryan Singer, USA: Twentieth Century Fox.

Yirka, Bob (2020), "Theorists Calculate Upper Limit for Possible Quantization of Time," *PhysOrg*. Available online: https://phys.org/news/2020-06-theorists-upper-limit-quantization.html (accessed March 2021).

"Your Home for Short-Term Trading," *NADEX*. Available online: https://join.nadex.com/offer-nadex-general/?CHID= 1&QPID=239744197&gclid= Cj0KCQiAyJOBBh DCARIsAJG2h5fE9GUudsEA6e7UJs1zpZymiO3 TyvbBpP0KZLT5tgdn4w7Jmhqnh SEaAmIPEALw_wcB&gclsrc=aw.ds (accessed June 2020).

Zizek, Slavoj (2009), *The Parallax View*, Cambridge, MA: MIT Press.

Zuckerkandl, Victor (1969), *Sound and Symbol: Music and the External World*, Princeton, NJ: Princeton University Press.

INDEX

Aben, Bart 92, 97
Abramovic, Marina 168-9
accelerationism 195
Adorno, Theodor 57-8
Aristippus 130-1, 134, 141
Aristotle 60, 105, 135-6
Arthur, Richard 106-7
Augustine 59-60

Bacon, Francis 124
Badiou, Alain 7, 109, 119
Barthes, Roland 170-1
Bellour, Raymond 174-5
Benjamin, Walter 57
Bentham, Jeremy 135-7, 165-6
Benveniste, Émile 5
Bergson, Henri 89, 92, 112-13, 206-8
Bernardi, Franco ("Bifo") 142
Boyer, Carl 113-17
Braudel, Fernand 71-7, 163-4
Bray, Oliver Pierre 180

Calculus 113-20
Chladenuis, Johann Martin 130
cinema 173-9
climate change 19-20, 80
Covid 21-2
Cowan, Nelson 88-97
Cyrenaics 130-5, 141

death 39-58, 62, 64
De Beauvoir, Simone 42-54
Dedekind cuts 30, 109, 111
Deleuze, Gilles
  Anti-Oedipus 201-4
  Cinema 173-5
  Difference and Repetition 191
  Logic of Sense 191
  "Postscript on Control Societies" 193-6
  Proust and Signs 192-3
Deleuze, Gilles and Félix Guattari

A Thousand Plateaus 189-92, 200-9
"*Mai 68 n'a pas eu lieu*" 199-200
Derrida, Jacques, 171-2
Descartes, René 107
desire 55-6
De Warren, Nicolas, 30
Dilthey, Wilhelm 112
disjunction 136-7, 207-9
Dodd, James 30

Eichenbaum, Boris 169-71
eidetic variation 11, 16, 50
employment 156-7
ephemera 14, 167-9, 180
Epicurus 131
Ernst, Wolfgang 81, 101
event 62-3, 66-74, 81, 107-8, 153, 194, 199

Fads 14, 157-8
Fanon, Frantz 9
finance 14, 154-7
fluctuations 76-8
Foucault, Michel 193-4, 197

Game Theory 138
Gauthier, David 139
Go 19, 177, 205
Godard, Jean-Luc 174-7, 179
Guattari, Félix
  "*La causalité, la subjectivite et l'histoire*" 196-7
Gyekye, Kwami 130

Hegel, G. W. F. 18
  Aesthetics 37-8, 182-5
  Philosophy of History 78-82
  Philosophy of Mind 183
  Philosophy of Nature 28-9
  Science of Logic 33-8, 117-20, 203, 206

Heidegger, Martin 61–4
history 31–3, 59–82, 86, 193–200, 207
Husserl, Edmund 11
  Analyses Concerning Passive and Active Synthesis 110–13
  Crisis of the European Sciences 31–2
  Lectures on Internal Time-Consciousness 30, 60–1, 87–8
  Logical Investigations 25–6, 31–2
  Origin of Geometry 32–3
  Philosophy of Arithmetic 109–10

interim 17, 55–6
interruption 201–4
intersubjectivity 32–3, 47, 182–5
investment 151–4

Jouet, Jacques 180–1
Joyce, James 124
Jump cuts 175–7

Kafka, Franz 15
Kant, Immanuel 26–8, 110, 171–2, 195
Kierkegaard, Søren 41–2, 134
Kojève, Alexandre 182
Kubrick, Stanley 178

Lacan, Jacques 144
last minute 7, 41–2
leakage, temporal 204–7
Leibniz, Gottfried Wilhelm 115
Le Lionnais, François 179–80
Levinas, Emmanuel 141–2
limit 33–8, 114–20
literature 82–6, 169–71, 179–82, 185–7
longevity 58

Maimonides 102–4
Malabou, Catherine 217
Matsuzawa, Tetsuro 96–7
Mbiti, John 17
McLuhan, Marshall 5, 124
measure 5, 18, 28, 60–1, 70–1, 73, 112, 119, 126–41, 203
memory 20, 29, 45–50, 87–99, 189–90, 200
  memory loss 98
Menken, Marie 178
Menon, Gautham 175–6

Merleau-Ponty, Maurice 25
microhistory 77
Mill, John Stuart 139–41, 149
missions, religious and medical 162–4
modernity 31–2, 52, 56, 81–2, 157
monochronos 131–3, 142
montage 173–9
music 37–8, 111, 170–1, 182–5, 205–6

Nabwana, Isaac 178–9
narrative 4–5, 60–71, 79, 82–6, 96, 177
Newton, Isaac 115–16
next 30–1
Nietzsche, Friedrich 77
numbers, small 109–20

O'Keefe, Tim 131–3
Olson, Charles 15, 185–7
Oulipo 179–85, 187

painting 171–2
Perec, Georges 180
performance art 157–9
Peris, Daniel 219
physics of time measurement 5, 8, 18, 101–2
planned obsolescence 12, 14, 158–9
plasticity 97–8, 108, 217
Plato 105, 121–9
pleasure 130–5, 141
post-futurism 142
propinquity 135–8
Protagoras 123
Proust, Marcel 83, 192–3
psychotherapy, brief 144–51

Queneau, Raymond 179–80, 182, 185

recency 32–3, 95
relationships 164–6
repetition 5, 81, 111, 190–5, 200
Ricoeur, Paul 59–71, 82–6
risk 77, 152–4

sand mandalas 14, 168
Sarr, Felwine 159
Sartre, Jean-Paul 45, 47–8, 66
scarcity of time 41–2, 48
Schoenberg, Arnold 84

Schopenhauer, Arthur 54–8
Seneca, Lucius Anneaus 133–4
Shakespeare, William, *Love's Labour's Lost* 129–30
short circuit 12, 19, 202
short cuts 12, 19, 120, 170, 177, 212
shortest time 13, 101–2, 107–8, 112, 114
short selling 154–5
short stories 169–71
short term semiotics 196–7
short termism in politics 9–11, 159–62
short-window events 153–4
Simiand, François 76–8
Sober, Elliot 107–8
Sorabji, Richard 104–6
speech, short 121–30
speed 4, 8, 16, 24, 71, 101, 134, 173, 192–8, 206–7

Stockhausen, Karlheinz 84–5
structuralism 74, 84–6, 169–73
subtraction 109–10, 190
suicide 40–1, 56–7

tense logic 17–18, 69, 187, 202
term limits 12, 160
time atoms 102–7
trends 66, 71–6, 157–8
Tsouna, Voula 133–4

utilitarianism 135–41

value of the short term 10–11, 54–8, 121–66
Vertov, Dziga 173

Zizek, Slavoj 19

www.ingramcontent.com/pod-product-compliance
Lightning Source LLC
Chambersburg PA
CBHW071824300426
44116CB00009B/1431